To an exce
woman + fire...

An Introduction to War

The Journey of a Medic's Heart
An American story inspired by true events

Love,
Linda

Linda Seebeth

Acknowledgements

This story is told in honor of all who "strive to save lives."

Gratitude to members of the 236th, 23rd and 196th for contributing to the story and helping to save John's life. Special recognition to George Waters, Joe Kralich, John Lysinger, and Richard Mosher. Thanks also to Billy Hughes, Coleman Nockolds, Rusty Capece, Sarah Haynes, and other friends who shared details and offered support.

Throughout the years of research and writing, two men generously gave their time and knowledge. Loving appreciation to "brothers" Gary Weaver and Robert Long. Some of the difficult missions described in the book were actual shared experiences of John and Robert, as they often crewed together. Gary and Robert added important details and historical accuracy. In their honor, I created and named characters based upon Gary and Robert. All other characters are fictional—except for the professors and doctors who influenced John and saved his life.

Writing about the subject of war was sometimes emotionally overwhelming to an old peacenik. Thanks to my friends and family, who carried me through. Special credit to Kris Adair, who deeply listened and motivated me when I was stuck. And thanks and appreciation to my wonderful daughters, Elisa and Lynmarie. As ever, you are a source of joy and inspiration to me.

To the one who introduced me to war—and encouraged me to complete the mission—I am blessed to be married to a man whose caring heart continues to fly Dustoff for all humanity.

I had never heard of Dustoff before meeting and marrying John. Previously, I shut my ears and eyes to war—except to be against it. After hearing about Dustoff, I was filled with awe. It took remarkable courage and compassion to fly into a hot LZ for the sake of another. Dustoff had the highest casualty rate of any other aviation group in Vietnam (1/3 of their men were KIA or WIA). Although this book relates the experiences of one man during a certain slice of history, it also seeks to impart the eternal caring spirit represented by the call sign Dustoff.

Chapter 1

He made it through high school by the skin of his teeth, which fortunately were one of his best features. Naturally straight rows of pearly whites illuminated a trademark smile on a handsome, boyish face. In less than two decades he'd already wrung a lifetime of mileage out of that bright smile. It served as a balm throughout his childhood, helping to soothe his younger brother and sister when their mother sank into her regular bouts of deep depression. The smile had been a mask, concealing the craziness inside their tract home from the guys in the neighborhood and later from friends at school. Framing contagious laughter, that same smile was a passport. It allowed him to traverse a variety of social turfs in his suburban high school and gave him passage onto the cobblestone streets of Germantown, the tough North Philadelphia neighborhood where his grandparents lived.

And Christie said it had been his smile that first caught her attention at the record hop that Friday night. She and a couple of her classmates from Saint Hubert's decided to check out the Goodwill Fire Hall in Bristol to see if the crowd really went wild when the DJ played the borough's namesake hit, "The Bristol Stomp." Christie often repeated the story of how she'd noticed his smooth moves from across the room as he danced with another girl. Watching that unruly lock of blond hair tumble across his forehead, Christie claimed she was determined to be his next dance partner. She deliberately bumped against him when the song ended and Martha and the Vandellas began to sing about nowhere to run and nowhere to hide. According to Christie, when she reached for his outstretched hand and looked into the sky blue eyes that accompanied the megawatt smile, she knew their hearts, as well as their feet, would soon be dancing to the same beat.

While his smile may have charmed Christie, it was a total waste of wattage on Miss Crutcher. The Vocational Commercial Art students at Bensalem High School maintained one English teacher for their sophomore, junior, and senior years, and he had the misfortune of being assigned to Miss Crutcher. In all three years, the stern sour-faced woman didn't find anything funny about his jokes – especially if the other students did. She had no tolerance for late homework, even if he'd been up half the night struggling with a two-and-a-half-inch water hose helping to put out a warehouse fire with the Nottingham Fire Company. His volunteer work as a Junior Firefighter meant zero if he didn't turn in his conjugated verbs. Miss Crutcher never gave him any slack, like the time he was supposed to bring in a magazine article from home. She didn't understand that when his mother moved out during his freshman year, she took her subscription to the *National Enquirer* with her, leaving nothing to read in the house and sometimes nothing much to eat.

Perhaps because Miss Crutcher viewed the world through fish-bowl-thick lenses she couldn't relate to being part of history in the making. Admittedly, the 1960s weren't as revolutionary as when the Founding Fathers were around and Thomas Jefferson penned the *Declaration of Independence* in a second-floor room on Market Street, but Philadelphia was still an epicenter for new trends. Take fashion, for instance. He and his friends dressed Philly conservative, a look that laced suede Desert Boots on the feet of teenagers across the country. And *Bandstand* had been a popular local show before Dick Clark prefaced the name with *American* and turned it into a national phenomenon.

He and his friends didn't just watch dancing on television— they lived it, never missing a chance to attend a record hop where Philadelphia's rich harmonies and doo-wop sounds were brought to life by the Geater with the Heater—Philly's iconic radio personality and emcee, Jerry Blavat. Music and dance gave his teenage years meaning. They were his heart and soul and a refuge from his childhood pain. Winning first place in local contests made dancing a source of pride. Yet thanks to Miss Crutcher, he seemed to spend as many hours in detention as he did on the dance floor.

Truthfully, he wasn't getting great grades in most of his subjects, but it was English that put graduation in jeopardy. He might have scored higher on his final paper if he had been allowed to pick his own topic. Instead of trying to write about *The Danger of Indifference to Public Affairs*, it would have been exciting to write about the stories of bravery and adventure he heard from the Pennsylvania State Troopers who stopped by Howard Johnson during his late shift as a busboy. The fate of his diploma all came down to his second attempt at the English final. Sitting alone in the classroom with Miss Crutcher, he remembered fighting to keep his focus on the exam. The sounds of his classmates' laughter echoed from down the hallway as they lined up to enter the auditorium to rehearse the graduation ceremony. When the high school band began to play "Pomp and Circumstance" he swallowed hard, wondering if he would get to wear a cap and gown. A few days later he was told that he would. Miss Crutcher must have passed him out of kindness – or maybe she dreaded the thought of working with him for another year.

Despite struggles with English, his artistic talents won him a partial scholarship at the prestigious Hussein Art College. He contemplated the opportunity only briefly, reluctant to reenter the academic environment he was so relieved to exit. Plus, there was no money to pay the remaining college expenses. If he had to work and commute to downtown Philadelphia for school, there wouldn't be enough time for the one thing that had meaning in his life – Christie. So when his dad arranged for him to get a full-time job at Bond Bread, he released the dream of college to the reality of making enough money to provide for the things he needed – like the upkeep of his car for the half hour drive to Christie's Levittown home – and money for dances and movies – and dinners out – and an engagement ring – and eventually an apartment when he and Christie got married.

He was an excellent worker, but getting to the bread factory to begin his janitorial duties at five in the morning proved to be a difficult task, particularly if he'd been out with Christie the previous night. His frequent lateness was an embarrassment to his dad who worked in the same building and had only been late six times in twenty years. Still, his competence earned promotions, and he went from cleaning the toilets and the huge kneading machine to making buns, and in only a few months he operated the complicated bread-wrapping machine. While he was proud of his achievements, one day it struck him that he was performing the same job as his dad. Deep within, he was discontent. Did he really want to be a bread wrapper for the rest of his life?

He didn't want life forced upon him; he wanted to be a force in life. He wanted to contribute to the world in a meaningful way. Having grown up watching Westerns and war movies, he knew there were bad guys out there along with meek and innocent who needed protecting. Stirred by the restlessness of youth, he felt a magnificence in his soul that spurred him to become more. Answering this call, John Neil Seebeth III followed the footstep of his namesakes before him. In December 1966, he enlisted in service to the United States Military. The Army would help him be all that he could be.

Chapter 2

"Johnny! What a surprise! Hang on a second."

John could picture Christie struggling to untangle the phone line and yank the receiver into the garage for privacy. During his senior year in high school he had just about lived with Christie's family, preferring the chaos under her roof to the loneliness under his own. John heard the familiar commotion fade as Christie moved to a quiet corner away from her parents and four siblings. As she wrestled with the mouthpiece, her jagged breath traveled from Philadelphia to Baumholder, reminding him of the intimacy he dearly missed. She was his one and only.

"Okay," Christie sighed. "As soon as I walked in the door, Tracy handed me the phone and said it was for me."

"You weren't there when I called last week, so I thought I'd try again."

"I went out with some of the other aides from the hospital last Friday."

"That's not what Annie said. She said something about a couple of Marines."

"Listen, my sisters don't know everything about my where-abouts."

John pulled at the coiled cord in the phone booth, knotted by nervous fingers of numerous soldiers before him. "All right. Forget it. I don't want to pay for a long-distance argument."

"I can't wait to get out of this house," Christie complained. "My parents are driving me crazy, and between my sisters and their boyfriends, I never have any room for myself."

"I miss you, Christie."

"I miss you, too, Johnny. My friends at work think it's so neat that I'll be living in Germany soon. Did you find out when I can come?

"I miss you, Christie."

"Yeah, I know. You've been there for almost three months. When am I going to be able to come over?" she probed.

"That's the thing, there's a rumor we're going to be redeployed back to the States."

"What?" Christie's tone sounded more like his Sergeant than his sweetheart. "When is that going to happen?"

"We don't know for sure. We're not supposed to talk about it, but no more dependents are being allowed to come to Germany."

"I'm beginning to not believe you, Johnny. We originally planned to get married after you finished your basic training in North Carolina. You were supposed to have a two-week leave, but you ended up going to Texas."

"We've already been over this, Christie. It wasn't just me. All the guys being sent to Fort Sam Houston had their leave canceled. They wanted us to get our specialty training right away because of the medic shortage," he justified.

"And I couldn't join you in Texas," she pointed out.

"Because that was an intense ten weeks. Plus, you weren't allowed to join me until I was assigned my permanent duty station."

John closed his eyes, and the memory of standing in formation back at Fort Sam came to mind. He remembered watching the young Lieutenant walk down the line and hand out orders. At the time, John was so preoccupied with his troubled romance, along with long hours of studying, he was oblivious to the tensions associated with a Vietnam assignment. As each man in the company received his orders, the Lieutenant uttered "Europe" or "Nam." Some men's faces dropped in despair to hear Nam. Others beamed with relief when Europe was announced as their assignment. John noticed that most Black and Hispanic men received orders to Vietnam. In addition, white men with discipline problems were also assigned there, which confused John because a competent medic could mean the difference between life and death. Didn't the soldiers in the war need the very best? Like the majority of men given orders to Europe, John was assigned to Germany.

Opening his eyes, he finished his thought to Christie, "And once I got assigned, we had to save some money for your plane ticket and a place to live."

"But now you're saying I can't come at all, and you can't tell me why. I don't understand, Johnny. You never used to let anyone boss you around, and now you expect me to believe that you can't do anything to make things different? I thought you got some kind of promotion."

"Yeah, I was promoted to Private First Class, but I'm still the lowest rank around here. Believe me, I don't give orders—I take them. That's the way it is in the Army." A loud rap on the door of the phone booth grabbed John's attention. In response, he forcefully held up his hand to the soldier who just knocked, signaling him to back off.

"I've been patient, Johnny, but I can't wait any longer!" Christie's words were punctuated with sniffles. "I need to get out of my parents' house, I can't stand it here anymore. And I'm sick of emptying bed pans at the hospital."

"Christie, please...."

The determined soldier cracked open the door of the phone booth. "How much longer are you gonna be, because I want to make a call before midnight?"

"Give me a break!" John responded, shoving the door shut. "Asshole," he uttered under his breath but loud enough to be transmitted across the phone lines.

"John Seebeth! I can't believe my ears! You never used to use that kind of language," Christie exclaimed.

"I wasn't talking to you. A guy was trying to...."

"Have you been drinking?" Christie demanded. "You've been drinking, haven't you?"

"I had some beer." In actuality, he had just polished off a liter-sized glass boot of German beer and May wine mixed. The combination had become a nearly nightly consumption and—twenty minutes ago—made this phone call seem like a good idea.

"You've changed, Johnny. You never used to swear, and you never used to drink. What other bad habits have you picked up?"

The image of Miss September 1967 popped into John's mind.

He had just flipped the page to the new month this morning. The Playboy calendar hanging in his wall locker was his first, having bought it at the Fort Sam PX. John's typical teenage male admiration of the female form had been ratcheted up a few notches since joining the Army.

"Christie, I love you."

"What's that singing?" Christie quizzed, referring to a cacophony of voices in the background.

"...leaving on a jet plane, don't know when I'll be back again...."

"It's some of the guys. They're singing along with the juke box and..."

"Juke box? Where are you, anyway?"

"I'm at the Budapest. I told you about the Gasthaus across from the dispensary."

"Right. Guesthouse. You mean a German beer joint. Are there some cute German Fraüleins there to keep you satisfied, too?"

"Damn it, Christie, why are you...."

"That's it, John Seebeth. You're not the same person I wanted to marry. It's over between us. I'm going to start dating other guys."

A couple months later, the rumors of redeployment turned out to be true. Unfortunately, so did the speculation about Christie's involvement with a Marine. While John held hope that he and Christie would reunite when he got back to the States—as they had done after their last long separation—he knew there was nothing he could do to speed up his date of departure. He just had to wait for orders.

In December, those orders came down. The US announced plans to withdraw 28,000 troops from Europe in 1968. As medical support for the 1ˢᵗ Armored Division, John's ambulance company, the 565ᵗʰ, was scheduled to depart with Old Ironsides in May. It would take seven months to complete the massive withdrawal, code-named Operation REFORGER (Redeployment of Forces Germany). Since 1949, the Army had maintained infantry, mechanized infantry, and armored units in Europe after signing the North Atlantic Treaty Organization (NATO) agreement following World War II. NATO provided formal military cooperation among European nations and serves as a shield against any future communist attacks.

The US and a host of NATO countries moved into Smith Barracks at Baumholder in 1951. Formerly a military training camp and major hospital complex of the Third Reich, the German government had relocated over eight hundred families and a dozen villages to make way for the nearly 30,000-acre facility.

When John first arrived in Baumholder in June of 1967, he'd scarcely unpacked his duffle bag before the 565ᵗʰ received orders for a NATO mission. John didn't follow current events and rarely read a newspaper, so he had little understanding of the conflict in the Middle East, which resulted in his company lining up their fifty ambulances at a nearby railroad yard. He vaguely remembered hearing something about it on the car radio when he and Christie drove home from getting blood tests for their marriage license. The news reported that Israel had launched preemptive airstrikes against Egypt, Jordon, and Syria, obliterating the air forces of those nations. That was early June, right at the end of John's two-week leave before reporting to Baumholder. He was so absorbed in saying goodbye that John never imagined his company would soon be involved in the residuals of that Israeli-Arab War. Even if he were interested in world politics, the complicated jockeying for resources in that area was beyond his ken.

John's company remained in convoy formation at the railroad yard for several days, ready to roll at a moment's notice. One medic stayed with the ambulance at all times while the other went to the mess tent and took latrine breaks. The buzz circulated that if orders came down to load their ambulances onto the waiting flatcars, they would be bound for Egypt. Nothing escalated, and the 565th was ordered to rescind alert status and return to the company area. They were not called for another NATO mission during the rest of John's ten months in Baumholder.

Since Baumholder was home to the largest concentration of US combat soldiers outside of the United States, the announcement of REFORGER caused a flurry of activity for personnel sending their dependents Stateside. Families had to transfer school records, find homes for pets, pack up their households, and prepare for a new life at a different Army base. John had mixed feelings about leaving Germany. As far as an assignment, Baumholder had been a piece of cake, often seeming like an eight-to-five job. Most of his time had been quite enjoyable—especially after meeting Karen.

Karen and her girlfriend were at the Budapest one November night when John and his buddies arrived for their regular recreation of drinking glass boots of beer and playing Foosball. Cute and precocious, Karen looked older than her sixteen years. John was a shy guy, but her forwardness erased their three year-age difference. They hit it off right away. Both were recovering from recent breakups, and both understood how disrupting the military could be to relationships. Karen's father was a career soldier, an E-6, so she lived on base with her family and attended the American high school, which she hated. Karen wanted to quit school, but John wouldn't hear of it. He told her if she dropped out, she best look for a new boyfriend. Karen remained in school, and they continued to date. They found it amusing that whenever they went to one of the seventy Gasthäuser in Baumholder it was John, rather than Karen, who would be asked for ID.

During his remaining five months in Germany, John walked a little taller because he was one of the few soldiers who had a pretty girlfriend waiting for him when he got off duty. Karen's parents generously welcomed him to their table for home-cooked meals, often extending the invitation to a few of his buddies. The homesick guys greatly appreciated spending time in a family atmosphere. John accompanied Karen and her family on picnics and day trips where he was introduced to Bavarian charm and breathtaking landscapes. Instead of bearable, life outside the Army was pleasurable, largely because of Karen and her family.

When it came time for him to leave, Karen alluded to marriage, but John knew his heart still belonged to another. Although he and Karen were close, there was a line of intimacy he would not cross—not if he hoped to reconcile with Christie. Christie was not the forgiving type, so he didn't need to place any additional obstacles between them. Well, in reality, there was an obstacle that John was fairly certain he wouldn't share with Christie. But it was a matter of the body, not the heart.

John hadn't planned on joining several other medics on a week-long trip to West Berlin and Amsterdam, because—other than beer and cigarette money—he was saving most of his paycheck for Christie's arrival. However, when he received a small package from Christie that contained her engagement ring and a letter confirming everything she had said over the phone about dating others, John was forlorn. His buddies convinced him that a vacation was exactly what he needed to pick up his sagging spirits. He quickly put in for a pass and made arrangements to travel with them.

Riding the train across the European countryside was a visual pleasure, but nothing was quite as eye-popping as the red-light district in Amsterdam. Walking the couple blocks from Central Station to the old neighborhood that dated back to the 16th century, John was taken with the quaint buildings leaning at odd angles and overlooking tree-enshrouded canals. Modernized and upscale, it looked nothing like a seedy side of town. Strolling along the narrow alleyways, John couldn't believe the beauty of the prostitutes who were sitting or standing behind the large picture windows under the inviting red glow. He had never been to a prostitute before, but he had seen some of the sleazy-looking whores that congregate around military bases. The women in Amsterdam were nothing like them. John noticed the nearby pubs, cafés and coffee shops were filled with a wide array of customers, not just GIs and lonely old men.

Holland's honest, pragmatic attitude toward sexuality was vastly different from his own puritanical culture. Acknowledgment of the fact that there will always be a segment of society who seeks the services of prostitutes led to the Dutch government's regulation of the industry. By eliminating the pimps, drugs, and organized crime rings, prostitutes remain healthier, safer, and of consenting age. Despite dire warnings that such openness would encourage promiscuous behavior, the exact opposite proved true. The Netherlands maintains one of the lowest rates of teen pregnancy in the industrialized world. In comparison, US rates are among the highest.

After shopping the brick storefronts, John selected a woman who looked like centerfold material. He was awkward and eager, like any inexperienced teenager, and in her skillful hands, it was over before it began. But she was gracious and allowed him to stay while she patiently answered his many questions. John had to ask how someone so beautiful could possibly be a prostitute. It was a surprise to learn that she had a husband and young son upstairs where they resided in one of the apartments of the three-story building.

John left the red-light district with a little more self-assurance and, unexpectedly, a higher opinion of women. The interaction with the prostitute actually helped erase some of the confusing, hypocritical messages about sex he'd received from his mother. He and his buddies departed Amsterdam and continued on to West Berlin. John couldn't speak for them, but he never sought the services of a prostitute during the remainder of his time in Germany. Anyway, it was soon after returning from vacation that he met Karen. Naturally, the guys bragged about their escapades, so Karen knew about his visit to the red-light district. He had no reason to conceal anything from her, still believing his future was with Christie. When John said goodbye to Baumholder, he said goodbye to some wonderful memories, and he thought he said goodbye to Karen, too.

***

Following the overseas flight from Germany to England Air Force Base in Louisiana, members of the 565th were now packed in a military bus and approaching their final destination.

"This place is flatter than a fuckin' pancake," a voice boomed, arousing the busload of weary soldiers.

John had to agree. He had been staring out the window for the past hour. Never having been to Louisiana before, he didn't know what the landscape would be like. It sure didn't resemble Germany. Nevertheless, John was glad to be back in the States. He was finally on the same continent as Christie. As soon as possible, he would put in for leave and go to Pennsylvania to sort things out with her.

"Welcome to Fort-fucking-Polk," another voice droned.

John's foot tapped in restless anticipation as he wondered what these new surroundings would bring. His body was anxious to stand and stretch. When the bus slowed as it neared the Fort's gates, John spotted a billboard displaying the silhouette of a combat soldier. The bayonet of the soldier's M-16 pointed at a small, shadowy figure wearing a cone-shaped hat. The words Bong a Cong were emblazoned across the bottom of the billboard with lightning-shaped letters. As the bus passed through the gates, John glimpsed another sign: Welcome to Fort Polk, Birthplace of Combat Infantrymen for Viet Nam.

Chapter 3

"Hey, Seebeth!"

John's scowl lifted into a wide smile when he caught sight of a familiar face from the 565th approaching on the sidewalk.

"Hey, Norton! How's it hanging?" John gave the tall man a playful punch on the shoulder.

Jim Norton wasn't a medic, and he never frequented John's regular watering hole, the Budapest. However, when John visited the company office area back in Germany, the two often traded wit over Norton's desk in the finance department.

"I haven't seen you since Baumholder," John commented.

"It's hard to believe that we've been at Polk for almost three months," Norton remarked. Wiping perspiration from his brow, he asked, "Can you believe this heat and humidity? Fortunately for me, I'm in an air-conditioned office most of the day."

"That must protect you from the mosquitoes. Geez, they're the size of small aircraft here," John jested.

"And just as fierce. Well, what would we expect to come out of Tigerland?"

Jim referred to a portion of Fort Polk's nearly 200,000 acres filled with dense, jungle vegetation. The Louisiana swamp area had been converted into Vietnam-like terrain for realistic advanced infantry training. Tigerland was the infamous final stop before soldiers were shipped off to Vietnam.

"It's a lot different than Germany," Jim reflected.

"You can say that again." John's smile faded as the realization of his predicament came back to mind.

"How's it going for you?" Norton inquired.

"This place is one big bummer," John complained, looking up into Norton's Army-issued, black-framed glasses. "I'm going to request a transfer out of the 565th. I'm fed up with this whole scene."

"Whoa! Where are you going to go? Transferring out of the 565th is a sure ticket to Vietnam."

"I'm going to apply to jump school and become a paratrooper."

"Damn! That sounds like a one-way ticket to Nam," Norton exclaimed. "You know, the 565th is pretty well situated here. We're on permanent call for NATO. We have standby orders to return to Europe in case of an international crisis, so we can't be sent to Nam. Lots of guys would give their right arms to get into the 565th. And some guys that didn't get in probably gave their right arms in Vietnam." Norton scoffed at his own sarcastic comment.

"I'm tired of all the bullshit," John grumbled. "I'm a trained medic, but all I do is take care of a cracker-box. I'm sick of being married to an Army ambulance and trying to make myself look busy on the motorpool line, and I've had it with all the goddamned, chicken-shit inspections."

Norton stood quietly and listened to John spill his frustrations. When John took a breath, he voiced, "What's so different here than what you were doing in Germany?"

John turned his head to watch several soldiers walk out of the commissary. Norton was right. It had been the same Mickey Mouse bullshit back in Baumholder where there were few requests for the services of the 565th's fifty ambulances. At Fort Polk, the most common requests came from the fort's firing ranges during shooting practice. There were also calls from Tigerland when a soldier sprained an ankle or suffered from heat exhaustion. After transporting the injured soldier to the infirmary, the ambulance would return to the motorpool line where it could again wait for weeks to be the vehicle on-call.

Each day, six days a week, week in, week out, John and the rest of the medics were required to be on the motorpool line overseeing the care and maintenance of the ambulances. Aside from washing the vehicle's interior and exterior, they checked the battery and radiator fluids and made sure the gas tank was topped off. The exact same maintenance procedures had been performed the day before— and the day before that—and the day before that—regardless of the fact that most of the vehicles hadn't even moved a mile. John would remove the vehicle's logbook from the glove compartment and record a daily entry to verify that the procedures had been meticulously followed precisely according to regulations. He found the tasks so repetitive, he swore he could do the routine blindfolded. John figured that his checking and rechecking of the dipstick was the most wear and tear his ambulance received.

The company was on the motorpool line for eight hours, although the overall routine actually took about two. It became a creative challenge to stretch two hours of work into a full day. Compared to his hard labor at the bread factory, John concluded it was more difficult to pretend to look busy than to actually do work. Several Sergeants walked the line to answer questions or help with problems but mostly to make sure that everyone was complying with the maintenance duties and not slacking off. They played a cat-and-mouse game with the medics who often relieved their boredom by congregating in the back of an ambulance to shoot the bull or play pinochle. John realized his life needed greater purpose when his biggest sense of accomplishment was to pull one over on the Sergeants—or occasionally win a hand of pinochle.

Every other week the company commander and his entourage would walk the motorpool line and conduct a vehicle inspection. John would stand at attention in his starched fatigues and spit-shined boots beside his assigned ambulance. While his vehicle was examined for infractions, his heart pounded at the dread of being gigged. If the slightest trace of battery acid erosion was found, or if a vehicle's tire pressure was determined to be under or over inflated, an overnight or weekend pass would be taken away—an unthinkable thing to do to a guy for a little too much air. Playing a make believe game of toy soldier with its constant harassment was getting real old for John. Most of the personnel stuck on the motorpool line griped about the pettiness, but they were willing to stomach it. John couldn't. He was churning on the inside and needed more of a reason to get out of bed in the morning.

Turning back to face Norton, John granted, "You're right. It's the same bullshit it was in Germany. Nothing's changed—except my tolerance level." After a pause he uttered, "And my good buddy, Billy, and a lot of the old timers have left."

"Yeah," Norton confirmed. "I noticed that a number of the draftees finished their two-year stint and have been discharged back into civilian life. The paperwork of their replacements crossed my desk."

John shrugged his shoulders. It was hard to see Billy and the others go. He missed the cohesiveness and camaraderie he had known in Germany.

"Well, you have to admit," Norton appeased, "there are plenty worse jobs in the Army. You could be in an armored division or the infantry and out in the field in all kinds of weather, eating Army rations, sleeping in a pup-tent, covered with dust or rolling around in the mud."

"I know," John agreed. Even though his job in the 565th was routine and monotonous and the inspections were a pain in the ass, he knew many Army jobs were much dirtier and more difficult and dangerous. In comparison, his work wasn't strenuous; he remained relatively clean and dry; he ate cafeteria-style food three times a day; and he slept on a mattress.

"Don't you have a girl in the States?"

"That's over," John brusquely stated. He pressed his lips together and lowered his gaze to the toe of his boot. All optimism of reuniting with Christie had been deflated by a phone call. She told him not to request a leave. She said that she and the Marine were really serious and were talking about getting married. John still contemplated making the trip; however, after calling Christie's house and talking to one of her sisters, he decided to wait. Hopefully, this thing with the Marine would run its course. Even if he had gone back on leave, where would he have stayed? His mother had remarried and moved to New Jersey, and his father had sold their home and was also remarrying.

"Do you socialize here?" Norton questioned. "There's a swimming pool and bowling alley on base, plus a tennis court and beer garden."

"Yeah, sure! The possibility of socializing at that corrugated-roofed, steel-tabled, piss-serving beer garden is nonexistent," John sneered. "After drinking good German stout out of a glass boot, I can't drink that watered-down near-beer out of a paper cup. If you want a real beer you have to go outside the fort, and I've been to that hellhole Leesville. It's nothing like Baumholder, that's for sure." John tightened his jaw as he thought about the good times he and his buddies had at the Budapest. It was a friendly place. He'd met Karen there. Leesville offered no such opportunity for casually meeting girls. It was a harsh soldier's town with women to match.

Norton removed his glasses and wiped sweat from the bridge of his nose as he inquired, "What do you have left, another year?"

"Eighteen months. And I don't want to spend it doing this chicken-shit job. I'm applying to jump school." John pulled himself to his full height of five feet nine inches. There was something about being a paratrooper that elicited pride and accomplishment. At basic training, John had observed the paratroopers with their berets and bloused boots. Fort Bragg was the home of the 82nd Airborne Division and the US Special Forces, the Green Berets.

John had witnessed how those soldiers commanded admiration and respect simply by walking into a room. John desired a noble presence like theirs. He knew if he tried hard enough, he could be one of them, instead of being an inconsequential ambulance polisher.

"Seebeth, if you're really willing to go to that extreme to get away from the 565th and Fort Polk, why don't you consider flying aboard helicopters? I hear rumors about a new helicopter medical evacuation unit being formed."

"What's that about?"

"I don't know all the details," Norton began, "but I heard the new unit is looking for committed volunteers. They need medics, pilots, crew chiefs, and other support personnel.

"Thanks for that lead, Jim. I'm going to look into it."

"Well, good luck to you, John."

As the two shook hands, Norton advised, "If I had to make a choice between the two, I'd pick the helicopter assignment over jumping out of an airplane." Taking a step toward the commissary, he rotated to face John and chuckled, "To me, it doesn't make any sense to willfully jump out of a perfectly good plane."

John followed through on his initial idea and submitted an application to jump school. He bought a pair of jump boots and started running every afternoon to get in better shape. Performing ambulance maintenance hardly prepared him for the strenuous physical demands of a paratrooper. He also requested a transfer to the new helicopter ambulance unit Norton had mentioned, figuring whichever came through first would hold his destiny. It was a surprise to hear from the ambulance company so soon. Three days after submitting his request, John had an interview scheduled with the 236th Medical Detachment Helicopter Ambulance Unit.

The morning of his interview, he took extra care in dressing. His hair had been trimmed the day before to remove any trace of curl from his forelock. No need to shave, as he had not yet grown facial hair. To him, it was timesaving. To some of his stubbled and whiskered buddies, his peach-fuzzed, baby face was a target of teasing. Standing tall in his starched fatigues and Brasso-polished belt buckle, John was confident about his appearance and determined to be reassigned to a more challenging and meaningful job.

"I'm here for an interview with First Sergeant LaForge," John announced as he entered the 236th Orderly Room. He noted that the lanky soldier bent over the filing cabinet was wearing a Specialist E-4 patch on his sleeve. John had been promoted to the same rank soon after arriving at Fort Polk.

"You must be Specialist Seebeth," the soldier established after checking paperwork on his desk.

John nodded. Despite the fact that the office was not air-conditioned, the man appeared cool and neatly attired.

"I'm Roy Reynolds, the Detachment Clerk." Motioning to several folding chairs against the wall, he directed, "Take a seat. Sergeant LaForge, who is acting First Sergeant, will be here shortly."

"How many job slots are open?" John queried as he leaned his stiff spine against the hard metal.

"There will be four officers, ten warrant officers, and thirty-four enlisted personnel in all," Reynolds replied. "Most of the support staff, like me, have already been selected by the Detachment Commander, Major Jackson. He's the one responsible for organizing the 236th."

"Did you volunteer for your job?" John wanted to know.

"I was recruited by Major Jackson. He went around to the different holding companies looking for people with the right mix of skill and personality. I was honored to be selected."

Reynolds stopped to answer the phone while the word honored reverberated in John's head. Currently, he was at an emotional and intellectual dead end, so the idea of having a job worthy of honor appealed to him.

When Reynolds hung up the phone, he asked John, "How did you hear about Dustoff?"

"Excuse me?"

"Have you ever heard of the term 'Dustoff'?"

"I don't believe I have."

"That's the radio call sign for the Army's medevacs. They took that name because when the helicopters make pickups in dry fields the rotor wash blows dust, dirt, poncho liners, shelter halves, and whatnot all over the men on the ground." Reynolds moved several folders to the corner of his desk before continuing, "Instead of frequently changing radio call signs—like other units—Dustoff has become the permanent call sign for all Army helicopter ambulance units assigned to medical command in Vietnam. It avoids confusion and facilitates better evacuations. So the 236th will have the call sign Dustoff, too."

John smiled as he listened. He liked this talkative guy, Reynolds.

"From what I've learned since joining the unit, the Army began using helicopters to evacuate the wounded in Korea, but aeromedical evacuation has become a highly organized, crucial operation in Vietnam." Reynolds paused while carefully inserting a document into the typewriter on his desk. "It really boosts troop morale to know that if one of their own gets wounded, a helicopter ambulance will be there within minutes. One guy in particular, Major Charles Kelly, is credited for getting the Army to designate choppers to the sole purpose of picking up the wounded. Before that, the wounded had to wait for a chopper that might be delivering supplies or providing general support tasks. Legend has it, Madman Kelly, as he was nicknamed by those who knew him, was quite the swashbuckler."

Brimming with curiosity, John soaked up every detail about this potential assignment.

"Kelly left an almost mythical legacy of flying into impossible situations to rescue the wounded. Really, it's the very best our national character has to offer—Americans risking their lives to save others."

John silently agreed. This job was speaking to his soul.

"And now with over half a million US soldiers in Vietnam, more medical evacuations are needed," Reynolds explained. "So the 236th and 237th are being formed."

"Where's Major Kelly today?"

"He piloted his last mission four years ago. Major Kelly was mortally wounded during a rescue mission." Reynolds turned his attention to a stack of papers on his desk. In a quieter tone he confided, "The grunts told him to turn back because enemy fire had increased and conditions were too dangerous. But in Kelly's no-compromise, no-hesitation style, he told them, 'When I have your wounded.' He really set the standard for Dustoff's bravery."

The office door banged open and John reflexively jumped to his feet. A short, heavyset man entered and stomped into the adjoining office without acknowledging John or Roy Reynolds. As he walked by, John couldn't miss the wide pools of sweat darkening the man's shirt and a bulging belly overlapping a belt buckle in bad need of polishing.

After a few minutes of silence, Reynolds stood and walked into the office. He returned and said to John, "First Sergeant LaForge will see you now."

The First Sergeant gestured for John to take the only vacant chair in the cramped room, directly across from his desk. John lowered himself into the chair and eyed the beefy man who had an unlit cigar stub protruding from the corner of his mouth.

Briefly glancing at an open folder, LaForge looked up and declared, "Says here you grew up in Pennsylvania."

"Just outside Philadelphia, sir," John affirmed.

"Myself, I'm a Cajun boy. Louisiana born and bred."

John smiled politely, recognizing a deep accent.

"All right, Specialist Seebeth. Explain your reasons for wanting to transfer to the 236th."

John took a breath and looked straight into LaForge's eyes. He talked nonstop for several minutes about his frustration with his current situation and his desire to find a more challenging and fulfilling job opportunity.

LaForge listened while chewing on his cigar butt. The smoldering heat caused perspiration to collect on his forehead. In the eyes of John's impeccably dressed First Sergeant with the 565th, the unkempt appearance of First Sergeant LaForge would be considered gig worthy. All the same—after listening to Reynolds' description of Dustoff—John reckoned he would kiss LaForge's ass in the middle of the fort's parade ground in order to get transferred to this new unit.

When John finished speaking, LaForge asked, "Do you understand what the mission of Dustoff is and how dangerous it can be?" Without waiting for an answer, he bent his big body forward and rested his forearms on top of the open folder. Clasping his hands together he stated, "The 236th has been given five new UH-1H Bell Hueys, and the only purpose of these helicopters is to be used as ambulances to save people's lives. And the only responsibility of the crews that fly these helicopter ambulances is to make sure that the mission of saving lives is carried out successfully. These helicopters and their crews are going to be sent to Vietnam in the near future."

John slowly wiped his palms against his thighs but kept his focus on the Sergeant.

"The stakes are high for each mission," LaForge admitted. "There's a war going on over there, and the enemy—he plays by a different set of rules. Our helicopters have a big Red Cross on them, and according to the Geneva Conventions, they're unarmed. But those Commie dinks, they don't honor them humanitarian efforts. You see, our country plays by the rules, but the enemy has no problem using that Red Cross for a bull's eye."

John swallowed hard but maintained the neutral expression on his face.

"Ya know, the injuries you'll see in Vietnam ain't nothin' like what you've had to deal with in your ambulance company." LaForge shifted the cigar to the opposite corner of his mouth. "In the cargo bay of that chopper, you're gonna see shit you ain't never seen. You're gonna see guys die from a puncture wound caused by a tiny piece of shrapnel." He held up his stubby fingers to indicate a fraction of an inch. "And you're gonna see guys blown apart with massive tissue damage and blood loss, yet they're still alive. A Dustoff medic has to deal with multiple casualties. You could find yourself in a situation where you have a dozen patients onboard and they be suffering from all kinds of traumatic wounds. The flight medic has to make some damn hard choices. He has to make life-and-death decisions. And while you're tending to your patients, you could be constantly shot at by the enemy. I'm not going to lie to you. Dustoff crews have a high casualty rate."

John listened silently, feeling the color drain out of his face despite the heat and humidity.

"I'm trying to make it as clear as possible, because we don't need to go through the trouble of training flight medics and then have to reassign them because they can't hack the situation." LaForge's voice bounced off the walls of the small office after bellowing his last remark. Leaning back in his chair, he scrutinized John's face.

John didn't move. His palms were sweating, but he kept his rigid mask in tact.

"Well, what's your decision, Specialist Seebeth? Do you understand the danger and responsibility? Do you still request a transfer?"

"Yes, First Sergeant La Forge. I understand the danger and responsibility, and my request for a transfer still stands."

LaForge nodded and took the cigar stub out of his mouth as he explained the next steps in the interview process. John heard the words, but his head was spinning. Up until this moment, he hadn't thought much about Vietnam, and he certainly didn't have an understanding of how dangerous and gruesome the job of a flight medic was when he submitted his application to the 236th. The magnitude of his decision was beginning to sink in. Exiting the First Sergeant's office, John saw another smartly dressed soldier waiting to interview with LaForge. John read the nametag on his uniform: Hartman. As he hastened out the door, John noticed that Hartman's cheeks were flame-red, quite a contrast from his own ashen face.

Walking from the building into the hot sun, John's stomach turned over. His mind told him not to worry about First Sergeant La Forge's dramatic remarks. He pushed his thoughts to more positive ones, like the sense of pride and accomplishment he would feel symbolized by the crewmember wings he would wear on his uniform. Plus, he would be doing an honorable job of saving lives. Making a change from his safe routine involved a level of risk, but it was a risk he believed worth taking.

When word came down that he was being transferred out of the 565th and into the 236th, John buzzed with excitement. He felt a smile form on his face as he realized that the time had finally arrived for him to say goodbye to that olive-drab, Red Cross-clad, cracker-box ambulance he had diapered for so many months. John was eager to share his news. He decided to head to the commissary and get some change to make a phone call. Maybe he'd call his mother. She always told him he'd never amount to anything, so won't she be impressed to hear about his job—his important job that follows the honorable tradition of Major Kelly. John decided to get enough

32

change to make a call to Germany, too. He wanted to share the news with Karen. It would be really nice to hear her voice again.

***

Wearing his field jacket, John walked up the dropped rear doors of the Lockheed C-141 Starlifter. It had been a relief to stretch his legs and wander around the Yokota terminal during a several-hour layover while the plane refueled. The cramped seating of the aircraft allowed limited leg and elbowroom between men. A versatile workhorse, the C-141's main hold could be rapidly configured for different missions. Today, a combination of passengers and cargo were being transported to Vietnam.

John and fellow members of the 236th, along with the other new company, the 237th, lumbered along the aisle of the monstrous, military transport and returned to their aft-facing seats. Most of the men were sluggish, still recovering from the heavy drinking of Miller Lite the night before. They didn't know who provided the cases of beer, but they willingly followed the tradition of getting wasted-ass drunk before going off to war.

"I'm still pissed," a guy from the 237th walking up the ramp in front of John complained. "Why did they have to destroy my whole roll of film? I had some nice pictures of my girlfriend on that roll."

"Are you still bitching about the MPs confiscating your film when we left England Air Base yesterday?" his buddy asked. "You weren't the only one, they took everyone's film if they caught them taking pictures."

"Well, why didn't they tell us we couldn't take pictures instead of destroying our film? I just wanted to show my mother the plane

33

we took out of Alexandria. And I would have really liked to have shown her a picture of the Alaskan mountains when we stopped to refuel in Elmendorf."

"My uncle is stationed at Elmendorf," the other soldier commented, "and we met up during our stopover. I wanted to take a picture of us, but he told me to put the camera away. They don't want any pictures of the C-141s. He said it could be a security risk because they have thirty or forty Starlifters landing there every day."

The soldiers' conversation faded from earshot when John reached his row and threaded himself through the narrow space to reclaim his seat next to Tom Hartman. He and the flush-faced soldier from LaForge's office both ended up as medics with the 236th. Even though it lacked half its authorized number of medics, the 236th was declared combat-ready and departed from Fort Polk yesterday. Furthermore, a last minute loss of two members left the unit even shorter. One of their medics was reassigned because his wife just had a baby, and her requests to keep her husband Stateside must have been made to the right offices. Also, one less aircraft mechanic would be going to Vietnam with them. Rumor had it that when the mechanic was home on leave the week before departing, he shot himself in the foot. Rather than avoiding Vietnam, he would end up going later when his foot healed.

Before sitting, John held up a fifteen-inch, black velvet canvas stretched on a wooden frame. Impulsively, he bought the oil painting from a vendor in the terminal.

"What do you think she's saying to him?" John quizzed Hartman.

Tom studied the figures depicted on velvet. A smiling, gray-haired Oriental woman was whispering into the ear of a balding, long-bearded, Oriental man. The man's wide grin and sparkling eyes glimmered with joy.

"She's probably telling him that there's liquor instead of tea in the teapot she's holding," Hartman offered. Tom's reddened cheeks revealed his exhaustion.

"What do you think?" John probed the guy sitting behind Tom, "What's she saying to him?"

"She's telling him to get ready. She just slipped an aphrodisiac in his teacup."

"Nah, look at his face," interrupted another soldier. "He already got off! And she's telling him she's going to give him another blow-job tomorrow."

Laughter circulated in the vicinity as John enticed more guys to guess what the little old lady was saying to the man. Each suggestion became raunchier than the last, elevating the mood of the tired men until it was time to settle in for takeoff.

"Next stop, Viet-fucking-Nam," someone from the other side of the aisle yelled.

"Whatever possessed you to buy that silly painting?" Tom questioned, slumping down in his seat.

"I guess she spoke to me." John chuckled as he placed the painting under his own seat, stuffing it beside his helmet and the rest of his web gear.

It was dark outside when they boarded, but John would have enjoyed seeing the lights of Japan from the air. That was impossible, because other than the front windows for the pilots, there were no windows in the back of the 168-foot C-141. John felt insignificant inside the Starlifter's cavernous cargo compartment. He could only see the back of a lot of heads and, in the far rear of the aircraft, stacks of palettes loaded with equipment.

Turning toward Tom he asked, "Do you think they'll have a turkey dinner for us when we land? Ya know, tomorrow's Thanksgiving."

After a lapse of silence, John noticed Tom's chin was resting upon his chest. Hartman had slipped into another restless catnap—about the only sleep they could grab on this uncomfortable flight. Even though he had lost all sense of time, John automatically glanced at his watch and was almost surprised to see a wedding band on his left hand. He could scarcely recall the sequence of events that led to his marriage six weeks ago. The long distance telephone call to Karen on the day he was accepted into the 236th resulted in a renewal of their correspondence, which led to her coming to the States for a visit. And the visit somehow ended up with a wedding.

John closed his eyes, but his mind was racing too much for sleep. Running through his head were the recollections of his two-week leave last month. He arrived at Philadelphia International Airport in early October to stay with his mother and her husband, Eduardo. It had been a long time since he had seen his mother, plus she had gained a substantial amount of weight. John didn't even recognize her at the terminal and walked right past her at the gate. She excused his oversight but made her disapproval of his new job assignment loud and clear.

"What were you thinking, volunteering for Vietnam? I don't know why anyone in their right mind would want to fly around Vietnam in a helicopter," she berated.

Everyday, his mother reminded him of how foolish he was for signing up to fly Dustoff.

On his first day of leave, John drove eighty miles from his mother's house in Lakehurst, New Jersey to Christie's home outside Philadelphia. Her family was overjoyed to see him. Christie was not. A date had been set for her wedding to the Marine, and John's hidden hopes of rekindling their relationship were doused for good. The drive back to Lakehurst was long and painful as Christie's final rejection sank into his bones. Finally nearing his mother's home, John took some comfort in knowing that Karen would soon be arriving from Germany for a visit.

Since John's mother never attempted to conceal her disapproval of Christie, it was a surprise when she warmly welcomed Karen into her home. Nevertheless, his mother wouldn't even consider John's request of allowing them to share a bedroom.

"I enforce a no hanky-panky rule under my roof," his mother piously declared.

As John curled up on the couch each night, he was angry at his mother's hypocrisy. He remembered waking up when he was nine years-old and finding her dressed in a fancy negligee, entertaining her boyfriend in the living room while his father was hard at work at the bread factory. How dare she now assert such priggish morals!

John opened his eyes after being jostled in his seat. Hearing the sound of the C-141's engines, he knew the airship had begun to taxi toward the runway. Leaning back, he considered how his own life had rolled out of control a few weeks ago. There had been no discussion of marriage when arrangements were made for Karen's visit. Yet, almost immediately after her arrival, Karen teamed up with his mother and began lobbying for a baby. Following a few days of coercion from both of them, John relented. Why not? The more he learned about Vietnam during his flight training, the more he began to believe he might not make it back alive.

Karen was now seventeen but still in high school. Her dislike of school was evident, but there was never a discussion about how her education would be affected by marriage. Of course, his mother had only been seventeen when she gave birth to John, so Karen's age was never an issue for her. As much as Karen's parents liked John, they would prefer that their only daughter wait until she finished school. But Karen was not one to ask for permission. Naturally, her parents could not attend the wedding on such short notice.

Looking back, it seemed that the idea of marriage culminated from three things: Karen's desire to escape her unhappy situation in Germany; his mother's desire to have a grandchild in case her son died in Vietnam; and John's desire to have sex. Undoubtedly, the news of Christie's upcoming wedding also influenced his receptivity to the idea.

John decided that if he were going to marry, he wanted to be married in his childhood church. He had it in his heart that he would only be married once, and he wanted to do it right. It involved making a number of 200-mile roundtrips from New Jersey to the Calvary Memorial Methodist Church outside of Philadelphia to make wedding plans. His mother and Karen tried to persuade him to get married by a justice of the peace in Lakehurst.

"Why go through all the trouble and expense? Getting married is getting married," his mother nagged. "It doesn't matter if you do it in a church or in a courthouse."

His mother's words held little meaning. She had been married twice by a JP. Obviously, she hadn't taken her first marriage vows to his father very seriously.

"If we get married by a JP," Karen urged, "we'll have more time to be together. Or else, it's gonna take your whole leave just to make all the plans."

Despite their arguments, John held his ground and insisted on marrying in the only church he had ever known. Making arrangements for the wedding did end up using all but three days of leave, but he and Christie had planned a church wedding, so how could he settle for anything less? To John, marriage was sacred. His childhood church—especially through the music and hymns—represented the place where he first experienced the divine presence of an infinite greatness. He wanted his marriage to be different from his parents', so he was adamant about having a consecrated ceremony.

Shaken by the movement of the C-141, John straightened and looked around. The aircraft must be getting in position for take-off, because he could hear the high-pitched whine as the engines reached full throttle. He wrestled with his body, trying to stretch his cramped legs, but there was little room between the jump seats. He felt extremely uncomfortable, particularly when the night before his wedding came to mind. He and Karen were alone in his mother's house, talking and caressing on the living room floor.

"Johnny, make love to me," Karen had suddenly whispered in his ear.

After using every ounce of self-control throughout the entire time they had known each other, John was angry that she would make this request on the eve of their wedding. Tomorrow they would be married in the Calvary Memorial Methodist Church. Karen would walk down the aisle wearing a white gown and veil sewn by Eduardo's mother. John would stand at the altar in his Class A dress uniform. He was only twenty, but in a week's time he had rushed around and organized everything. He had used every cent of his own money to pay for it all, even borrowing money from his high school buddy, Eddie, in order to have a two-day honeymoon. Tonight, after days of restraint, Karen wanted to fuck.

"Sure! You want to fuck?" John raged. "Okay, let's fuck. And oh—by the way—I don't love you."

All the stress of the past hectic week, along with the tension of living under the same roof with his mother, plus the pressures of the pending Vietnam assignment exploded in John's harsh words. They brought tears to Karen's eyes. She promised that in time he would learn to love her. Nonetheless, it was not a good beginning to their marriage.

When Karen joined John in a small trailer outside of Fort Polk, the honeymoon soon came to an end. Growing up in a dysfunctional household hadn't exactly provided him with a good role model for how to be a loving spouse. His biting remarks—well learned from his mother—would make Karen cry. Insensitively, he even dug up an old picture of Christie and showed it to friends right in front of Karen. No, he had not been a very loving husband. Who could blame Karen for not being a devoted wife? She played the role of housewife for a few weeks, but after a short time became bored and wanted to see other people. When John came home from a busy day at the Fort's infirmary, he just wanted to kick back and have a few beers. If he walked in the door and found their trailer empty, he became incensed. His irritation and anger multiplied if he had to retrieve his wife from a nearby tavern.

Twirling the wedding band round and round his finger with his thumb, John felt his stomach flip. Maybe it was the Japanese food he ate at the Yokota Air Base. Maybe it was from facing backwards in the plane for so many hours. Maybe it was the uncertainty of his future.

Karen had cried when they parted. He put her on a plane to New Jersey before he left. She would stay with his mother, and he would send money each month to pay for her expenses. Now that he was on the other side of the world and about to enter harm's way, Karen's love seemed ever more important to him.

John was thrust rearward and the seatbelt pressed against his chest as the Starlifter began its ascent. He knew they were headed for Da Nang, but he didn't know it was the busiest airport in the world. In 1968, Da Nang had more landings and takeoffs than Chicago's O'Hare. To be honest, John would have had a hard time locating the country of Vietnam—the heel of Asia—on a world map, let alone the city of Da Nang. He would be flying missions to save soldiers' lives, but he really didn't understand what the war was about. What was Communism, anyhow? And why was it so bad we had to go to war to keep it from spreading? Unexpectedly, the memory of Miss Crutcher entered his thoughts. The topic of his final English paper, *The Danger of Indifference to Public Affairs* suddenly carried new meaning.

Chapter 4

John scraped the remaining scrambled eggs to the side of his paper plate with a plastic fork. Finished with breakfast, he tossed his trash into a large bin at the end of the mess hall. John had no complaint about Army food. It was similar to what he knew from his high school cafeteria. Compared to the TV dinners served at home, he'd considered the meals he ate as a busboy at Howard Johnson gourmet, so Army rations were okay by him. When John and his unit landed in Da Nang nearly a month ago, a Thanksgiving dinner had been waiting for them. The new arrivals chowed down on turkey, unaware that twenty US soldiers would be leaving Vietnam in body bags by the end of that Thanksgiving Day.

Exiting the mess hall and heading back to his unit's area for morning formation, a salty breeze felt cool against John's face as he stepped along the PSP, the interlocking perforated steel panels that served as sidewalks throughout the sandy shores of the complex at Red Beach. PSP had been invented during World War II for use as runways. In Vietnam, the steel plates seemed to be everywhere, including the flight line and sidewalks around the compound. Approximately six miles north of the city of Da Nang, the 236th was co-located at Red Beach with a transportation battalion and several other maintenance support units. It was obvious the quarters of the 236th had been the former encampment of the 1st Cavalry, because the 1st Cav's insignia of a yellow Norman shield with a baldric and horse's head had been stenciled all over the plywood buildings when the 236th first arrived. John heard that the 1st Cavalry Division had been relocated to ward off enemy threats near Saigon.

Other than driving a jeep across Highway 1 to buy cigarettes from the huge PX at the 1st Marine Division facility known as Freedom Hill, John rarely wandered from his unit's area. The 236th was tucked into a small corner of the large aviation installation called "The Paddock." The Paddock was one of forty-five US installations and sixty-five South Vietnamese installations housed at Da Nang's immense military base. The Da Nang Vital Area (DVA) encompassed nearly fifty square miles of territory with cantonments stretching from Red Beach to Marble Mountain and the Cau Do River. In 1968, the DVA supported two-thirds of the Navy's strength in Vietnam. In addition, it supported 7,000 US Air Force personnel, 81,000 Marines, and about half that number of Army personnel from seventy-three battalions. Also, the DVA was home to over half a million Vietnamese civilians who had been driven from their countryside villages by bombings and military sweeps. Swarming to the cities for safety, displaced peasants relocated into makeshift shantytowns crowded close to the military installations where many sought employment. Throughout Vietnam, millions of refugees became dependent on the American bases for survival.

John noticed the morning sky was beginning to fade from red to blue. Since the sand was a magnificent white, he wondered if the Marines who first landed here in 1965 tagged the beach "Red Beach" because of the spectacular reflections of the sunrises upon the sea. While the 3rd Marine Division was officially the first ground force sent to Vietnam, Zeke, the unit's Radio Operator and a buddy of John's, insisted that the US government had been involved years earlier.

"Do you really believe so much could be accomplished in only three years?" Zeke challenged. "I was talking to a member of the Navy's Construction Battalion, and he said the Seabees have been in Vietnam for at least ten years. They dredged ports and improved canals. I mean, how could they have built hundreds of miles of roads and dozens of bridges and airfields in such a short time?"

"Well, maybe they hustled," John suggested.

Ezekiel Goddard attended college a couple of years before being drafted, perhaps giving him a more skeptical eye than John. A big, silver peace sign hung alongside the dog tags around his neck. Zeke was none too keen on the structure of military hierarchy.

"Look at the number of medical facilities here," Zeke argued, adjusting his black-rimmed, standard-Army-supply eyeglasses. "The 236th is one of twenty-five detachments under the command of the 67th Medical Group. And the 67th is one of four or five major elements of the 44th Medical Brigade. I read in *Stars and Stripes* that there are 5,283 hospital beds in Vietnam." Zeke was a regular reader of *Stars and Stripes*, the official daily newspaper published by the US Armed Forces.

"I heard the Army's 95th Evacuation Hospital in Da Nang just opened in April," John mentioned.

"Yeah, that's the eighth hospital that the 67th oversees. I read

45

there are nearly twenty US hospitals here. I don't know what it's like in Philly, but I tell you, Trenton, New Jersey could use a new hospital or some reconstruction dollars to patch some potholes." Zeke ended the conversation by saying, "Don't be a fool, get back to school, control your drool, and think thoughts that are cool."

How could John possibly respond to that? He laughed as Zeke walked away on his skinny, bowed legs.

From the mess hall, John stopped by his plywood hooch. Hooch was slang for their barracks and referred to the simple thatched dwellings of the Vietnamese peasants. He grabbed a new pack of unfiltered Lucky Strikes from his footlocker. Since arriving, John and the rest of his unit had built partitions inside their hooches and filled and stacked sandbags outside them. He shared the hooch with Tom Hartman and two other medics.

Peering over at Hartman's bed, John knocked on the dividing wall.

"Hey, Tom! What are you doing? Formation is in ten minutes."

Half-dressed, Tom sat up and replied, "It's my stomach. Man, I feel nauseous."

"Can you make formation?"

"Yeah, I think I'll be okay." Tom moaned as he thrust his arms into the sleeves of his olive-drab fatigue shirt.

The two joined about twenty other men already standing in line. The pilots and officers were not required to report to morning formation, nor were workers in the detachment's Operations Office, such as Roy Reynolds. Soon, acting First Sergeant LaForge's bulky body stepped forward to deliver the day's announcements.

"Just a reminder," LaForge barked, "I don't want to hear about any of you men going into that miserable collection of huts known as Dogpatch." LaForge referred to the small South Vietnamese civilian city of tin shacks huddled right outside the base. "That place is a refuge for deserters and AWOLs, along with drug peddlers and infected prostitutes. There could be Viet Cong agents and terrorists mingling around there, and since you can't tell the difference between Charlie and a friendly peasant, do yourselves a favor and keep the hell out of Dogpatch."

One of the crew chiefs, Robert Long, kept his focus on the ground as LaForge spoke. Robert had already made a few acquaintances in Dogpatch.

After an unpleasant incident outside Fort Polk in Leesville that ended up with John spending a night in jail for the only time in his life, he didn't have to be reminded about dangers lurking off base. He stayed clear of Dogpatch.

LaForge spat the soggy cigar stub into the sand before resuming. "It's okay to go down to our area of beach here to swim and sunbathe, but be on watch for strong wind and waves. The weather here can change fast, so don't get carried away in the water and end up on the other side of the concertina wire. That side of the beach is full of land mines and God knows what. Be alert at all times. You never know where those sneaky, slant-eyed gooks are gonna be."

John glanced over at Tom and noticed that his face and neck were brighter than Red Beach at dawn, but he seemed to be holding together so far.

"The wood I requisitioned from the Seabees has arrived," LaForge continued, "so those of you who aren't flying today's VIP missions can work on constructing our unit's clubhouse. And, I hap-

47

pened to get my hands on a case of Bicardi, so I'm trading some bottles of rum with the Marines to get enough lumber to build that handball court you want, too."

LaForge's news was met with whoops of approval, John's included.

"All right," The First Sergeant commanded, regaining silence. "I need a medic to volunteer to go down to Chu Lai today and train with the 54th Medical Evacuation Unit for a week. You're gonna shadow an experienced medic for some on-the-job-training. Now that our choppers are all assembled and up and running we're gonna begin flying serious rescue missions. Which of you medics volunteers to go first?"

John didn't hesitate. He was the only medic to raise his hand. Later, Hartman would tell him that he saw LaForge's eyes roll when John's hand shot up. LaForge had apparently formed an impression of John and Tom as being a pair of goody-two-shoes.

As the men broke formation, Zeke reached for a cigarette. "At least that fat ass doesn't put us through those nit-picking inspections that were part of our routine back in the States," he quietly commented about LaForge. "Probably because he's the raunchiest one in the unit."

John grinned. Zeke's own rumpled fatigues would definitely have gotten him gigged outside the war zone.

Zeke finished lighting his cigarette and added, "But you know, I'd even put up with inspections to *get back to the world*." Zeke used a common phrase among soldiers. Get back to the world meant to get back home to the good ol' USA.

As Tom approached, Zeke remarked, "Hartman, you are one red

dude today."

"I think I have a stomach flu," Tom muttered.

"Aren't you supposed to fly a VIP mission?" John asked.

"Yeah, we're picking someone up at the airport and taking him to the 95ᵗʰ, but I should be okay by then."

"Well, good luck," John offered as he moved toward his hooch to pack his flight bag. "I'll see you guys in a week."

"And good luck to you," Tom called as he headed in the direction of the latrine.

"Have a Merry Christmas in Chu Lai," Zeke wished while turning toward Operations to begin his shift. "Hope you get to see Bob Hope," he yelled over his shoulder.

John couldn't grasp the realty of Christmas being a few days away. Compared to last year when he was in Germany celebrating with Karen's family in a wintry, postcard setting, the ninety degree heat of Da Nang made the holiday seem surreal. What a contrast! Not that Vietnam wasn't beautiful. Aboard the helicopter traveling almost sixty miles south to Chu Lai, John was struck with the awesome beauty of the land. Several miles west of Da Nang, a chain of towering mountains protruded from the flat coastal plain, abruptly rising without any softening foothills. From the sky, Vietnam was a verdant tapestry of soaring mountains and braided rivers spilling across vast, fertile deltas. In the distant hinterlands, John could distinguish otherworldly rock formations. It was almost unbelievable to think a war was taking place in this lush environment, except numerous pockmarks on the scenic terrain were evidence of war's fury. John knew the massive soup bowls were bomb craters from B-52 Stratofortress strikes. Without question, the most devastating weapon of the war, the Boeing eight-jet heavy bomber flew 1,200 sorties every month in 1968, with each sortie dropping twenty to thirty tons of bombs. By the end of the war, the US would leave the land bomb-scarred, having blasted 23 million craters into Vietnam's landscape.

Most of the flight to Chu Lai the helicopter flew "feet wet," or low over the ocean. Flying above the water avoided artillery fire while providing a view of the glistening white beaches along the shores of the South China Sea. The pilot said they were near Hoi An when they spotted the battleship, the USS *New Jersey*. Before landing, John had a view of the mid-sized city, which in reality was the Army-Marine-Navy Base at Chu Lai.

"Welcome to the 54th. I'm Rich Bernardo."

John shook hands with the tall, black-haired medic he would be shadowing. When assigned to Bernardo, the Operations Officer for the 54th told John he was one of their best, having recently been awarded the Silver Star for displaying gallantry while giving medical aid to the wounded during extreme combat conditions. This combat-seasoned medic would have a lot to teach him. It was a surprise to learn that Bernardo was only four years John's senior. Something about his dark eyes made him appear much older than his twenty-four years. After tossing his gear on a cot in Bernardo's hooch, John met the other members of the crew.

Over the next week, John went up and down with Bernardo and crew as they responded to requests for medical evacuations at all times of day and night. John was an extra pair of hands, and like the crew chief, did not act without Bernardo's direction. During his training at Fort Polk, John had sutured bodies badly beaten from bar fights in Leesville. He'd seen how stabbings and shootings could mince flesh. He also witnessed a couple of bodies chewed up in car accidents, but nothing prepared him for the extreme mutilation he would see in the cargo bay of a Dustoff chopper. Sergeant LaForge hadn't exaggerated during his interview when warning about the shit he'd see.

It was late afternoon when a call came in to pick up two Vietnamese civilians. The landing zone (LZ) was considered not "hot", which meant no enemy fire was taking place in the vicinity. Nevertheless, Bernardo warned John to treat all LZs as hot because the enemy often refrained from firing their weapons until the Dustoff chopper had loaded its patients and begun its ascent. The added weight slowed takeoff and provided an easier target. A direct hit by a rocket-propelled grenade (RPG) could turn a helicopter into a huge, deadly fireball. A hit to any of its crucial moving parts could cause a chopper to fall out of the sky and crash, making the chances of exploding even greater, as JP-4 jet fuel was notorious for igniting upon impact. The enemy targeted helicopter ambulances because they knew it was a real blow to the morale of the ground troops to see their rescuing angel go down with their wounded comrades onboard.

When the skids of the 54th's chopper touched ground at the LZ, John watched as two litters were quickly loaded into the cargo bay. A Vietnamese girl was on each stretcher, and John guessed they were both in their early teens. One girl had shrapnel wounds all over her body. Despite a horrified expression on her face, she was conscious. The other girl had a two-foot long, two-inch diameter tree branch protruding from the side of her abdomen. She was dead. John noticed that her body was half covered with mud, as though she had been partially submerged in a rice paddy. What was their story? What in the world happened to them?

John watched as Bernardo keyed his helmet mike and spoke to the pilots.

"I do not locate an exit wound with the tree branch," Bernardo reported.

The pilots' responses were unheard by John, since he was not wearing a helmet with earphones and a microphone. Dustoff crews wore helmets fitted with audio equipment connected to an internal intercom system because the Huey was a particularly noisy helicopter. When in forward flight, the tip of the advancing 48-foot diameter rotor blade breaks the speed of sound, creating a small sonic boom. The characteristic "whomp, whomp" sound of the Huey made in-flight communication difficult without an intercom.

Switching off his mike, Bernardo shouted and gestured to John, "I'm not going to touch or probe near this girl's wound because she could be booby trapped." Bernardo continued to swab blood from the other girl's shrapnel wounds and added, "It's highly unlikely that she is, but we can never underestimate the ingenious ways Charlie tries to kill us."

John nodded his understanding and looked down at the dead girl's face. Even in death, she looked sweet and innocent. It was hard to imagine that she might carry a bomb inside her.

The pilot had radioed ahead and requested an x-ray machine be set up in a bunkered area. When they landed, one girl received medical treatment, and the other was x-rayed to see if the branch was connected to a small explosive device imbedded in her body.

John helped Bernardo wash down the cargo bay and recheck supplies while waiting to hear if the girl with the tree branch was booby-trapped. As it turned out, she was not.

"Those girls were in the wrong place at the wrong time," Bernardo summarized. "You see, an artillery shell can strike a tree and cause it to blow up, sending splintered pieces of tree everywhere. The branches are like missiles and fly through the air at high velocity, impaling anything in their path."

"So that girl was speared with a flying tree branch," John confirmed.

"That would be my guess. When bombs explode, everything around can be blown to smithereens, and all kinds of potentially lethal objects fly through the air. You'll see bone fragments or rock pieces as deadly as bullets."

"She was so young and innocent," John murmured, still thinking of the image of the dead girl's face.

"John, I'm going to give you some advice," Bernardo stated as he put his hand on John's shoulder. "And I ask you to trust me on this because I've been through it, and I know what I'm talking about. When you evacuate a wounded patient, especially if they're severely injured, your job is to treat them, drop them off at a medical facility, and then erase them from your mind. You've got to forget about them. There's nothing more you can do. The rest is up to the doctors, themselves, and their God. In order to maintain your own emotional sanity, you have to move on and do the job you've been trained to do."

Sitting on the edge of the cargo bay, both medics lit a cigarette and inhaled deeply.

"You're married?" Bernardo clarified, pointing to John's wedding band.

"Yeah," John replied, glancing down at his hand.

"Any kids?"

"No." The last letter from Karen verified that she had not become pregnant.

"Well, I have a three-year-old son, and it's especially tough when the victims are children," Bernardo reflected. "It's easier for me to deal with the pain of treating wounded grownups, maybe because I know it's grownups who are making this war, and it's the grownups who are killing and maiming each other. The children are the war's unintended victims. They're the innocent ones. They're the ones who will eventually have to live with the results of what the grownups have wrought—that is, if they manage to live at all."

"Come on, let's go!" the pilot ordered Bernardo and John.

"Another call?" Bernardo questioned.

"It's Christmas Eve! We're going to see Bob Hope," the pilot answered, taking his seat behind the controls.

The chopper landed on a pad very near the location of the USO show. John was hit with a wave of throbbing, wild excitement as soon as they stepped into the rear of the crowded amphitheater. The place felt like a rowdy party, packed with enthusiastic soldiers all gathered to watch Operation Holly—the name of 1968's production. John kept his eyes on the miniskirted Golddiggers as they gyrated and kicked to the heart-pounding music. For a moment, he forgot about the Vietnamese girl impaled by the tree branch.

Thunderous applause welcomed Bob Hope to the stage. He began his routine with a reference to the second manned mission of the Apollo space program and the three astronauts who were looping around the moon right at that very moment. "I don't know what's the big deal about sending three men out to the moon when there are 500,000 men here wanting to *get back to the world.*"

John and the crew didn't stay long enough to hear Bob Hope's entire monologue. They missed seeing Ann-Margret and Miss World, too, but they had to return to their station in case there was another call for a medevac.

Their chopper had taken a hit on Christmas Day, and the crew agreed it was a great Christmas present to have received no serious damage. Bernardo informed John that he had also received another gift.

"You're no longer an FNG," Bernardo proclaimed. He used the soldier's slang meaning Fucking-New-Guy. "Now that you received enemy fire, you officially had your cherry broken." Bernardo slapped John on the back. "Glad the 54th could be of service to you!"

Christmas night, the base was showing *The Green Berets*, and John and Bernardo found seats in the packed room to view it. John was especially interested in watching the movie, because his mother said it frightened her when she and Eduardo saw the new release at a theater in Lakehurst. In fact, the film made her so angry, she stopped talking to her son because he volunteered for Vietnam, even refusing to say goodbye when he left. In Chu Lai, the soldiers found the movie to be funny more than frightening. Their frequent catcalls and jeers ridiculed the unrealistic action and preposterous dialogue. The Chinese and Korean actors hardly resembled the Vietnamese they were supposed to portray, not to mention the Caucasians dressed as Viet Cong. After a helicopter crash sequence when an unscathed John Wayne burst out of a downed chopper and hit the ground running, the roomful of soldiers in Chu Lai burst out in laughter.

John's training with the 54th ended three days after Christmas. Bernardo had been a wealth of information, and John knew he would be a better medic because of his time with Rich Bernardo. Back in Da Nang, John checked his M-16 and .38 caliber revolver at the unit's armory located in the supply room. He then walked over to the other side of the building to the Operations Office. The acting mail clerk handed him just one letter. It was from his kid sister. Nothing from Karen. He'd been gone a week, how could there be no mail from his wife?

That night, sleep eluded John as he lay on his mattress in the medic's hooch. He pushed the radio and ashtray to the side of the crude shelf he had built so he could better see the framed picture of Karen. It was an old picture, taken in Baumholder. He was waiting for her to send a new one. Sitting up, John was about to call over to Tom but then remembered Hartman was down in Chu Lai. He had volunteered to follow John for training, although he would be shadowing a different medic. Reclining again, John closed his eyes. A conversation with Bernardo came to mind. They had been talking between missions on their last day together when Bernardo spoke words John would never forget.

"Do you understand the purpose of your patient protector?" Bernardo asked, referring to the .38 caliber pistol worn by members of the Dustoff crews.

John put his hand on top of the holster carrying his sidearm. Like

John and Bernardo, most medics preferred wearing a hip-holster to the shoulder-holster pilots favored.

Without waiting for a reply, Bernardo continued, "You saw how we don't allow the grunts to bring their weapons onboard and how hard it was for some of them to part with their M-16, but we can't take the chance of having an accidental discharge. Not only does it put the other passengers at risk, it poses a danger to the helicopter itself. So in the event your chopper is shot down or forced to land, your unarmed patient's safety is your paramount concern."

Taking a deep breath, Bernardo resumed, "If it appears that your position is about to be overtaken by the enemy and there's no hope of rescue and it seems like a sure thing that you're going to be captured, it's the medic's duty to explain the situation to each of the patients. And after they hear the medic's assessment of the situation, they can exercise their choice about whether or not they want to be taken prisoner. If the wounded soldier doesn't want to be taken prisoner, then you pass him your .38 so he can shoot himself in the head."

"Right!" John snickered. What kind of a fool did Bernardo take him for? Surely he was bullshitting. None of John's instructors at Fort Sam Houston ever mentioned anything like this during medic training.

The expression on Bernardo's face remained somber. His dead-serious eyes told John this was not a joke. This was for real. John's smile disappeared and his shoulders sagged as he continued to listen carefully to this experienced and admired medic.

"If the patient doesn't want to be taken prisoner but doesn't have the heart to shoot himself, then that will be your job." After a pause, Bernardo added, "And I advise you to keep the last bullet for yourself."

John still had a hard time believing this wasn't a joke. Never did he remotely fathom that his patient protector might be used to shoot his own patient. A look of shock and disbelief must have lingered on his face because Bernardo persisted in driving the point home.

"Remember the American soldier we picked up the day after Christmas? The one who'd been tortured by the Viet-fucking-Cong?" Bernardo questioned.

"How could I forget him?" John sighed. It was the first time he had witnessed a body that had been wracked by torture. Images of the soldier and the stench of his rotting flesh were permanently imprinted in John's senses. He remembered how baling wire had been wrapped so tightly around the soldier's arms and legs that it cut to the bone. Plus, the man's hands and feet had been cut off. In the nearly hundred-degree heat, the body was decomposing rapidly. The horrific memory of the bloated corpse filled with squirming maggots still haunted John.

"Just think what that poor guy suffered," Bernardo lamented. "Which would you prefer? Would you rather have your hands and feet hacked off one-by-one with a machete? Or would you take a bullet to the head?"

Tossing on his side, sleep was more distant than ever as John struggled to convince himself he would be able to perform the ultimate duty of patient protection. "If I am ever in such a dire situation, I will never allow myself to be taken prisoner. I will shoot myself first." John replayed that mantra over and over in his head.

A whining mosquito had found its way inside John's mosquito net. It was lusting for his blood just like Charlie. With the aid of his flashlight, he won the battle with the mosquito and stretched out in search of sleep once again.

The night air was suddenly pierced with thunder from the sea. It sounded exactly like a locomotive, but John knew it wasn't a freight train.

"That's the Navy clearing its throat," Zeke announced the first time they heard the noise. "In actuality," he elaborated, "I read in *Stars and Stripes* that the battleship, named after my very own home state, is floating along the coast and broadsiding Vietnam at night with its 5-inch and 16-inch shells." Zeke explained that it took 300 to 600 pounds of gunpowder for the USS *New Jersey*'s powerful guns to blast a one ton shell over twenty miles inland. "Just think, those shells are the size and weight of a VW beetle," he added with a smirk. "Imagine what it would be like to be bombarded by one of those puppies in the middle of the night. Yeow! Jumpin' Jack Flash! It's a Gas! Gas! Gas!"

Sleep became even more elusive for John as he thought he felt his hooch vibrate from the concussive booms of the *New Jersey*'s cannon blasts. Instead of sheep, he pictured VW beetles hurling over his head, flying past Da Nang to who-knows-where. He lay in bed praying none of the rounds fired short.

Chapter 5

January 4, 1969

Dear Johnny,

HAPPY NEW YEAR!!!!!!

Your sister sez you're mad cuz I don't write more. Well, OK!!! Here's a letter!!

Things are kind of bad right now. I hope you don't get mad at me but I'm just going to say it—Johnny—I don't like your mother very much. She is rude to me!! When she found out I'm not pregnant she said it was due to you being a D-E-S baby. D-E-S is short for a drug the doctor gave her when she was pregnant with you. They found out later that D-E-S hurts babies. Boys can never make a baby of their own.

Oh, Johnny, I'm so sad and so sorry I had to tell you this. I think your mother should of told you. Why didn't she say something when she talked so much about us having a baby?

Now you see why things are bad here. I can't stay. I'm moving to West Virginia to stay with Grandma Flora. I go on Monday Jan. 6. I really need some more money to pay for things.

OK!! I will send a picture of me. But my hair is too short!! I got it cut so no dye is left. It's way too short. But it will grow by the time you get back. I'll NEVER dye it again!!!

I miss you. Hope you are saving lots of lives.

All my love and heart,

Karen

John folded the slip of paper inscribed with Grandma Flora's address and phone number and tucked it into his wallet. He reread Karen's letter one more time before sticking it inside his flight bag. John looked over at Jim Owens, a pilot, stretched out on his mattress and sound asleep. The crew chief, Ted Wilcox, was in the same position on his mattress. Lying on his stomach, the helicopter commander, Steve Goodman, was busy writing, probably a letter to his wife. Rising from his own bed and reaching for a cigarette from the front pocket of his fatigue shirt, John stepped outside the hooch where the Dustoff crew was quartered at LZ Baldy.

LZ Baldy was a large, stationary firebase (or fire support base) located about twenty miles south of Da Nang and was now serving as a resupply point for the 196th Light Infantry Brigade. General Westmoreland, Senior military commander of the United States forces in Vietnam, pioneered the idea of firebases as a war tactic. Unlike previous wars, where opposing troops scrimmaged along front lines for territorial conquest, there were no actual fronts between armies in Vietnam. Westmoreland pointed out that the Western front in Vietnam was a thousand miles long. To take advantage of his better-armed and more mobile helicopter troops, General Westmoreland dotted the landscape of South Vietnam with innumerable firebases. Often circular in shape to conform to the dictates of the terrain, fire support bases in the mountainous region near Da Nang were commonly located on high elevation vantage points. Initially cleared by blasts, bulldozers, and a defoliant such as Agent Orange, troops and supplies were then transported in by helicopters. Howitzers and large-caliber guns were positioned to achieve interlocking fields of fire with neighboring firebases.

Firebases allowed Westmoreland to employ a strategy called "search and destroy." Patrols would maneuver from the bases, searching for enemy troops and caches of weapons and rice. When contact was made, soldiers would call in artillery and air support, and if needed, more infantry could quickly be airlifted via helicopters to surround and annihilate the enemy force. Since commanders were taught to use generous volumes of firepower instead of manpower to accomplish their military objectives, the American military would end up expending more than eight million tons of artillery on targets in Vietnam—roughly four times the tonnage dropped during World War II and the equivalent of 600 Hiroshima-sized bombs. Westmoreland's strategy was one of attrition. He wanted his superior firepower to kill Viet Cong guerillas and the North Vietnamese Army (NVA) faster than they could be replaced.

The US military divided South Vietnam into four military zones, and the 236th's area of operations (AO) was located in the first, northernmost one. The I Corps region consisted of five provinces, including Quang Ngai, the birthplace of Ho Chi Minh. Forbidding landscape in I Corps favored the enemy. Triple canopy jungles, steep peaks, and deep ravines made it difficult to shove the NVA out of their mountain redoubts. With almost no natural landing zones, even for agile helicopters, I Corps remained a stronghold of the NVA and a hotbed of guerilla resistance throughout the entire war.

Taking a last deep drag from his unfiltered Lucky, John walked the short distance from the Dustoff crew's hooch to the aid station. While some firebases were no more than cleared hills lined with bunkers and razor wire, LZ Baldy's almost five square miles included an aid station, which was permanently attended by Company C of the 23rd Medical Battalion, Americal Division in direct support of the 196th Light Infantry Brigade. Out of the 500,000 US troops serving in Vietnam in 1968, the Chargers, as the 196th nicknamed themselves, were among the 80,000 soldiers actually involved in combat operations that year.

This was John's fourth rotation at LZ Baldy, also known as Hill 63. Fire support bases were often named for their physical characteristics, and the bald rock outcropping in the center of Baldy may have inspired its name. Firebases were also named after officers or fallen heroes, and Baldy could have been named to honor Colonel Paul A. Baldy, Sr., an advisor to the South Vietnamese Army in the early 1960s. Frequently named after wives or girlfriends or named for reasons unknown to the current occupants, firebases could be renamed several times in their lifespan. Other times, a firebase was moved to a new location but retained its same name. A firebase could be operational for hours, days, or seasonally. Some firebases, like LZ Baldy, were considered permanent because they were in continuous existence for years. Since its establishment as a firebase, Baldy had evolved from rudimentary underground bunkers to sandbagged GP medium tents, and currently, wooden buildings with corrugated steel roofs. The 196th had originally scrounged up a couple of helicopters to evacuate their wounded, but now Baldy housed a Dustoff crew.

In addition to flying missions out of Da Nang, the 236th maintained a one-aircraft field standby at Baldy in order to reach wounded soldiers in remote areas more rapidly. Generally, a pilot, copilot, medic, crew chief, and chopper were assigned to the aid station for four days before returning to Red Beach. A fresh four-man crew and helicopter would then be stationed at Baldy for four days until they were replaced. While the medics held to this four-day rotation system, sometimes the crew chief and his chopper stayed longer or sometimes were replaced sooner, depending on the condition of the aircraft and the need for periodic maintenance inspections. The crew chief remained with the same chopper, as it was his job to keep that bird in the air. Also, during busy days at Baldy, the pilots could surpass their allocated number of flying hours, and then two fresh pilots were brought in to finish the four-day rotation.

Meanwhile, two choppers and their crews were always on-call in Da Nang as first and second standby. The 236th answered medevac requests from north of Da Nang and as far south as Tam Ky. Their AO was over 2,000 square miles and stretched east from the South China Sea and west to the Laotian border. Although the 236th primarily provided support to the Army's Americal Division and Special Forces units, they also evacuated wounded US Marines as well as soldiers from the Army of the Republic of Viet Nam (ARVN) or "Arvins", which was military slang for the US-trained South Vietnamese Regular Army. In addition, Dustoff supported troops from the Republic of South Korea. Despite being a tenth of the size of the US forces, Korea's troop size was significantly larger than any other members of the Free World Military Forces (comprising Australia, New Zealand, the Republic of the Philippines, Taiwan, and the Kingdom of Thailand) who were the US allies in this war.

With so much time either on-call in Da Nang or stationed at Baldy—and without the 236th's full allotment of medics—it seemed to John that he was always flying. At times, as in the case of this rotation, John was back in Baldy after only eight days in Da Nang. This morning, when John walked toward the aid station, he saw a figure quietly standing and looking in the direction of the rising sun. John recognized the familiar, friendly face of the ranking senior medic with the 23rd, Sergeant Gary Weaver. Gary was a nice guy, ten years older than John, and a source of much information.

"Good morning, John," greeted Gary.

"Good morning, Sergeant Weaver," John halfheartedly agreed, wondering if there could be anything good about it. This was his last day of rotation on Baldy, and a good day would be an uneventful one.

"Thankfully, it was a quiet night," Sergeant Weaver sighed, almost in prayer. "Only one mamasan outside the gate this morning bringing a child with high fever and chills—probably another case of malaria."

Vietnamese civilians commonly brought their sick and wounded to the aid station for medical treatment. Especially after an active night of firefights, a long line of injured women, children, and old men would be waiting outside Baldy's entrance gate in the morning. The 23rd had earned the trust of the villagers because of their regular MEDCAP visits (Medical Civil Aid Program). Members of the 23rd willingly volunteered to drive to nearby hamlets and treat sick civilians. Thus, when medical assistance was needed, civilians did not hesitate to seek help from the docs at Baldy.

"And there were no sapper attacks last night," Sergeant Weaver added. He referred to Viet Cong or NVA commandos who snuck into Baldy's perimeter armed with explosives. "No attacks since a week ago when we found a guard and his dog with their throats slit in that bunker over there." Gary pointed to an area by the airstrip, just beyond the chaplain's hooch. "It's amazing how they avoid all the

66

claymores and squeeze their nearly naked bodies through the razor wire. Of course, sometimes they don't, and we see their remains in the morning." Pulling a pack of Salems from his pocket, Gary positioned a cigarette between his lips.

"Last time I was here, sappers were setting off satchel charges almost every night, but you couldn't figure out how they were getting in," John recalled. "Did you ever figure it out?"

"Yeah! The SOBs had a tunnel from outside the perimeter all the way to the center hill."

"Those shrewd little fucks!" John exclaimed.

"After we destroyed the tunnel, the nightly visits ceased." Gary lit his cigarette and took a deep drag.

"Hey, Sergeant Weaver, I thought you didn't smoke," John commented, ready to light another cigarette of his own two-pack-a-day habit.

"I didn't. I gave it up four years ago, but something about being on Baldy makes a cigarette necessary," Gary chuckled.

"How are the two grunts we brought in yesterday?" John inquired. "The ones with heatstroke."

"I think they're going to be fine. They're sound asleep in that new air-conditioned ward we built." Gary referred to a rustic plywood hooch attached to the back of the aid station. Like other structures on Baldy, the company built it using plenty of ingenuity to improvise needed materials along with lumber Chaplain Bartley seemed to miraculously scrounge from Da Nang. The windowless room was insulated with Styrofoam packaging salvaged from boxes of resupply ammunition. A row of cots and a small, generator-operated air conditioner at each end completed the new ward.

"The one guy was in pretty bad shape," John stated, remembering how he had worked quickly to untuck the soldier's pants from his boots and loosen his belt and shirt before starting an IV. After picking up a number of men suffering from heat exhaustion, John had devised a system for keeping full canteens within easy reach. He would shower the nearly unconscious soldier with water from a string of canteens he had roped together, and the rotor wash from the chopper would provide instant cooling.

"He's better now that he's been rehydrated," Gary remarked. "We'll see how he is in three days. I'll tell you, heatstroke will kill a guy as fast as a bullet. Good thing you Dustoff boys got to him in time."

"Well, that's our job, Sergeant Weaver. We're just trying to be there for them."

"And these guys deserve the best," Gary affirmed as he extinguished his cigarette and entered the aid station.

John followed him inside and watched as Gary headed to the rear ward carrying an IV bottle of Ringer's lactate. Rather than lying around the messy, unpartitioned Dustoff hooch, which was perpetually covered with layers of dirt kicked up by the aircraft, John often spent time between missions honing his skills in the aid station. Starting an IV on a large-veined patient in a helicopter was challenging enough because of the vibrations and sudden movements of the chopper. Starting an IV on a Vietnamese patient was even more challenging because of their small veins. Although most Vietnamese were very cooperative and tolerant, John knew they wouldn't sit still forever and take his repeated attempts at sticking them with a needle.

Before checking with Sergeant Weaver to see if he could lend a hand, John stopped at the Tactical Operations Center (TOC), which was a closet-sized room in the front corner of the aid station where a Radio Transmission Operator (RTO) was stationed around the clock. Calls for Dustoff missions came in through TOC, and it was where John could make a telephone call to the 95th Evacuation Hospital. He had called every day to check on the condition of a young Vietnamese boy the crew had delivered there three days ago. While seriously wounded South Vietnamese soldiers and civilians went to the Provincial Hospital in Da Nang, American soldiers and Vietnamese children received state-of-the-art care at the 95th.

Rich Bernardo had warned John to drop off his patients and forget about them. And John had been pretty good about heeding his advice. But then he picked up that little Vietnamese boy. He was probably around 10 years old. He had stepped on a land mine, and the explosion had ripped off his legs. He was in real bad shape. After the boy was placed in the cargo bay, John immediately started an IV to help maintain blood volume. Looking at the boy's shattered body, John felt helpless. The trauma was so severe, it was amazing the little guy was still alive. Splintered bones and torn tissue hung just below his small abdomen, and his severed body oozed fluids. Not knowing what more he could do, John kneeled beside the stretcher and gently stroked the top of the young boy's head. Unconscious but still alive when the helicopter landed at the 95th, that kid was going to need a whole lot of luck to come through this.

"I'm calling to check on the condition of the Vietnamese boy who lost his legs," John explained to the nurse who took his call.

After several moments she returned and said, "That boy died during the night."

John's chest grew heavy as he took a breath. Holding back tears, he left the aid station and walked past the bunker in front of the Dustoff crew's hooch to the outer row of buildings at the edge of the LZ. John leaned against the sandbags piled high against Graves Registration, where a soldier's remains were registered before his final journey home. The dead wouldn't hear his sobs. John wasn't sure why this kid's death hit him so hard. Somehow that youngster's survival represented hope that perhaps all this craziness could be overcome. John cried about the boy—the loss of a young life's promise. He cried about the letter from Karen, aching for her softness and the comfort of her arms. And he cried about the horrible reality of war. This was totally fucked up.

Bernardo's words reverberated in his head. "If you don't forget about them, you're only asking for problems. You've got to forget about them and move on."

John finally understood where Bernardo was coming from and why he warned him to stop caring. Wiping his eyes and lighting a cigarette, John told himself, "My job is to treat them, drop them off at a medical facility, and then erase their image from my consciousness."

John straightened as he heard the familiar sound of two Pratt and Whitney radial engines coming in for a landing. Turning toward Baldy's one-quarter mile airstrip just a few hundred feet away, John saw the Caribou approaching. The tactical airlifter was designed to operate in the most primitive of conditions with STOL (Short Take Off and Landing) capabilities. Caribous made regular stops at Baldy bringing in supplies and troops, and on their return trips, they evacuated the dead.

John set out toward the Dustoff crew's hooch and saw the RTO running in the same direction with a mission sheet in hand.

"You've got an urgent!" the RTO yelled when he spotted John. Of the three categories of missions—urgent, priority, and routine—this was the one where speed saved lives.

John entered the crew's quarters and saw the pilots studying the coordinates of the pickup location on the large topographical map hanging on the hooch's wall.

"Good to go?" the crew chief, Ted Wilcox, asked John. Wilcox blinked his eyes, still blurry from sleep. The side of Ted's face was red and creased where his head had been resting on top of his arm just a few moments ago.

John nodded. He and Wilcox dashed out of the hooch and ran 100 feet to the sandbagged revetment where their helicopter was parked. As soon as he got there, John untied the main rotor blade from its locked position and swung it ninety degrees while Ted wiped mist and dust from the windshield with a couple of towels. John grabbed his body armor, which he kept on the right side of the cargo bay where he sat on the floor behind the copilot's seat. He threaded his head between the OD (olive drab) fabric-covered, twenty-eight pound plates. Ted had already inserted his body between his chicken plates, as their turtle-shell armor was referred to, and was now giving the chopper a fast safety inspection. Climbing into the cargo bay, John rechecked his medical supplies. Everything he needed for a mission was kept in place inside the chopper. Putting on his flight helmet, John made sure it was plugged into the aircraft's intercom system. He pressed the switch on the cord that ran between his helmet and the intercom jack to be certain his microphone was operational.

Within minutes, the pilots were harnessing themselves into the aircraft while conducting a preflight check. John was back outside making sure everything was clear around his side of the chopper. Men had been killed from unwittingly walking into the blur of the Huey's tail rotor.

"Clear?" Steve Goodman, the aircraft commander, questioned without a hint of turmoil in his voice.

John keyed the switch to his helmet mike. "Clear," he replied, mimicking Goodman's calm tone.

"Clear to start," crew chief Wilcox responded, clicking on his own switch and using the same composed manner of speaking. Wilcox stood outside the helicopter with the visor of his helmet down. He kept his eyes on the exhaust in case of a hot start.

Goodman began the start sequence. The transmission slowly whined, and the overhead blade began to turn. When it rotated at thirty percent of operating RPM, Goodman flipped on the overhead fuel switch. With Wilcox on one side and John on the other, they each helped slide an armored plate next to the pilots' seats and assisted them in closing the front doors.

When the outside of the aircraft was secure for takeoff, John and Ted jumped into the cargo bay. John sat unbelted upon a 2-inch-thick, 12-inch-square armored plate capable of stopping a .30 caliber round. He faced aft, overlooking the cargo bay. Wilcox belted himself into the left side hellhole, as the unarmored jump seat was called. With his back to the transmission wall, Wilcox sat by the open cargo bay doors facing outward.

Goodman did not have to say "clear" prior to takeoff, because John and Ted automatically anticipated the procedure. From where he sat behind the copilot, John scanned the ground and sky in search of possible hazards. No aircraft approaching. No wandering personnel in the immediate vicinity. John double clicked the switch on the cord attached to his helmet mike to relay that all was clear on his side of the aircraft.

In a split second, Wilcox performed the same double click on his switch to convey that his side of the aircraft was clear. Wordlessly, the crew functioned like a well-oiled machine.

"Roger that," affirmed Jim Owen, the copilot, as he worked on setting radio frequencies.

Goodman pulled pitch, and the helicopter jerked upward. Pushing the cyclic stick forward, the helicopter nosed over and gradually gained air speed. In no time, it reached 120 knots and began climbing.

John listened as Owen described the nature of the wounded. Five US soldiers had been hit with an RPG. Two were unconscious. One was a triple amp.

"The Blue Ghosts are flying in ahead of us," Goodman's voice related matter-of-factly over the intercom. He was referring to the Huey Cobras, the world's first helicopter gunships, flown by the 196th's air cavalry out of Hawk Hill. A Cobra's fuselage was only about a yard wide, providing an extremely narrow profile when viewed straight on, thus making it difficult to hit as it dove directly toward its target. To support a variety of tactical situations, Cav gunships carried a banquet of weaponry and warhead combinations.

"The Ghosts are going to keep Charlie's head down while we fly in for the pickup," Goodman added.

After flying over rice paddies and hedgerows for twenty minutes, John now strained to listen to the intercom as Goodman made contact with the RTO on the ground.

"See that tree line to the south at three o'clock?" the RTO hollered. "That's where we're taking fire."

Goodman flew in a circular holding pattern at about 1,500 feet while the Cobras, or "Snakes" as they were called, strafed the tree line again. John could see red clouds surrounding the area. The Blue Ghosts were using warheads, which contained 2,200 fleshettes—or steel nails—with fins stamped on one end, resembling tiny darts. A solid-fuel motor would propel the warhead to supersonic speed in less than two seconds, and the rocket would explode a few hundred feet above the terrain, leaving a red dye cloud to mark the release point. From there, the shower of nails would strike the ground in an elliptical pattern approximately the size of a football field.

"Dustoff, as soon as we give them a dose of Willy Pete, you can come on down," one of the Cobra pilots relayed. The pilot used the soldier's jargon for white phosphorus, a chemical the US employed in aerial bombs as well as in explosive rounds from artillery, mortars, or rockets. WP started white-hot fires, impervious even to water. When it hit the skin of a living creature Willy Pete would continue to burn until it burned right through the body. To prevent the enemy from quickly scraping it off, Dow Chemical added polystyrene to their product, which, according to one medic, made it stick like "shit to a blanket." Trying to scrape it off only caused it to spread and burn in new places.

John recognized the huge puff of white smoke produced by the explosion of WP. When some US ground troops were unlucky enough to be in the path of a Willy Peter strike, John knew if the stuff couldn't be cut out of the flesh, the only way to stop it from burning was to prevent it from interacting with oxygen. Using water, Pepsi, or even urine to wet the soil, a mud poultice was scooped up and patted onto the wound to seal it from air.

"All right, Dustoff, we'll keep an eye on Charlie for you while you go in," a Blue Ghost's voice crackled over the intercom.

"What is your recommended approach," Goodman questioned.

John heard Goodman state that they were coming in from the North, away from the tree line where Charlie had been. His stomach tightened when he felt the helicopter start to make its descent. From his position on the floor seated upon his small lead pad, John looked out the open cargo bay and spotted the Cobras flying above in a tight circle. The din of the transmission overwhelmed all other sounds as John strained to hear the chatter and military jargon through his helmet earphones as the RTO on the ground communicated with Goodman. In the background, barely audible, John could hear the grunts' panicked voices. His body craved a cigarette, but his patients would be onboard in only moments, and he had to steel himself for whatever would be arriving in the cargo bay. When the chopper touched down, John jumped out and directed the loading of patients.

"Let's go," Goodman urged in a controlled voice. Like most of the pilots, he maintained a sense of calmness in the midst of chaos, despite being anxious to get out before Charlie got a good aim.

Five big men were literally thrown into the back of the chopper. As soon as they were onboard, John keyed his mike and communicated to Goodman with as few words as possible. "Go," he said.

Concurrently, the guys on the ground backed away from the

helicopter and melted back into the bush. The helicopter rose about ten feet and rotated 180 degrees. Its nosed dipped as it accelerated and flew out the same way it came in.

John was on his knees, already assessing the wounded. Glancing at each man, he checked to see if any of them were spurting blood. No ruptured arteries. Okay. Is everybody breathing?

"Hey, buddy. Look at me now," John yelled to one guy who was drifting out of consciousness. The patient's head was wrapped with blood-soaked gauze, but the bleeding was controlled. "Stay with me, now," John shouted again, making contact by gently grasping the young man's shoulder. Startled, the soldier returned from his haze and was able to focus on John with one unbandaged eye. "You're on your way home. Hang in there." John encouraged.

John wedged his body in between two others and gave them a brief check. One was crying and kicking a leg up and down, but he was conscious. He had some serious shrapnel wounds, especially to his left leg. Blood from his bandaged thigh pooled together with blood from the other soldiers all over the floor of the cargo bay.

"Watch him so he doesn't roll out!" John shouted and gestured to crew chief Wilcox. Dustoffs regularly flew with the doors of the cargo bay wide open, making it necessary to keep a watch on frantic patients as they could come dangerously close to falling out.

John's attention then went to a soldier who was struggling to breathe. He wasn't wearing a shirt, so John could readily lift the Ace bandage wrapped around his upper torso. John examined the Vaseline gauze that covered a sucking chest wound. The bandage was intact, but this guy's breathing was too labored. John bent over and raised the patient's head. Wilcox's hands were immediately upon the patient's shoulders, helping to rotate him to his side. Lowering the blood-saturated Ace bandage, John saw an unbandaged exit wound on his back. No wonder he couldn't breathe. Tending to multiple injuries was challenging enough for a field medic, but the pressure of bandaging while taking enemy fire explained why exit wounds were sometimes missed.

"You're gonna be okay, buddy," John consoled as he stretched his body to reach a foil packet containing a Vaseline gauze. Ripping the packet open, John pressed it against the wound. He then held a handful of cotton gauze on top of it while reaching into his medic's bag for a new Ace bandage. John quickly wrapped it around the man's body to secure the gauze bandage on his back in place.

"You've got a ticket home," John reassured, shouting to be heard above the whir of the transmission. The guy was half conscious but breathing better when John squeezed between the next two soldiers. He had to stop and adjust his body armor. The chicken plates made maneuvering in the cargo bay awkward. The extra thirty pounds could throw him off balance, and the edge of the plate would some-times jab him in the gut as he squatted and kneeled over his patients. After repositioning his armor, John bent over to examine another unconscious patient.

"Oh my God! Oh God!" the soldier beside the unconscious man bawled.

John put his hand on the crying guy's head. "Hang in there, you're gonna get treatment soon!" The patient had a bad shoulder wound but was alert—the only ambulatory one of the five.

Reaching for a bottle of fluid, John started an IV on the uncon-scious soldier who was in really bad shape. Both legs and an arm were shredded. John checked the tourniquets to see if they needed adjusting. The soldier was breathing but remained unconscious.

"No! This can't be happening!" the sobbing soldier continued. "No! No! It isn't right!"

"Just a little longer," John promised, yelling over the Huey's noise. "Hang in there!"

John looked across the cargo bay floor. All the patients were alive. He keyed his microphone and reported the nature of the injuries to the pilots. They would call the information ahead to the aid station so there would be litters waiting, along with a ready medical team.

"Please God! Don't let this be happening!" the soldier kept repeating, clutching at John's shirtsleeve.

John felt the speeding chopper begin its descent. He called over to the young soldier with the bandaged eye, "Hold on, we're on our way. Stay with me, we're almost there!"

Okay. They were all still alive—two of them barely. The wails of the one soldier were pitiful, but everyone reacted differently to being wounded. John had seen big Marines cry like babies for their mothers, and he'd seen others not even flinch despite life threatening injuries. The guy that was crying now wasn't that seriously wounded.

"Larry, look at you! How can this be happening? Oh God! This can't be happening!" the soldier weeped. To John he said, "He's got a wife and two kids!"

Now John realized—the soldier wasn't crying about his own injuries. He was crying for his buddy—Larry. John fought a lump in his throat as he watched the distraught soldier hanging onto his brother-in-arms.

As the Huey made its approach to Baldy's Aid Station, several US soldiers standing near a bunker along the perimeter waved towels and fatigue shirts, trying to get the Dustoff's attention.

"What do those guys want?" Pilot Goodman asked.

From his side of the cargo bay, Ted Wilcox could see six or seven men frantically gesturing and pointing to a soldier prostrate on the ground. "Looks like there could be an injured man," Wilcox spoke into his helmet mike. He moved his arm from side to side to let the guys below know their signal had been seen.

Goodman continued to the aid station, lowering the helicopter onto the faded Red Cross painted on the landing pad. A group of doctors and medics ran out to the chopper. The wash from the rotor created a windstorm of swirling dirt and debris, causing the men to firmly grip the litters. John remained in the cargo bay to assist the litter teams in unloading the patients, starting with the most critically injured. When Larry was placed on a litter, his buddy climbed out of the cargo bay to follow him. Sergeant Weaver quickly approached, ducking to keep the whirling dust out of his eyes. John watched as Gary took hold of the distressed soldier and guided him into the aid station behind Larry.

After the last patient was unloaded, the pilot announced, "Let's go see what those guys want back along the perimeter."

"Clear right!" John affirmed.

"Clear left!" Wilcox reported.

It took less than two minutes to reach the bunker, where several soldiers were bent over one of their buddies. The pilot found a relatively flat area to rest the helicopter's skids. John unplugged his mike and jumped out. One of the soldiers ran over to him.

"This is fucked, man. He took it right in the fucking face. Jesus Christ! Goddamn it! This is so fucked!"

John hurried over to the circle. For a moment, he couldn't believe what he was looking at. A soldier was lying on the ground with a live 40-mm round imbedded in his head. To John, the guy's face seemed like it was made of wax because there was no blood or spewing brain matter. It looked like someone had pressed a big, fat, several-inch bullet into the soft wax of this guy's face right where his eyes were supposed to be. It was a peculiar-looking injury, to say the least. Amazingly, the guy was still alive, although unconscious. John ran back to the chopper, plugged in his mike and related the circumstances to the crew.

While the pilots called Baldy's Aid Station to see how to deal with a soldier with a live round in his head, John heard the story of how it happened. The soldiers were on guard duty along the perimeter. This guy was leaning back against a sandbagged wall. Fighting sleep, his head would drop forward when he dozed. Another soldier a short distance away was loading his M-79 grenade launcher when it accidentally discharged. Because the guy was so close, the round didn't spin the necessary number of revolutions to cause it to detonate, otherwise most of the soldiers in the vicinity would have been wounded, and some could have been killed.

The Dustoff crew transported the patient to the aid station but waited on the helipad while the doctors sought advice on what to do with him. After no more than ten minutes, a couple of medics emerged carrying a litter. The patient with the live round in his head was brought back over to the waiting chopper. Dustoff would now ferry him to the USS *Sanctuary*, a fully equipped hospital ship anchored in the Gulf of Tonkin and specializing in neurological injuries. Meanwhile, the standby Dustoff crew from Da Nang was on the way down to LZ Baldy in order to maintain coverage.

John immediately jumped out of the cargo bay as the litter team approached. Without speaking, they performed the familiar routine of loading the litter into the cargo bay. John took hold of one handle as the first medic released it and moved to the other side to clasp that handle with both hands. They then positioned the litter on the cargo bay floor, and all three medics helped push it in place. Although the Huey was equipped with straps to hold three stacked litters—plus one litter on the floor for a total of four patients on stretchers—John and the other Dustoff crews soon learned to dispense with litters in order to fit more patients onboard. When patients were suspended by the litter straps, it was almost impossible for the medic to reach across the stacked litters to treat the wounded on the other side of the cargo bay. Furthermore, taking time to insert the litters into the straps made the Dustoff more vulnerable and wasted precious seconds at a hot LZ.

After the patient was in position, the medics from the aid station stepped away while John climbed back into the helicopter. In his usual swift motion, he placed his right foot on the floor of the cargo bay and grasped the unused overhead litter strap with his left hand to swing himself inside. Only this time, the strap broke. The weight of John's body armor catapulted him right on top of the patient's litter, and John's knee landed just two dangerous inches from the soldier's face and the live round. John's heart raced, and his body broke out in sweat. He didn't know what it would take for that 40-mm round

81

to detonate. He was just glad his knee hadn't tested the possibility of turning them all into a big red-orange fireball.

"Are we clear right?" Goodman's voice sounded over the intercom.

Steadying himself, John clamored back to his position. "Clear right," he stated, feeling dampness from his perspiration-soaked shirt.

There was nothing he could do for this patient on route to the hospital ship except pray that the live round didn't blow them all up. John examined the piece of strap still clutched in his left hand and discovered why the unbreakable webbing gave way. The frayed strap revealed a hole where a bullet must have ripped through. John didn't know when that happened. While loading patients, it wasn't unusual to hear a round whisking by. Yet sounds and commotion all became background noises as he focused on getting the job done. Tossing the broken strap beside his medic's bag, he pulled out a Lucky and inhaled the calming smoke.

As the Dustoff chopper approached the big white ship marked with Red Crosses, John listened to the voices over the intercom while Goodman received landing instructions.

Someone onboard the USS *Sanctuary* announced, "Congratulations! You've set a record. You're the 1,000th medevac landing this month."

It was a relief to be back in the air without the guy with a live round in his head. For a few minutes, the beauty of the crystal-blue water and pearl-white beaches soothed John's tension as he puffed on another unfiltered Lucky Strike. Later, John would learn that their patient didn't survive. Probably just as well. What would remain of that guy's face once the round was removed?

After returning to Baldy, the crew went over to the small mess tent where Sergeant Weaver had set aside meals for them. The roast beast, as the frequently served meat was called, and cold boiled potatoes were better than nothing. They hadn't finished eating before the RTO ran over with a mission to evacuate an amputee.

This time, Dustoff flew out to a village somewhere in the jungle. When the helicopter landed at the pickup site, the only person to be put on the aircraft was a Vietnamese woman carrying an infant wrapped in a blanket.

John keyed his helmet mike. "Weren't we supposed to pick up someone who was reported to be an amputee?"

"That is correct," Goodman responded.

"Well, the woman who just got onboard has all her appendages."

"What about the baby?" Copilot Owen asked. "Check the baby to see whether it has all its arms and legs."

As soon as John heard Owen's words he thought, "Oh, shit! It's the baby!"

The woman squatted in the middle of the cargo bay floor. John motioned for her to hand him the baby. A terrified look came over her face, and she clutched her child even closer.

John keyed his helmet mike again and said to no one in particular, "Sometimes I really hate this job."

John gestured for Wilcox to help him hold the Vietnamese woman so he could examine the baby. The woman reluctantly handed her child to John. As soon as he took hold of the infant, the woman pressed her empty hands together in prayer and bowed her head over and over again to John. She repeated words he didn't understand, but he knew she was pleading with him to not hurt her baby.

John slowly unwrapped the infant from the dirty blanket and found that the baby was missing one of its arms. There was a tourniquet tied tightly just above the wound. Examining the wound more closely, its edges appeared smooth and straight. The trauma had to have been made by a sharp instrument such as a knife or machete. It appeared someone had cut the baby's lower arm off. It could have been the result of an accident, but since this was a combat zone and John saw crazy things all the time, he was convinced that someone had purposely cut off this baby's arm.

The baby was conscious and not overly upset with his condition. John was actually amazed at his calm reaction. John put a fresh dressing over the infant's wound, wrapped him back up in the blanket, and handed the bundle back to a grateful but sad mother. For the rest of the flight, John's mind struggled to understand why anyone would do such a thing to a baby.

The crew was called on one more mission before their rotation at Baldy ended. On this mission, they picked up a severely wounded South Vietnamese soldier in the middle of a rice paddy. As soon as the ARVN was placed inside the cargo bay, he stopped breathing. John detected a faint heartbeat. Quickly reaching in his bag, John removed a plastic airway and inserted it into the man's mouth. John tilted the patient's head back, cleared the respiratory passageway, pinched the man's nose, and breathed a few of his own breaths through the resuscitation tube. In his rush to treat the patient, John neglected to put a piece of cotton gauze over his end of the plastic airway. During one puff of breath, the Vietnamese soldier suddenly vomited and some partially digested rice shot through to John's end of the plastic tube. John's involuntary inhalation caused him to swallow some of the man's last meal. Immediately removing his lips from the end of the plastic airway, John turned away from the unconscious soldier and began to cough and gag.

Knowing the man was not breathing and would soon die if he didn't get air into his lungs, John struggled to gain control of his own urge to retch. Reaching into the center of his being, John vigorously shook his head to clear it, grabbed some gauze from his medic's bag and purged all other thoughts and sensations from his mind. Totally concentrating on what he was doing, John once again started to puff breaths through the cleared plastic airway into the soldier's lungs.

The man started breathing but soon stopped again. John promptly resumed giving him mouth-to-mouth resuscitation with the help of the plastic airway. When the chopper landed, the Vietnamese soldier was breathing on his own as he was transferred onto a litter and taken into the aid station. John started to climb out of the cargo bay but began retching uncontrollably. He fell out of the chopper. In the shadow of the evening, and on all fours like a dog, John threw up his guts on the helipad. Thankfully, it was the last mission of this rotation. The crew would be back to Baldy soon enough, but it would be a long time before John would be able to eat rice.

Chapter 6

"Hartman missed all the fireworks," Zeke stated sardonically after finishing a swig from a can of Coke, his preferred breakfast drink.

"He probably had his own fireworks down at Baldly," John replied, taking a glug from a carton of Foremost chocolate milk.

"The RTO at Baldy said they could see the explosions from there, so Hartman probably caught the light show." Leaning back against his folding chair, Zeke held up a newspaper. "*Stars and Stripes* reports that Da Nang was the hardest hit." Reading aloud, he continued, "24 Feb 69—Reds Pound US Viet Bases. Fifty rockets pummeled US and ARVN military bases surrounding the city of Da Nang beginning about 2:30 a.m. There was no evidence that the rockets had hit the densely populated city itself. The Communists appeared to be aiming at military installations exclusively." Looking up from the paper through the thick lenses of his black frames, Zeke commented, "Gee, what does that tell us? Yankee go home!"

"It looks like the shitter took a hit," John mentioned. "It's blasted with fragment holes."

"That's going to be a pain in the ass!" Zeke chortled.

"And that huge explosion that rocked the ground during yesterday morning's formation was an ARVN ammunition dump," John added. "That was five hours after the initial rocket strikes."

"OooEEEEE! What a spectacular scene that was!" Zeke laughed. "I thought 'ol LaFart was going to shit himself when that big boom let loose."

"He seems to avoid putting his fat ass anywhere near combat," John grumbled.

"Yeah, I see that he maintains his flying hours by scheduling himself for the safest of VIP missions," Zeke sneered. "I was talking to an RTO down in II Corps, and he said their First Sergeant is a senior medic like LaForge. And their First Sergeant flies his fair share of evacuation rotations. Not like our Top."

Zeke used the unofficial but commonly used term that referred to non-commissioned First Sergeants. Because they were at the top of the company or unit's enlisted ranks, they were nicknamed Top.

"Lately," Zeke verbalized, "Top's prime mission is to oversee the building of the clubhouse. The roof was barely up before he started selling beer from behind the 2x4s."

"What's that wild thing I see following him everywhere?" John asked, raising his eyebrows high as he and Zeke rose from the table and threw out their trash.

"Ha! That's right, you were at Baldy when he started bringing that Vietnamese woman around a few days ago. That's Sucky Fucky."

"Excuse me?"

"You heard me right," Zeke affirmed as they left the mess hall and headed back to their area at Red Beach. "Her ugliness doesn't

88

seem to affect her popularity. Have you noticed she doesn't have any teeth?"

"I haven't been close enough to get a good look. And I don't think I care to!"

"What are you doing after formation? Are you on call?" Zeke questioned as they each lit up a cigarette.

"Unless all hell breaks loose, I finally have a couple days off, so I'm going to drink as much beer as possible and maybe play some volleyball on the beach. I've gotten out of shape." John flexed his right arm muscle in mock exaggeration. "I used to put away a glass boot of good stout every night in Germany, so I've got a lot of catching up to do."

"Well, if you're still standing when I finish my shift, I'll come work out with you." Zeke raised his own skinny arm and imitated John's motion of pretending to lift a can of beer to his lips.

The rest of the morning, John kept busy hammering nails in the almost-finished handball court. It had already become a place where enlisted men and officers mingled together off-duty. Unlike other units, there was less official hierarchy amongst the Dustoff crewmembers. For one thing, several of the Warrant Officer pilots were only 21 years old—younger than some of the medics and crew chiefs. Those young pilots enjoyed hanging out with enlisted men their same age. Shirtless, on the handball court, they were all just young guys playing a game. Plus, when a four-man crew did their rotation at Baldy, they were nearly as close as any husband and wife. The medic, crew chief, and pilots flew together, ate together, shit together in the four-hole latrine and slept in the same hooch. They were never outside shouting distance of one another during their entire four-day assignment.

John was a guy who really enjoyed socializing, and he was friendly with most everyone. However, the changing nature of the crew's rotation schedules seemed to inhibit close friendships. Upon arriving to Vietnam, many original members of the 236th had been exchanged for personnel from other units to prevent everyone's 365-day tour of duty from ending on the same day. And while John related to the other medics, he hardly got to socialize with them, because if they weren't flying, he was. John randomly flew with a variety of pilots according to their own rotation schedules. Furthermore, sometimes John flew missions with unfamiliar choppers and crew chiefs on loan from other units when the 236th's own birds had been shot-up or were receiving routine maintenance. Although he became acquainted with a number of different men, some of John's closest associates were the guys he saw regularly in the unit's compound, like Zeke Goddard and Roy Reynolds.

When John noticed a blister had formed on the palm of his hand, he retired his hammer and checked the progress of a slot-car track some of the guys were building. He then went over to Operations where Roy Reynolds was sitting behind his desk. Roy smiled when John entered.

"Hey, John! You returned safely from your rotation at Baldy, but you end up being here when we got rocketed," Roy exclaimed, running his hand over his neatly combed brown hair.

"Yeah, that was some kind of fireworks," John agreed as he slouched in an empty chair.

Roy picked up several papers on his desk. "I was just reading about the damages. The Marine facility at Marble Mountain was hit, and the Air Force base was hit, but remarkably, there were no casualties. And, fortunately, the fires in the fuel pipelines didn't spread and ignite any of the storage tanks." Roy raised his focus from the papers in his hand and noted John's distracted expression. "Everything all right?"

John shook his head. "How can anything be all right here? Just like always—SNAFU—Situation Normal All Fucked Up!"

Roy put down the papers. Older than most of the men, he often offered counsel and a sympathetic ear to many of the young soldiers. He faithfully lived his upstanding, Midwestern values, never cursing or drinking despite John's constant efforts to gibe him into corruption. "So was there a letter waiting for you from Karen when you got back?" Roy inquired.

"I'm lucky if I get two letters a month," John complained. "Shit, it seems like Hartman gets a letter every fucking day."

"Well, I know he corresponds regularly with his mother," Reynolds offered.

John snickered with disgust. "I got a letter from my mother yesterday. Actually, it wasn't a letter. It was an envelope with this inside it." He stood and reached in his pants' pocket and took out his wallet. Opening the leather billfold, he removed a newspaper clipping and handed it to Roy.

"She's lovely," Reynolds commented about the picture of the bride. "Is this your sister?" After a pause of silence as Roy read Christie's wedding announcement, he handed the clipping back to John. "I guess she's not your sister."

"We used to be engaged." John studied Christie's smiling face. He thought she looked exceedingly beautiful. The wedding announcement stated that her mother had made the velvet bow and veil she was wearing in the picture. She and the Marine were married on Valentine's Day. All her sisters were bridesmaids and wore burgundy velvet dresses also sewn by their mother. John put the clipping back into his wallet.

"So, your mother sent you that announcement—because why?" Roy wondered. "Did she go to the wedding?"

"No, my mother never liked Christie."

"And your mother didn't include a letter in the envelope, just the wedding announcement? I think I'm missing something here." Roy wrinkled his face into a frown.

"My mother's the type to pour salt in your wound."

"She must be very different than Tom's mother. Maybe it's just as well she doesn't write more. With all the wounded you see, you don't need any salt."

"Well, you'd think my wife could write more often. I hate mail call. I fucking hate it."

"John, you have to be patient with your wife. She's young, and she doesn't have any idea what life is like for you here."

"She's probably fucking some longhaired Jody now that she's down in Virginia." John referred to the mythical name for the guy who was fucking a soldier's wife or girlfriend. Just as Charlie was a soldier's enemy in Vietnam, Jody was his enemy back in the States. "I think her old boyfriend used to live in Virginia," John continued.

Roy picked up a pencil and began tapping it on his desk like a schoolteacher. "John, it doesn't do you any good to think like that. This is your day off, why don't you go down to the beach? Or have you checked out the clubhouse? It's almost finished."

"Yeah, I'm planning on doing some serious drinking today, and

I'm about ready to start," John proclaimed. "Come on, let me buy you a beer."

"Kind of you to offer, but no thanks. You know I don't drink."

"Hey, I didn't drink either before I joined the Army, but it goes down pretty easy once you get started."

"Well, thanks anyway, but I've got to get back to work." Reynolds picked up a folder from a stack on his desk. Glancing up at John, he commented under his breath, "You'll probably find First Sergeant LaForge at the clubhouse. It seems to be his new office."

"I see he has a girlfriend."

"Oh, please!" Roy scanned the area, making certain no one was within earshot.

John laughed as he stood and announced, "Well, I'm off."

"Take care of yourself, now." Roy warned, knitting his eyebrows together in concern. "Don't go too wild."

On his way over to the clubhouse, John noticed new changes in the compound. Wood frames were under construction where concrete sidewalks would soon be poured, and Vietnamese workers were now seen in the 236th's area. John observed a half-dozen peasant teenagers filling sandbags, a job he had once performed.

Sure enough, LaForge was in the clubhouse, his stocky arms leaning against the unfinished plywood bar. John recognized the man across from him. Bart Buckman was a crew chief and super-sized guy from Alabama. He and LaForge held plastic cups, and an open bottle of Seagram's Seven Crown sat between them.

"Hey, Seebeth!" Buckman greeted. "Get your ass over here and have a drink."

"Looking good in here. I see you got electricity," John commented as he caught sight of the naked light bulb hanging from the ceiling of the approximately 14x24-foot room. "Are you open for business?"

"I reckon we can find some medicine for a 236th medic," LaForge responded with his usual cigar stub poised in the corner of his mouth. "What'll it be, soldier?"

John looked on the wall where a crude stenciled sign had been hung: Beer 15¢, Soda 15¢, One shot of whiskey 25¢. "I'll have a beer, Sarge."

LaForge pulled open the door of a white refrigerator positioned at the end of the bar. It had been transported on the same ship that brought their helicopters and other supplies and was now plugged in and well stocked with beer. "Ya want Bud, Miller, Schlitz, Hamms, or Ballantine?"

"Budweiser."

John popped open the 12 oz. can of beer just as LaForge was called back into Operations.

"Mind the shop, 'til I get back," LaForge ordered Buckman.

John saw Sucky Fucky stand up from behind a stack of wood and follow LaForge out the door.

"So how was your rotation at Baldy?" Bart asked while refilling his plastic cup.

"Same old fucked-up shit," John replied, chugging the remaining contents of the cold can. "How about another?" he blurted as he reached in his pocket and pulled out a Military Payment Certificate worth five cents and one worth ten cents. MPC was the only currency issued to GIs, and they jokingly referred to the small, colorful paper bills as Monopoly money.

Supplying him with two cans, Bart insisted, "Here. This extra Bud's for you. You could use a beer holiday."

John held one of the cool cans against his forehead before popping the tab and taking another giant swig. "I heard your bird took some hits," he said to Bart.

"Shit, yeah. We were way out there somewhere in East Jesus. I don't know where the fuck we were, probably across the border in Laos. We started taking small-arms fire like we do whenever we fly over AK Valley."

Bart referred to Song Chang Valley, which the grunts nicknamed AK Valley in honor of the AK-47 Soviet-manufactured combat assault rifle, the basic weapon of the Communist forces. The 196th's frequent contact with the NVA in the Song Chang Valley was met with the explosive popping sounds of the AK-47. Similarly, the nearby Communist-dominated Hiep Duc Valley was dubbed Death Valley because of the incessant nose-to-nose contact with the enemy that resulted in a high number of US casualties.

Bart downed the remaining contents of his plastic cup. "The tail rotor drive shaft was shot to hell. Looks like a .51 cal round went through it. I don't know how the fuck we made it back in one piece. So now, my bird's in the maintenance tent waiting for a part, and my ass is gonna be on the ground for a couple days," Buckman smirked, the smell of Seagram's on his breath. "But that's okay by me. We've been getting into hot shit no matter where we've been flying lately. Time to fucking relax." He poured himself another hefty shot.

John finished the second beer in no time and was smiling when he opened his third.

"Ya know, Top's got some girls here," Buckman slurred.

"Yeah, I noticed that group of sandbaggers doing our old job."

"No, not them. I speculate those young, gook sandbaggers are relatives of Sucky Fucky," Bart drawled. "Did ya notice his new business partner—Sucky Fucky?"

"Yeah, she's a real looker," John jested. "What kind of business is he doing with her?"

"Cheap labor for one thing. And like I was saying, since he hooked up with Sucky Fucky, girls have been around. There's a hooch maid in the crew chief's hooch today, and she does more than the laundry if you know what I mean."

At first, John didn't know what Buckman meant.

"It's only five bucks, and she's a cutie pie—for a slant-eyed slope-head," Bart elaborated.

When John heard LaForge barking orders at someone just outside the clubhouse, he finished his fourth beer and told Buckman he was headed for the beach. The rays of the afternoon sun felt like a furnace blast as John walked toward the medic's hooch to put on the Levi cutoffs he wore for swimming trunks. He passed the group of young Vietnamese sandbaggers and was reminded of what Buckman said about the hooch maid. The thought of her whirled in his head as he stepped along the sandy walkways. Why not go see her? He was alive today, but the way things were going, John believed there was a good chance he could die tomorrow. It would really help if he could talk to Karen, but there was no way for him to call her from here. And why didn't she write more? She wasn't working but couldn't find time to write. What was she doing—fucking some Jody? With the end of his life dangling in front of him, John didn't want to die without being with a woman ever again. Karen knew about his visit to the red light district in Amsterdam, so she knew about the ways of soldiers. The hooch maid was here and available. The Top Sergeant brought her here, so how could John question the appropriateness? Hell, this could be his last day alive.

Changing direction, John walked toward the crew chief's hooch. Upon entering, he thought it was empty, but when he walked past a partition, he spotted her. She didn't look like a prostitute. Her black pants and white blouse told him she was a peasant. She looked young—not more than sixteen. John felt shy and awkward, like he was back on the canteen dance floor wanting to ask a pretty girl to dance.

"You," John pointed at her. "You and me...."

The girl dropped her gaze to the floor. She seemed shy, too, as she slipped one leg out of her silk pajama bottom.

Somehow their bodies made the connection. His blond hair and pale blue eyes were a stark contrast to her black hair and eyes. Her rosebud breasts hardly resembled the voluptuous female forms on the wall of his hooch, nor did they come close to filling the red, lace bra of Karen's hanging beside the Playboy calendar. But she was a female, soft and feminine. With all the blood and killing surrounding them, these two human beings shared a tender moment. John's body shuddered a release. He gulped back sobs, and she held him. He clung to her warmth and softness, gently stroking her long, straight hair.

"Your name?" John pointed to her face, brushing his fingertips against her cheek, relishing in the sensation of silkiness. "What is your name?"

She gestured to herself. "Xuan."

To John, it sounded like she said Sue Ann.

"I'm John."

"Babysan," she quietly giggled, using the pidgin term meaning baby.

"I wish I didn't have to go," John murmured. He heard men talking outside and sure didn't want someone to walk into the hooch right now. John reluctantly lifted himself from the bed and pulled up his fatigue pants. He hadn't removed his boots. Reaching in his pocket, he pulled out a five-dollar MPC bill.

Xuan quickly slipped her leg back into her pajama bottom. She shook her head no when he handed her the currency. "Babysan," she uttered, lowering her focus downward.

"No, you should take it. I—I had a good time. You earned it," John rambled as he held the bill out to her, realizing she didn't understand English.

She pushed his hand away and stretched her arm to cup the smooth skin of his whiskerless face with her palm. "Babysan," she whispered, the corners of her mouth rising into a smile.

"Sue Ann," John faintly voiced as he returned her smile.

He walked all the way back to his hooch before thinking about lighting a cigarette. He decided to forego his afternoon at the beach. After only two puffs, John butted the Lucky in the ashtray next to Karen's picture on the small shelf he had built. Lying on his bed, he instantly fell asleep and slept better than he had since arriving in Vietnam.

John probably would have slept right through the night until the next morning if Zeke hadn't come by his hooch to rouse him, reminding him of their vow to get in shape.

"Let's go, Seebeth! You're not going to wimp out on our work-out, are you?" Zeke implored. "Wilcox and Long are meeting us in two minutes."

John and Zeke were standing outside smoking cigarettes when crew chiefs Ted Wilcox and Robert Long approached.

"What's shaking?" Ted said as he swung his arm around John's neck and squeezed it with the crook of his arm. "We saw some shit on the last trip to Baldy, didn't we, doc?"

Before John had a chance to agree, Long responded, "When don't we see shit?"

"I see that you guys have already hit the sauce," Zeke commented.

"Yeah, we pitched in and bought one of those small refrigerators at the PX," Ted replied, releasing the headlock on John's neck. "Now we have our own supply of cold beer in our hooch."

"What can't you buy at that Freedom Hill PX?" Zeke scoffed. "You can order a brand-new car or buy a deluxe stereo. Hell, that PX is better stocked than the one back home at Fort Dix."

"Why are we going to the Enlisted Man's Club?" John questioned. "Why not just drink cold cans from your new fridge?"

"Because there's a band playing at the club!" Ted ran ahead and shuffled his feet in an exaggerated dance move. Spinning around to face the others, he added, "And there are women in the band."

"Filipino women," Zeke specified.

"Tits are tits and ass is ass," Ted responded as he gyrated his hips. "Ooooo, baby!"

"We only get to see slant-eyed women," Robert realized aloud.

"Not the pilots," John commented. "Robert, remember that night at the 95th when you and I sat outside with the bird while Owens and Frasier were in the China Beach Officer's Club?"

"That's right," Robert concurred, "we're sitting in the cargo bay while they're partying with the round-eyed nurses and donut dollies."

"Ya know," Ted continued with his own thoughts, "We pick up lots of guys—and occasionally females, too—with VCS written across their foreheads with grease pencil. I've never thought about it, but who the hell are they?"

"VCS means Viet Cong suspect," Robert stated.

"Victor Charlie," John offered, using military phonetics for the letters V and C.

"I know that," Ted replied, "and I know that Victor Charlie is the enemy, but they look just like regular peasants. How can we tell who the fuck is who? At least the NVA wears uniforms."

"Viet Cong stands for Vietnamese Communist. Cong means communist in Vietnamese," Zeke explained. "Viet Cong is the label the South Vietnamese government gives to any rebels who oppose them. The VC don't call themselves VC. They call themselves the NLF, or National Liberation Front. And the North Vietnamese Army doesn't call itself the NVA. They call themselves the People's Revolutionary Army."

"What are you, some kind of fucking gook-lover?" Ted accused Zeke.

"Cool your jets, dude!" Zeke warned. "I like to learn about my surroundings, and I was talking to the translator, Hoang."

"Hey, did you notice Hoang wasn't around when we were mortared the other day?" Robert interjected. "He probably told them

100

where to point the rockets."

"Yeah, are we supposed to trust all the Vietnamese working for us?" Ted challenged. "All the sandbaggers and hooch maids—how do we know they're not VC?"

"Hoang said that working for the Americans puts him and his family at risk, but he can't refuse the chance to make good money," Zeke pointed out. "Hoang said he makes more money in one week than he would in a year, and he hopes to send his son to college in England, so it's hard to refuse that kind of money."

"Same with the prostitutes," Robert offered. "They support their whole extended families."

"That's something you'd know about," Ted teased as he slapped Robert on the back.

"I have a few friends in Dogpatch," Robert admitted, "and they're some nice people, so shut the fuck up. I visit an old man who runs a sawmill, because I used to work at a sawmill before I was drafted. The guy was cutting some beautiful teak. He said the French planted teak plantations during their occupation."

"Hoang said that most peasants don't support communism," Zeke contributed. "He said they don't even understand what it means. They just want to stay on the land of their ancestors and they want the occupiers out."

"Who the hell are the occupiers?" Ted interrupted.

"We are, asshole," Zeke asserted. "First, the Chinese occupied Vietnam, then the French and Japanese, and now it's the US of A." Zeke stopped to light a cigarette.

"Well, enough of this shit," Ted criticized. "Like they say, the only good gook is a dead gook. Right now, it's party time, and I don't want to think about anything except drinking beer and watching a live woman shake her ass."

After walking for ten minutes, the four men were within sight and sound of the large Enlisted Man's Club on the other side of the Paddock. A couple of already drunk soldiers were standing outside the building, yelling and gesturing to a few others walking in the opposite direction. John noticed that one group of soldiers was black and the other white. He couldn't hear what the groups of soldiers were saying to each other, but he knew it wasn't friendly. John heard about racial tensions between soldiers, but it was not something he experienced in his unit. Dustoff strived to save lives no matter what color the packaging. As they neared the club, John could see a soldier's forehead was cut open and blood smeared the side of his face. His fatigue shirt was ripped at the shoulder. A Military Policeman stood to the side, speaking into a walkie-talkie. Another MP emerged from the doorway with a bedraggled soldier in tow.

"What the fuck is this shit, man?" the black soldier said to the black MP. "I ain't putting up with shit from that white ass. Who's my fucking enemy here? No VC ever called me nigger. Goddamn white man's war."

The MP seemed to have things under control as John and his friends neared the entrance. Men from all over the compound congregated at the club, and sometimes all hell broke loose.

Tinny music from an electric piano floated out the front door as John, Zeke, Ted, and Robert walked in. After procuring a round of beer, the four men stood to one side of the smoke-filled room and watched the band perform under the glow of colorful stage lights, which gave the whole club a reddish glow.

The voice of the keyboardist for the Filipino band sang in a monotone, phonetic way, "C'mon, c'mon, c'mon, bebee now. Twis an' Shou."

Three female singers in spray-on white pants moved to the music with subtle tease. They repeated the song's refrain with expressionless faces and voices. It didn't deter the crowd of drunken soldiers from whistling and whooping and hollering and shouting obscenities. The atmosphere of the club made John think that this was probably what Deadwood was like during the days of the Wild West. MPs were on high alert as drunkenness slipped into warring chaos.

After several hours and many more beers, the foursome left the club and stumbled back to their unit's area. Ted and Robert had their arms draped over each other's shoulders as they sang at the top of their lungs, "Wild thing, you make my heart sing. You make everything GROOVY." Since those were the only lyrics they could remember, they kept repeating them over and over.

"You guys sound like a broken record," Zeke complained.

Zeke wasn't much of a drinker, claiming to be naturally high. The guys agreed with his claim. Zeke didn't need alcohol to act crazy. And as far as John knew, none of his friends in the 236th took drugs or smoked marijuana.

"You're awful quiet tonight," Zeke said to John. "It's usually your off-key voice that would be singing the loudest.

John snorted and continued walking.

"And you'd be the one dancing and kicking like a wild animal."

"Yeah, well, maybe I'm still half asleep."

Suddenly, in the shadows ahead, John and Zeke watched Ted stumble head over heels. Robert buckled in laughter as his dancing partner lay sprawled on the sand. His three upright buddies struggled to get him back to his feet and half dragged him to his hooch, where he passed out on his bunk. The others soon did the same on their own.

Chapter 7

"All right!" Hartman exclaimed. "The Yankees won the opening game of the season! They beat the Washington Senators 8 to 4. And they're favored to beat the Tigers when they go to Detroit on April 11th. Hey, that's this Friday."

"Who gives a fuck?" John grouched. This was one of those rare stretches when both he and Tom Hartman weren't flying at the same time. Lying on his bunk, John reread the same two sentences of the letter he started writing to Karen an hour ago. It was a struggle to put his thoughts on paper. John had just returned from another rotation at Baldy, and his head was pounding with a hangover from last night's boozing. The breeze from his portable fan did little to ease the day's ninety-five degree heat and did nothing to cool his rising irritation.

"You know, the Mets have some strong players this year and...."

"Seriously, Hartman. I'm not interested in hearing about New York's baseball teams. After what Zeke said last night about over 33,000 men having been killed—more than in the whole Korean War—how can you care so much about baseball?"

John's comments were answered with silence from the other side of the partition. Rotating to his side, John propped his head against his knuckles. He didn't follow the politics of the war, so that wasn't why he was upset. He was just sick of all the carnage. It had been a particularly busy four days at Baldy, and quite honestly, he was feeling a strange sort of heartache. Over the past month, John had seen Xuan a half-dozen times. He looked forward to their brief moments together. Their intimate connection, however fleeting, was about the only thing that felt real to him. But now she was gone.

Rolling on his back and covering his face with his hands, the poke of a metal bracelet bumped against his cheek. Xuan had given him the bracelet the third time they had been together.

"To babysan," she had said, pointing to his heart and then sliding the bracelet on his wrist. It was a Vietnamese friendship bracelet, probably pounded into shape by a resident of Dogpatch. "Babysan number one," Xuan hastened to add. She used a phrase that meant "the best." Even if they didn't know any other English, most Vietnamese knew the term "number one" and its opposite, "number ten."

John and Xuan didn't communicate through spoken language, but they shared something the rest of the world might not understand. In actuality, John didn't understand it himself, yet his heart couldn't deny the sweetness he felt when he saw her. She never accepted his money. During the minutes they spent together, the smiles and playful giggles became as important as the sexual release. John moved his hands away from his face and opened his eyes. He wore the friendship bracelet on the same hand as his wedding ring. Right or wrong, those moments of tenderness with Xuan had been a source of peace for him. And then suddenly, she disappeared from his world without explanation. And there was no one he could ask about it.

Just trying to find out if Xuan was in the unit area and where she was located had been a challenge every time John saw her. If he couldn't discreetly discover her whereabouts from Buckman or other crewmembers, John had to resort to asking LaForge, and he hated letting that man have one up on him. Wincing, John recalled the ordeal he went through a couple of weeks ago when he had no choice but to ask LaForge.

Standing at the bar in the clubhouse, John had already finished a couple of beers before reluctantly bringing up the subject. "So, Top," he began in a casual sounding tone, trying to conceal his desire to see Xuan, "are there any hooch maids here today?"

LaForge slowly refilled his glass with Seagrams, taking his time placing the bottle on the shelf before raising his head to acknowledge John's question. "Why should a nice married boy like you want to know the whereabouts of a hooch maid?" The heavily built man chewed on the cigar stub in the corner of his mouth as he directed his eyes at John.

John wanted to ask if LaForge's wife knew about Sucky Fucky, but he kept that thought unexpressed. Instead, he pretended to be supremely interested in crushing his empty Budweiser can with one hand, hating to be at the mercy of this less-than-honorable man.

When Sucky Fucky leaned over and whispered into LaForge's ear, his head jerked back and his face curled into a smirk. To John, LaForge taunted, "Now, do you want any 'ol hooch maid, or do you have a hankering for a particular one? Cuz Sucky Fucky here says she'll clean your hooch for you."

John could still hear the mocking tone of LaForge's horselaugh. LaForge and Sucky Fucky convulsed with laughter while John tightened his lips and squeezed the beer can even harder. That afternoon was the last time John saw Xuan. She never appeared in the unit area again after that day.

Today, Tom's ranting about baseball wasn't the real cause of John's annoyance. The letter John was attempting to write to Karen was the true source of his anguish. Desiring honesty in his marriage, he felt compelled to confess what took place between him and Xuan. However, John had a hard time explaining something that he himself did not fully comprehend.

Ted Wilcox burst into the medics' hooch, and his booming voice broke into John's thoughts. "Hey, anyone interested in going to Freedom Hill? Reynolds got a jeep and said we can make a fast trip to the PX. If you want to go, get your asses over to Operations, pronto!"

John shoved the unfinished letter under his pillow and climbed out from the mosquito net that covered his bed. He walked around the partition to where Hartman was stretched out on his bunk. Like John, Tom kept his area neat and orderly, but the similarities ended there. While John had a Playboy Calendar and Karen's bra prominently displayed, Tom had a Rocky and Bullwinkle Sports Calendar and a poster of the Yankees' schedule hanging on his side of the wall. And while John could hold all the letters he received over the past four months in the palm of one hand, it seemed that every person in Tom's town in upstate New York must have sent him a letter, because his stack of mail nearly overflowed his footlocker.

"I need a carton of cigarettes, so I'm going to ride over with them," John related.

"I'll pass," Hartman proclaimed.

"Do you want me to pick up anything for you?"

"Nah, I'm fine."

John stood quietly for a moment. He noticed a new photo of Tom's high school girlfriend had been added to his shelf. Her sweet face smiled beside a plastic statue of the Virgin Mary and a framed, 8x10 photograph of Tom's whole family gathered around the Christmas tree, taken last December without him. John sighed. "So, you think the Yankees are going to have a good season?"

Tom spread apart his mosquito net and looked over at John. "They've got some pretty strong players this year."

John tightened his lips and nodded. "Damn Yankees."

"Hey, could you pick me up a bag of Fritos?"

"Sure thing," John replied as he ran out to catch up with the others.

John had flown a VIP mission in the morning, so he was wearing his flight suit when he walked into the PX. The unit's emblem was sewn above the breast pocket. On the emblem was a Red Cross with white wings coming out from each side. Above the Red Cross was the word Dustoff, and just below was the unit's motto: Strive to Save Lives.

As John stood in line, two Marines came up to him. They were slogging their M-16s over their shoulders, barrels pointing downward. Judging by the thickness of the red dirt on their battle gear, they looked like they had just come out of a long stay in the bush. John wondered if they could be with FORCE Recons, Marines who made extended foot patrols deep into unfriendly territory to gather information about enemy base camp locations, supply lines, and troop movement. In addition, these trained men sometimes performed assassinations and body snatchings of high-level enemy officers.

"I see the Red Cross on your uniform," one of the Marines said to John. "Do you fly on the helicopter ambulances?"

"Yeah, I'm a flight medic," John explained, thinking how he'd hate to have to lift this hefty fellow to the chopper's top litter rack.

Tears formed in the Marine's eyes as he put his arm around John's shoulder. "I've got to tell you, man. I appreciate what you guys do."

John bowed his head in acknowledgment, a little overwhelmed by this big Marine's emotion.

"I just want you to know that my squad came under enemy fire, and a couple guys got wounded. My best buddy from high school was one of them," he stated, his voice cracking. "The Dustoff ship was called in, and I'll tell you, they openly disregarded their own safety. They flew into that hot LZ and picked up our wounded. I really appreciated what those men in that chopper did, and since I couldn't thank them, I want to thank you."

John walked a little taller the rest of the afternoon. It wasn't the first time he'd been thanked by guys on the ground. Those who flew Dustoff developed a special sense about themselves, which was constantly reinforced by such encounters. After leaving the PX, Roy drove them back to the 236th's area. They were approaching the main entrance of the compound, marked by a twenty-foot rotor blade partially buried in the ground with "The Paddock" painted on the top end, when they heard the terrible sounds of women wailing. The men didn't speak as they drove by the graveyard where a

Vietnamese funeral was taking place. Since their unit area intruded into the burial grounds, it was not uncommon to hear and see funeral processions. A twenty-five foot killing zone lined with concertina wire and dotted with land mines and bunkers separated the graveyard from the perimeter of the compound. As the jeep passed by the crying women, John wondered who was responsible for the death of their loved one—the US or VC?

Reynolds had no sooner pulled up to Operations when the RTO approached the jeep and announced to John, "They need another chopper up. Harrison's bird is unflyable, and the 1-up crew is out on a mission, so you need to get over to the flight line."

"Where's your equipment?" Roy Reynolds asked John.

"It's on Long's chopper from this morning's VIP."

John jumped back on the jeep, and Reynolds sped him over to the flight line where Robert Long was preparing his helicopter for takeoff.

"This is for Hartman," John yelled as he tossed a bag of Fritos onto the seat and headed toward Robert's bird.

Within minutes, the crew was onboard and proceeding toward a train wreck. They didn't know what to expect on this mission, since there was no radio contact with the men at the site. A gunship had called in the crash after catching sight of it from the air.

Soon after leaving Da Nang and heading north toward Hue, the railway steeply rises upward toward the Hai Van Pass. The name means "Pass of the Ocean Clouds", because the peak of the mountain is in the clouds while its foot is close to the sea. The rail line curves through tunnels and hugs the edges of sharp inclinations to climb over 1,500 feet to the summit before descending toward Hue.

The US and South Vietnamese Armies regularly transported supplies via the railway, making the trains frequent and prized targets of the enemy.

The Dustoff crew flew for about thirty minutes before spotting a dark, sleek locomotive that had been pulling about ten boxcars and ten flatcars stacked with palettes and lumber. One section of the train had been blown apart, and the remains of several cars were twisted at odd angles where the tracks ran along the edge of a nearly vertical embankment. As Warrant Officer Stanton circled the area several times, the thundering thumping of the Huey's rotor blades was almost deafening as the sound reverberated off the rock-ribbed walls. Looking down, John noticed a number of South Vietnamese soldiers standing on the mountainside guarding a perimeter, their M-16s silently aimed at an invisible enemy. When the helicopter passed by again, several ARVNs appeared on top of one of the flatcars and were frantically gesturing to the Dustoff.

"They want us to come down," Long stated as he observed the waving men.

"I don't see any wounded," the copilot declared. Without radio contact, the crew had no way of knowing what the situation on the ground was.

"The initial call said they had casualties," Stanton related. And after a pause, "Well, we didn't come all the way out here just to turn around."

"Anyone in the vicinity is certainly aware we're here," the copilot commented, referring to the amplified sound intensity of the chopper echoing against the mountain.

"What's the best way to set this up?" Stanton questioned over the intercom.

112

Staring out the open cargo bay door, John thought this had to be a mission impossible. He didn't see how they were going to be able to land along this narrow passage where the tracks ran along the natural ledge of the mountain landscape. They hadn't brought the hoist, and at this particular location, Stanton couldn't bring the helicopter close enough to land directly on the flatcar because the Huey's rotor blade would strike the adjacent rock cliffs. John's stomach flipped when he looked beyond the tracks and saw waves crashing and breaking into foam far below.

Warrant Officer Bill Stanton was only 21 years old, but other crewmembers recognized him as a rare example of man and machine melded into one. Somehow Stanton managed to lightly perch one of the chopper's skids lengthwise on top of a stack of plywood along the outer edge of the flatcar.

Several more ARVNs must have clambered onto the flatcar from the opposite side, and they now approached the helicopter hauling a litter with a patient belted to it. John reached up to the intercom controls on the ceiling of the cargo bay and flipped the switch to "live" position, so he would not have to key his mike to speak to the pilots and crew chief. In open mike position, his helmet mike would remain on and transmit every word he spoke while leaving both hands free to load patients. John kneeled at the open cargo bay door and watched the South Vietnamese soldiers bring the patient closer. Even if the ARVNs spoke English, it would be impossible to verbally communicate with them, because all sounds were lost to the Huey's reverberations.

The South Vietnamese soldiers exerted much force to lift the stretcher at a difficult angle, straining to push it toward the cargo

113

bay. John realized that the ARVNs could not raise the litter high enough, so he lowered himself out of the cargo bay and onto the skid while Stanton held the helicopter in position. With his back to the ARVNs, John bent his knees and twisted his left arm back and downward, trying to grab a handle of the litter. He wasn't wearing a safety strap, and his right hand's grip on the smooth, wide lip of the small side door didn't provide a particularly strong handhold. Maintaining a Huey in a hover was no easy task, but Stanton kept the bird relatively motionless while John strained to reach hold of the litter. As the ARVNs struggled to push the stretcher upward, the rotor wash swept debris in their faces and blew their uniforms snug against their skin. The strong wind dislodged one of the ARVN's caps, and out of the corner of his eye, John caught sight of it tumble beyond the skid and fall toward the distant, swirling froth and boulders beneath them.

In any other circumstance, the spectacular view on this sunny afternoon would be beautiful, but at this moment it was terrifying. John knew the pilots had the same view through the chin bubble, the curved windows along the floor of the cockpit that allowed them to see the ground below, and he knew it took intense concentration to keep this chopper in place. Plus, they were hovering out of ground effect, which made the pilot's job technically even more difficult. Stanton was constantly adjusting the controls to maintain height, position, and direction while fighting the wind currents coming off the ocean. Despite the intermixing of updrafts and downdrafts from the mountain, Stanton held a stable hover.

From his sideways position, John caught a glimpse of two more

ARVNs trying to climb on top of the flatcar. They were lugging a second litter. From John's vantage point, all activity on the other side of the train car was hidden from view. Taking a breath, John forced himself to keep his focus on trying to get the first patient—strapped to a litter—onboard. When the ARVNs shoved upward, he finally was able to clutch the litter handle. John wrestled to pull the handle up while crew chief Long—on his hands and knees on the floor of the cargo bay—leaned out and grabbed the other handle, making sure not to pull too hard and wind up falling out the opposite open door. Finally, they were able to slide the patient up against the pilots' seats, allowing room for the next litter. If the patient had been a large American soldier rather than a small-stature Vietnamese, they might not have been able to accomplish this tricky maneuver. Noting that the soldier was bleeding from his ears, John turned his attention back to the train car. In the back of his mind he couldn't help but think that somebody had just blown up this train, and he wondered where the enemy was now—possibly on the mountain above them, positioning an RPG to blow up the rest of it. Shoving that thought out of his mind, John forced his concentration back to what he was doing. Keeping his mind focused on what was right before him was the only way he could overcome thoughts of worry and fear.

The same effort continued as the ARVNs then lifted the second patient. Balancing the stretcher at an awkward slant, they aimed it toward John's feet. John again bent down on the skid, stretching to reach the litter handle. Before grabbing it, he glanced down at this patient and realized the man did not have a head. John was looking down into a dark cavity where a blood-smeared flap of skin—all that was left of a neck—was folded in on itself where this man's head should have been.

Immediately straightening, John spoke into the open microphone of his helmet, "Mr. Stanton, the second patient is not alive."

"Are you certain?"

"Yes, sir. He has no head."

"Then we won't take him; we're not evacuating the dead," Stanton directed.

John waved the ARVNs off and gestured for them to pull back, but it was obvious they wanted John to take the litter as the group of South Vietnamese soldiers shouted and motioned in protest.

"They're not too keen about us not taking this guy," John exhaled into his mike.

"We're not taking their dead," Stanton insisted.

It was the aircraft commander's call, and John was relieved they wouldn't have to sweat to load a second litter onboard while hovering in this precarious position. The strenuous effort could not be justified for the dead.

Clambering back up into the cargo bay, John signaled all clear, and Stanton tipped the bird away from the mountain. Relieved to be in motion again, John started an IV on the patient as they headed to the Provincial Hospital in Da Nang. They certainly never had training for the mission they just flew. Like many of their missions, it was OJT—on-the-job-training. But they had pulled it off, and no one had gotten hurt.

Later that day, the same crew flew a mission to pick up a wounded member of a K-9 unit. John watched a soldier scramble over to the chopper with an 80-pound dog slung over his shoulders. From the looks of it, the handler had carried his dog a long distance to get to the LZ. Like the other military dogs John had evacuated, this dog was a large German shepherd, a magnificent creature. Probably accustomed to being ferried about in helicopters, the dog seemed relaxed as it stretched out on the cargo bay floor, panting beneath the leather straps of its muzzle. It had shrapnel wounds on its body and was bleeding from the ears, similar to the South Vietnamese soldier the crew had rescued from the train hours earlier. The dog probably took a concussive blast as it ranged ahead of a patrol.

John had been told there were hundreds of dogs serving in all branches of the US Armed Forces in Vietnam, and they were given the same priority as other US soldiers. Employed as scout or sentry, a dog had one of the most dangerous jobs in combat. Many soldiers owed their lives to their dogs. John had heard heroic tales of dogs getting shot but still continuing to attack the enemy. The K-9 teams must have been pretty effective, because the Viet Cong offered a high bounty for their capture.

Watching as the handler bent over and massaged his fingers deep into the scruff of the dog's neck, John witnessed the incredible connection the two shared. The protective loyalty between man and dog was so profound there were reports of dogs refusing to leave the side of their dead handlers. The relationship was almost magical and explained why some handlers re-upped for another tour of duty just to remain with their dogs.

Before the day was over, John received word of another mission. Without even knowing what it was, John knew he wouldn't like it because he really disliked flying night missions. The call was to pick up a seriously wounded Marine. Although the Marines had their own evacuation system, the 236th frequently answered calls to pick up Marines for one main reason—they were wounded Americans in need.

John had been puzzled about why Marines made frequent evacuation requests from Army units until a Marine explained several reasons to him. For one thing, Marine helicopters were used for dual-purpose missions and would not necessarily have a Navy corpsman onboard to tend to the wounded. Marine missions combined insertion and extraction of troops, resupply, and medevacs; whereas the one dedicated mission of Dustoff helicopters was human rescue, and they always had a medic onboard. Also, the Marines flew larger, older, and slower aircraft, such as the CH-34 Choctaw, the Sikorsky S-58, which had been an Army workhorse since 1955. As piston-driven engines gave way to turbine-engined helicopters, the Marines acquired the Boeing Vertol CH-46 in 1964 for medium-lift cargo transport. However, not only was the tandem-rotor Sea Knight a huge target, it required more room to land. In contrast, the Army's fast and nimble UH-1 could dart in and out of hot LZs, proving to be the best machine for the mission. When first ordered into production, the Army designated Bell's utility helicopter as HU-1 and officially named it the Iroquois. The HU-1 designation gave rise to the nickname Huey—a name that stuck even after the aircraft was re-designated as UH-1. The Huey became the legendary machine of the Vietnam War, and the Dustoff pilots who flew them were highly skilled. Resembling teenagers behind the wheel of a souped-up hotrod, Army Dustoff pilots tended to be younger warrant and commissioned officers as opposed to the high-ranking officers who often flew the Marine helicopters. While the Marines didn't fly at night or in the rain, the instrument-rated Dustoff pilots flew in all conditions. Their ability to fly in and out of insecure LZs contributed to the vaulted reputation of Dustoff pilots. The Marines on the ground understood the differences in capabilities between their own helicopter medevacs and the Dustoff helicopter ambulances clearly marked with a Red Cross. They recognized that if they wanted to get their wounded brothers back to a hospital for urgent care, Army's Dustoff would get the job done. Sometimes, however, the Marines didn't play by the rules, and as John would soon discover, this was one of those missions.

Flying to a pickup site at night made the war seem surreal to John. As he peered down through the night sky, it was easy to spot where the action was. The darkness revealed a mind-blowing display of lights and energy. There would be raging fires, explosions, and tracers flying every which way. Tracers were rounds of ammunition that had been chemically treated to glow so their paths could be followed. When a soldier fired his automatic weapon with tracers interspersed between bullets, the tracers would burn a certain color and allow the soldier to see where his barrel was aimed. The bad guys had one color tracers and the good guys had another. From above, the tracers created continuous, unbroken lines of red and green, yet John knew there were actually four regular bullets between each tracer round. Sitting on his seat in the cargo bay, John would smoke cigarette after cigarette while watching different lines of color crisscross the ground below. Occasionally, one would rise toward their chopper or at another aircraft in the vicinity.

During a night mission when the raging battle was so visible, John would become fretful as the chopper circled above while waiting for the okay to come down for the pickup. He could do nothing but sit in the cargo bay and wait until it was time for his job to begin, and then it would be all action for him. Meanwhile, sitting and waiting inside an aircraft flown by another human being made John feel like he was not the master of his own fate. Listening to the chatter of the pilots and men on the ground through his earphones, hearing blasts in the background and seeing flashes of explosives below, John would be bombarded with sensory input that triggered his active imagination. With time to dwell on various possibilities, his mind would create a continuous stream of "what ifs" as unbroken as the trail of tracer rounds. And some of those "what ifs" had morbid outcomes. In response, John's left knee would shake uncontrollably. He would grab it with both hands but couldn't keep it still. As soon as the chopper began to make its descent, John became so involved with his duties that if his knee was still shaking, he didn't notice. It was only while he was sitting in the chopper, circling and waiting, that his damn knee would be telling him how he was feeling on the inside.

On tonight's mission, thankfully, there was no enemy fire. Stanton was circling at about 1,500 feet searching for their contact on the ground where they would touch down and pickup the wounded Marine. It was a dark night with no moon, and there were no strobe lights, flashlights, or aerial flares to mark the position of the men on the ground. The RTO directed them to the side where a couple of Marines would be holding up a Zippo lighter.

In a sea of darkness, the pilots spotted the feeble flicker of flame. Crew chief Long inserted a color cartridge into the M-79 grenade launcher and fired it, launching a magnesium burning parachute flare that would illuminate the area for thirty seconds, long enough for the chopper to get on the ground. The helicopter descended into the dancing shadows cast by the eerie white glow of the rocking parachute flare.

"One hundred...seventy-five...fifty...twenty...ten..." Long announced the distance from the ground over the intercom. He had the unique ability of being able to visually calculate their height above ground level, and it helped Stanton land the helicopter on a little clearing in the jungle. Quickly, the Marines lifted their wounded buddy up to the cargo bay as John helped position him on the floor. The helicopter immediately lifted off, and John began to examine the patient using a flashlight with a red lens cover. On night missions, it was standard procedure to use red lamps inside the cargo bay because they gave off less light and were supposed to minimize the risk of becoming an enemy target. With the flashlight in one hand, John scanned the patient from head to toe. Although most of the man's body was wrapped in a rubber poncho, John detected something peculiar. The wounded Marine appeared to be lying on his back with his head facing upward, yet the toes of his boots were pointing downward as though he were lying on his stomach.

John gestured for Robert to hold the flashlight. Rotating the patient's head, John checked his pupils and found them dilated. The Marine's face, even under the red light, looked ashen and lifeless. Examining the patient for vital signs, John found no pulse or breath. With Long's assistance, John unwrapped the poncho and discovered this guy's problem. The middle of the man's body was a pool of black tar. Under red-tinted lights, blood did not appear red but black and shiny, only adding to the hellish feeling of nighttime missions. John observed that the tattered remains of the patient's flak jacket were enmeshed in the splintered bones and shredded flesh of his chest. The extent of trauma was so severe, his heart and lungs looked like they had disintegrated. The guy had probably stepped on a booby trap known as a bouncing Betty—an antipersonnel mine with two charges: the first propels the explosive charge upward, and the other is set to explode at about waist level. Looking down at the Marine's chest, John knew there was no way this Marine could have survived a blast that basically split his body in two. The guys on the ground surely knew he was dead when they requested the medevac. Dustoff would never have risked flying a night mission to evacuate the dead.

The general rule was that the deceased could wait until the next resupply helicopter landed. Yet, on rare occasions Dustoff would sometimes evacuate the dead along with the wounded during tactical emergencies when the men on the ground were in heavy contact with the enemy and it would be advantageous for them to move rapidly to another location. Since American soldiers take pride in not leaving their dead buddies behind, they might ask the Dustoff pilot to help them out by picking up their dead. Otherwise, the grunts would have to carry them to the new location, slowing their progress at a time when speed was a crucial variable. The guys on the ground were very appreciative of Dustoff's cooperation at such times.

However, there were good reasons why Dustoff didn't pick up the dead. The presence of the dead on the chopper had a demoralizing effect on the wounded being evacuated at the same time. They undoubtedly knew each other, and it was disheartening to have a dead buddy lying nearby on the cargo bay floor. It was also demoralizing to the Dustoff crew, whose mission was to save lives. In addition, weight was a critical issue during rescue missions. At the upper limit, the Huey could handle about a dozen US wounded, but with that much weight, the chopper was slow to take off and gain altitude. Carrying the dead would add weight that could put them all at risk, especially when there was enemy contact. Furthermore, as often happened, the Dustoff ship could be returning from one pickup and receive a call for a second urgent mission. Dead bodies onboard would occupy space and weight that should go to the critically injured. Therefore, Dustoff stressed to the ground troops that they picked up the wounded, not the dead.

When John finally plunged inside his mosquito net and stretched out on his bunk for the night, his fingers found the unfinished letter to Karen under his pillow. Exhausted from this day, he couldn't begin to think about writing to her now. He was frustrated and angry—with the dishonest Marines—and about Xuan's inexplicable disappearance. And there wasn't a damn thing he could do about either one of them.

Chapter 8

April 24, 1969

Dear Johnny,

How's my firstborn child? You don't know how much I miss you. You always make things right. My health is not good. The doctor said my heart was OK. He doesn't know why I get out of breath. It upsets me to watch the news on TV or hear about the war.

Remember that show you liked? *The Smothers Brothers Comedy Hour*. CBS took it off the air. Tommy Smothers said too much about the war. I didn't like that. I like *Bonanza* better anyway.

I'm fed up with Eduardo. He can be so stupid. I'm not going to say more but we need to move out of Lakehurst naval housing and he needs to find a civilian job.

Are you still sending Karen money? She should get a job. It made me mad that she sat around the house all day in her nightgown. Your brother and Eduardo didn't mind, but I thought it wasn't proper. She hasn't called since she moved out in January. I don't think your wife is very polite.

Your sister will graduate from high school in June. Don't forget to send her a card and gift. Your brother is OK. He'll move into Lakehurst's enlisted men's billets. Now we won't have his rent to help out.

It was sad, but we had to put Digger to sleep. The other dogs are fine.

You never say what your job is like. Aunt Helen asked and I told her you saved lives.

Be careful for the sake of your worried mother. I'll send you our address as soon as we find a place. I don't know what we're going to do.

Love,
Mom

John almost wished there hadn't been a letter waiting for him this day. A month had passed since he'd written to Karen about Xuan, and he was anxiously waiting for her reply. Even with the few letters he received, he'd almost prefer no mail than such a complaining one from his mother. Stuffing the letter into his shirt pocket, he headed to the mess hall.

John had been up since the crack of dawn to meet the rest of his crew at Operations at 0500. They were flying a daily routine mission nicknamed the milk run. Without breakfast or coffee, and in the quiet of the red-tinted mornings, a crew from the 236th would follow the zigzagging river through Da Nang and make the ten-minute flight to the 95th Evacuation Hospital at China Beach. The serenity and beauty of the early hour faded when they landed and began loading their patients. These guys were the worst of the worst and were on their way out of Vietnam. On these missions, the medic and crew chief took the time to carefully load the stretchers onto the chopper's litter straps, making certain that IV bottles and drainage tubes remained secure. Usually, the Huey was filled to capacity with four litters of critically wounded patients. Some mornings, the crew would have to fly several trips to transport all the tattered bodies to the Da Nang Air Base. There, they went to the northeast corner of the airfield where a Starlifter would be parked with its rear doors dropped. A number of attendants waited for the Dustoff helicopter and took control of unloading the wounded. Some litters were walked onboard, and some were placed on gurneys and rolled up the ramp of the cavernous air-ship. John didn't know how many units brought patients from other hospitals to fill the C-141. He just thought the milk run was a sad mission.

After completing the morning's mission, John entered the mess hall where Zeke and Ted Wilcox were eating breakfast. Sliding his tray onto the table next to theirs, he couldn't help but notice Zeke's new duds.

"Hey," John remarked to Zeke, "how come you don't look like your usual rumpled self?"

"I'm wearing my new Nomex flight suit," Zeke replied, extending his arms to fully display the olive drab shirt, which resembled their fatigues except the fibers were created with a heat and flame resistant chemical developed by DuPont. "It's kind of stiff and scratchy," Zeke complained as he rubbed the woven fabric with his left hand.

"Why are you wearing it then?" Robert Long asked, setting his tray on the table and pulling up a chair. "Are you preparing in case the commo bunker gets hit again?" Robert referred to the communications building where a corrugated-steel shipping container had been attached to the Operations building after the radio hooch took a direct hit last month.

"Yeah," Zeke considered, "I suppose the Nomex could be useful if we get mortared when I'm inside that windowless CONEX."

An acronym for CONtainer EXpress, CONEX shipping containers were a common sight in Vietnam. In addition to transporting a variety of items, the shipping containers provided covered storage and were employed as command posts, dispensaries, portable stores, and bunkers. For the 236th, a CONEX now served as the radio room.

"I see you've piled another layer of sandbags around your CONEX," Ted noted, "with at least three layers deeper on the roof."

"Radio transmissions are an essential part of Dustoff, dude," Zeke pronounced, pushing his black-rimmed glasses back into place on the bridge of his nose.

"Ever since the CO's hooch took a direct hit," John commented, "most of the buildings in the unit have been fortified a layer thicker and higher."

"How can we be sure that the gook sandbaggers we hire to fortify the buildings aren't telling the VC where the important targets are?" Ted scoffed. "I still think Hoang is the one who gave Charlie the coordinates of the RTO's hooch. I haven't seen him around lately."

"I don't think Hoang is going to be translating for us anymore," Zeke explained. "Last week he went home and found his wife and son with their throats slit."

"Jesus!" Ted uttered.

The men sat in silence for a moment as they digested that news.

"Anyway," Zeke continued, "I didn't get the uniform just in case we take another hit. I've volunteered to be 5th man," he announced, waving his plastic fork in a salute. "I'll be helping to protect your asses."

"All right for you, Mr. RTO man." Robert gave Zeke a slap on the shoulder.

Although Dustoff crews consisted of four men—a medic, crew chief, and two pilots—recently they began taking a 5th man along on missions when enemy fire was reported. The 5th man was known as a patient protector. From his cargo bay lookout and with his M-16 poised and ready, the 5th man also provided protection for the crewmembers. The clerks and mechanics who flew as 5th men were volunteers, receiving no payments for their efforts.

"And this Nomex suit will prevent me from becoming a crispy critter." Zeke stated, using the slang term for burn victims.

They had all seen the charred skin of guys who were caught in rocket fire. The ensuing heat and flames did a real number on those soldiers, especially if they were trapped inside a vehicle or tank. Burned so badly, their skin was black and crisp.

"How did you manage to get a new suit?" Ted Wilcox queried, shoving his chair back as he spoke. "I tried to get a new pair of flight gloves from that guy in charge of supplies. Man, he's a prick deluxe! He said there's nothing wrong with my gloves and I didn't warrant a new pair." Addressing John, he said, "Doc, you know how my gloves were covered with blood and shit, and after being soaked in all those body fluids they got stiff and smelled, but that asshole wouldn't give me a new pair."

"I bet if you came up with a ten dollar bill, you would have gotten yourself a new pair," Robert smirked as he stirred more sugar into his coffee. "There's a lot of money to be made in the black market of war, and that prick in supply seems to be part of the underground feeding frenzy."

"Instead of going home *good* soldiers," Zeke quipped, "some plan to go home *rich* soldiers."

"Like our first sergeant," Ted groused.

"And the mess sergeant," Robert said in a low voice, moving his head toward the door of the mess hall where a 55-gallon drum was located. "You notice how we now separate our food waste from the plastic utensils and paper plates? That's because the mess sergeant sells that barrel of food scraps to the dinks in Dogpatch."

"No way!" John protested, abruptly pushing his plate aside. He did not want such a thing to be true.

"Don't be so naive," Robert replied as they all rose from the table. "The mess sergeant sells to a local chief who sells to the people. Just like the prostitution rings, the black market payoffs go up the chain."

As John scraped his food into the 55-gallon drum, he wondered if Xuan's situation was so dire that she was now forced to eat the American's plentiful wastes.

Walking toward the unit area, John and Ted stopped to light a cigarette.

All of a sudden Zeke burst out singing, "You know that it would be untrue—yip, yip, yip! You know that I would be a liar—zippity-doo-dah!"

His rough imitation of José Feliciano's version of the Door's song couldn't be ignored.

"What the hell is wrong with you?" John wanted to know.

Pulling a lighter out of his pocket, Zeke straightened his right arm. "I'm going to test out the Nomex to see if it really is fireproof," he replied. "Come on baby light my fire," Zeke sang as he flicked his Zippo lighter until it produced a flame.

Robert, Ted and John stopped and watched as Zeke held the blue flame a couple of inches under the fabric of the sleeve of his outstretched arm.

"Light my fire, light my—YEOWZA! SON OF A BITCH!" Zeke hollered as he yanked the flame away from his arm. His face winced in pain.

"Well, the shirt didn't burn," Ted noted.

"FUCK! My arm is burnt!"

John carefully rolled up the sleeve of Zeke's shirt to expose blotches of redness and a blister. "You damn fool! You've given yourself a second degree burn," John scolded.

"Anyway," Ted remarked, "it's good to know we won't ignite."

"Yeah, what a relief—we'll bake instead of broil," Robert sneered.

A sudden, shrill sound pierced the air and sent all of them hustling to Operations. One of the mechanics had created the warning whistle by removing the horn from a deuce-and-a-half—a two and a half ton truck. The high-pitched blare could be heard throughout the unit area and alerted the Dustoff crew that a mission had been called in.

Since John was on standby, his crew would not be the ones to respond to this morning's warning horn. However, later in the morning, the 2-up crew flew a routine mission south to Tam Ky. John had flown the same mission before, and although not as regular as the milk run, Da Nang Dustoff often flew to Tam Ky to pick up a chopper-full of civilians and ferry them to the Provincial Hospital in Da Nang. Today, similar to other days, six mothers and their young children along with two elderly women and an old man were crouched on the cargo bay floor, their small bodies huddled together with fear etched on their faces. Since the peasants were often reluctant to board the helicopter, John speculated that flying must have been a cultural shock for people whose former mode of transportation had been an ox-drawn cart.

Today, John was glad to be flying with two pilots he really respected. They were career soldiers who had already completed two prior tours in Vietnam. After additional training, they were now serving another tour as Dustoff pilots. When dressed in their Class A uniforms, the left side of their shirts hung heavy with all the decorations, awards, and insignias collected over their years in the military. Rows of ribbons displayed their valor, and numerous badges boasted their accomplishments, including paratrooper wings and CIBs (Combat Infantry Badges). Warrant Officer Parker was nicknamed "Pops", because, in his later thirties, he was one of the oldest Dustoff pilots. Formally with Special Forces, Pops was a father figure whose quiet presence commanded respect and authority. Captain Smith was in his early thirties and stood six feet tall with a barrel chest. His chiseled features and crew-cut made him resemble the model for Hasbro's 11-1/2 inch GI Joe doll. Previously an Army Ranger, Smith was the unit instructor pilot and conducted himself with a certain bravado that caused shoulders to straighten and backs to stiffen when he passed by. Both men were role models for many of the younger members of the 236th. John greatly admired Parker and Smith and was glad to be flying with them this day.

After the long roundtrip flight to Tam Ky, Captain Smith took the helicopter to Marble Mountain to top off the fuel tank. John didn't know the crew chief very well, as Adam Wheeler was fairly new to the unit. Still, the routine at the fueling station was the same, no matter who the medic or crew chief. The highly explosive nature of JP-4 jet fuel dictated certain safety procedures be strictly followed. With helmet visors down, the crew chief would operate the fuel pump while the medic stood ready with a fire extinguisher in hand. The pilots remained in their seats with doors open and door armor slid back to facilitate a fast emergency exit.

By the time the crew returned to the unit area at Red Beach, the mess hall had stopped serving lunch, but as he often did for the crews who were flying, Roy Reynolds loaded up plates and set aside meals for them. Pilots Smith and Parker pulled up the only spare chairs in the Operations building and began to eat. Standing, John balanced a paper plate of soggy spaghetti and wilted salad in his left hand while leaning his body against the plywood where a doorway had been cut to access the CONEX radio room. With eyes on the RTO, John stabbed a cold meatball with a plastic fork and was about to take a bite when his attention was captured by a crackling voice coming through the radio transceiver. John set the meatball back on his plate and watched the RTO—seated at a small desk—write rapidly in response to the request for a medevac.

Over the static, John discerned that a CH-34 helicopter, a chopper not known for its air worthiness, had crashed in a valley somewhere west of Da Nang, and a couple of crewmembers had been injured. John heard the RTO repeat that there was currently no enemy contact.

Sounding like an easy pickup, John turned his attention back to eating lunch. Crew chief Adam Wheeler was standing on the other side of the doorjamb, shoveling spaghetti into his mouth while also watching and listening to the RTO. Just as John was about to put a forkload of tightly wound spaghetti into his own mouth, additional information started coming in over the radio. John's eyes and ears were again glued to what was happening in the CONEX.

The fuzzy voice described the steep terrain and thick jungle canopy of the pickup location. "Please be advised, we are requesting that the helicopter be equipped with a hoist. A forest penetrator is needed to extract these guys."

This no longer sounded like an easy pickup to John. Hoist missions were always tricky and much more likely to be a target of enemy fire than regular missions. The chopper became a sitting duck as it held a hover for fifteen or twenty minutes while a cable was mechanically lowered to the troops below. After the men on the ground secured the patients to a seat apparatus known as a forest penetrator, the cable was recoiled, and the patient was lifted to the chopper. John had never received formal training in operating a hoist. Like other crewmembers in Vietnam, he had just been turned loose on it.

After the RTO in the CONEX finished transcribing the coordinates of the pickup site to a standard mission form, he walked over to Captain Smith and handed him the duplicate sheet. At that moment, pilot Steve Goodman and crew chief Robert Long strolled into Operations, followed by the copilot and medic of the 1-up crew. They, too, had missed lunch, but Reynolds had also set aside paper plates of spaghetti for them. John nodded to Robert, silently offering respect and condolences, thinking that as part of the first on-call crew, Robert would soon be flying the hoist mission.

Captain Smith stood as he greeted the other pilots. "Here," he said to Steve Goodman, gesturing to the chair where he had been sitting. "You can sit here." Holding up the mission sheet he added, "This is a priority, not an urgent, so you go ahead and eat. We've already eaten. We'll take this one."

Adrenaline exploded in John's body when he heard Smith's words. Although he hadn't eaten a bite of food, John was feeling indigestion at the thought of a double—or triple—canopy jungle hoist mission. He watched Adam Wheeler set his half-eaten plate of food on a desk and exit Operations. John set his own uneaten plate beside it and followed Wheeler's lanky body out the door, mentally preparing for a mission he thought Robert would be flying.

A jeep transported the crew to the flight line. As they approached Wheeler's helicopter, they drove past Bart Buckman, who was standing in the next revetment where his own chopper was parked. Buckman's head was just visible above a wall of metal shipping containers that once held rockets or helicopter engines and were now filled with sand and stacked side by side, several rows high around each chopper.

Buckman waved and called over, "Hey, what have you got?"

"A hoist mission," Wheeler announced as he untied the rotor blade of his bird.

Captain Smith walked toward the left side of the chopper to take his position as aircraft commander. Removing his sunglasses, he squinted in the bright sunlight as he paused to wipe a smudge from the lens. Glancing across the revetment at Buckman, he asked, "Do you want to go for a ride?"

Buckman told the jeep driver to let Operations know that he would be going along on the mission. He then brought his helmet, armor, M-16, and hulking body over to Wheeler's bird to join the mission as 5th man.

John was busy checking his medical equipment and examining the hoist.

"The monkey strap is missing," he informed crew chief Wheeler. The monkey strap was a four-foot safety belt that looped around the hoist operator's waist and clicked onto a D-ring fastened to the chopper floor, securing the operator as he lay on his belly lowering and raising the cable.

"It probably was left behind on the other bird," Wheeler guessed. "When they moved the hoist to my chopper, they must have forgotten it."

John looked down the flight line. The hoist had come from a chopper three revetments away. He was about to race over to get the strap when he heard the ignition of the Huey's engine. Watching the overhead rotor blade begin to turn, John made a fast assessment—the day was sunny and clear and no enemy contact had been reported. Rather than hold up the mission by running for the monkey strap, John decided to take his chances, as only his own safety would be at risk.

Within the 236th, there was an internal debate about who was best suited to operate the hoist. Some believed the crew chiefs were more qualified because the hoist involved manipulating a motor-driven device and crew chiefs better understood the functioning of machinery and aerodynamics. Presently, the 236th assigned the operation of the hoist to the medic, presumably because it was connected to the patient and patients were the medic's responsibility.

While flying the milk run this morning, John had noticed an extra cord dangling from the ceiling and connected to the onboard intercom system. Wheeler explained he was in the process of rewiring his chopper to accommodate the 5th man, because lately, more and more regularly, increased enemy activity necessitated a patient protector accompany the missions. Some of the crew chiefs always seemed to be working on ways of better facilitating the missions, but this afternoon, with a 5th man on board, Wheeler's rewiring revealed some serious glitches. John's helmet was plugged into the rewired socket, and it did not allow him to communicate directly with the pilots. He could hear Mr. Parker, but he could not hear Captain Smith. Furthermore, Buckman—who shared the same jack—was the only crewmember able to hear John. John would talk through his helmet mike, and then Buckman would have to relay his words to the rest of the crew.

Despite the intercom problem, John felt confident as they headed to the pickup site, because this mission benefited from the rare experience of having both his respected role models piloting the aircraft. John pulled out his pack of Lucky Strikes and smoked a cigarette during the twenty-mile trip to an area the Americans had dubbed "Elephant Valley." During the early years of the war, wild elephants were frequently sighted in this jungle-blanketed, mountainous region of I Corps. The NVA used trained animals to transport supplies along otherwise impassable, treacherous terrain. Since elephants provided value as pack animals for the enemy, they became fair game for extinction, and eventually elephants were no longer seen in Elephant Valley.

When the Dustoff crew approached their destination, the Alley Cats, gunships of the 282nd, helped vector the medevac into position above the ground unit. The guys on the ground popped a smoke canister to indicate where to lower the forest penetrator. John heard Mr. Parker comment that the winds must have become more turbulent because the Alley Cats reported that the smoke from the burning CH-34 had been rising straight up earlier, but now the red indicator smoke was drifting horizontally as it rose above the trees. John spotted the smoke and promptly positioned himself on the floor of the cargo bay, lying upon his stomach. Captain Smith moved the aircraft over the dense treetops and lowered the chopper into a depression on the slope of the mountain.

With his head and upper chest extended over the edge of the cargo bay door, John looked down through a hole in the thick jungle canopy to the ground below. Whoa! Those guys were way down there! Never having performed a hoist mission from this height, John would have to lower the penetrator 150 to 200 feet. Of all the times to not have the monkey strap! While John waited for orders to begin operating the hoist, he heard Buckman give feedback to Smith about how far the tail boom was from the surrounding treetops. John glanced to his right where Buckman sat in the hellhole—the outward-facing seat beside the transmission. Wheeler sat in the hellhole on the opposite side of the chopper and was also keeping a sharp eye on the tail rotor and overhead blades. In preparation, John grasped the remote control with his right hand. It was attached to the hoist by a coil of electrical wiring.

Smith maintained a hover in an opening scarcely wider than the width and length of the Huey. Buckman told John that Captain Smith gave the order to begin lowering the hoist. John pushed the conical switch on the remote control, allowing the cable to slide through the glove of his left hand, which loosely circled and guided the line. The cable began to gradually unwind and send the bullet-shaped forest penetrator with its seats in upright position down to the guys waiting on the ground. The whirring sound of the hoist's motor was nearly drowned out by the thumping beat of the main rotor blades and the constant racket coming from the Huey's transmission. John watched the cable delicately thread its way through the tiny hole in the canopy. At one point, the penetrator became caught in the trees, so John reversed the direction of the cable, raising the penetrator before sending it back into the forest again. Concentrating as it continued its journey, John was thinking that so far everything was going all right. There was no enemy activity, and the penetrator was nearly to the ground.

When the apparatus finally hit the jungle floor, it took a few minutes before the guys below were able to bring the injured over to its location. As John discovered, the wiring of his headset also prevented him from hearing any communication with the men on the ground, so he maintained his focus on the penetrator to keep on top of the action. John watched the guys on the ground lower the paddle seats, realizing they were going to hoist both injured men at once. After he saw them attach the chest belts to the patients, John waited for the command to start reeling in the cable.

"We're taking weight," John announced as soon as Buckman relayed Smith's command and John pressed his thumb against the cone-shaped control of the remote. It was Standard Operating Procedure (SOP) to inform the pilot when the hoist's cable was activated so the pilot could compensate for the down-pulling load.

"We're taking weight," Buckman repeated to Captain Smith, who had the difficult task of maintaining a hover without allowing the helicopter to drift in any direction.

On today's mission, with the cable extended nearly to its full length—along with the extra burden of evacuating both patients at once—the helicopter immediately responded by dipping downward on its right side. To regain balance, Captain Smith maneuvered his hands and feet, constantly adjusting the controls.

"Tell Captain Smith to keep it steady," John directed to Buckman as the cable appeared to move toward the aircraft. From his limited view above the treetops, John momentarily had an eerie sensation of not knowing if the cable was moving toward him or if the helicopter was drifting toward the cable.

"We're drifting right," John reported as the cable came even closer to the aircraft. He leaned farther out the cargo bay to view his patients who were now thirty or forty feet in the air.

Buckman reiterated the message to Captain Smith, "We're drifting right."

Through the narrow opening in the jungle canopy, John could see the men standing on the ground below. No one was waving or acting strangely to indicate a problem. Captain Smith had ordered him to bring up the penetrator, and no one had ordered him to stop. Yet, as the cable came close to touching the chopper's skid, John had a sinking suspicion things were not right.

"We're drifting too far to the right! We need to stop drifting!" John yelled into his open mike, not sure he was using the proper nomenclature to describe what was happening.

Buckman again relayed the message to Smith.

"I'm running out of left cyclic," Captain Smith said into his mike. Buckman then echoed to John, "We're running out of left cyclic."

John didn't understand what running out of left cyclic meant. His focus remained on the forest penetrator. It was disappearing under the helicopter, and John feared his patients could be dragged through the trees. His eyes darted up to the emergency cable-cutting device on the hoist. The toggle switch was protected with a red plastic cover to prevent accidental activation. Flipping the switch would cause an explosive charge to fire against a guillotine that would sever the cable and free the chopper from an entangled line, which could pull it down. Knowing the pilots also had a device that could slice the cable in an emergency, John mentally registered where he would have to extend his arm if he received an order to cut the cable. He quickly returned his concentration to the skid where the cable was now bent around it, and his patients were completely out of sight.

Suddenly, the Huey gave a sharp jerk. John didn't know the main rotor blade had just sliced through a tree, but he knew they were in serious trouble when he felt the chopper tilt and twist in reaction. He released his left hand from the cable and slid farther back into the cargo bay as the chopper slowly pivoted to the right. The aircraft gave an even greater, heart-stopping jerk when the tail rotor struck another tree and completely snapped off the tail boom. In the next moment, John saw the remainder of the snapped cable curl up into the air like a giant whip, lashing into the path of the main rotor blade. From his position on the floor of the cargo bay, John could see clear, unobstructed blue sky where the usual blur of the rotor blade should be, and an abrupt silence replaced the usual thumping sounds. Oh, shit! The main rotor blade was gone.

Pushing down through the trees and spinning out of control, the fuselage slammed through the forest, banging and crashing as it knocked off tree limbs and spewed leaves and branches in all directions. John dropped the remote control on the cargo bay floor, searching for a way to hang onto the aircraft as it continued to thrust forward through the jungle while pivoting right in a tight circle. Now, he could kick himself in the ass for not taking time to get the monkey strap. If the chopper spun over, he'd be like a dishtowel in a clothes dryer and tumble right out through one of the open cargo bay doors. A rapid scan of the area around him revealed two large black springs behind Parker's seat. John grabbed hold of the sturdy coils and held on for dear life. The resounding blows of the helicopter ripping through the trees came to an end when the Huey scraped against the bottom of a rocky ravine and skidded onto its nose. The chopper then tipped over onto its right side, settling in a dry creek bed.

Startled to find himself alive after impact, John regained his senses and knew he had to get out of that helicopter before it burst into flames. The horrible grinding of the engine reminded him he had to move quickly. Everything that had not been fastened down prior to the crash—including John—had slid forward and was now strewn about in the space between the floor and the back of the pilots' seats. Uncurling himself from where he was wedged behind Parker's seat and the hoist, John stood, trying to regain his footing amidst the debris. The cargo bay area was raised higher than the front end of the aircraft, and the floor was tilted at a steep angle. The open door on the right side, where John had been leaning out just moments ago, now pressed into a rocky creek bed. Thankful that he seemed to be all right, John looked up and saw Wheeler and Buckman dangling from their jump seats. Their seat belts held them at the waist while their upper bodies had been thrust sideways. Although dazed, they both appeared to be conscious.

John searched for Captain Smith but found his seat empty. What could have happened to him? How could he have exited the aircraft so fast? John wondered if he had blacked out and therefore missed seeing Smith free himself from his armored seat and harness to climb out of the aircraft before anyone else. Looking carefully, John noticed that the armored plate that slides into position on the left hand side of Smith's seat was still pulled forward. Captain Smith could not have gone out his door. Then John noticed the windshield was missing. Smith must have gone through the windshield. But how could he have been thrown through the windshield if he had been harnessed in his seat?

John next looked in the direction of Mr. Parker. He appeared to be conscious, but the front of the aircraft on Parker's side had taken the brunt of the impact, pushing the instrument panel against him. In an undamaged aircraft, a pilot would have to fully extend his arm and lean forward a bit to be able to touch the instrument panel. Now, the instrument panel was right up against Parker and concealed the view of anything below his upper chest. Pops Parker squirmed in the armored seat that had prevented him from being crushed.

"I think I'm trapped. I'm trapped in this seat," Parker shouted. His voice was barely audible because of the intense noise coming from the laboring transmission. The turbine engine was still running.

Buckman yelled over to John, "I can't reach the seat belt to release it."

John balanced himself on the upward angle of the cargo bay floor by bracing against the legs of the pilot's seat. Stretching up, John was just able to reach the release mechanism of the seat belt. He pushed it and rapidly moved out of the way as Buckman came tumbling down, rolling to the same place where John had ended up after the crash. John then moved to the other side of the cargo bay and extended his arm to release Adam Wheeler's belt, who then somersaulted to the same position.

Regaining their balance, Buckman and Wheeler both climbed up the left side of the cargo bay and pulled themselves over the edge of the upward-facing door, jumping to the ground below. When John saw them both disappear out the opening, he started to follow them to safety away from the permeating odor of JP-4 fuel.

"I'm trapped!" Pops Parker's voice was heard over the abrasive, grating sound of the engine. "Hurry! This bird is going to blow up any moment!"

John released his hold on the brink of safety and sank back down into the cargo bay area. As much as he desired to get out of this aircraft, there was no way he could abandon Pops. Regaining his footing on the floor's nearly vertical and awkward angle, John maneuvered over to Parker's armored seat.

"This bird is going to blow!" Pops called. "Do something!"

John faced a real dilemma. Even though he was free to flee a pending explosion, he knew he couldn't leave Pops. But what could he do to help? Blood raced through his veins as he searched for a way to escape the orange fireball that was surely about to devour them. He remembered that their survival packs, located under the jump seats contained a handheld hatchet. But what the hell was he thinking? Parker was surrounded in metal. A hatchet wouldn't be of any use.

"HELP!!!" Parker hollered at the top of his lungs while pushing and struggling to get out of his seat and repeating that the helicopter was about to explode. Out of fear and frustration, John clutched the back of Parker's seat. His admired role model and father figure was stuck here. Pops was hysterical, which convinced John that this experienced soldier knew what was coming down. Continuing to rotate at a fast rate, the insistent clamoring of the transmission was the last sound John believed he would hear. Gripped by panic that they were both about to be engulfed by a giant fireball, John violently shook the back of Parker's seat and joined in his yelling. The transmission whined and scraped, and John and Parker screamed when all of a sudden a loud outcry pierced the air.

"Parker! Shut the fuck up! And shut down the aircraft!" The familiar voice of Captain Smith broke the spell of doom that had overcome Pops and John.

Parker, now silent, stretched his left arm up to the overhead control panel, where he hit the fuel cutoff switch and started pulling breakers. The engine and transmission immediately responded with a slacking in RPMs and a quieting of the obnoxious din.

Pops Parker must have figured out that he was still buckled into his safety harness, because he reached under the instrument panel, unlocked the lever, and released the device that restrained him at the shoulders and hips. After moving the cyclic control stick that had been pressing against his thigh, Parker slid out from between the armor seat and instrument panel and moved to where John was standing in the cargo bay.

Astonished at how easy it was for Parker to free himself, John regained his bearing and said, "Lets get out of here!"

They both climbed out the upward-facing cargo bay door, the same way Wheeler and Buckman had exited. Once on the ground, they spotted Captain Smith lying in front of the chopper where— seconds ago—his shouting voice had penetrated their panic.

"I can't move!" the Captain moaned. "I think my leg is broken."

John looked at Smith's position on the ground and then up to where the windshield had been. He concluded that Smith must have released his shoulder harness and safety belt before the aircraft slammed into the ground.

"We need to get away from the aircraft, because it could still blow." Captain Smith waved his arm as he spoke, gritting his teeth in pain.

John and Parker each took hold of one of the Captain's arms and dragged Smith up the steep, rocky ravine away from the downed aircraft and heavy fumes of the JP-4 fuel. Knowing that a broken thighbone—the largest, longest, and heaviest bone in the body—was one of the most painful breaks one can experience, John was not surprised when Captain Smith bellowed and cried in agony as they pulled him up to a path along a narrow ledge. John examined Smith's leg and concluded that he did indeed have a broken femur. It needed to be set, but John's medical supplies were back in the chopper.

"I'm going to get my supplies," John announced to the pilots, and without waiting for a reply, he scurried back down the ravine. Approaching the underbelly of the aircraft, John's nostrils flared in response to the strong odor. He could see gouges in the exposed fuel cells where JP-4 was dripping. Finding a slim opening where the cargo bay door pressed against the bank of the creek bed, John got down on his hands and knees and crawled into the cargo bay area from that tight passage. He searched the cluttered interior and gathered his scattered medical supplies. Since Dustoff medics were not authorized to carry morphine, he hunted for one of the standard-issued first-aid kits attached to the frame above the pilot's and copilot's seats. He had been told that the first-aid kits contained morphine, and after watching how Captain Smith had responded to being dragged up the ravine, John knew an injection of painkiller would ease his distress. Unlatching a kit from above Parker's seat, he broke the metal seal and rummaged through the canvas bag for painkilling drugs. None were there. John decided there was no use exerting the time and effort to reach the chopper's other kit, because if one sealed kit didn't contain any drugs, the second one probably didn't either. Clutching his medical supplies and squeezing his body through the small space, John climbed back up the ravine, frustrated that he didn't have any morphine to relieve Smith's pain. What the fuck was the point in sealing the first-aid kits if they didn't contain narcotics?

John finished setting Captain Smith's femur with two splints and an Ace bandage when an American in well-worn camouflage fatigues suddenly appeared along the ledge where John was kneeling.

"How bad is he?" the man asked, slightly pushing his boonie hat back to get a better look at Smith.

"He's got a broken femur," John replied. "I did my best to set it, but I don't have anything to give him. Do you have any morphine?"

"Follow me."

John glanced at Parker, who appeared dazed as he sat beside Smith. Motioning that he would be going with this guy, John followed the man along the trail into thicker jungle. They continued for a couple hundred feet until arriving at a clearing where the rest of the patrol was located. The crashed CH-34 smoldered nearby.

A quick glance informed John that the patrol consisted of six to eight ARVNs and two American advisors all wearing the same tiger-stripe camouflage. John knew that brimmed boonie hats were the most common headgear for Special Forces, but with no markings on their clothing, these guys could be Army or Marine. Both had teams performing secret missions deep into enemy territory. Because the US government denied that American troops were in North Vietnam or Laos or other places in Southeast Asia, these guys wore sterile uniforms with nothing to distinguish their person or equipment—no labels of name or rank, no dog tags, ID cards, no indication of country, not even an engraved Zippo lighter that could identify them as US soldiers.

In actuality, these soldiers were part of CCN (Command Control North), an operational arm of the MACV-SOG (Military Assistance Command/Vietnam-Studies and Observations Group). SOG was a super-secret organization responsible for strategic reconnaissance, special operations, psychological operations, POW rescue, wire-taps, sabotage, assassinations, and other clandestine activities. CCN operated in I Corps and their AO included Laos and North Vietnam. This team comprised two American Special Forces soldiers and eight indigenous mercenary troops. They had been inserted by helicopter into Elephant Valley for a training mission. Even though Elephant Valley had a reputation for being a very dangerous place, CCN only used it for training purposes. If a team couldn't make it in Elephant Valley, it had no chance at all in their true target areas.

The guy John was following picked up a rucksack from the ground, pulled out a syrette containing a single dose of morphine and handed it to John. Thanking him, John retraced his steps back to

Parker and Smith. In his urgency to relieve the Captain's pain, John swiftly uncapped the syrette and stabbed the needle into Smith's injured left leg. Uh-oh. When the needle stuck Smith's thigh, something didn't feel right. Captain Smith was wearing a one-piece flight uniform that had pockets in both the sleeves and pant legs. Unbeknownst to John, Smith was carrying a small notepad in the left thigh pocket of his uniform. Damn! John had inadvertently stuck the syrette into the notepad. Damn it all! John cursed himself for not administering the shot in Smith's upper arm.

John jumped up and stated, "I need to go get another syrette from those guys." Making his way past a field of boulders rising from the dry creek bed, John stopped when he heard the familiar sound of a Huey moving very slowly over the treetops. Immediately, he reached into the front pocket of his armored breastplate and pulled out a pencil-sized emergency flare. Screwing the flare into a small firing device, John shot it into the sky over his head. As he followed the flare with his eyes, a Huey with no markings on it appeared in the clearing above him. The door gunner, seated in the hellhole behind a door-mounted .30 caliber machine gun, spotted John and signaled to him with his free arm. John waved back and made exaggerated movements with his arms to indicate where Smith and Parker were located along the ledge. The gunner waved acknowledgment to John, and the chopper followed the direction where John had pointed.

John continued along the trail until he found the same American advisor, but there wasn't any more morphine. The guy had given him the last dose. Damn it all, again! Arriving back at their position on the ledge, John looked around but only saw Mr. Parker sitting on a big rock.

"What happened to Captain Smith?" John inquired, noticing that Pops maintained a steady gaze on their downed Huey.

"Mr. Parker, what happened to Captain Smith?" John questioned again.

Without taking his eyes from their wrecked bird, Parker finally said, "A chopper took him."

John scanned the sky overhead. It was buzzing with aircraft, but none was visible in their vicinity.

"Mr. Parker, perhaps we should go over to where the patrol is located," John suggested.

"We'll stay by the aircraft," Parker replied, keeping his eyes fixed on the destroyed chopper.

John stood beside Parker and joined him in staring down the ravine at the wreckage for several minutes. He figured all the activity assuredly announced their whereabouts to Charlie. And if US Special Operation forces were involved, the enemy couldn't be far. Concerned about their vulnerability from their open position on this path, John faced Pops.

"I'm going back over to the patrol," he declared. "They have a field radio, and I'll see if they know what's in the works for getting us out of here."

Back in the jungle clearing, as John approached the patrol, he noticed two bodies lying side-by-side on the ground. Were these the two guys that had been on the hoist? Were these his patients? John swallowed hard.

"It all started with a fucking headache."

John quickly turned toward the guy who had spoken—the same

guy who had helped him earlier. The man's eyebrows pulled tightly together, producing deep grooves on his forehead.

To John's confused expression the guy further explained, "I had this pain-deafening headache, and a couple of the others were sick, too, so I radioed for a chopper to come take out the patrol."

John nodded with understanding, realizing that this guy must be the patrol leader.

"The AC of the 34 said he was hovering at max power and could only pull one man out. So he left to burn off more fuel and then came back in again. That time, the engine failed and it crashed—killing one of their crewmembers. And one is missing." Pointing to the smoldering wreckage, he added, "Probably burned in the crash. We called in your medevac to pick up the injured pilot and RTO, and now they're dead, too. All because of a splitting fucking headache."

John didn't know what to say. He stood silently and watched the patrol leader's fist as it repeatedly clenched and released, clenched and released.

All of a sudden, the sky broke loose and a hard rain started to fall. The other American who had been talking on the field radio walked over to John and the patrol leader, raindrops dripping from the brim of his tiger-striped boonie.

"There's not going to be any more rescue attempts until this weather system passes," the radio operator relayed. "And we've heard some single shots fired north." To John, the radioman clarified, "The NVA use single shots as a mode of communicating with each other. They're probably curious about what the fuck all this commotion is about."

"You and your other crewmembers should come over and wait with us until we get hoisted out," the patrol leader informed John. Glancing skyward he added, "It could be a while."

John said he would go recount the information to the only other remaining crewmember, Warrant Officer Parker. He didn't know what had happened to Wheeler and Buckman. Finding his way along the trail, John was aware that the sky no longer buzzed with aircraft. Other than the pounding rain, all was silent. Parker was still sitting on the rock, seemingly in his own world as rain dripped off his nose and flattened his crew cut. John reported all he had learned about the current situation, trying to convince Parker of the wisdom of joining the patrol. However, Mr. Parker insisted they stay with the bird. John suggested that if they were going to remain in their present position, he would go back down to the aircraft in order to obtain weapons, ammunition and their survival kits.

"Don't go near the aircraft. It could blow," Parker stated.

"Sir, there's a possibility we could be stuck out here for hours. The patrol reported enemy activity, and our M-16s are down in the chopper. Mr. Parker, Sir, if we're going to stay with the bird, we don't want to be caught with only our .38s."

"Stay away from the chopper. It could still blow."

Unlike the normally confident, capable role model John knew, Pops wasn't making sense. It made John wonder if Parker had hit his head during the crash. Since John was gruesomely aware of how the enemy treated their prisoners, and considering that he and Pops were practically unarmed, John chose to disobey a direct order. He proceeded down the side of the rocky ravine back toward their Huey.

Snaking into the aircraft the same way he had done before, John grasped two M-16s. He found an M-79 grenade launcher under the debris, but when he picked it up, he saw it was broken where the barrel attached to the stock. Unfastening several cloth bandoleers full of loaded cartridge magazines from where they were hanging on the stretcher posts, John draped them over his shoulders. After grabbing a small metal ammo box, he squeezed through the crawl space and scaled the ravine. Parker was still seated on the rock and didn't speak as John laid the weapons and ammunition on the ground next to him. John then returned to the aircraft and detached the overland survival kit from where the canvas sack was belted on the floor. He dragged it out of the helicopter and hauled it up the ravine.

As he deposited the kit on the ground, another thought entered John's mind. "Mr. Parker, what about the maps and radios?" he asked, imagining that enemy patrols would soon be crawling all over the wreckage and sifting for useful materials.

"Stay away from the chopper. It could still blow," Parker repeated.

"Sir, our maps and radios could be useful to the enemy if…."

"Don't worry about the maps or radios."

John took a few steps and pointed his M-16 in the direction of the Huey, seriously considering firing a magazine into its underbelly. With JP-4 spilling out of the fuel cells, John knew that even in the pouring rain, a few rounds would produce a major explosion. Yet, he had already disobeyed Parker's orders twice and had not been given an order to blow up the aircraft. Besides, if two chopper crashes hadn't caused the NVA to come investigate, a huge fireball would surely arouse their attention. John controlled the urge to squeeze his finger and lowered his weapon. Instead, he concentrated on setting up a defensive perimeter, because he and Parker were out in the open.

"Mr. Parker, I'm going to go over there and see if I can find a better position," John stated, following his instinctive urge of self-preservation.

John walked about twenty yards until he came to a place where the steep ravine gentled into a more gradual incline. Near the top of the slope a concentration of four-foot-tall boulders provided cover from the rear and a lookout over a seventy-five-yard field of rocks to the thick jungle below. The area was forested, but not as densely wooded as the surrounding jungle. John figured that he and Parker could place themselves in the middle of those rocks and have fairly good cover.

When he returned to Parker, John described the location and recommended they move there. "Sir, it will provide us with better concealment, and we can still see the chopper."

Pops Parker glanced up at John and returned his gaze to the downed Huey without uttering a word.

Pointing in the direction of the rock slope, John added, "It's right over there, Sir, just twenty yards away, and we'd still be close to the chopper."

John waited, but Parker maintained his unresponsiveness. Was Pops in shock? Or, as a former Green Beret, was he so confident in his hand-to-hand combat skills that he saw no need to take defensive measures? John didn't know what to think as he watched Warrant Officer Parker sit in the rain and stare at the wreckage.

"Mr. Parker," John said louder. "I'm going to that area right there," John exaggerated his pointing movement. "Do you want to join me?"

"No," Parker responded without moving his gaze.

Carrying his medical equipment and the survival kit, John found a place on the ground, surrounded by a cluster of large rocks. As rain poured down on him, he examined the M-16, making sure all the magazines were readily accessible. He unholstered his .38 and checked the chamber, making certain it was loaded. John then opened the survival kit and took a fast inventory: food, water, first-aid supplies, hatchet, flashlights, flares, smoke grenade canisters, and wool blankets. Cradling the M-16, he snuggled into the rocks and scanned the clearing below. What if the NVA appeared out of the jungle? What kind of fight would John put up? And if Charlie snuck up behind him and wrestled him to the ground, did he have what it would take to kill another man? As a medic, John breathed life back into bodies; would he be able to look into someone's eyes and take the last breath from one? He was definitely out of his element. He belonged in the sky flying around in a Huey. Shivers ran down his spine as he grappled with thoughts of killing—rather than saving—lives.

John had been sitting between the rocks for several hours when the rain stopped almost as abruptly as it began. After about fifteen minutes, he heard a slow-flying helicopter somewhere nearby. From where John sat above the rock field, he had a clear view of the unmarked helicopter when it appeared above the trees. Stopping and holding a hover position, a rope came flying out of its cargo bay, and a man dressed in camouflage fatigues repelled down. As soon as the guy touched ground, the rope was pulled back into the departing aircraft. John watched as the fellow descended the slope where he and his backpack disappeared into the dense jungle.

Another fifteen minutes passed as John sat and wondered who that guy was. Had he spotted John's position on the rocks? All at once KA-BOOM! Several explosions startled John. Sounds of crashing trees followed. He glanced over to his right and spotted Mr. Parker still immobile on the rock. Looking downward to the left toward their Huey, he could see it was not burning. Nervously directing his watch to the trail, John wondered if the enemy had stumbled upon the US-led ARVN patrol. He hadn't heard any other gunfire, but he held his M-16 ready. As he pondered the puzzling situation, John saw the patrol leader appear out of the jungle and run toward him. John stood to be seen.

"Come on!" the patrol leader yelled when he saw John. "We're being taken out."

John left his medical supplies and climbed back to the path, bandoleers draped over his shoulder and weapon in hand. He noticed that Mr. Parker was already walking in the direction of the patrol leader. Entering the area where the rest of the patrol was located, John could see a number of trees had been blown up and were now scattered on the ground. The man who repelled down from the hovering chopper must have brought some type of explosives to enlarge the clearing around the wreckage of the CH-34. The clearing still wasn't large enough to land a helicopter, which meant they would be extracted by hoist.

John heard the helicopter before he could see it. When the CH-46 twin-rotor aircraft became visible above the trees, the Sea Knight appeared huge compared to a Huey. Four heavy-caliber machine gun barrels protruded from its forward and aft doors, two on each side. More than halfway down the aircraft's underbelly there was a square hatch. As the helicopter positioned itself and began to hover, John watched a forest penetrator descend from the open hatch. The familiar sight caused John's heart to accelerate. Here we go again.

John and Pops Parker were put on the penetrator together. When the cable began to sway and spin, John tightened his grip and kept an eye on the tree branches, kicking them back when they came too close. The ride up to the belly of the Sea Knight seemed to take forever. Once released from the penetrator, Parker and John belted themselves into jump seats and waited for the rest of the patrol to be hoisted up. Wrapped and secured in ponchos, the dead crewmembers were also brought up. No one was left behind.

The Sea Knight first landed at Marble Mountain where the weary patrol and the bodies of the dead were evacuated. Then it proceeded to the 95th, where John and Parker were dropped off. Medical technicians at the hospital checked John, bandaging a small cut on his right shoulder. John asked about the rest of the crew and was told that Wheeler and Buckman had been airlifted out of the jungle before it started to rain. They had been treated hours ago. Wheeler was in a body cast because of back injuries, and Buckman had back and leg contusions. Captain Smith's femur was fractured, and Mr. Parker had abrasions on his nose and shoulder. They would all remain at the 95th for additional treatment, but John was released back to his unit.

After being led to a radio room in the hospital where he was told a chopper from the 236th was being sent to pick him up, John paced the floor and approached the RTO.

"Could you please radio back to my unit and ask them if they would send a jeep instead?" John requested. "I don't want to get back into a helicopter just yet."

The RTO nodded and made the call for John. A few minutes passed before the reply came back. The RTO turned to John and said, "The message is that you're to come back on the chopper. No jeep is coming for you."

"Would you mind asking again if a jeep could be sent? I'm not ready to get on another chopper."

A few more minutes passed and John could hear the voice of the RTO from the 236th. "The Commanding Officer is giving you a direct order, 'Be on that chopper!'"

It was dark outside when John boarded the Huey. Even though it was nighttime, being back in a helicopter wasn't too bad after all. The familiar sights and sounds from the cargo bay almost felt comforting as they flew to Red Beach. When they landed at the flight line, John refused a jeep ride and told the driver he would walk to the unit area. He needed some time alone to decompress. Reaching into the pocket of his body armor, John pulled out his pack of Luckys. His hand shook uncontrollably as he lit a cigarette and deeply inhaled. Stepping on unsteady legs, he could feel his whole body trembling as he walked to the 236th's area. As usual, the perimeter was lit with a glow of drifting parachute flares, which turned night into artificial day. A staccato of explosions echoed in the distance, sometimes reverberating closer and louder, reminding him that the war continued. Releasing a long exhalation, John felt relief that his five-hour nightmare in Elephant Valley was finally over. Miraculously, the crew had all survived a helicopter crash. For four others, including his two patients, luck had run out, and the day had not been so fortunate. When you're in the middle of war, you just never know what kind of a day it's going to be.

Chapter 9

"Hey, Reynolds, do you know if my R&R has been approved?" John asked as he slumped into the chair beside Roy Reynold's desk. Folding his arms across his chest, he watched Roy stuff a stack of papers into a manila envelope.

"You just put in your request a couple days ago," Reynolds reminded, "and remember, R&R decisions aren't made at the unit level." Glancing over at John's slouched posture, he added, "All your paperwork was submitted, and I don't foresee any problems. You'll meet the in-country requirements by the end of this month. You have to be in Vietnam for six months to qualify for Hawaii."

"I want to let Karen know as soon as possible so she can book her flight."

"Well, you'll be put on the end of the list, and from what I've seen, there's at least a three-month wait. Your R&R will probably come up mid-August."

"Not until August?" John gasped. He fidgeted with his lighter, rotating and flicking it several times before reaching for his pack of cigarettes. Three months seemed like an interminable wait. He had just waited a whole month to receive a letter from Karen.

That long-anticipated letter finally arrived a few days after the helicopter crash; however, reading it provided little consolation. Karen's words were light and newsy with no explanation of why she hadn't written in a month and no response to his confession about Xuan. Instead of clarity, the letter left him even more confused. John wanted to see Karen now! How could he wait three months before looking into her eyes to see if she still loved him? How could he wait three months to know if she was being faithful—or if she was seeing her old boyfriend who lived in the same town as her Grandma? He needed to get things straightened out right away!

"Have you considered going someplace else?" Roy questioned. You only have to be in-country for three months to go to Hong Kong, and I think Singapore and the Philippines. You probably don't want to take your wife to Bangkok," Reynolds remarked derisively. "I hear it's become an American brothel."

"So, is that where you're going for your R&R?" John ribbed.

"I should say not!" Reynolds exclaimed, pursing his lips. "I'm thinking of going to Australia, but you have to be in-country for ten months before you can go to Sydney. Or maybe I'll go to Tokyo. That only has a six-and-a-half month in-country requirement."

"Hawaii is the shortest distance for Karen to fly," John related as he tapped an unfiltered Lucky on the corner of the desk.

"Danforth just returned from his R&R in Hawaii," Reynolds stated. "He and his wife stayed at the Hilton Rainbow Towers on Waikiki, and he said it was really nice."

John fantasized about being in a romantic setting with Karen for a week. Realistically, it wouldn't matter where they were staying, because he'd probably never want to leave the hotel room. Extending the cigarette toward Roy, he asked, "Do you want a smoke?"

"You always offer, and I always say, 'no, thank you.' When will you get the message—I don't smoke!"

"My mission is to have you smoking, drinking—and using profanity—before we leave this place," John said with a grin.

"Haven't you heard the expression—you can take the man out the Midwest, but you can't take the Midwest out of the man?"

"What the hell does that mean?" John lit the cigarette and took a deep inhalation.

Roy shook his head and smiled. "Never mind! Let's change the subject. Have you heard anything more about the crash investigation?"

"I haven't heard a thing since that Major interviewed me a couple days after the crash—that was the Sunday before last." John took another long drag from his Lucky Strike. "I only met with him for about ten minutes, and honestly, he asked the dumbest questions. Like, 'Can you describe how to operate the emergency cable cutting device?' I mean, what's to describe about flipping a toggle switch? And he seemed so concerned about me not having the monkey strap—as if that caused the crash!"

"It's unbelievable that you were the least injured." Reynolds took two steps to the filing cabinet and murmured, "Somebody was watching over you."

Unconsciously, John reached for the medal he wore around his neck along with his dog tags. Before departing for Vietnam, his father had pressed the Saint Christopher medal into his palm. "To watch over you," his dad had whispered while wiping a moist eye.

Closing the cabinet drawer and returning to his seat, Roy

recounted, "I heard the members of the crash investigation board couldn't get here for a couple days because of the increased enemy activity in the Da Nang area. And when they got here, they wanted to go to the scene of the accident, so we provided a chopper for them—Long's ship. But the area was insecure, and they were told they needed a gunship escort. Of course, the gunships were busy, so they had to wait, and they weren't pleased about the delay." In a lowered voice, Roy said, "And I don't think First Sergeant LaForge was happy to have the brass hanging around the company area for so long."

"Was the chopper still there?" John wondered, recalling those five hours on the floor of Elephant Valley.

"I guess it was difficult to find, but they finally spotted the wreckage through a small hole in the jungle canopy. They wanted ground troops to go over to it, but only isolated patrols of Special Forces were in the vicinity, and it would be a two-day march to the crash site."

"How's Wheeler doing?" John wanted to know. "And the others."

Holding up a sheet of paper, Roy divulged, "I was just about to fill out this form on Wheeler. He's heading out of country. Buckman is doing better, but he'll get a new MOS (Military Occupational Specialty) and won't be flying anymore. Mr. Parker won't be flying with the 236th anymore either, but I'm not informed about those decisions."

"Considering what could have happened, we were pretty lucky," John surmised.

In a quiet voice, Roy criticized, "I can't believe you weren't given any time off. I mean, to schedule you right back to flying without some down time...."

"Well, I did have time off from flying. I rode along with the water truck one day." John had enjoyed the distraction of accompanying the driver of the OD water truck that had the 236th's numerals painted on the bumpers in white. They drove to the Army water facility at Da Nang where a purification truck was positioned alongside the river. John fastened one end of a hose to the intake valve on their truck while the other end attached to the swinging, overhead filler pipe of the facility. After filling the two 300-gallon water buffaloes on the back of their truck, they returned to Red Beach, and John helped recharge the storage tower where they showered. Maneuvering the rubber hose brought back memories of his work as a junior volunteer firefighter. The water run had been a diversion for John, but it certainly didn't make him want to drink the stuff. The water actually upset his stomach, and he completely refrained from drinking it after Long discovered that he didn't need to use chemicals to develop his photographs. Plain water from the compound developed them just fine.

John took a last draw on his cigarette before standing and extinguishing it in the sand-filled butt-can nailed onto one of the support columns of the building. Flicking sand and sticky strands of tobacco from his fingertips, he thought about asking if Roy had heard anything about him receiving a medal. The day after the crash, Warrant Officer Samuels, who was also the unit's Awards Officer, stopped John on the sidewalk outside of Operations. Samuels told him he had been recommended for a Silver Star for his conduct after the crash, especially for staying with Parker. Wow! John was dumbstruck at the mention of a Silver Star! But that was two weeks ago, and he'd heard nothing more since. Anyway, John didn't believe he was deserving of such an honor. He was just doing his job. And he was still feeling down from the emotional pain of losing his patients in the accident. How could he be recognized when two lives had been cut short that day? No, he wouldn't bring up the subject to Reynolds. Better to let those thoughts hang there unexpressed.

"Are you going to the club for steaks?" John inquired as he moved toward the door.

"I thought I smelled something burning besides your cigarette." Roy fanned the air with his hand before looking at his watch and then out the screened window in the direction of the clubhouse. "It's sixteen hundred hours on Friday. Time for First Sergeant LaForge to fire up the grill."

"Maybe you'll let me buy you your first drink later," John called as he walked outside.

"Not likely!" Roy's laughing voice drifted through the doorway.

Quite a few men had already gathered around the fifty-five gallon drum that had been sliced in half vertically by a welder's arc to create a grill large enough to barbecue a multitude of steaks. Lately, the unit was having a cookout almost every week.

"Hey, Doc! It's my turn to buy you a beer!"

John glanced behind him and recognized the familiar face of a Navy corpsman beneath his cover—a soft OD baseball cap with a Marine emblem on the front. John and this guy had been drinking together at the club a few weeks ago.

"Hey, you're back in town," John acknowledged as they greeted each other with an improvised dap—an elaborate handshake involving shoulder slaps and finger snaps. Originally introduced by black soldiers, various versions of the dap became a ritualistic greeting for those who had humped the boonies in Vietnam.

"I'm Martin," the corpsman reminded John's baffled expression.

"I remember you," John nodded, recollecting his face but uncertain if Martin was his first name or last since the guy was not wearing his fatigue nametag but a red t-shirt with the letters USMC emblazoned on the front in black. Martin was part of the Marine Corps Combined Action Program (CAP), which embedded a squad of Marines and a Navy corpsman in hundreds of villages in I Corps in an effort to build positive relations with the villagers. The program attempted to counter the perceived war against the peasant society that Westmoreland's tactics fostered when livestock, homes, and water supplies of the villagers were ravaged during search and destroy missions. In between assignments, CAP Marines sometimes stayed in a vacant hooch in the 236th area, where they would unexpectedly appear, disappear, and in Martin's case, reappear. Even though Martin and John were both "docs," they didn't say much about their work. Instead, they perused *Hot Rod* and *High Fidelity* magazines, comparing the sleek lines of Chevy's Camaro Z/28 and Ford's Mustang Mach 1 and discussing the merits of the new Dual turntable and Sherwood receiver. And, of course, they talked about their sweethearts.

John followed Martin into the air-conditioned room where an abbreviated sign on the outside of the building read: 236 MED DET HEL AMB DAYROOM, meaning this was the clubhouse of the

236th Medical Detachment Helicopter Ambulance.

"Look at the fancy new ceiling!" Martin noticed, referring to the two overlapping parachutes that now hid the metal and plywood roof. "You've redecorated." Shifting his gaze to the direction of the bar, Martin added in a lower tone, "And you redecorated your bartender, too."

Instead of First Sergeant LaForge, a Vietnamese woman had become the main barkeep. Doe was young and attractive, especially compared to Sucky Fucky. One day, like Xuan, LaForge's shadow inexplicably disappeared from the 236th's area, never to be seen again.

John's eyes examined the small club's interior. Walls had been painted white, and the plywood had been decorated by torching and staining. Each passing month provided more centerfolds from *Playboy* and *Penthouse*, so there were more naked women on the walls, including an oil painting on black velvet. There were also more bottles of booze on display. Behind the bar were bottles of Smirnoff Vodka, Ronrico Puerto Rican Rum, Calvert Soft Whiskey, and Seagram's Seven Crown. A new neatly lettered sign revealed that the price of all drinks had been raised a nickel.

"Last time you bought me a beer, it only cost you fifteen MPCs," Martin joked, raising his voice to be heard over the country music playing on the reel-to-reel deck behind the bar. "But now I have to spend twenty to return the favor!"

After a number of beers and a juicy steak, John and Martin sat at the small table inside the clubhouse and were dealt into a game of pinochle with crew chiefs Robert Long and Ted Wilcox. Unlike

Germany, where John played pinochle almost every day, it was a rare event for him to participate in a card game in Vietnam. Martin only played a few hands before leaving, but Zeke arrived to take his place as John's partner.

"There'll be prostitutes here tonight," Robert commented as he shuffled the deck. "I saw the big man put the canvas cover on the three-quarter ton."

"Say what?" John questioned, chomping on a fried potato stick from the can he had purchased at the bar.

"Tonight's Friday. The club will be rocking. If it's a weekend and LaForge puts the cover on the truck, you can bet he's on his way to Dogpatch to pick up some girls," Robert further explained.

"I wouldn't call them girls," Ted corrected. "They're hardcore whores with their teased hair and miniskirts and makeup. And that's the reason they're here."

John had seen the new breed of women LaForge was now bringing to camp. Men from all over the Paddock came to the 236th area when LaForge brought in Vietnamese prostitutes. The first time John saw a long column of guys standing in line, he wondered what was happening. When he found out they were waiting to take their turn with a prostitute who used a bucket to rinse between customers, John was disgusted at the sight.

"I never met a man like Top," Robert said under his breath. "If you've got a taste for it, he's the man to see if you want to get laid or make some cash on the side."

"Vietnam gives you an opportunity to act like a heathen and live out all those deep secrets inside you," Zeke reflected.

"You'd think Major Jackson would do something about LaForge," Ted complained.

"The Old Man must look the other way, because he has to know what's going on," Robert ventured. "If he doesn't, he's a lousy Commanding Officer."

"I know he knows what's going on," Ted affirmed. "Because I went to his office and detailed the dirt to him, but he doesn't seem to do anything. Nothing's changed."

"Jackson is a fly," Zeke blurted. "He eats shit and he bothers people." Talking with his cigarette dangling from his lips as he arranged the cards in his hand, Zeke continued, "Did you hear what he did to O'Brien?"

When the others shook their heads, Zeke told the story. "The other night when O'Brien was on duty, an urgent call came in at about 0200."

"I know," Ted interrupted. "Patterson woke me to take that one. An ARVN lost his leg."

"Yeah, Patterson was the runner that night. He was asleep on the cot when the call came in. O'Brien was reading a book in Operations, trying to catch some kind of breeze through the screen instead of sitting in the CONEX. He said he got up to answer the call but didn't get to the radio in time. Anyhow, the guy called again for an urgent Dustoff. This time O'Brien was on the horn and sent Patterson to wake the crew and drive them to the flight line. Meanwhile, O'Brien is sitting by the radio when all of a sudden Jackson walks in. He must have heard the call from his hooch next door. Well, the Old Man pulls the .45 out of his holster, walks up to O'Brien and holds the pistol up to his head! Jackson tells O'Brien, 'I could legally shoot you for dereliction of duty.' O'Brien was scared shitless." Taking a deep drag from his cigarette, Zeke concluded, "So you bet your sweet asses that I answer every call first time."

"I heard Major Jackson is leaving," John stated.

"Yeah, the Old Man is being promoted to headquarters some-where," Zeke sneered. His can of soda clinked against the peace medallion around his neck as he leaned forward to gather the pile of cards on the table.

"You know, I flew those REMFs out to the site of your chop-per crash," Robert announced to John, referring to the officers who had investigated the crash. To Robert, almost all officers were REMFs—Rear Echelon Mother Fuckers. "And I enjoyed breaking their balls."

"How'd you do that?" John chuckled.

"I made them roll their sleeves down." Robert smirked and threw back a shot of rum. "They were prancing around in their starched fatigues busting our chops for Mickey Mouse uniform infractions. When they went to board my bird, I told them they had to roll down their sleeves, even though it was hotter than hell and their shirts were so perfectly sharp-creased and pressed."

"What'd they do?" Ted queried.

"They rolled down their goddamn sleeves!" Robert triumphed. "I told them it was SOP to fly with sleeves down in case of fire, and they couldn't get on my chopper unless they complied."

"I would've liked to have seen that!" Ted released a loud whistle before putting his lips on his beer can.

"Did you hear anything about their investigation?" Robert ques-tioned John.

"No. I was interviewed, but I haven't heard anything else."

"Well, if you ask me, Buckman should've never got on that

bird," Ted evaluated. "There wasn't any enemy contact. Why take that extra weight? They had five crewmembers, they had the hoist onboard, and the fuel tank was almost full, plus they hoisted both patients at once from that height."

"Buckman didn't ask to go along," Robert clarified. "Captain Smith invited him. How could he refuse an officer?"

"That's true," Ted admitted. "Smith fucked up by asking him."

"I would've grounded the bird," Robert asserted, straightening his tall torso. "The crew chief has the right to do that."

"Wheeler was probably too timid, being pretty new to the unit," Ted conjectured while reaching for a smoke. "How's he gonna stand up to the pros—Captain Smith and Pops Parker? Besides, he doesn't have a steel pair like you!"

"Well," Zeke summarized, looking at John through his black plastic frames, "even if mistakes were made, the intention of your mission was a heroic effort. Just like all your missions, you live the motto of the 236th everyday: We strive to save lives." Zeke lifted his soda can, and everyone around the table raised their arms together.

"Fucking A," they each repeated.

Darkness filtered through the couple of small Plexiglas windows of the clubhouse. Top entered the crowded room and took his place behind the bar. With his usual cigar stub stuck in the corner of his mouth and cap cocked back on his head, LaForge stood beside Doe and took drink orders. John had never seen most of the guys who wandered in and out of the small room, but they all seemed to know the First Sergeant.

"Hey Long," Zeke called before bursting into song. "It took me by surprise, I must say, when I found out yesterday. Don'tcha know

172

that I heard it through the grapevine—yeah, yeah, yeah, Oh I heard it through the grapevine...."

John snapped his fingers to Zeke's attempt at Marvin Gaye's new hit. Growing up with the soul-throbbing sounds of Philadelphia, John greatly preferred Motown to what, according to his musical background, he considered the hillbilly music played in the club.

"Okay, Goddard," Robert scowled. "What did you hear through the grapevine?"

"I heard you had a close call when you were at Baldy yesterday and got suckered into a VC ambush."

"Christ on a crutch! That was a close call." Robert leaned back in his seat. "Goddamn gooks got on the Dustoff radio band and gave us coordinates for an urgent pickup. The voice came over the radio in perfect English. Sounded like an American, not a dink. They popped a smoke and we began our approach. All of a sudden we're taking fire from a .51 cal machine gun. Holy shit! The tracers looked like red basketballs coming at us." Robert paused to sip his drink. "We got out of there in a hurry."

"Where was that at?" Ted asked.

"About nine klicks west of LZ West."

"Was it the firebase just built last month?" Zeke questioned after swallowing a sip of orange soda. "The one so far out into NVA territory they named it LZ Siberia?"

"Yeah, those guys are really out there," Robert concurred, "not much bigger than a football field with nothing but foxholes and artillery perched on it."

"It overlooks the Hiep Duc Valley Resettlement Camp," Zeke explained, pulling out his pack of Kools and lighting a cigarette before shuffling the cards.

"What's with the resettlement camps?" Ted wanted to know.

"It's part of the pacification program. It's where the refugees are placed after they leave their land." Zeke dealt the cards as he continued. "Westmoreland's strategy basically gives the peasant three choices: he can stay on his land, but the land usually becomes a free-fire zone, so he could be shot at or bombed at anytime; he can join the Viet Cong and then we'll do everything we can to kill him; or he can move to an area under South Vietnamese government control and become a refugee. Some of the camps are surrounded by barbed wire and have armed guards watching over them."

"That's fucked, man," Ted grumbled. His voiced boomed throughout the room during a quiet pause between songs. "I thought we're supposed to be fighting communism and spreading freedom and democracy."

"Well, the only way to control the VC slipping in and out of the villages is to destroy the village and move the peasants to resettlement camps," Zeke elaborated. "And there are plenty of Americans back home questioning that strategy. My sister wrote that students are rioting in protest on college campuses. Last month, three hundred students took over the Administration building at Harvard and...."

"Goddard!" LaForge's gruff voice shouted out from behind the bar. "Shut the fuck up! I don't want to hear you spouting your peacenik shit in here. Shut up or get the fuck out."

The guys finished the card game in silence until Robert asserted in a hushed tone, "Those sissy-ass college students should come over here and help us end this war instead of making so much trouble back home."

"Yeah," Ted agreed. "If they came and fought, we could all get out of here sooner. But they get their student deferments and avoid being drafted. I'd like to see those longhairs' asses on the front lines. Isn't it better to fight communism over here instead of on our own soil where our women and children will get hurt?"

"Hey, Doc!" Zeke suddenly interjected. "I forgot to congratulate you for giving birth to a baby boy."

"Uh, that would be my patient who gave birth, not me," John corrected.

"Seebeth buys no more beers tonight," Robert insisted as he reached over and slapped John on the back. "We all take pride that a birth took place on one of our choppers." Holding up his plastic cup, he toasted, "Here's to Doc Seebeth and a successful delivery."

"Yeah," Ted hastened to add. "It always bothers me to have someone die on my ship. It's great that we had a birth. Here's to you, Doc."

The guys clinked their plastic cups and aluminum cans while John beamed but insisted he couldn't be credited for the birth. He was 2nd-up that day in Da Nang when a call came from LZ Baldy to ferry seven ambulatory patients and one on a stretcher to the 95th Evacuation Hospital. It was a mission he had flown numerous times before, as Da Nang Dustoff routinely transported patients in need of additional treatment from the 23rd Med Aid Station to the 95th.

On this mission, after the litter was situated, the seven US soldiers climbed aboard the chopper and John instructed them where to sit, positioning three in the hellholes and having the others sit on the floor around the litter. They would not require any treatment on the twenty-five-minute flight. Their medical problems consisted of fevers, an earache, stomach disorders, foot problems, a snakebite, and one patient was going to the 95th for an eye exam. The patient on the litter was a young Vietnamese woman close to her ninth month of pregnancy. Although she was having some contractions, the doctor at the 23rd Med felt she wasn't ready to deliver.

After making the pickup, the helicopter ascended to its normal flying altitude of two thousand feet and proceeded to head north toward Da Nang. They were in the air five minutes when the Vietnamese woman started experiencing sharp pains. John keyed his helmet mike to ask the pilot if he had correctly understood that this woman was not supposed to be close to delivery. The pilot radioed the 23rd Med and then related back to John that in the doctor's opinion, the woman should not be in labor. However, if she seemed to be, they should get her to the 95th Evac as soon as possible. Observing the way the woman was moving and watching her face grimace in pain, John was convinced that she was definitely experiencing contractions. He requested that the pilot change the mission classification from priority to urgent, and the helicopter immediately increased speed.

John felt a sense of nervousness, because he had never delivered a baby before. The only instruction he received was during his medic training at Fort Sam Houston nearly two years ago where he was required to watch a couple of films about childbirth. In contrast, he'd had plenty of experience treating people injured by the instruments of war. It was ironic that he was better prepared and more at ease bandaging a patient with a gunshot wound than delivering a baby. He could handle someone who was blown apart but felt unprepared and uncomfortable assisting in the natural act of childbirth.

Something else was making John feel uncomfortable as well. The US ambulatory patients began to act like a bunch of clowns when the woman reached down to lower her black pajama bottoms. Pointing and laughing, hooting and hollering, their sexual innuendoes created a carnival-like atmosphere. John knew they must be stressing the woman, because their actions were stressing him out—and embarrassing him. Why were these guys carrying on in such a disrespectful way? John attempted to pull the woman's pants back up, shaking his head no. The woman would have no part of it. She was going to give birth and that was that. When the woman pulled her pants down to her ankles the catcalls increased. John felt his face flush when he yelled at the soldiers, asking them to give her a break. Most of them stopped, but a few assholes kept at it.

If the woman was making any sounds, John couldn't hear her above the loud grind of the transmission and continuous beat of the rotor blade slicing through the air. Maintaining control, the woman was handling the situation better than the rest of them. Raising her knees while keeping her feet flat on the stretcher, she spread her legs, and the crown of the baby's head appeared. John placed his hands under the emerging infant, his left hand wearing a blood-stained Nomex glove. Eventually, the whole head appeared. Soon after, John found himself holding a wiggling dark-haired baby covered with the fluids of birth. The woman raised her black, loose-fitting shirt, baring her breasts. She motioned for John to hand her the baby, which he did without delay. He watched her put the newborn up to her breast, where it began to suckle. Mother and baby were still connected by the umbilical cord. By then, all the soldiers in the cargo bay sat in silence and awe as the Vietnamese mother breastfed her infant.

In a few minutes, the helicopter landed, and the patients were taken into the hospital. When the chopper was back in the air a call came in from the RTO at the 95th.

"Dustoff 602, congratulations on your successful delivery. Both mother and son are doing fine. And please advise your medic, he's now the godfather of a baby boy."

Several aircraft in the vicinity were monitoring the radio transmission, and they also broke in and congratulated the crew for a job well done. So when the guys were toasting John in the clubhouse tonight, he knew they were really toasting the creation—rather than the destruction—of life, and the joy of a birth instead of the usual suffering and death on their choppers.

"Are you staying for tonight's stag flicks?" Ted asked everyone at the table while gathering the cards into a pile. The card game was over, and they were ready to quit for the night.

"Nah, I don't want to watch that shit." Robert related. "I'm gonna go drink my own booze. If anyone wants to stop by for a nightcap, the bar in my hooch is open." Under his breath he added, "I don't want to give this one any more money."

"Rumor has it that the first movie shows a donkey fucking a woman," Ted said. "Ya can't miss that!"

"Yes, keep the troops content and satisfied," Zeke snorted in a whisper while rising from the table. "Give them ice cream, pizza, steaks, hooch maids, swimming pools, and stag movies."

"Where do they get the movies?" John wondered.

Gesturing his head toward LaForge, Ted revealed, "The big guy gets them from the Korean laundry. You know, the one by the entrance to the compound. And tonight's movies are supposed to be far-fucking-out."

John took his time leaving the clubhouse. He was curious. Back at Fort Sam Houston, he'd heard about carloads of guys driving across the border to Tijuana where they would attend a live performance of a woman and donkey. Standing in the doorway nursing his beer, John waited for the movie projector to start up so he could catch a glimpse of the unimaginable. It was an eye-popping sight but did nothing for him except make him a little sick. He left the club, passing the line of men still waiting for their turn with the prostitute.

Arriving back in his hooch, he saw a light in Hartman's room. Parting the beaded divider purchased at the PX and hung for privacy, John saw Tom sitting on his bed writing a letter.

"You're not missing much at the club tonight," John informed him.

"I'm beat," Tom declared from inside his mosquito net. "I'm either flying and my adrenaline is pumping, or I'm in a constant state of exhaustion."

"Same for me."

Raising the ballpoint pen in his hand, Tom explained, "And I need to finish this letter to Gail."

"Hey, I put in for my R&R. Karen and I are going to meet in Hawaii," John proclaimed. "We were only married for six weeks, and we've been apart now for six months."

"R&R in Hawaii sounds real good," Tom concurred.

"Yeah, but Reynolds said there's a three-month wait, so my R&R won't come up until August. That's such a long time to wait. I wish I could see her right away."

"Damn!" Tom cussed. "I know what you mean. I really miss

Gail." Pointing to the letter he was working on, he added, "We're sort of making wedding plans."

"All right to ya," John said as he backed out of Hartman's doorway. "Well, I'm going to turn in." He took two steps and separated his own beaded divider to enter his room.

Lying on his mattress, John heaved a sigh and thought about his godson. What a miracle to welcome a new life amidst so much death and devastation. He wondered what kind of life that baby would have in this war-torn country. Would he grow up to be a fucking VC? John's thoughts turned to his R&R and how much he wanted to hold Karen in his arms. It was painful to think about her because he missed her so much.

"Hey, John?" Hartman called over the partition.

John cleared the emotion from his voice. "Yeah?"

"Miller said that you were the first helicopter on the scene when you flew over that downed Dustoff yesterday. I was wondering if one of the medics who trained us was onboard."

John couldn't respond for a minute. His crew had been on their way to a pickup when news of a crashed Dustoff came over the radio. Since they were in close proximity, the pilot immediately flew to the crash site to offer assistance. Approaching the area, they could see the wreckage over 1,000 feet below. When John learned the downed bird belonged to the 54th, Rich Bernardo came to mind, along with the picture he had shown John of his wife and three-year-old son. Before descending, the RTO on the ground frantically instructed the 236th Dustoff to get out of the vicinity. The 54th's helicopter ambulance had gotten caught in the crossfire of .51 cal rounds, and the enemy was still in the area. John's crew quickly departed without knowing what was what.

Finally, John asked Hartman, "Do you know how they made out?"

"I heard there were no survivors—all four were KIA."

Silence hung in their hooch for several minutes.

"Hey, John?"

"Yeah?"

"You wear a Saint Christopher medal around your neck, don't you?"

"Yeah."

"My mother wrote that the Pope kicked 200 saints off the Universal Calendar of Saints on May 9th, the exact same day of your crash. Saint Christopher was one of them."

John reached for his dog tags and fingered the medal from his father. "So, Saint Christopher doesn't protect me anymore?"

"Hell, no!" Tom responded. "You were the least injured in that crash. I'd say he's got more power than the Pope gave him credit for."

"Man, I just want to get the fuck out of here," John murmured. "I want to get away from all this perversion and carnage. I'm really sick of all the blood and suffering."

"Amen to that, bro."

Chapter 10

"Welcome to Hell," crew chief Robert Long uttered under his breath as he and John jogged over to the landing pad at LZ Baldy. It was late afternoon on the third day of their rotation at Baldy, and they were about to assist in a grim job nobody wanted to do, but all available hands pitched in to help. The task of unloading a chopper full of dead soldiers was the stuff that could give young men nightmares for the rest of their lives. In silence, bodies were lifted from the aircraft and placed upon litters. Rigid bodies—frozen in horrific positions of terror, faces twisted in shock, limbs locked in ghastly, outstretched poses. Flaccid bodies—big and bloated and alive with squirming maggots. Bodies so dismembered their remaining pieces were collected in plastic baggies. Bodies that had baked in 100-degree heat and now emitted a repugnant stench so vile they reeked to high heaven.

Today, there were six dead soldiers from the 196th infantry stacked onboard a Huey gunship. The pilots wore their gas masks to avoid breathing the nauseating odor fanned inside the chopper by the rotor wash. John lifted the shoulders of one body and hardly reacted when the detached head rolled out of the cargo bay and landed on the helipad with a thud. Sergeant Weaver steadied the litter handle as John bent down to pick up the head and place it on the stretcher beside the rest of the body. Somberly but hastily, the bodies were carried past the Dustoff hooch to the neighboring building, Graves Registration. There, an eighteen-year-old kid from a rural town in New York State took charge of dealing with the dead.

Reed Humboldt was drafted before he enlisted, and he served in the infantry before volunteering to work in Graves Registration. Perhaps because he was a big guy, he was given the big responsibility of meticulously caring for the remains of fallen soldiers. Already a Sergeant, Reed supervised a clerk and two grunts assigned to the task of processing the dead at the Division Collection Point located at LZ Baldy. Bodies from various areas of I Corps were delivered to Baldy by truck or by air. Reed and his assistants would remove the deceased's clothing and put the body into an olive-drab, six-handled rubber bag. Each body had to be examined by a doctor, and Reed's observations often helped the doctors determine the cause of death. The personal effects of each soldier were put into an envelope, labeled, and would eventually be sent to next of kin. From Baldy, remains were shipped to Da Nang, which was one of two fixed and well-equipped mortuaries in-country. The other was located in Tan Son Nhut, just outside of Saigon. At the mortuaries, positive identification was made, sometimes using laboratory procedures to supplement traditional methods such as dental and fingerprint comparison. The bodies were embalmed and vacuumed-sealed in aluminum coffin shipping containers. Those who had lived east of the Mississippi River were sent to Dover, Delaware, and those who had lived west were sent to Oakland, California.

At Baldy, a 15 × 20-foot walk-in cooler held as many as twenty bodies, but today it was full to capacity. Reed directed John and the others to deposit the remaining bodies in the adjacent refrigerated CONEX that could hold another six. Two generators kept the rooms refrigerated. The noise of their engines joined the constant background whirring of the other generators that provided power at Baldy.

When the chopper was evacuated, it immediately departed. John and Robert walked toward their hooch. Stopping outside it and facing the aid station, John reached for his pack of cigarettes.

"Hey, can I bum a cigarette?" Robert asked.

"Sure," John replied as he extended the pack of Lucky Strikes to Robert. After lighting his own unfiltered Lucky with a Zippo lighter, he lit the one dangling from Robert's lips. When the metal device clicked shut, John commented, "I didn't know you smoked."

Rubbing his right jaw, Robert replied, "I don't, but I've got a helluva toothache, and I thought smoking might numb it."

"There were a lot of casualties today," John remarked after exhaling a long line of smoke and glancing over at the now vacant helipad.

"Yeah, and I heard the RTO say that another gunship just called in. It's on its way with two more dead," Robert stated. "But they said they're covered. They've got enough hands to unload this one."

John nodded as he saw several medics from the aid station holding litters and congregating in the fifty-something-foot space between the building and the landing pad.

Massaging his jaw, Robert added, "One of the grunts at Graves said that, if possible, Sergeant Humboldt likes to keep the bodies here for a few days because sometimes the guys in the field find a random arm or leg a couple days later."

John took a deep draw from his cigarette. "The wards are full, too. Sergeant Weaver said three guys came in by truck with food poisoning."

"What did they do, eat something in a village that made them sick?" Robert questioned, butting the half-smoked cigarette and cupping the right side of his face.

"Yeah, or it could even be baked goods from Mom—they spoil fast in this heat and humidity. Or sometimes the guys go against regulations and take a quick drink from a cool stream without using their water purification tablets," John further explained. "But Sergeant Weaver said this is nothing compared to last December when over fifty guys came down with food poisoning. He said the chapel and supply room were overflowing with sick guys. They had to line them up outside, and there weren't enough litters for them all."

"Fifty guys? That had to be a mess!"

"Can you imagine? And with so few latrines, he said guys were puking and shitting everywhere." John looked up at the sound of the incoming gunship.

Above the whomp of the approaching Huey's rotor blades, Robert yelled, "How did so many get food poisoning?"

"They traced it to the gravy in their Christmas dinner," John shouted before the noise of the arriving gunship made verbal communication impossible.

John put his hand over his eyes as the ship's rotor wash sent dust and debris fiercely flying through the air. Rather than approaching along the prescribed route above the flight line, this helicopter swooped down directly over the buildings, creating a swirling dust storm and causing the metal roofs of the hooches to shake and rattle violently. Suddenly, the roof of the chaplain's hooch lifted up and sailed skyward before crashing to the ground. Sergeant Weaver had been running to the aid station and was right there when the roof went airborne. John and Robert watched Gary race over to the chopper as soon as the gunship's skids touched the landing pad. His hollering and gesturing made it clear that he was pissed.

"Looks like Sergeant Weaver is jumping on that pilot's ass," John observed in a loud voice.

"He needs to set him straight," Robert affirmed. "That stupid maneuver could have killed someone."

After the helicopter was unloaded, it quickly lifted off. John and Robert walked toward the aid station and heard Gary rage to others, "He was in such a hurry to get treatment for the one injured soldier onboard, he didn't think about how he could have caused even more injuries."

"I bet he won't repeat that mistake," John predicted as he and Robert watched a red-faced Sergeant disappear into the aid station.

Just then another medic walked out of the aid station. Spotting John and Robert, he announced, "A call came in for Charger Dustoff at West—a routine." The medic then continued toward the Dustoff hooch to alert the pilots.

When in Da Nang, their medevac's radio call sign was *Da Nang Dustoff*, but at Baldy where the Dustoff crew and chopper provided direct support for the Chargers, the 196th Light Infantry Brigade, Americal Division, their call sign was *Charger Dustoff*.

Ten minutes after receiving the call, the Dustoff crew was in the air and on their way to a nearby fire support base known as Hill 445, or LZ West. When the 196th's area of operations moved north a couple of years ago, they established a row of firebases in the hotly contested Hiep Duc/Que Son Valleys. War strategists knew that—forcedly or willingly—peasant farmers in the large fertile basin provided valuable supplies for the toughest and largest enemy force in the area—the 2d NVA Division, with 7,000 well-trained and well-equipped battle-hardened soldiers. In theory, the strategists believed that creating a wall of firebases on top of 1,500-foot vantage points, approximately four miles apart, would allow the lowlands to be monitored and supply lines stanched, driving the enemy out of the Annamite Mountain Range. In reality, lush jungles covered with triple canopy growth of teak, mahogany, and other tropical hardwoods, along with rushing rivers and deep gorges, provided plenty of natural hideouts for the NVA and VC units to conceal their operations.

Like other firebases, the summit of LZ West had been scalped of foliage to create a clear lookout and better aim for the howitzers. Although both Baldy and West were encircled with a perimeter of concertina wire and mine fields, Baldy had evolved to almost luxurious conditions compared to the crude foxholes and bunkers on West. Helicopters were the only way to bring supplies and troops in or out of the fire support base. LZ West loomed high above the southeast end of the Hiep Duc Valley, providing artillery and mortar support to the infantry that patrolled the surrounding countryside. Brave men of the 196th humped up and down the steep slopes of West and other nearby firebases with eighty-pound rucksacks on their backs. They swept the land, patrolled the Song Chang and Song Thu Bon Rivers, and crawled through underground tunnels to find and destroy the enemy. The basins of Que Son and Hiep Duc were soaked with the blood of American and Vietnamese men fighting for control of the region.

Had John known the Vietnamese name for the mountain that LZ West now occupied, he certainly would have agreed with the appropriateness. *Nui Liet Kiem* referred to a "Mountain of Leeches," and many times the patients at West were covered with leeches when loaded onboard the chopper. The leeches fell out of trees and onto the grunts as they hiked through the surrounding jungles, and after picking up a leech-covered patient, the rotor wash would send leeches flying everywhere in the cargo bay.

This afternoon's pickup involved two ambulatory soldiers who had reported to the battalion aid station, which was located in an underground bunker in the center of LZ West. Later in the day, the Dustoff crew performed several more hill-hopping missions to pick up the sick call at other nearby firebases. It was deep into the evening after John had stretched out on a dusty mattress in the perpetually dirty Dustoff hooch when a call came in to evacuate a seriously wounded Marine with a gut wound.

Knowing in advance that they would be transporting the Marine to the Naval hospital in Da Nang, the standby crews in Da Nang were alerted. Assignments would temporarily shift in order to maintain continuous coverage at Baldy. The 1st on-call crew in Da Nang flew down to Baldy, and the 2-up crew in Da Nang moved to 1-up position for a couple hours until John's crew completed their mission. The crews would then slide back to their original assignments.

Upon reaching the pickup site, John was ready to hand a litter to the guys on the ground so they could bring the wounded man over to the chopper. GIs who received gut wounds generally expressed a great deal of pain and were usually brought to the medevac on a litter with their intestines spilling out of the ragged tears in their skin. Often they were unconscious. Tonight, three figures walked out of the darkness and up to the chopper. With the aid of two men, the patient approached the helicopter on foot. This guy was conscious. His arms pressed upon a large bloodstained abdominal bandage that covered the exposed parts of his entrails. It looked like he was cradling his guts as he slid onboard.

"It's more comfortable for me to sit up," the patient communicated to John.

John nodded and motioned for Robert to help him slide the guy to the center of the floor, where they leaned his back against the wall that housed the chopper's transmission. Considering the injuries, John didn't expect the patient to be as lucid as he was. John guessed the man to be in his mid-thirties and recognized that he was a Marine Gunnery Sergeant, or Gunny Sergeant as informally nicknamed. A Gunnery Sergeant in the infantry is typically in charge of a company-sized group of Marines or over a hundred personnel. They have a reputation for being tough as nails. John heard that in the Marine chain of authority, first there was the Gunny Sergeant, then God, and then your mother and father.

In flight, and under the red lighting of their nighttime mission, John checked the Sergeant's abdominal bandage, bending forward to hear what his patient was trying to say.

"I've been given an injection of morphine," the man related, "and right now I just need to get to a hospital."

"Yes, Sir," John assured him in a voice loud enough to be heard over the clamor of the transmission. "That's exactly what we intend to do." John had seen the letter "M" written on the man's forehead with grease pencil and knew it meant morphine had been administered. Since 236th medics didn't carry morphine, there was no danger of overdosing in flight. However, the hospital would be alerted by the "M." Reaching for his medical supplies, John gestured and shouted, "I'd like to start an IV on you." The flight to the Naval Hospital in Da Nang was going to take about twenty minutes, and John wanted to get some fluids running into his patient to offset the loss of blood.

The Sergeant indicated that it was okay to give him an IV, so John set up an IV solution bottle and hung it from a hook attached to the ceiling of the helicopter. Next, he unwrapped an IV start-up kit. Crew chief Long came over and held a flashlight so John could better see what he was doing. The flashlight had a red lens cover that diffused the beam of light. The tinted lighting was far from optimal when trying to thread a needle into a vein while flying aboard a helicopter at night, but it would have to do.

While the wounded Sergeant leaned back against the wall, John attempted to insert an IV catheter in his vein but couldn't get it to go in. Realizing he had botched the first attempt, John pulled the needle out and tried again. Thinking he had it in position that time, John slowly released some IV solution, only to see a bubble of fluid begin to rise, indicating the catheter was not in place. Pulling the needle out of the patient's arm, John tried once more to insert the IV needle into the skin over the vein, probing the inner catheter around in his arm, but saw it again wasn't right. All the while, the Gunny Sergeant sat patiently—holding his guts with his right arm as John continued to poke about in his left. Being doped up on morphine probably dulled the man's sensations to John's repeated needle sticks.

John desperately wanted to help this deserving Marine; however, his own anxiousness and frustration increased with each failed attempt. What should have been a routine procedure, he couldn't get right tonight. In reality, the patient was probably in vascular shock. With such severe loss of blood, a person's blood pressure can quickly bottom out, causing veins to collapse. At the time, John had no explanation for his inability to help the severely wounded Sergeant. When the aircraft finally dropped the patient off at the hospital, John felt dejected. He couldn't believe he couldn't perform something he knew he should be able to do. On the flight back to Baldy, John sat upon his armored pad on the floor. Facing to the rear, he gazed out the open cargo bay door into the dark night sky.

The next morning, John awoke to the sound of an incoming Caribou. Surprised to find himself alone in the Dustoff hooch, he dragged his exhausted body off the mattress to locate his other crewmembers. As he walked out of the hooch he turned to glance at the words someone had recently painted over their door in capital letters and white paint—*WE GOT A PAIR*. Yeah, it did take balls to fly into some of the hot situations where Dustoff flew.

A medic at the aid station told John that Robert was over at the dentist's hooch. John found Robert Long seated in what looked like an old barber's chair. The dentist for the brigade was stationed at Baldy and had just finished extracting two of Robert's wisdom teeth. Compared to a modern dental office, the device used for drilling, powered by pulleys, lines, and an air compressor, resembled an antique.

When John commented about the rustic equipment, the dentist laughed and informed them, "After losing power, I've had to finish procedures with a handheld flashlight and a drill run by a stationary bicycle." Tapping on the back of the chair that held Robert, he added, "And this chair is better than the webbed lawn chair we had before."

As Robert rose from the seat, the dentist comforted, "You'll feel a lot better with those out."

John and Robert walked over to the mess tent, where they joined the two Dustoff pilots.

"I'll pass on eating," Robert mumbled, rubbing his swollen and purple right jaw.

When a medic from the aid station ran into the hooch to inform the crew they had a mission, John turned to Robert and asked, "Are you okay to fly?"

"Ab-sha-lutely."

Minutes later, the Dustoff ship was balancing its skids upon a dike beside an expanse of rice paddies. It brought back memories of the first time John had landed on a rice paddy berm five months ago. Then, the Dustoff pilots had spotted a partially submerged Huey, and not knowing the circumstances, they decided to go down and see if there were survivors in need of help. Perched on an embankment between paddies, the pilot had ordered John to go over to the crash site and take a look.

John had jumped off the skid and into a rice paddy, immediately sinking up to his chest in water. His body armor weighted him deep into the muck, and for a moment he thought his career as a medic had ended. When his feet found resistance, he eventually made his way over to the chopper. He was apprehensive as he approached, because more often than not, downed aircraft were booby-trapped. There were no bodies inside the helicopter and no personnel nearby, so John made his way back to his own chopper. Afterwards, his leap into the rice paddy became the subject of many jokes. Since that experience, John never again jumped into one.

This morning as the Dustoff chopper landed on the dike, John's skin moistened from the triple-digit temperatures common in this mountain-surrounded basin. The rotor wash provided the only circulation of the valley's muggy heat. Two American soldiers appeared from a nearby hedgerow half-dragging a fellow soldier whose arms were draped around their shoulders. Hopping with one foot held out front, this guy had stepped on a punji stick. Along the narrow wood line that bordered the paddy, John saw a number of peasants squatting on the ground with their arms tied behind their backs. They were, no doubt, being questioned about the punji stick.

Punji sticks (or stakes) were nonexplosive booby traps made of sharpened wood or bamboo. They were concealed by vegetation or mud and sunken along trails where American soldiers were expected to walk. Strategically placed, sometimes obvious sticks protruded from the ground, baiting the soldier to step around them and right onto a hidden stick. Often they were smeared with human or animal feces to promote infection and increase their wound potential. Most soldiers stepped on them, but occasionally a soldier would dive for cover during a surprise attack and end up being impaled by a number of punji sticks. Compared to the American's sophisticated and expensive weaponry, the primitive punji stick was remarkably effective in removing a GI from combat status for three weeks or more.

Since bamboo grew everywhere, the simple trap could be fashioned and placed into position by women and children, explaining why John saw several women among the peasants being detained and queried today.

After delivering their patient to the aid station where he would have his wound cleaned and receive a dose of penicillin, the Dustoff crew flew a couple of routine missions before responding to a call to pick up a wounded NVA officer. Like the Gunny Sergeant they evacuated yesterday, the NVA officer had a bloodstained bandage covering a serious gut wound. Unlike the Gunny Sergeant, this guy had not been given a shot of morphine. And instead of taking him to a hospital for treatment, the Dustoff crew had orders to deliver him directly to a military compound outside of Da Nang.

"The RTO says to tell the medic not to give this guy any pain medication," the pilot related to John over the intercom as the litter holding the enemy prisoner was shoved onboard headfirst. "He says the brass at the compound want him in a talkative mood."

In flight, John examined the patient, noting he had been shot twice in the abdomen with at least one bullet exiting his back. This guy had to be in tremendous pain. In John's usual routine of treatment, he reached for an IV bottle and opened a startup kit. He found a vein on his first attempt and had no problem starting the IV drip.

Scooting back to his armored plate on the floor, John stretched his legs to the right to avoid the litter that was positioned perpendicularly in front of him. This angled John in direct view of the patient's head. It was the first time he had ever been face-to-face with a live North Vietnamese Army officer. He'd evacuated plenty of Viet Cong suspects dressed in civilian garb, but here was an actual enemy soldier wearing what was left of a khaki military uniform. Surprisingly, this officer was young. He appeared younger than John—perhaps just a teenager. He looked too small and helpless to be causing so much trouble in this country. His face glistened with sweat as his head moved back and forth on the stretcher. John knew the guy had to be hurting, because he'd seen hardened soldiers with holes in their midsections writhe in misery and cry out for their mothers in a delirious state. Yet, this little bastard made no sounds. His teeth were clenched, but he uttered no cries of agony.

As John scrutinized the person stretched out before him, he became consumed by a growing feeling of hatred. This guy symbolized everything that was wrong in this place. This guy and his commie buddies were the reason why America was in Vietnam. They were responsible for all this suffering and killing, all this maiming and carnage. If it weren't for them, John could be home with Karen. He could be back where bodies are healthy and whole—not bloody and missing appendages. This son-of-a-bitch and those like him had turned this place into a living hell. And John hated him. Glaring at the enemy, John squinted his eyes to send daggers of hatred to this guy's heart. Shame on this fucking bastard and his evil ways! John was happy that this goddamn gook was going to die a miserable death. *Once you and your kind are all dead, there will be peace— and the killing will stop.*

The patient turned his head left and his eyes suddenly locked with John's. But rather than fear, the soldier's eyes radiated strength and confidence and—John couldn't believe it—they radiated contempt! This defeated and humiliated enemy, this undernourished kid in his tattered uniform, this wounded and bleeding body about to meet its maker should have been feeling helpless and scared shitless. Instead, he conveyed a sense of surety and self-justification. As he flashed an arrogant gaze at John, his eyes implied that *he* was the better man. *He* was the one more committed to his beliefs. *He* would endure the fires of Hell to be victorious—not only as a soldier—but as a human being. *I'm in control, and I stand for something that you know nothing about.*

John wanted to get up and kick him. He felt like picking up this fucking guy and hurling him and his insulting eyes out the open cargo bay door.

The movement of Robert's hand grabbed John's attention. He was giving a thumbs-down sign right above the prisoner's head. John nodded in agreement, thinking that this NVA officer was bad news. But Robert also could have meant that this guy was soon going to meet a very unpleasant future.

When the chopper touched down, several stern-looking military police rushed forward to take the wounded prisoner of war into custody. The prisoner made no sound when his litter was roughly dragged from the helicopter, but his eyes continued to shoot darts of defiance. As the chopper lifted off, John watched the stretcher being carried into a building. Silently wishing the interrogators luck, John couldn't help but believe they could torture the shit out that kid, but he wasn't going to tell them squat.

On the flight back to Baldy, John felt uneasy. He didn't feel victorious. He didn't feel superior. Something gnawed at him, but he couldn't exactly put his finger on it. What if circumstances were reversed? Would John hold up as well? Did he possess deeply held beliefs that would get him through such a hell on Earth? And what were his own deep beliefs? For the remainder of the day, John was restless. He felt a confusing inner disturbance but wasn't able to put his finger on it.

The next morning was overcast and cloudy. John and Robert sat in the cargo bay of the parked helicopter waiting for a fresh crew to arrive and replace them. They both said good morning when Sergeant Weaver walked over to them.

"There's some bad news," Gary started before looking away. "We lost a really good man yesterday. Chaplain Bartley was killed."

"I'm very sorry to hear that, Sarge," Robert responded.

"How...?" John began.

"Their vehicle ran over a land mine...in the vicinity of Toan Lun Village...about seven miles south of Da Nang. Nobody expected trouble there." Gary coughed and stopped to light a Salem. "He was taking part in a TV documentary about chaplains in Vietnam. They were all killed—three members of the film crew, two Marines, and Chaplain Bartley."

John knew Chaplain Bartley had earned three Purple Hearts and a Silver Star without ever picking up a weapon. In addition to his role as counselor, Chaplain Bartley lifted the troops' morale by bringing them steaks and other welcomed supplies. The Padre also provided sanctuary for the troops by building four chapels, including one on Baldy.

"We're going to gather in the chapel on the hill," Gary explained. We'll have a memorial service for him later, but right now we're just going to support each other."

"We're headed back to Da Nang, Sergeant Weaver," John stated. "We're just waiting for our replacements to arrive, but we send our condolences to all who knew him."

"He was a great man, and he'll always be a hero in our hearts," Gary proclaimed.

Robert quietly agreed, "I'm sure he'll be welcomed to Heaven."

Chapter 11

June 1969

Dear Johnny,

I want to go to Hawaii but I don't have any money for a ticket. You'll be back at the end of November. Soooooo, that's not so far from August!!!

Grandma Flora said if I want to stay with her I have to get my diploma. I'm taking GED classes at the Community college. They are so much better than high school!!!!

My hair is growing out. It's almost down to my chin. My friends at class say it looks good. I hope you like it. Sorry I haven't sent a picture but I'll send one soon.

Lots of love to you! Good luck!

Love,

Karen

John collapsed on his mattress to reread the letter, searching for something he might have missed the first dozen readings. He had to get back to the flight line, but he needed a minute to pull himself together. Still shaking from what he considered a major fuck-up, John's anger was killing him, and this morning it almost killed his crewmates as well. He drank hard last night after returning from

Baldy and reading Karen's letter. At first he was elated to find mail from his wife, because more often than not, mail call was a source of disappointment and depression for him. The thrill of receiving a letter soon faded after reading the one-page note. It raised more questions than it answered. What was Karen doing with all the money he sent each month? Other than fifty bucks for snacks and smokes, he sent her the remainder of his $560 paycheck. And that included an extra $55 combat pay and an extra $55 hazardous duty flight pay. Why wasn't there enough money to meet him in Hawaii? Why didn't she write more? And undoubtedly because he was scarred by childhood memories of his mother's infidelities, one question obsessed him most—was Karen being faithful? John feared she was not. Getting good and drunk was the only way he could stop those incessant questions and the downward spiral of his thoughts.

This morning he awoke with a dry mouth and a throbbing head. He was cursing Karen as the chopper lifted off to fly a routine mission when a pair of F-4 fighter-bombers approached from John's side of the helicopter. It was John's job to watch for anything that could endanger their rotor blades and tail boom—be it trees, buildings, wires or low-flying aircraft. John was so absorbed with his angry thoughts that he missed seeing the Phantoms zooming towards them. There was no collision, but the wake of the screaming jets created a tornado-like vortex that rocked the helicopter for a moment of helpless terror. The pilot quickly steadied their chopper, but the crew was rightfully pissed at John's failure to provide a heads-up.

As soon as they completed the mission and returned to the flight line, John rode back to the company area in a jeep. He walked into Operations and asked if he could speak to the new Commanding

Officer. Major Jackson had recently been replaced by Major Evans. Roy Reynolds told him he could find the Major in the CO's hooch, so John headed in that direction, his face and neck a burning red.

"Yes, Specialist Seebeth?" Major Evans inquired after being saluted.

"Sir, I'm having problems with my marriage, and it's affecting my job. I need to go back to the States and get things straightened out with my wife, and then I'll be able to come back and do my job better. Right now, I'm having a hard time concentrating. And Sir, my drinking is beginning to interfere with my job."

"Are you drinking during your duty hours?"

"No, Sir. Absolutely not, but last night—after getting a letter from my wife—I drank a lot of beer, and I was hungover this morning, and I put the crew at risk by not seeing a pair of zoomies approach. I need to ease my mind and go see my wife and make sure everything is okay between us."

John described the incident with the F-4s while Major Evans sat silently and nodded.

When John finally stopped speaking, Major Evans knotted his gray eyebrows and rubbed his chin while stating, "You know, those fighter bombers can come upon you in a blink of an eye. They practice intercepting aircraft and can blow by at 350 mph or more, and their afterburners leave a powerful wash."

"Sir, I was thinking about my wife, and I failed to see the jets, and I failed to give the pilot a heads-up."

After a long pause, Major Evans related, "Your circumstances do not qualify for an emergency leave, so it's not possible for you to go Stateside. But, I'll tell you what I'll do. I'm meeting my wife in

Hawaii in a week, and while I'm there, I'll give your wife a call and see what the situation is." Major Evans shoved a notepad and pen in John's direction. "Write her phone number down."

John pulled out his wallet to remove the folded piece of paper with Grandma Flora's address and phone number written on it. He'd never called it himself because there were no telephones available for the troops to phone home, so he carefully copied the number onto the pad beneath Karen's name and wrote "wife of Specialist John Seebeth" in parentheses.

The Major set the paper to the side of his desk. "And by the way, Specialist Seebeth, are you following orders and wearing your Nomex flight gloves? I don't want to see you without those gloves on your hands."

Major Evans was a pilot, and he occasionally flew VIP or routine missions. When John had crewed with him, the Major noticed that John kept his right glove tucked inside the front pocket of his body armor.

"Yes, Sir. I do wear them. I mean, I always wear my left glove, but it's really hard to thread a vein with those gloves on. So I keep my left one on, Sir, but I remove the right one. It's better for having contact with my patients."

"Well, that is against regulations, Specialist. I need you to keep those Nomex gloves on at all times while in flight."

"Yes, Sir," John replied. He saluted, did a 180, and exited the CO's hooch. It was not the outcome he had hoped for.

Stopping by his own hooch to grab a pack of cigarettes, he didn't respond the first time Hartman called his name.

"Hey, John, is everything okay? Aren't you supposed to be at the flight line?" Tom questioned.

"Yeah," John finally acknowledged. "I'm just grabbing some cigarettes."

"Boy, Sunday was a really sad day," Hartman bemoaned from across the partition. "June 8th, 1969 will go down in history as a really sad day."

"Are you talking about Chaplain Bartley being killed?"

"No," Tom sighed. "I heard about that. Boy, that makes it an even sadder day. I was thinking about Mickey Mantle retiring. He announced his retirement at Yankee Stadium on Sunday to a crowd of over 60,000 people."

"I'll talk to you later," John interrupted. "I've got to get back to the flight line."

"I'm going down to Baldy in the morning," Tom informed him, "so I'll catch you when I get back."

"Well, keep your head down. Charlie's out there," John warned as he departed.

Back at the flight line, John entered the tent where the unsung heroes of Dustoff were hard at work. The maintenance crew had a hand in saving all the lives, because they made sure the helicopters were flyable. Often working sixteen-hour days, their mission was to keep the birds safe and airworthy.

Sonny, a Spec 6 and the head of maintenance operations, greeted John with a wave and a smile as he walked toward a helicopter parked in the huge cylindrical tent. A couple of men were busy working on the chopper.

Passing John, Sonny said, "You take care and fly safe today, okay?"

John thought Sonny was one of the nicest guys in the world. His upbeat outlook inspired a positive attitude. It was comforting to know that the flight crew's safety was in Sonny's care.

Searching for one of his buddies, John entered the makeshift office of a guy he had known since Fort Polk. Paul's office was more like a small shack built inside the maintenance tent. It contained a homemade desk and shelves, which were piled high with repair parts manuals. Like John, Paul was now a Spec 5. As the Helicopter Repair Parts Specialist for the 236th, Paul was in the rear with the gear. He kept a PLL (Prescribed Load List) of maintenance supplies and repair parts for the maintenance crew. Paul went the extra mile—sometimes using whatever means necessary—to find specialty parts for Sonny. Since he wasn't in his office, John was about to search for him along the row of CONEX containers that served as Paul's warehouse when a call came in for an urgent mission.

The pickup site was along the coast, several miles south of Da Nang. It was a hot LZ with reports of enemy fire, so they were being escorted by gunships and carried a 5th man. Approaching the pickup site, John looked below and saw a ring of APCs inland on the sand, circled like a wagon train. Essentially an armored box on tracks, the M-113 was the ultimate American Armored Personnel Carrier. It was able to transport about a dozen troops, and with its mounted weapons, could be employed like a light tank. In the center of the circle of APCs, the men on the ground had popped a smoke canister. A guy stood near the yellow smoke and gestured to show the descending Dustoff chopper where to land.

Knowing the patients were Vietnamese civilians, John prepared to jump out of the cargo bay as soon as the skids touched ground to separate the wounded from the unwounded. Picking up an injured civilian often meant picking up the family, because clusters of people tried to board the chopper in an attempt to stay with their loved one. Today, only the wounded were inside the circle of APCs. Amid the dust storm of sand stirred up by the rotor wash, John's adrenaline pumped overtime as he directed the loading of patients. Seven were onboard, and John motioned to the remaining two when—pffft! pffft! pffft!—some ten hits of automatic weapon fire kicked up a line of sand about twelve feet from where John was standing.

John heard the pilot's voice over the intercom, "Let's go, let's go, let's go!"

Pushing the last patient onboard, John quickly jumped into the cargo bay and gave an all-clear into his helmet mike. The pilot radioed the gunships, alerting them that the Dustoff was lifting off and would be flying back north low-level over the water. Rising above the commotion below, John listened to the radio chatter as they flew out of that hot LZ, their patients safely evacuated.

After dropping the wounded Vietnamese civilians at the Provincial Hospital in Da Nang, the chopper returned to its revetment on the far end of the flight line. Today, John was flying with crew chief Scott Jared, a newcomer to the 236th. Jared began the routine maintenance and inspection of his bird that crew chiefs performed after each flight, while John headed back to the maintenance tent to grab some bottles of hydrogen peroxide. As he trotted along, intense heat radiated from the corrugated steel panels that made up the sprawling flight line. Despite the high temperature, John couldn't help but notice the beauty of the surrounding land. The white sandy beach and western horizon of towering mountains rivaled the setting of any luxury resort.

Entering the cavernous maintenance tent, John walked to the end where a CONEX container filled with medical supplies was located. Gathering what he needed, John returned to the helicopter and started his usual routine of washing down the cargo bay floor. It was his responsibility to clean off the blood, extraneous body fluids, and even tissue and bone fragments strewn across the floor of the helicopter. Blood was a powerful corrosive, so it required thorough removal, especially from the seams and cracks. Since water was in short supply at the flight line, he liberally poured pint-sized bottles of hydrogen peroxide over the cargo bay floor and used a handful of 4 × 8 cotton gauze like a sponge. John tossed a saturated handful aside and ripped open several more packets of gauze to finish wiping the pink, foamy mess.

"Sure is hot," crew chief Scott Jared said to John as he poked his head inside the opposite cargo bay door from where John was cleaning.

"Yeah, it's hot all right," John concurred while gathering up a big gob of soaked gauze.

"I heard about your race against time," Scott informed John while checking the wires of the intercom.

"When was that?"

"I heard the pilots talking about when you landed in a field and mortars were coming toward the left side of the aircraft while your patient was being carried to your right side."

"Yeah, that was a funny moment," John could say now that it was behind him. He remembered watching two soldiers bringing their wounded comrade toward the chopper. Footing was uncertain as they traipsed across the freshly plowed field. Behind John, through the other cargo bay door, he could see explosions of dirt as mortar rounds hit the field. The strikes were in the distance, but each round brought the bursts of dirt closer and closer to their bird. Rotating to face his patient, John motioned for the soldiers to hurry. He then turned back to see how the gooks were progressing in walking the mortar rounds in, wondering if Charlie would get lucky and suddenly lob a Hail Mary right on them. Looking back and forth through the cargo bay doors, John was relieved when the patient won the race against time and was safely evacuated.

John climbed out of the cargo bay and was about to take the bloody gauze to the trash bin but stopped when he heard Jared yell.

"Holy shit! Holy shit! She took a couple hits." Jared pointed to the bullet holes as he spoke. "One in the main rotor blade and one in the tail boom."

Jared's chopper was no longer flyable, so Robert Long and his ship replaced him as the 1-up crew. John moved his medical supplies, body armor, helmet, and armored seat over to Long's helicopter a couple revetments away.

After a busy day of flying, they were called for a nighttime mission John would never forget. The crew flew along their customary route over the water as they headed back down the coast. They flew farther south than they had flown earlier in the day to a village right off the beach. John had probably flown by that village many times before, but tonight it was a blazing inferno. Grass huts burned out of control, flaming trees and vegetation seared the dark sky, and civilians ran frantically in all directions. The pilots had no radio contact on location, so they had no idea what to expect and no idea what had taken place in this village. All crewmembers were on high alert as the chopper descended.

A sole Marine wearing a soft cap was the only US personnel John observed. As soon as they landed, the Marine ran over to the chopper and spoke to the copilot. The pilot then communicated through the intercom and told John to throw all the litters out the cargo bay door. John slid four litters onto the ground where they were immediately picked up and carried away by Vietnamese civilians. In a short time, the litters were carried back to the helicopter, with each litter now holding two or three wounded and bleeding children. John quickly unloaded the children off of one litter and placed them in the middle of the cargo bay floor. He unloaded another litter. And then another. All children. Some had lost limbs. Some had head injuries. Some were screaming and crying. Some had the look of near-death. John had no time to examine or stabilize any of them, because the litters kept coming. An empty litter would disappear into the darkness only to return with another load of severely wounded children.

The scene was overwhelming. John couldn't fathom what caused this tidal wave of children's bodies. So many little bodies. This was insane! Why the fuck were there so many wounded children, and what was he going to do with them all? And they didn't stop. More bodies kept coming. There were so many he had to start stacking them on top of each other like firewood.

The mothers were hysterical. They ran up to the chopper sobbing and screaming their babies' names, desperately trying to climb onboard to remain with their children.

"Sir, the mothers want to come with their children," John reported to the pilot through his helmet mike as he placed another child on the pile.

The pilot twisted in his harness to glimpse the sight in the cargo bay behind him. "The litters?' he asked John.

"Still coming," John responded.

"Then no mothers," ordered the pilot. "No room."

While John lifted a child off the stretcher, a mother scrambled up into the cargo bay. John grabbed the woman by the back of her shirt and threw her down onto the sand. The mother quickly got up and tried again to get to her child. John continued whirling—loading a child and then turning and hurling a mother from the chopper. From inside the cargo bay, Robert tossed out the frantic and weeping women who got past John and made it onboard.

In about five minutes there had to be thirty children piled in the cargo bay. There were too many to count. John reached for an infant positioned on one end of a litter. The tiny thing was frothing at the mouth. When John picked up that baby, he just couldn't stack it on the pile. Keying his helmet mike, John told the pilot they had enough. Cradling the infant in one arm, he slid over to his armored seat on the floor. Robert ejected one last mother from the cargo bay as he and John informed the pilot they were clear for takeoff. John glanced at the ground below. The remaining litters and their blood-ied contents shrank into the darkness. In between John and Robert, a wriggling, howling pile of children were stacked three and four layers deep.

Looking down at the baby on his lap, John noticed brain mat-ter protruding from a wound on the side of its head. With his ungloved right hand, he put a finger into the tiny mouth to clear it of debris. John checked to see if breath was coming out of its mouth. There was none. Putting his mouth directly on the infant's, John tried to resuscitate the child. He continued giving mouth-to-mouth while facing the surreal sight before him. Under the red lights of the nighttime mission where blood resembled shiny black tar, the stack of wounded children dribbled with glistening blackness.

When they landed at the 95th Evacuation Hospital, a small army of medical personnel swarmed up to the cargo bay to remove the children, strap them onto gurneys, and wheel them into the hospital. A pair of hands gently lifted the baby from John's arms and vanished. John and Robert sat in numb silence in the now empty cargo bay where irregularly shaped puddles and smears of glossy black tar were scattered on the floor.

Back in the air, they received a call to return to that village. There were still more wounded children to be evacuated. Dismally, they had to repeat the procedure. They piled more bloody children into the cargo bay, chucked more mothers out the door, and finally dropped the second and last load of shattered children to the 95th.

When he first started flying, John would have been so emotionally shaken by evacuating that many children, he would have shed tears. But not anymore. After nearly eight months of witnessing all kinds of horrible trauma, it had been a long time since John cried over a mission. The last time was over five months ago during monsoon season.

John would forever remember that patient. And he would vividly recall that particular mission because of the weather. Often times, dealing with the elements could be as scary as dealing with the enemy, and that night the zero visibility made the mission a perilous one. The crew was asleep at LZ Baldy when a call came in to evacuate a seriously wounded soldier from LZ West. They gathered in the aid station by the radio to discuss what they were up against. The RTO at West reported that the firebase was socked in with rain and fog. The aircraft commander asked if the patient's condition was grave enough to warrant flying an evacuation mission during such uncertain weather conditions. When they were told the patient had a severe head injury and was in great pain, the crew made the decision to fly the mission.

Other than pouring rain, it was fairly clear flying from Baldy to LZ West, but once they reached the base of West, heavy rain and dense fog reduced visibility to zero. The pilot switched on the searchlight and flew in low, just above the treetops. The sound of the rotor blades was muffled in the fog. As they slowly came up the side of the mountain with their high beam on, the RTO at West talked the Dustoff to the top where strobes and flares marked the landing pad. The patient was put on a litter and loaded into the chopper headfirst. After lifting off, John no longer paid attention to the weather. He didn't think about being in a helicopter 1,500 feet above ground. He didn't think about speeding through the air at 100-plus knots. And he didn't think about the dangers of a night mission. John became totally absorbed in attending to his patient.

The patient was thrashing his arms and legs so wildly that John motioned for the crew chief to hold him so John could examine the guy's head. Under the red lighting, the patient's hair appeared to be matted with shiny black tar. The guy's jaw and chin were also smeared with black, so John searched all over his scalp for the source of blood but couldn't find a wound anywhere on the patient's head. John sat back a second and rethought the situation. He had been told that this guy was in a bunker when an RPG struck and collapsed the bunker on top of him. Looking at the patient's face, John noticed that blood continued to slowly trickle from the corners of his mouth. With no apparent head wound, John surmised that this soldier had been crushed under the weight of sandbags, causing internal injuries and bleeding from the mouth.

The guy was in tremendous pain. He rolled around and flailed his arms so much that John worried he would knock one of them right out of the cargo bay.

"I want to die! I want to die!" the patient cried.

John bent closer to try to convince him to live. The crew chief wrestled to hold the guy as John positioned his own face just inches above his young patient's face. Supporting the guy's bloody head in the crook of his left arm, John maintained eye contact and kept talking and asking questions. Where was he from? Did he have a girl? What was her name? The patient's thrashing calmed as John got him to dialogue. John encouraged him to hang on. Yet, the patient was in such pain, he persisted in expressing a desire to die.

Arriving at Baldy, the medics recognized that John was keeping this guy focused. They slowly and carefully removed the litter so John could climb out of the cargo bay while keeping the patient's head cradled in the elbow of his arm.

"Stay with me," John demanded. "You're going to be going home to Susan," he consoled, maintaining close connection as the patient was carried inside the aid station. His head was still nestled in John's left arm when the doctors at Baldy made an incision in the patient's chest wall and inserted a chest tube to drain one lung. In a moment, the rubber glove used as a receptacle was filled with blood. The docs repeated the procedure on the other side of his chest while

John kept eye contact and coaxed him to hang in there.

Then, John watched the patient's eyes dilate and knew he was watching the departure of life from the body. John didn't move a muscle, but it felt like he'd just been slammed in the chest. The emotional hit to his heart was almost as hard to take as a bullet. John withdrew his arm and—still wearing his helmet and body armor—walked outside the aid station. He'd been profoundly changed by the intense encounter with the young man—and by watching life pass from his deep blue eyes. That blond-haired kid could have been John. Now he was gone from the earth. Drawing ragged breaths, John was pissed at him for dying. The guy had escaped, but John had to remain in this Godforsaken place. Leaning against the sand-bagged wall, John shed the last tears he would ever shed in Vietnam. Even after evacuating two loads of wounded children tonight, John's heart had become so armored, he had no more tears to shed.

Chapter 12

"He's everywhere! He's everywhere!"

John rolled to his side after listening to a morning episode of *Chickenman*—the most fantastic crime fighter the world has ever known. Even if he didn't have his own transistor radio turned on, enough radios were blaring around Red Beach to keep the daylight hours filled with sounds. Most everyone listened to AFVN (American Forces Vietnam Network). AFVN first broadcast from Saigon but quickly expanded from the Delta to the DMZ, and a station in Da Nang transmitted a clear signal to the 236th's area.

Radio had become an important instrument of war since American Forces Radio Service was first established under the War Department in 1942. The broadcasts transmitted useful information—such as reminders to take malaria pills—and played popular music that provided the servicemen with a touch of home. Primarily, radio was a vital tool for countering enemy propaganda efforts. Like the infamous Tokyo Rose, the Communist Radio broadcasts of Hanoi Hannah encouraged GIs to question the war and their participation in it. Thus, the US government hired aspiring actress Chris Noel to remind American servicemen of their duty, honor, and patriotism. John rarely listened to her nighttime show, *A Date With Chris*, which was taped a week earlier in L.A., but he had her sexy pinup displayed on the wall of his hooch.

This morning, John tried to go back to sleep after chuckling at *Chickenman*. He lay on his bed fully dressed in his one-piece flight uniform, easier and more comfortable than his two-piece Nomex. His boots were on the floor, quicker to slip on since he purchased a zipper insert at the PX. Getting dressed fast was crucial, as John was on-call with the 1st-up crew. They'd flown a mission sometime after midnight, and being on-call, he was not required to report to morning formation—if it even occurred. Formation was a way of accounting for all personnel, but First Sergeant LaForge had ceased having regular formations months ago. Now he only called formation if they were under attack or had a decoration day.

Tossing to his other side, John knew he wouldn't be able to fall asleep. Not with all the thoughts running through his head today. Foremost in his mind was the ongoing confusion about Karen. John had been so eager for Major Evans to return from his R&R in Hawaii that he kept checking with Roy to confirm the exact hour the Major would be back in the company area. John ended up being at Baldy on the day Major Evans returned, so it took three more days before John would be able to talk with him. Finally, that long anticipated moment came, but like their first conversation, it did nothing to assuage John's worries.

"What can I do for you, Specialist?" Major Evans inquired as John entered the CO's hooch.

"Sir, you were going to call my wife when you were in Hawaii and see what the situation is about our marriage."

"Yes," Major Evans replied as he scratched his chin. "That's right."

"Were you able to get a hold of her, Sir?"

"Yes. Oh, yes. We talked, and she's a nice girl. It's all a big misunderstanding. Everything's fine, so you can do your job without worrying. It will all be straightened out when you get back home."

Thinking of that conversation, John rolled from side to side on his bed several more times and then decided to get up and grab some chow before being called to another mission, which he surely would. Walking along the concrete sidewalk to the mess hall, he heard a familiar wail. It was Zeke. No matter what time of day, even at this early hour, Zeke had taken to howling like a mournful dog whenever the Tommy James and the Shondells song, "Crystal Blue Persuasion," came on the radio. He said the song made him homesick and made him long for the new vibration being ushered in by their generation. John liked the music and rhythm of the song well enough, but he thought the lyrics were bullshit. How could they sing about tomorrow bringing a new day—a day when all nations would have peace and good and brotherhood? Obviously, they didn't know what was going on in Vietnam. Every new day here just brought more death and destruction. And the song encouraged you to look to your soul and see that love is the answer. Well, John had seen plenty of souls leave this planet because of very unloving circumstances. No, that song's message was bullshit. It only made him think about all that free loving going on back in the States—and Karen was there taking classes with those longhaired mother-f....

"Hey, Seebs." Crew chief Ted Wilcox interrupted John's runaway train of thoughts. He was exiting the mess hall as John entered. "Don't eat too much," Wilcox mocked, alluding to John's wiry, 145-pound frame, "my bird won't handle the extra weight."

"I'll see you at the flight line," John replied, "after I stuff myself to maximum capacity."

John was finishing breakfast when Zeke walked into the mess hall.

"Have you been listening to the giant leap for mankind?" Zeke asked.

"You mean the astronauts walking on the moon? It's been on the radio all morning."

"Yeah, the world is glued to the tube watching the Apollo mission. But as far as I'm concerned, July 20th, 1969 is just another day of B.S.," Zeke proclaimed while lighting a cigarette.

"That was yesterday," John corrected. "Today is Monday, July 21st."

"Well, back in the States, it's still last night." Zeke explained. "And I bet no one is thinking about Vietnam." Holding up the June 20th issue of *Time* magazine he had been reading, Zeke showed the cover to John. It displayed a full-page face of a tired-looking GI. The caption stated, "Starting To Go Home." "My sister sent this to me, but this was last month. Yesterday, July 20th, Nixon said that his Vietnamization plans were misconstrued. Instead of a staged withdrawal, he now only *hopes* to de-escalate." Stopping to take a drag from his cigarette, Zeke concluded, "So, July 20th is just another day of monumental B.S. I don't see how we're ever going to get out of here if the peace talks got stalled over the shape of the conference table."

"What's that about?" John mumbled before taking a swallow of chocolate milk.

"The Paris peace talks, you know, the negotiations that started over six months ago—in January—and are supposed to end this goddamn war. North Vietnam wanted a circular table so everyone would have an equal place, but the South, which is basically the US, wanted a rectangular table to show the two sides. I mean, if they can't even agree about the shape of the fucking table, how can we start withdrawing troops?"

"I don't see any slow-down in calls for evacuations," John commented. "We're busier than ever."

As if on cue, the runner entered the mess hall and told John he needed to get to the flight line. They had an urgent.

Onboard the chopper, John learned they would be evacuating a civilian with possible gunshot wounds. In the air, Da Nang Dust-off flew south along the coast and then inland to the pickup site. The rotor wash whipped up a swirling sandstorm as they landed. Through the flying debris, John detected the approaching litter as it was carried toward them. He saw the patient's small hands waving frantically in the air. Jumping out of the cargo bay to help guide the stretcher onboard, John almost lost his grip when he looked down at the young Vietnamese woman.

The grotesqueness of his patient's wound momentarily knocked him off balance. The woman had no mouth. The bottom half of her face had been ripped away, and the front of her neck was chewed and ragged. As the chopper climbed back into the air, John set aside all thoughts and focused on providing life-saving aid. He kneeled beside the woman—her eyes were locked on his, urgently pleading for help. The way she flailed her arms and pointed to her face, John immediately understood that she couldn't breathe. He quickly grabbed his aid bag and pulled out the metal trachea tube. Peeling back the blood-soaked cloth that someone had draped over her torso, John couldn't find any semblance of a trachea. Where there had once been a chest, only bits and strands of pulverized flesh remained. There was no gushing blood, no main arteries severed, just a heap of black-and-red gristle from under her nose to above her navel. Wondering what could have caused such a wound, John probed inside her upper chest, anxiously searching for a trachea— anyplace he could get air into her lungs. He pulled aside loose flesh with one hand and positioned the tube over a point of entry with the other. Before inserting the tube, the woman's arms dropped to her side. John looked into her eyes and watched her pupils dilate. The panic departed as her eyes glassed over and became liquid tranquility. Perhaps because the rest of her face was so hideous, her eyes seemed hauntingly beautiful. John sat up and placed his hand on top of her head, almost a gesture of apology for not being able to comfort those desperate eyes. He remained kneeling by her side. Instead of a loving family member, it was John—a total stranger—who had shared the final intimate moments of this person's life.

When they landed at the Provincial Hospital in Da Nang, John silently observed the woman's body being removed from the chopper. It had been disturbing to watch life pass from her expressive eyes. Looking at her mutilated vessel, he had a feeling this woman's soul would be restless for some time. And who could blame it?

Later in the week, John was in high spirits knowing that he would soon have a few days off. Maybe that explained his conduct on a mission he would never be proud of. They had a call for an urgent evacuation, an older Vietnamese man with a gunshot wound. When they landed in a valley dotted with cultivated fields, several GIs shoved a litter onto the cargo bay floor. The patient's civilian garb suggested that he was probably a farmer. He was unconscious and had lost his left arm below the elbow. As the man was boarded, John noticed a tourniquet had already been applied to the stub. Bleeding had stopped, so this wound was not brand new. Nonetheless, John reached for an IV start-up kit as the chopper began its ascent. Suddenly, when the chopper was already several feet above ground, in through the cargo bay door flew an arm. It landed on the floor with a plop. Shredded and terribly discolored, it was obviously the amputated arm of the unconscious papasan. John picked it up and keyed his helmet mike.

"Look at what just came flying through the door," John remarked, amused and bewildered by the incident, since amputated body parts generally arrived upon the same litter as the patient. The 5th man and the crew chief eyed the arm as John clawed the air with it, just like the disembodied hand he had seen years ago in an episode of Boris Karloff's TV show, *Thriller.*

Setting the arm on the floor, John tended to his patient and inserted an IV. As they neared Da Nang, John detected that the papasan was stirring and beginning to regain consciousness. John had the bright idea of placing the discolored and disconnected appendage at an odd angle right by the old man's face. He again keyed his mike to alert the others of the impending show, just like something from Boris Karloff. When the papasan came to, he opened his eyes and saw his amputated hand abnormally positioned beside his head. He screamed at the freakish sight and instantly lost consciousness again. John didn't know if anyone else thought his joke was funny, because he was too busy laughing at it himself to notice.

When Friday finally arrived, John greeted it with eager expectancy. Not only did he have time off, he had arranged for something he had never done before. If asked how the arrangements were made, John couldn't recollect. He knew he must have been stinking drunk at the time, and he knew he must have negotiated the arrangement with First Sergeant LaForge. Tonight, a prostitute would use John's bed to conduct her business, and when she had accommodated the line of customers, she would remain with John for the rest of the night. The thought of standing in a line for an hour or more to spend a couple of minutes with a prostitute never enticed John. He had not been with a woman since Xuan. However, the idea of cuddling a woman in his bed—a female with curves and softness—well, that must have motivated him to make Friday night's arrangements. Any guilt about fidelity had been alleviated by the lack of correspondence from Karen. Only one letter last month, and it didn't explain why there wasn't enough money to meet in Hawaii.

Tonight, John was giddy with anticipation. He settled into a night of beer-drinking at the clubhouse. Even the shit-kicking music seemed pleasant this evening. Every so often he would step outside and see how the line that wrapped around his hooch was progressing. He sat on top of the sandbags, laughing and shooting the shit with the guys in line as though he were the host of some gala event. When midnight came and went, John made more frequent trips to check the status of the line. He was beginning to feel tired and impatient. Around 0200, he actually barged into the hooch and pointed to his wristwatch while Scott Jared was taking his turn with the prostitute, jokingly urging Scott to hurry things along. John was so drunk and exhausted by the time he got to bed, he wouldn't remember if the night met his expectations. But he certainly would remember the next morning.

John was sound asleep with the prostitute beside him when First Sergeant LaForge shoved aside the beaded room divider and barged into his room. It was 0800, and Top was spitting mad. At first, John couldn't figure out what was going on. He was still half drunk and exhausted, but LaForge's stormy presence in the doorway made it clear that the First Sergeant was absolutely pissed. What was his problem? Confused and uncertain, John and the prostitute roused their naked bodies from the bed.

LaForge leaned against the doorway, his thick arms folded across his chest. He had no intention of moving until John was dressed and reported to formation, which Top had inexplicably decided to call this morning. Under the gaze of the First Sergeant, John shoved his legs into his one-piece flight uniform while the prostitute slipped into her miniskirt. John was red with embarrassment and bristled with anger as he fastened his boots. Why was Top harassing him this way? For God's sake, it's not like he had snuck the prostitute into his bed. LaForge had orchestrated the whole evening. There were probably a couple of other prostitutes climbing out of other guys' beds this morning as well. So why was he getting on John's ass for not reporting to an unscheduled formation?

The First Sergeant took a step back to allow John and the prostitute to pass through the doorway. John quickly glanced at the woman. No chance for any parting words, though she seemed to be taking the whole thing in stride. Older and unlike Xuan, this woman had probably seen all kinds of stuff in her short lifetime.

Standing in formation with just a handful of other guys, John was filled with fury and humiliation. Things appeared very different to him this morning. Over the past eight months, every time First Sergeant LaForge had requested help for a mission or duty, John had willingly volunteered. He had done his best and given his all. Yet, instead of being appreciated for his efforts, John was being royally harassed by his First Sergeant. Well, fuck him! Fuck this mess. And fuck this whole fucking war.

Chapter 13

John hurriedly started an IV drip on all three patients. The soldiers were lucky to be alive and on the way to the 95th Evacuation Hospital. Just a few minutes ago, the Dustoff chopper picked them up near their overturned tank. The tank was probably an M60 Patton, but flipped upside down, it was hard to identify. Diesel-fueled M60s were gradually replacing M48s as Chrysler Corporation began production of 15,000 of them in their Delaware tank plant in 1960. Crewmen of older tanks were often badly burned when flash fires occurred inside the turrets. John didn't risk trying to start IVs on such crisp, blackened skin, knowing the patients would soon be in an emergency room equipped to deal with burn victims. Today's unburned patients were lucky. Three of the four tank crewmen were being evacuated for less serious injuries.

A big crater in the road marked the spot where the land mine had exploded and inverted the tank. It was humbling to see such a big piece of equipment lying on its back like a helpless turtle. Before setting the helicopter down, the pilots had to consider the best place to land, realizing that the area could be riddled with mines. 21-year-old Warrant Officer Bill Stanton was the aircraft commander today, and he decided to set the skids directly upon the tank's track marks on the dirt road. Since the tank had already traveled over that part of the road, the tracks should make a safe landing pad free from land mines. Soldiers on the ground quickly loaded the injured onboard the Dustoff chopper. Within minutes, they were being treated at the 95th.

Back at the flight line, John was busy washing down the cargo bay floor while crew chief Robert Long performed his routine maintenance tasks. Increased enemy activity this summer kept the crews constantly flying and their choppers in ongoing need of repair. Almost a month had passed since that fiasco with the prostitute, and other than a three-day leave in Saigon, John had been flying nearly nonstop.

After Da Nang was rocketed again in July, John and Tom decided to take an in-country R&R together. They were used to Da Nang being struck often—which is why it was nicknamed Rocket City— but that last attack was a little too close for comfort. It took out the CO's hooch, located directly across from their medic's hooch. Major Evans was not in the company area at the time, so he escaped injury. In the middle of the blasts and whistling rockets, John ran out of the bunker and back into his hooch to wake up Hartman, having to almost drag his fellow medic to safety. How in the world Tom could sleep through that ruckus was unbelievable to John. Tom explained that his sheer exhaustion allowed him to sleep through anything— and besides, he had grown accustomed to the constant background of explosions in the rocket belt. Following that near miss, John and Tom agreed they needed a break from a job they had performed practically every day for almost nine months. And that last strike convinced them to go sooner than later. In early August, John and Tom headed to Saigon. Hartman had the days off, but John had to trade duty with Willis Keaton, a medic who was another newcomer to the 236th. Appreciative for the time off, John told Willis he owed him a big favor.

It was almost a sensory overload to arrive in the congested city on a Friday afternoon. In 1969, Saigon had a population of over two million people, plus hundreds of thousands of refugees fled the countryside to seek protection along the city's outskirts after their villages had been destroyed by raids or bombings. Since arriving in-country John had seen little else but sand and hooches. The sights of paved streets, multi-story buildings, and billboards galore were reminders that civilization still existed. Elaborate French architecture, including the twin-spired Notre Dame Cathedral overlooking Kennedy Square, evidenced a history of colonialism. The familiar sounds of engines and horns could be heard as motor scooters weaved through the marketplace and trucks, taxis, pedicabs, cars, cyclos, buses, and bicycles crowded the steamy streets. Unusual, exotic smells wafted from restaurants and busy outdoor cafes. People in traditional garb peddled their wares along the sidewalks and storefronts. Miniskirted women strolled by fashionable shops. Youth gathered in public parks, where dazzling gardens and statues verified that this was the cultural and political capital of the Republic of Vietnam. No matter how much the hustle and bustle were reminiscent of a regular city, fear was in the air, and the large military presence made it impossible to forget that this was a war zone and Saigon was a capital under siege. Armed US MPs and South Vietnamese police were visible everywhere, patrolling the streets and maintaining order.

Tom would later tell John he feared they would spend their entire R&R in jail because John had gone ballistic when confronted by the white mice. Dressed in white helmets and gloves, the South Vietnamese police force were derogatively nicknamed white mice. Following a long dinner and lots of beer, John and Tom were surprised when two white mice stepped out of a jeep and approached them on the sidewalk. John and Tom were unaware that a curfew existed and unaware they were in violation of it, so they resisted the white mice's directives to climb into the jeep.

Not knowing and not trusting these guys, John launched a verbal attack. "Why are you fucking with us, man? We're here saving your asses, and you're giving us a hard time."

Fortunately, the South Vietnamese police had plenty of experience dealing with drunken GIs. The sight of a third policeman sitting calmly in the back of the jeep with a shotgun resting across his lap convinced Tom to persuade John to get into the vehicle. The white mice drove to a hotel and handed them over to several US MPs who were standing in front of the fortified building. The MPs escorted John and Tom into the lobby where they obtained a room for the night.

Too soon, their short reprieve from death and destruction ended. The two basically did what most soldiers did on R&R. In fact, R&R—Rest and Recreation—was dubbed I&I, which stood for Intoxication and Intercourse. They drank mightily and frequented the steam baths and massage parlors. One night, they hired a couple of bar girls to spend the night with them. Like other GIs, their constant state of drunken stupor made their three-day vacation from war mostly forgettable.

Today, the relaxation John enjoyed on his R&R two weeks ago was no more than a distant memory as he concentrated on wiping down the cargo bay floor and restocking medical supplies. The crew flew several more missions during the afternoon, and John performed the same cleaning ritual after each one. While John again walked toward the maintenance tent, the sun had already set and the heat of the day was subsiding. He stopped before entering the tent when he noticed the jeep approach.

"The Baldy crew got shot up," the driver shouted to John. "Everyone's okay, but their chopper took some hits. Where's Long?"

"Here he comes," John announced, glancing over at Robert, who was walking out of the maintenance tent and heading in their direction."

To Robert and John the driver stated, "I'll drive you back to get your stuff. Your crew's going to Baldy."

On the way back to the unit area, the driver repeated some of the details he heard in Operations when the radio transmission was relayed. The chopper was in the Hiep Duc Valley when it flew into a hornet's nest of enemy fire. None of the crewmembers was injured, but one of the hits to the chopper shattered an IV bottle the medic had just hung from a hook on the cargo bay ceiling.

John was in his hooch packing the few items he needed for a 4-day rotation when the plastic beads of his room-divider jangled and Willis Keaton walked in. Willis had been the medic onboard the shot-up chopper and was still wearing his body armor and flight helmet.

"You know the favor you owe me?" Keaton puffed, slightly out of breath. In the dim lighting, his short, stocky frame made a blurry silhouette against the plywood partition.

John nodded affirmatively, appreciative for his 3-day R&R in Saigon and eager to settle his debt.

"Well, I'd like to call it up now. I want to go back to Baldy. I'll trade places with you and fly with your crew."

John nodded again, silently wondering why Keaton would want this to be the repayment of his favor. Other than requesting the favor, John had never spoken to this new medic, so he didn't know Willis Keaton or his motivation to go back into the fireworks, especially after having an IV bottle explode over his head.

When Keaton thanked him and hastily departed, John began to remove the uniforms and toiletries from his flight bag. He suddenly stopped and glanced around the small space. This didn't feel right. It was his responsibility to be flying today. He had been flying with the same crew all day and they depended upon him. Just like some crewmembers tried to avoid flying with certain pilots, he knew some pilots preferred to not fly with certain crewmembers. Bill Stanton trusted John to be a composed and competent medic, and John felt like he would be shirking his responsibility to allow Keaton to take his place. John repacked the items he had just unpacked, grabbed his flight bag and rushed out of the hooch.

Willis Keaton had almost reached Operations where the jeep was parked and waiting to drive the crew to the flight line. John sprinted forward along the sidewalk and swerved around Keaton, announcing, "I still owe you a favor."

Keaton reached out, physically trying to grab John's sleeve, but John jackrabbited ahead of him and jumped into the back seat of the jeep. At any rate, John outranked him and it was his call to make.

John sat beside crew chief Robert Long. Zeke Goddard was already seated, clutching his M-16 and flying as their 5th man. As soon as Bill Stanton and a new pilot to the unit, Dave Collins, got into the vehicle, the jeep took off for the flight line.

It was pitch black when their chopper landed at LZ Baldy on the evening of August 19th. They flew a mission that night and were awakened to fly another around 0200. As they approached the pickup site, the sky buzzed with aircraft activity. High-voltage radio chatter filled the air with anticipation. From above, the colored paths of tracer rounds displayed an exchange of firepower. Random bursts of light in the surrounding slopes revealed the explosions of an ongoing battle. Parachute flares created eerie shadows as they drifted downward in front of the jungle-covered and rock-lined mountain walls. When their chopper descended, the perimeter of the landing area was illuminated much more than usual for a nighttime pickup. The severity of injuries to the ten evacuated soldiers indicated that something was coming down in this valley, but John didn't know what.

John, like most boots on the ground forces, did not have knowledge of the overall battle strategies dictating his endeavors. As a matter of fact, John didn't know if his patients were Gimlets or Polar Bears, as the 196th Battalions called themselves. He didn't know if they were from Alpha, Bravo, Charlie, Delta, or another company farther down the military phonetic alphabet. Sometimes he couldn't tell if a patient was Americal or 1st Division Marine. He just knew they were Americans in need, and that's all that mattered to him.

In actuality, this was the beginning of the Summer Offensive of 1969. By the end of the two-week battle, approximately 100 Americans would be killed and 400 wounded. Reportedly, NVA losses would be ten times greater. The Summer Offensive was the first major engagement since President Nixon, under intense political pressure, announced that the US would begin withdrawing troops. In July, a battalion of the 9th Infantry was the first to be extracted out of the 25,000 initially scheduled for withdrawal. That still left over half a million US troops in Vietnam, and for those in the mountainous region of I Corps the fighting continued to be as ferocious as ever.

Throughout the war, US combat commanders grappled with control of the Hiep Duc and Que Son Valleys. Both valleys were part of an approximately 10-mile-long and 3-mile-wide basin wedged between the steep peaks of the Annamite Mountain Range. The unbroken 750-mile Annamite Range extends northward into China, straddles the border of Laos and Vietnam, and runs southward into eastern Cambodia. The village of Hiep Duc was located in the southwest end of the basin in the province of Quang Tin, while the District capital of Que Son was located in the northeast area in the province of Quang Nam. The basin formed a natural corridor that weaved around smaller hills and provided lowland passageways from the mountains to the coast, becoming an important artery of the over 10,000-mile road network known as the Ho Chi Minh Trail. Throughout the basin's fertile floors, thousands of people lived in hundreds of hamlets growing rice as their ancestors had done for generations. Portions of the large basin were known by different names, such as Song Chang Valley, Hiep Duc Valley, Antenna Valley, Death Valley, Dragon Valley, Que Son Valley, AK Valley, Phuoc Valley, the Rice Bowl, Nui Chom, and Nui Loc Son Basin.

This area posed unique problems for the US military command. Their usual strategy of using copious amounts of air strikes had not been successful in knocking the enemy out of his mountainous redoubts. An intensified bombing campaign in 1969 saw over 240,000 bombing sorties flown by land and sea-based warplanes with an estimated 160,000 tons of bombs targeting the Ho Chi Minh Trail. Yet the enemy persisted. As much as land could provide protection from B-52 bombings, the hidden ravines, vertical ridges, and rock gorges offered as much protection as landscape could possibly offer and allowed the NVA to remain entrenched in this vital region. In addition to massive air strikes, Marines and soldiers swept the valleys over the years, succeeding in pushing the enemy back, only to have him regroup and resurface later.

On August 17th, small units of American Division soldiers from 4th Battalion, 31st Regiment Infantry patrolled the base of LZ West, searching for signs of the elusive enemy who had recently invaded the nearby resettlement camp at Hiep Duc. Days before, the enemy had mortared over 100 targets throughout South Vietnam with raids penetrating the perimeters of Baldy, West, and other fire support bases in the valley. During the course of policing the area around LZ West, Delta Company came under heavy enemy fire. The next day, 4/31 Bravo Company was searching for a rice cache northeast of Hiep Duc when they also drew intense fire. Both companies sustained high numbers of KIA and WIA as a result of their engagements with Regiments of the well-equipped and dug-in 2nd NVA Division.

The NVA had established artillery positions on a hill near LZ West. Hill 102 was dubbed "Million Dollar Hill" because millions of dollars worth of helicopters had been shot down during a previous battle when US forces fought to capture it. High command's orders to relinquish the hard-won territory was often discouraging to the guys on the ground, especially when the enemy returned to reoccupy it, having added concrete and steel reinforced bunkers. In the case of Million Dollar Hill, the NVA reclaimed it and established an effective anti-aircraft site. On August 19th, they succeeded in shooting down a Charlie-Charlie, or Command and Control (C&C) helicopter. Eight men were onboard, including a battalion commander, his sergeant major, and an Associated Press photographer. All would be considered missing in action until their bodies were recovered.

As the Dustoff crew evacuated ten soldiers in the early hours of August 20th, they did not know that military efforts were focused on locating the crashed C&C chopper and retrieving the bodies. However, the lights and activity in the darkened sky left no doubt that something major was happening.

Later that same day, just before noon, the crew evacuated a couple of men with heat exhaustion from LZ Center. After the patients were unloaded and the chopper parked in its sandbagged revetment, John and Zeke headed toward the Dustoff hooch.

"It's hot out there," Zeke commented.

"One of the medics told me it's almost 120 degrees on the valley floor," John responded.

"That, too," Zeke affirmed. "I meant the situation around West. I was talking to the RTO, and he said Charlie Company was just about surrounded, like they'd walked into a trap. The Blue Ghosts were taking fire trying to get to them."

John and Zeke took the remaining steps to the hooch in silence.

Plopping down on a dusty mattress, Zeke released one of his mournful howls.

John lifted his head from his bunk and eyeballed Zeke. "Why are you howling? I don't hear a radio."

"I'm miserable," Zeke complained as he removed his black plastic frames and rubbed the bridge of his nose. "I wish I was at Woodstock."

"What are you talking about?"

"My sister said she was going to a rock concert in upstate New York. It started on Friday, and that's where I'd like to be—listening to live bands playing good music and dancing." Grabbing hold of the peace medallion around his neck, Zeke lamented, "Lots of peace and love and YEOWWWWWWWW!"

Robert Long walked into the hooch and raised an eyebrow at Zeke. "Pull yourself together, man. C'mon, we've got an urgent."

They flew into the same general vicinity where the ground troops continued to search for the downed chopper. When the skids touched ground at the pickup site, crew chief Long kicked a couple of water blivets out the cargo bay door. Water was being rationed at LZ West, so the pilots agreed to drop some while they made the pickup.

It was chaos on the ground. The guys were soaked with sweat and looked exhausted as they heaved their wounded buddies into the cargo bay. There were a lot of patients, and their injuries were severe. Some wounds were bandaged with torn fatigue shirts. One of the guys told John they were running out of medical supplies and were short on medics—a number had been wounded or killed.

Keying his helmet mike and grabbing hold of his medical bag, John spoke to Warrant Officer Stanton. "Sir, they're short on medics. Should I stay on the ground and assist?"

Scarcely a second before Stanton ordered, "No."

There were fourteen wounded, and that was a big load for the Huey. The copilot reported seeing tracer bullets near his side of the chopper during their descent, so the pilots agreed to take all fourteen at once rather than risk another trip and give Charlie a chance to sharpen his aim. The last patient was onboard and the guys on the ground backed away from the helicopter when, suddenly, a soldier came running up to the cargo bay toting his M-16. Beneath the shadow of his helmet, this infantryman's face wore a frantic expression. His eyes said he had seen enough. John extended his arm, signaling for him to get back. The guy ignored John's directive and kept coming forward, placing one foot on the skid.

John again motioned him off while keying his helmet mike. "Sir, there's a guy here wanting to board."

"Is he wounded?"

"I don't see any injuries."

"No!"

Facing the guy, John shook his head no and forcefully waved him back. As the soldier removed his foot from the skid, John indicated they were clear for takeoff.

When Bill Stanton pulled pitch to climb out, the RPM dropped so low it triggered the low-RPM warning light. He had to reduce pitch and climb out straight and slow with no maneuvering. There were tense moments as they lifted up like a wounded duck.

Over the whine of the struggling transmission the sound of metal piercing metal cracked the air. John immediately knew they were taking fire, because a patient near his feet suddenly gave a convulsive jerk and spurted fresh blood. The guy had been lying on his stomach when a bullet came through the cargo bay floor and struck him in the gut. The patient had one bullet wound when he was loaded onto the chopper. Now he had two and was dead.

John heard the whoosh of something pass by his head at an incredibly fast rate of speed. More bursts ripped through aluminum until the Huey finally reached a safe elevation. The chopper made it back to Baldy, and after the patients were unloaded, copilot Dave Collins climbed out of his seat.

"The unlocking device of my shoulder harness took a hit," Collins told crew chief Long. "And I felt something warm on my thigh."

Robert examined the interior of the cabin, finding oil splashed over the instrument panel and windshield. "That's most likely oil on your leg and not blood," he related. "Looks like a spare oil can was hit."

The crew almost laughed in relief, especially for getting out of that tight situation and successfully completing the mission.

Robert studied the bullet holes on the floor of cargo bay and then inspected the exterior of his bird.

"Find any arrows?" John asked.

"Huh?" Zeke wanted to know what John was referring to.

"Seriously," Robert explained, "one time we came off a mission from deep in the mountains where a patrol of Special Forces was inserted, and when we got back, John found an arrow stuck in the tail boom."

"Yeah!" John exclaimed. "Can you imagine? They fired arrows at us! I expected to see a pterosaur flying at us next."

"Talk about a clash of ages," Zeke scoffed. "The most advanced aeronautical technology struck by a lowly arrow!"

Since Long's ship had taken a number of hits, it was ordered back to Red Beach so damages could be assessed and repaired at the maintenance tent. The 236th had to borrow a chopper from the 571st, stationed north of Da Nang in Phu Bai. The new chopper and crew chief joined John, Zeke, Bill, and Dave at Baldy.

Late afternoon of August 20th, they were called on a mission back to the area near the C&C chopper crash. Collins questioned the RTO on the ground: Where were they taking fire? What would be the best approach? They were advised to approach from one end of the horseshoe valley because automatic weapons fire was coming from the ridgelines. It was cloudy and overcast, so when Pilot Stanton communicated with the RTO, he asked them to pop a smoke grenade to reveal their position.

"We have your purple smoke," Stanton related and then proceeded to put the chopper into a steep dive, rotating in a tight corkscrew until a few hundred feet above ground. Bringing the helicopter out of its dive, Stanton accelerated to 125 knots. Through the open cargo bay doors, John watched rice paddies speed by as the chopper flew just ten feet above ground, swerving around trees as it approached the LZ. Nearing the smoke, the pilots became confused when they spotted a second purple smoke grenade a short distance away. The Dustoff began to draw enemy fire from the direction of both smoke grenades, so Stanton quickly pulled the tail of the aircraft toward the fire and then zigzagged up to a higher altitude.

Reestablishing contact with the RTO, Stanton agreed to try again, asking for another smoke grenade. Acknowledging yellow smoke, Stanton repeated the descent. He dropped the helicopter out of the sky hard and fast and then low-leveled it toward the pickup site. As the Dustoff approached, they caught sight of a second location of yellow smoke and again came under intense fire. Obviously, the enemy was monitoring their radio calls or had lookouts up on the horseshoe ridge. Stanton zigzagged out of there once more.

From a higher elevation, Stanton reached the RTO on the ground. "We want to come in and get your injured, but this isn't working. We're going back to Baldy. Call us when you secure the area and are better able to hand off your wounded."

No one felt good about leaving before completing the mission, but Dustoff wouldn't be doing anybody any good if they got punched down. They were never called back and subsequently heard that a wounded soldier died overnight.

The next day, on August 21st, they were called to evacuate a sick GI at LZ Ross.

"Goddard is napping," John reported to pilot Stanton.

"Let him sleep," Bill replied. "It's just a routine."

They picked up the patient at Ross and were headed back to LZ Baldy when the RTO from Baldy called to relate a request for an urgent Dustoff. It was not unusual for Dustoff to receive a second call while still in the air completing a mission. The urgent pickup was in the Hiep Duc Valley, where ground troops continued engaging with NVA and VC forces while maneuvering to retrieve the bodies from the C&C chopper crash. The area remained saturated with enemy forces. Since the patient currently onboard was not seriously injured, Dustoff would drop him off at a nearby firebase before proceeding to the urgent pickup. Stanton contacted LZ Center to inform them the Dustoff chopper was inbound to drop off their ambulatory patient and would then fly to LZ West to pick up the urgent.

On the way to the pickup site at West, copilot Collins made radio contact with the RTO on the ground. The news was not what the Dustoff crew wanted to hear. The ground troops were currently in contact with the enemy and receiving small arms and automatic weapons fire. The RTO suggested obtaining air support.

Collins contacted the gunships, but they were working elsewhere. It would take at least ten minutes for them to get to their location. Radioing back the RTO, Collins told him to advise the grunts on the side of West that the Dustoff would be down for the pickup in ten or fifteen minutes when the guns arrived.

The RTO relayed, "The platoon medic says that the patient can't wait ten minutes. He has multiple gunshot wounds to the abdomen and exit wounds in his back. He's in real bad shape and needs urgent care now."

Through the earphones on their flight helmets, John and the crew chief silently listened to the exchange between Collins and the RTO on the ground. John's mind was torn between waiting for the gunships and possibly having the patient die or flying down without the guns and facing a hailstorm of bullets.

Stanton's voice came over the intercom. "Does anyone have any suggestions about what we should do?" He was doing what many pilots did. Even though they had flown into hot LZs without gunships numerous times before, it was not normal operating procedure. If they were going to do so, the pilot wanted it to be a group decision.

After a long uncomfortable pause when no one answered the aircraft commander's question, Stanton nodded at Collins, who radioed the RTO and told him they were coming down without the gunships.

"This makes our fifteenth insecure mission in the last three days," co-pilot Collins reported to the rest of the crew.

"God go with us," John uttered over the intercom. He'd never said anything like that during previous flights into hot LZs, so he wasn't sure what compelled him to say it today.

Stanton corkscrewed the Huey down and speeded low-level to the pickup site, only to have to slow down and carefully lower the bird into a hover-hole barely wider than their rotor blades. The clearing might have been a bomb crater, because it was sunken below the ring of jungle. John saw trees, burnt and splintered—body parts hanging from some of them. As the skids neared ground in the tight circle, the sounds of bullets slicing through the air intensified. Explosions sent out shock waves and drove the men on the ground to run and seek cover.

The skids were about to touch ground, so John raised himself off his armored pad to crouch by the cargo bay door. He was just gaining his footing when WHAM! He was slammed backwards against the pilots' floor control panel. Bringing himself around, he crawled back to his spot on the floor behind the copilot. Wow! Something just happened, but John couldn't make sense of it.

"What was that?" Stanton's voice demanded over the intercom. "Did we take a hit to the hydraulics?" He questioned if the spray of warm fluid he felt on the back of his neck was something from the engine.

Sitting on his armored pad, stunned, John glanced to his left at the open cargo bay door and saw two grunts bent down low and dragging a third guy between them. Upon reaching the chopper, the guys stood and loaded the wounded soldier into the cargo bay. Their eyes widened when they looked at John. Their eyes reflected John's worst nightmare—like he had been hit or something.

As the helicopter lifted off, John keyed his mike to ask his fellow crewmembers what happened. He wanted to know if something happened to him. He believed something had, but he wasn't sure. Pressing the mike, he went to speak. No sound came out. Why couldn't he talk? Could somebody please tell him what was going on? Help! He reached his hand up to his throat and felt a mass of soft wetness. Pulling his hand away, he saw it was covered with blood. His own blood. John looked farther to his left and detected three splintered bullet holes in the Plexiglas window. So that was it. He had been hit in the throat with a bullet.

Settling back on his seat, John tried to maintain calmness. For the first time, he became cognizant of his patient. The man was lying on the cargo bay floor with a widening circle of blood unevenly pooling around his midsection. John watched helplessly as the guy flipped around like a fish out of water, twitching from head to toe.

Copilot Collins told the crew chief to see if he could help John and then encouraged over the intercom, "We'll get you out of here, John! Hang on!"

The crew chief on loan from the 571st came to John's side and helped remove his flight helmet and body armor. He reached into John's aid bag and grabbed some 4x8 gauze, putting it over the front of John's throat. With the gauze in place, John couldn't breathe. The magnitude of the situation was beginning to sink in. John was breathing through his wound.

John pointed toward an IV bottle and setup kit and then pointed to his arm, indicating for the crew chief to start an IV drip. The young crew chief tried at least three times to insert an IV, but without training, his trembling hands were unsuccessful. John signaled for him to pass over the needle, thinking he would thread his own vein. But it was difficult to concentrate, and his hands were shaking way too much. John threw the needle aside and looked at the patient prostrate near his feet. He noticed he was a black man and wore camouflaged Sergeant's stripes on the sleeve of his fatigue shirt. He also noticed that his body was motionless, no longer even a twitch. John gestured in the patient's direction, hoping the crew chief could be of some help to him.

Gazing out the open cargo bay door, emotion rose in John's chest. He couldn't believe he was hit. He'd seen so many who had been. Always, it was someone else. In fact, he began to believe he was immune to the enemy's bullets. He used to fantasize that he'd become a god-like creature with the helicopter for wings—an angel of mercy swooping down and picking up the wounded. With the power of God, he saved the near-dying and brought the dead back to life. Now, here he sat—a mere mortal—feeling powerless to prevent his own life from escaping. His blood was red, and his fear was real. He was a human being lost in the extraordinary drama of war. And it seems his luck had run out.

John didn't feel pain, but his battle to breathe put him in great discomfort. In the midst of his distress, unhappy thoughts of Karen intruded into his mind. She hadn't been writing, and he just knew she'd been fucking around on him. If anything happened to him, she would receive his government insurance of $10,000. Sitting there—

bleeding—angry thoughts of his wife circulated through his head.

Choking. Coughing up blood. John could hardly catch his breath. There was a labored sucking noise when he inhaled. He guessed his wound was swelling to the point that it was blocking off his ability to draw air. He was suffocating. There was a metal trach tube in his aid bag. Properly inserted, it would allow him to breathe. It was a relatively simple procedure, but he was the only one here trained to insert the tube. And he couldn't do it to himself. He couldn't even see his wound.

He couldn't see his own wound, but the image of another person's wound abruptly appeared in his mind's eye. They evacuated her last month, yet he could see her now as though she were right across from him. It was the grotesquely wounded young Vietnamese woman who had lost the bottom half of her face. The vision of the woman's horrible wound and painful death hung in front of him. John could see her saucer-like eyes filled with fear and bewilderment. Her omnipresent specter repulsed and frightened him. John gasped for breath and refused to see her image as his own. No! John would not accept that as his destiny. He would not become a roaming, tortured soul who couldn't find peace. Resisting the pull to follow the woman, John fought for his life.

It's not my turn! Not like this!

Chapter 14

John knew the distance from the floor to the ceiling in the cargo bay was less than six feet, but here he was looking down at himself from three times that height. It seemed impossible the space could have stretched to fifteen feet or more, yet the thought didn't trouble him. From above, he neutrally observed his body below, watching it gurgling and gagging and struggling to breathe. His elevated perspective gave him a sense of serenity, oblivious to the frantic activity of his crewmates.

There was chaos inside the cabin as Stanton pushed the Huey back to Baldy at maximum speed. All of the helicopter's radios had been knocked out except one, so Collins was busy trying to find a radio signal and alert the medical team at the aid station that John had been hit.

John was unfazed by the commotion until, in a flash, he rejoined his body and was overpowered by the realization he couldn't breathe. Coughing and spitting up blood, all he could hear was a tight wheezing sound as he strained to take air into his lungs. He wasn't in pain but had to fight the urge to panic. If he was going to die, he wanted to do it with dignity. No screaming, no crying, no acting like a wild man. Just do it with control and dignity.

In an effort to get his act together, John turned his eyes toward the open cargo bay door. Wow—the beauty of the countryside was amazing. The forest and sky were such vibrant shades of green and blue. The different textures of color so bright and vivid, it seemed like everything was alive and calling out to him. Instead of looking down at his body in the helicopter, he gazed outward at the magnificence. He was free from discomfort as he became part of what he was seeing. It was as though the molecules that made up John were moving apart and merging with the expanding molecules that made up the sky, sea, and trees. Fully conscious, he felt only peace as he transitioned into the vast oneness of the unfolding life of the cosmos. If this was death, it was nothing to fear. Really, it was beyond any love he could ever describe.

Suddenly, out of the blue—barbed wire. The sight of concertina wire intruded into his awareness when the chopper flew over the perimeter of Baldy. Instantly, John's consciousness snapped back into his body, and once again, he was in great distress fighting to breathe.

Aircraft commander Stanton was determined to get John to the aid station as fast as possible. When the chopper reached Baldy's outpost, he attempted a maneuver he had only heard about. He flew in low, tipping the helicopter to one side and pulling pitch until the rotor RPM went down. He lowered the pitch and then tipped the helicopter to the other side and pulled pitch again. He did this several times to quickly reduce speed in a short distance. Successfully saving precious minutes, Stanton brought the chopper in sideways— hot and fast.

John watched the ground race toward him. He could see the helipad. And there were his friends from the aid station in their sleeveless green smocks. The rotor wash rustled their hair as they squinted at the descending chopper. He was so close. If he could just hold on—but it was so difficult. Anxiety and fear overwhelmed him.

Sergeant Gary Weaver, along with a team of medics and docs, watched the Dustoff approach. As soon as Gary heard about John being shot, he dropped what he was doing and ran to the aid station. There was heightened emotion amongst the medical team. John was special because he was one of their own.

When the skids touched ground, medics ran forward with litters in tow. John knew the routine and knew time was running out for him. Coughing up blood, he didn't have time to be carried into the building on a litter. He pushed aside the litter and pointed to the patient on the cargo bay floor.

Dashing toward the aid station on his own two feet, John slowed when he spotted Zeke standing near the entrance. He looked in his friend's eyes and mouthed the words, "Zeke, I'm fucked up!"

The shocked expression on Zeke's face relayed the truth.

John continued inside with Sergeant Weaver at his heels. Knowing the layout of the aid station, John ran up to an empty litter where the medics directed him to lie down. He tried to comply with their instructions, but when he was on his back he began to convulse and retch on his blood. John jerked upright, frantically gesturing that he couldn't breathe. He saw copilot Dave Collins at his feet, trying to still John's kicking legs.

"I can't breathe!" John mouthed to him. No sound accompanied his words.

A young doctor put one hand on John's shoulder and held a

razor-sharp scalpel with the other. He looked John in the eyes and calmly stated, "John, you know what I have to do," and gently tried to push John flat on the litter.

John couldn't do it. He couldn't lie flat. Choking and gagging, his blood and mucous covered the green shirts encircling him. Hands grabbed him, held him, and stuck him with needles. The doctor's hand neared his neck, and excruciating pain pierced John's body. Instantly, everything around him went black.

Doctor George Waters, on TDY from the Air Force and assigned to the 23rd, stood to the side watching the young doctor probe around in the mangled flesh of John's wound. The process was taking too long. John was unconscious, but when Doctor Waters saw him turning blue, he pushed the younger physician aside and said, "Let's get an airway into this man."

Sergeant Weaver quickly handed a trach kit to Doctor Waters, who promptly inserted a tube that established a life-saving flow of oxygen to John's lungs. The medical team worked to stabilize John enough so he could be transported to the 95th.

Outside the aid station, the crew chief from the 571st examined the damages to his shot-up bird. There were holes in the fuel bladder, tail boom, windows, and fuselage. After the helicopter's engine had been shut down, the rotor blades collapsed and completely bent downward. They had been shot clear through and had only been held up by centrifugal force as the chopper sped back to Baldy. When the crew chief removed his flight helmet, he found one more hole. The hole in his helmet had a bullet lodged in it.

It continued to be bedlam on Baldy's helipad the rest of the day. At one point, five Dustoff helicopters were there at the same time. By the end of the day, sixty GIs had been medevaced to the aid station with at least twenty being life-and-death cases.

Another pilot from the 236th had overheard the radio calls about John being shot and anticipated the need to transport him to the 95th in a hurry. The pilot unloaded the ambulatory patients from his chopper, flew over to the station to refuel, and within minutes was parked at the helipad ready to fly John to the hospital. The flight from Baldy to the 95th generally took twenty minutes. Today, the pilot would get John there in eight.

Lying on the litter in the cargo bay, John awakened to the whine of the transmission and thumping whomp of the Huey's rotor blades. The familiar sounds reassured him. When he opened his eyes, he saw a face—only inches away—with eyes intently peering down at him. John couldn't move his head because a thick bandage immobilized his neck, but out of the corner of his eye he saw a pair of hands squeezing an ambu bag. Following the rhythm of the air bag, John noticed that his breath mirrored its action. The manual ventilation was providing his air supply—but he was breathing! He was alive and breathing! John could see plastic tubes connected to bottles hanging from the chopper's ceiling and figured they must be supplying him with fluids. Beyond the face in front of him, John saw more faces staring at him with concern. Unaware that the medical team had just restarted his stopped heart, John slipped back into darkness.

For the medical team in the cargo bay, the eight-minute flight was intense. Doctor Waters flew onboard because John's air passage would not stay open. He knelt beside John, closely monitoring his breathing. When John's heart stopped, Doctor Waters was able to bring him around with chest compressions and the artificial breath of the ambu bag. Concentrating on keeping John alive diverted the doctor's attention from the head-reeling view outside the open cargo bay doors. The pilot did not waste time gaining altitude, and at a speed of 160 knots, treetops flew by at a dizzying rate. The copilot continually checked gauges, making sure the Huey didn't overheat as the pilot pushed it to the max.

A gurney was waiting for John at the helipad when the Dustoff landed at the 95th, and a staff of nurses and medics rushed him inside to begin triage. John was frothing at the mouth and couldn't breathe. IV fluids had backed up in his heart and were seeping into his lungs. This time when his heart stopped, a defibrillator was used to shock it back to life.

After being stabilized, John was taken to x-ray and then pre-op. It was there he again regained consciousness. Blinking his eyes, the bright lighting in the room revealed that he was no longer in the helicopter. He was on a hospital table, unable to move his head because of the bandaging around his neck. Instead of a pair of hands squeezing a bellow bag, he could hear a mechanical respirator and observed a plastic hose connecting the device to his throat. Moving his eyes to the left, John could see a person over him. It appeared to be a nurse wearing a green surgical uniform covering all but her eyes. John saw she was using a pair of bandage scissors and then realized she was cutting off his one-piece flight uniform. The thought that she was going to see him naked made him blush. He couldn't believe he could feel bashful at this moment. Blackness began to descend upon him, but before he lost consciousness, John felt confident that everything was going to be all right. Having gone through this dreadful experience, having survived it so far, and now lying here feeling bashful, well, everything was going to be all right.

John was taken to surgery where an ENT surgeon inserted a plastic stent into the area by his larynx, which had suffered extensive tissue loss. Because so much flesh was missing, the surgeon had to thread a #26 wire completely through his neck in order to hold the stent in place. The wire protruded a couple of inches below each ear on the outside of John's neck where skin was still intact. To secure the wire, the surgeon affixed it to a four-hole shirt button on one side and a small piece of the stent tube on the other, which would reveal the size of the stent to physicians providing further care. In addition, the surgeon performed a low tracheostomy, installing a trach tube below the mutilated flesh of John's neck. From surgery, John was taken to the hospital's intensive care unit.

John had flown hundreds of missions to the 95th Evacuation Hospital without ever really understanding what a state-of-the-art surgical hospital it was. The 95th had a long and outstanding history of providing support for a field Army since the Office of the Surgeon General constituted the formation of a group of large military hospitals in 1928. The 95th was first activated in 1941 and became the first US hospital in Europe during World War II. Deactivated in 1946, the 95th was reactivated in 1963 and alerted for overseas movement. On 26 March 1968, the unit arrived on the sandy shores of Red Beach and began basic construction of a defensive perimeter, an access road, and tentage for billets. Within a month, the first 100 beds were operational, and within days, they were 99% filled. The end of May saw a 400-bed hospital and 2,476 admissions in the first sixty-three days of operation. In less than a year, the 95th moved from a tent hospital to a fixed facility with a staff of about thirty doctors and sixty nurses who valiantly treated the sick and wounded.

The 95th provided direct support to the Americal Division, which consisted of eleven battalions of light infantry, one armored cavalry squadron, two armored reconnaissance troops, an air reconnaissance troop, six battalions of artillery, and three battalions of assault helicopter squadrons. The 95th also treated Vietnamese children and soldiers from other units as well. Every doctor was a specialist, including chest, oral, and orthopedic surgeons, dermatologists and ENTs—like Dr. Clarence Sasaki, the Yale University Medical School graduate who operated on John. The medical personnel in Vietnam offered outstanding emergency care. From the frontline medics and Dustoff crews to the staffs of the rear area hospitals and hospital ships, the success of the 67th Medical Group was nothing short of spectacular. Of the Americans wounded in Vietnam who reached medical facilities, 97.5% of them survived. John was fortunate to be one of them.

John woke up in the intensive care post-op unit, recognizing he was in a hospital bed. He still couldn't move his head because of all the bandages; however the top of his bed was raised forty-five degrees, allowing him to move his eyes and look around. He could see several metal stands holding IV bottles with tubing hanging down and connecting to his body. One plastic bottle was attached to a rubber hose that was inserted into a nostril and down into his stomach. John heard the steady rhythm of a respirator, positioned next to the head of his bed and providing him with life-sustaining oxygen through the tube in his neck. On the other side of his bed, he detected a new and distinctive sound. A tube was connected to a different machine that was suctioning fluids out of his lungs. He even had a tube inserted into his penis and connected to a plastic bag hanging at the foot of the bed.

Peering across the room, John saw other beds lined against the opposite wall. On his right and left were more beds. All the beds contained the bodies of severely wounded men who had recently undergone surgery. Each was covered with a white sheet, and most were unconscious. Some had bloodied bandages and various types of medical equipment connected to them. Throughout the ward, John heard muffled hums of machinery emitting different types of noises. No conversations, only the groans and whimpering of men in pain.

Drifting in and out of consciousness, John felt intense pain when awake. A nurse would administer a needle of morphine, and he would nod out for three or four hours. Upon awakening, severe pain resumed, a nurse would return, and again he would nod off into oblivion. This would become the cycle of his existence.

During one of his waking moments, the device connected from the respirator to the opening in his neck became detached, leaving John unable to breathe. He flung his arms, trying to get the nurse's attention. A young Vietnamese boy was sweeping the floor and noticed John's thrashing. He came over to John's bedside and tried to put the apparatus back up to John's throat. A nurse rushed up and pushed the boy aside. She quickly reconnected the device, then faced the boy and gave him a scolding. With head bowed, the boy returned to his sweeping. John felt bad for the boy. He had just been trying to help. Unable to speak and explain the situation, John received another painkilling needle and left all concerns behind.

Two days later, the surgeon who had operated on him came to

his bedside.

"How are you doing, John?" Dr. Sasaki asked, although he knew John couldn't answer. "You experienced a gunshot wound to your throat," he explained, pointing to his own neck as he spoke. "The entrance wound was in the left anterior region in the area of the cricoid cartilage and thyroid, with an exit wound on the opposite surface of the right anterior portion of the neck. I performed exploratory surgery with the insertion of a plastic stent. And your condition was further aggravated by the over-replacement of fluids, resulting in acute cardiac failure."

John stared at the surgeon, feeling shaken as he tried to absorb all he was saying. He had so many questions, but unable to speak, the questions remained in his head unasked.

"Because of the severity of your wound," Dr. Sasaki continued, "you're going to be flown to the hospital at Clark Air Base in the Philippines. Reconstructive surgery is going to happen outside of Vietnam. So, tomorrow morning, you'll be taken to an Air Force medical transport plane and flown to the Philippines."

John squeezed his lips together tightly. It was hard to grasp the reality of all that had happened.

"Best of luck to you, John" the doctor stated as he placed his hand on John's shoulder. "And thanks for your brave service to the country."

As soon as the doctor departed, a nurse walked over to John's bed. "While you were sleeping, you had some visitors," she informed him. "Several members of your unit stopped by."

John was filled with emotion as he thought about his fellow crewmembers, wondering how long it would be before he would be back flying with them.

"One of your friends left this letter at the nurse's station, and he said to make sure that it was delivered to you." The nurse held up an envelope addressed to Brother John.

John's fingers fumbled when he reached for the letter, and it fell to the floor. The nurse quickly retrieved it. She was about to hand it to him again when she detected tears in John's eyes and saw his shoulders trembling.

"Would you like me to read the letter to you?"

John's expression conveyed that he would like that.

23 August 1969
Hi John!

I just don't know what to say. We all know you are going to be well and up soon. Zeke and myself took care of all your personal belongings and everything. So don't worry about that. Johnny, you're remembered in all our prayers. And especially mine and Zeke's.

Johnny, I just found out you're leaving in the morning. So I guess I'll only get to see you just a few minutes on the chopper to the airport. It would take me about three years to write down on paper what a great guy you are and one of the best and greatest buddies I ever had and have known.

So when you can write drop Zeke and me a line and let us know what is up. Johnny, I'll never forget you and all the great times we all had. I hope this letter brightens your day just a little.

Your Best buddy,
Tom

The next day, John was moved out of the intensive care unit and taken to the hospital helipad. It wasn't long before his gurney was wheeled out to a waiting chopper. He would be flying onboard the milk run—the routine mission he had flown so many times, but this time he was one of the severely wounded patients on the way out of Vietnam.

A familiar face looked down at John as his litter was pushed into the cargo bay. It was Tom! He was the medic on the flight. And another recognizable face smiled at John when his litter was positioned on the floor. It was Roy Reynolds! He flew along to say goodbye. The pilots enthusiastically greeted John, but in his drugged and delirious state, John wasn't sure who was beneath the sunglasses and flight helmets.

While Tom checked the other three patients already loaded into the cargo bay, John noticed the stark contrast between the white sheets and the charred and blackened skin of the guy on the adjacent litter. Although probably heavily medicated, the burn victim continued to writhe and moan in pain.

Once in the air, the pilots took turns looking back at John. They would mouth something, but their words were drowned out by the noises of the helicopter. Tom sat nearby and rested his hand upon John's shoulder. When they arrived at Da Nang Air Force Base, the chopper landed on the helipad. After unloading the other patients, Tom came over to John and pushed a patch into his hand. Bringing the piece of fabric up to his face, John identified the winged Red Cross of their unit's emblem. The 236th's Dustoff military insignia exhorted, *Strive to Save Lives*.

Before his litter was unloaded, John directed his eyes at the pilots who remained seated in the idling aircraft. Both pilots had rotated in their seats to face John, and both energetically lifted their arms in his direction with raised thumbs. Tom and Roy jumped out of the cargo bay when John's litter was unloaded. Tears streamed down their faces as they stood over the litter. Tom tried to bid his buddy farewell, but even if his voice could have been heard above the sound of the helicopter, he was choking back sobs and couldn't speak. John was crying as the litter team began to carry him toward the large transport aircraft. When would he see his friends again? They had shared so much together. Against this inhuman setting of war, they had forged deep bonds of brotherhood. Looking back at Tom and Roy, John held the unit's patch up high with his left hand. Above all else, members of the 236th nobly strived to save lives. With his right hand, John gave his friends the peace sign.

In an act of profound affection, to let John know he had touched him—and had succeeding in corrupting him—Roy threw John the finger.

Chapter 15

Western Union   Telegram

DONT PHONE. REPORT DELIVERY. CHECK DLY CHGS ABOVE 75 CENTS= =THE SECRETARY OF THE ARMY HAS ASKED ME TO EXPRESS HIS DEEP REGRET THAT YOUR SON, SPECIALIST JOHN N. SEEBETH WAS WOUNDED IN ACTION IN VIETNAM ON 21 AUGUST 1969 BY SMALL ARMS FIRE WHILE EVACUATING WOUNDED PERSONNEL FROM AN AIRCRAFT LANDING ZONE WHEN THE AREA CAME UNDER O=WR=SCK WITH AN AVULSIVE INJURY OF THE LARYNX. HE WAS INITIALLY HOSPITALIZED IN VIETNAM AND SUBSEQUENTLY EVACU-ATED TO THE PHILIPPINE ISLANDS. HE WAS PLACED ON THE VERY SERIOUSLY ILL LIST IN VIETNAM. HE HAS BEEN REMOVED FROM THE VERY SERIOUSLY ILL LIST AND PLACED ON THE SERIOUSLY ILL LIST. IN THE JUDGMENT OF THE ATTENDING PHYSICIAN HIS CONDI-TION IS OF SUCH SEVERITY THAT THERE IS CAUSE FOR CONCERN BUT NO IMMINENT DANGER TO LIFE. PLEASE BE ASSURED THAT THE BEST MEDICAL FACILITIES AND DOCTORS HAVE BEEN MADE AVAIL-ABLE AND EVERY MEASURE IS BEING TAKEN TO AID HIM. HE IS HOS-PITALIZED IN THE PHILIPPINES. ADDRESS MAIL TO HIM AT THE U.S. AIR FORCE HOSPITAL, CLARK AIR BASE, THE PHILIPPINE ISLANDS. APO SAN FRANCISCO. YOU WILL BE PROVIDED PROGRESS REPORTS AND KEPT INFORMED OF ANY SIGNIFICANT CHANGES IN HIS CONDI-TION. DELAY IN NOTIFYING YOU WAS DUE TO LATE RECEIPT OF THE REPORT FROM THE OVERSEAS COMMANDER=

THE ADJUTANT GENERAL DEPARTMENT OF THE ARMY WASHINGTON DC=

John had never before considered where the wounded GIs being evacuated out of Vietnam were headed. He probably assumed they were flown to the States for further medical treatment, so it was a little surprising when the surgeon informed him he would be going to the Philippines. As his litter was positioned on the large C-141 transport, John noticed the aircraft was filled with stretchers of wounded American soldiers. There were four rows of litters, and each row was stacked three-high, carrying about eighty litter patients altogether. At least twenty medical attendants moved up and down the aisles during the flight, adjusting the numerous hoses and equipment attached to the wounded men.

Like some of the other patients' onboard, John's precarious condition required that a doctor watch over him at all times. It was standard procedure for the seriously wounded with special circumstances to have an attending physician. John's doctor was going to the Philippines for an R&R and agreed to monitor John on the way. Since John had been heavily medicated, he remained unconscious for most of the flight; however several times he woke with a start, unable to catch his breath. The doctor right beside him would suction his lungs and regulate his air supply. Before drifting off again, John heard the groans and cries of his fellow Americans. Their expressions of pain permeated the din from the Starlifter's engines.

US involvement with the Philippine Islands dated back to the Spanish-American War in 1898, when a military installation was first established. The initial construction of Clark Air Base was completed by the mid-1920s. Named for the first US airman to fly in Hawaii, Major Harold M. Clark, the base underwent significant expansion following World War II. In 1960, the US Air Force began construction of a modern Regional Medical Facility. The 200-bed Clark Air Base Hospital was completed in April 1964. By the time John arrived at Clark in 1969, patient capacity had more than doubled and the medical facility played an important part in coordinating the treatment and evacuation of GIs from Vietnam.

The last few days left John exhausted, and the medications were jumbling his mind. He had no recollection of being removed from the large C-141 transport and being admitted to the hospital at Clark, so when John first regained consciousness, he was completely disoriented. He blinked open his eyes to the bright glare of a surgical light shining directly over his head. Lying prostrate on an operating table, the intense light blurred his vision, but he could decipher several shadowy faces partially hidden by surgical masks. Who were these strangers and why were they prodding at his neck and jabbing him with sharp instruments? The pain was unbearable.

Squinting, John discerned that the masked face hovering right above him had Oriental eyes. In his drug-induced haze, John's mind slipped back to his ever-present reality of Vietnam and confused him into thinking that the guy behind the mask was not a doctor but an enemy soldier. And instead of understanding that he was being given an exploratory examination, John was convinced that he had somehow been captured and was now being tortured. He gritted his teeth, holding hatred for the enemy in his heart as he looked up at the slant-eyed bastard who was poking him. The more the gook probed, the more John fought to conceal the severe pain. But it hurt so bad! His throat was on fire and felt like it had a thousand knife cuts. He bent his spine into the sustained pain, determined not to give this Communist motherfucker the satisfaction of seeing him break.

Fighting the pain, a memory of someone who had endured extreme suffering came to mind. John recalled the young NVA officer with a serious gut wound and remembered how that prisoner of war never surrendered to pain. If the enemy could hold it together, John could, too. Clenching his fists, he rigidly held his arms by his sides as the digging at his neck persisted.

After the doctors finished the exploratory examination, John was wheeled to a room where a nurse gave him another shot of Demerol. His clouded mind mixed hallucination with reality, and John continued to believe he had just undergone torture by the hands of the North Vietnamese. As the painkiller carried him to a state of complacency, John gave himself a pat on the back for not showing weakness in front of the enemy. Despite the terrible pain, he felt a sense of self-satisfaction for succeeding in holding it together. John closed his eyes and his pride was suddenly humbled. The haunting image of that wounded NVA officer swirled back into John's head and erased any satisfaction he had momentarily felt. Thoughts of that young enemy soldier cheated John of feeling like the better man. That guy never received a shot of painkiller—and never knew the safety and security of dozing off in a hospital bed. Soon, John left all thoughts behind, and the drug took him into a forgetful state of slumber.

"How are you today, Specialist?" a nurse asked as she entered his private room and stood beside his bed. "It's time for you to get up and take a short walk around the room."

It was John's third day at Clark. He had basically been unconscious his first couple of days, unaware that nurses had been attending to him hourly to suction fluid from his lungs, clean his wound, and change bandages. Over the last few days, his condition improved and he had transitioned from being dependent on the respirator to breathing on his own. Today, the nurse awakened him, determined to get John out of bed and walking. Although he had been swinging his legs to the side of his bed and sitting up, the nurse knew John had to start walking and moving to regain strength.

"Okay, we're going to disconnect you from the machines," she stated as she unfastened the vaporizing mask from around his neck. The nurse reached over and shut off the supply of warm, moist air where the vaporizer's hose attached to the wall. "Okay, now move your legs and sit up."

John would have preferred that the nurse simply give him another shot of Demerol and let him go back to sleep, but she was unwavering in her mission.

"Okay, now get your feet in your slippers." The nurse supported him with her arm and helped him stand on his wobbly legs. "Hold onto your IV stand and use it to balance. Push it forward as you walk. Come on now, slide your foot forward and take a step."

It took a supreme amount of effort for John to walk a dozen steps around the small room. His weakened 21-year-old body was soon fatigued and ready to return to his hospital bed for another shot of painkiller.

Later in the day, when a nurse came in to change his dressing, John mimed that he would like to write a note. With the pencil and pad of paper she gave him, John asked for a mirror. He wanted to see his neck. When the nurse returned, she handed John a mirror and then left him alone in his room.

Sitting upright in his bed, John took a breath and examined the reflection. He was shocked! He moved the mirror back to see the full image. Oh my god. Dropping the mirror onto his lap, he stared straight ahead, totally dismayed at what he had seen. His neck was hardly a neck. It was all screwed up. Extensive tissue loss left it looking like chopped meat. No wonder it emitted waves of warm, throbbing, piercing pain. Tears welled up in his eyes, and he began to whimper.

John held up the mirror and gazed once more. There were numerous black stitches closing two long incisions on each side of what resembled a raw meat patty in the center of his throat. The lengthy rows of stitches made it appear that his head had been sewn onto his body—just like a monster. And what was that—a button? It looked like a fucking button from his fatigue shirt, and it was attached to a wire sticking out of the right side of his neck. Tilting the mirror, he saw that the wire came out through the skin of the left side of his neck, where it wound around a quarter inch piece of plastic tubing. Those knobs and wires and stitches made him look just like Frankenstein's monster.

John set the mirror down and covered his face. If he couldn't stand to look at himself, how could anyone else look at him? His muffled sobs ceased when another shot of pain medication supplied tranquility.

Upon awakening several hours later, another nurse was standing at his bedside. She was about to perform the worst part of his treatment—suctioning his lungs. Every hour or so, a nurse would thread a rubber hose through the metal trach tube in his throat until it reached a lung. She would then poke around inside, sucking out as much of the secretions and unwanted fluids as possible from one lung and then repeat the procedure on the other. In addition to being exceedingly uncomfortable, John thought the sound of the suctioning noises alone would cause a person to gag, making him wonder if that was one reason he was in a private room. Next, the nurse performed another painful procedure—removing and replacing the metal trach tube. John would clench his teeth as she removed a crusted tube from the bloody mess of tissue and reinserted a clean one. The trach tube was held in place by cloth strings that were tied into a bow at the back of his neck.

John was still being fed by the tube through his nostril. Since it was difficult and painful to swallow, he kept an emesis basin nearby to drool into. Now that he had seen the sight of his neck, he craved the painkilling shots more than ever. They gave physical relief from discomfort and also provided euphoric escape from the devastating reality of his situation.

The next day, John was lying in his bed when a deep wail from somewhere out in the hallway sliced into the quiet of his room. The nurse, who had been making him get out of bed and walk, came to the side of John's bed. He penciled a note to ask her what the sound was.

"That was a patient who just came out of surgery," the nurse explained.

John's eyes asked more.

"He had to have part of his arm removed," she informed John while checking his tubes and hoses. "Like you, he was wounded in Vietnam, and he's upset because he played football in high school. He's having a hard time dealing with the loss of his throwing arm."

John knew the feeling. Since seeing his throat, he'd been miserable. How could he ever show his Frankensteinish neck in public again? What kind of future did he face? How could he go through life like this? And could Karen stand to look at her freak of a husband and love him like this? Such questions drove John into a state of emotional despair. After thoroughly stewing in his negative thoughts, he sunk into a dark and gloomy place.

The nurse, picking up on John's despondency, began to disconnect and move some of the hoses and equipment. "It's time to get out of bed and go for another walk," she announced. Smiling, the nurse cheerily chirped, "We'll go down the hallway this time. There's somebody I want you to meet."

After sorting out all the tubes, the nurse guided John to an upright position.

"You're doing fine," she encouraged as she supported John's left arm while he stepped forward and pushed his IV stand with his right.

Out into the hallway they walked. John could feel air on his exposed butt cheeks as his hospital smock swayed open with each step. His hand reached back to close the flap, but then he thought, oh well. He inwardly laughed and added it to all the other indignities he'd experienced so far.

The nurse directed John down the wide hall until they reached a room with four beds. Only one bed was occupied. On top of it sat a young red-haired man in a hospital robe. In the place of one of his legs was a bandaged stump that ended about mid-thigh.

"Hello, Danny. I have someone I'd like you to meet." The nurse introduced John to Danny and explained that Danny was a Marine who had his leg blown off about six weeks ago. "John is an Army flight medic, and he arrived here earlier this week," the nurse detailed. "It's hard for him to accept the disfigurement of his wound."

Danny shifted his body to face John, nodding his head with understanding.

"I thought maybe you could explain to John what happened to you, and how you feel about it."

"So you're a Dustoff medic?" Danny grinned, momentarily lightening the dark circles under his eyes. "Well, all right! I was medvaced after stepping on a land mine."

John cracked a smile, briefly swelling with the familiar glow of honor he felt whenever the dangerous job of flying Dustoff was recognized.

"Well, I know what you're dealing with," Danny stated, pointing to his bandaged limb. I couldn't believe that I lost my leg. I was pretty angry about it and couldn't adjust to the idea of going through life with only one leg. But, there's nothing I can do to make myself whole again, so I decided I'd better accept it and move on with my life."

John couldn't speak or nod his head, but he listened intently to this Marine, believing he was being sincere. Danny was probably close to John's age. He might be a little older, because his freckled forehead was grooved with deep lines of stress.

"I'm even going to have my prosthesis painted olive-drab instead of flesh-colored," Danny snickered. "I figure since everything in the military is OD—and since my leg is a result of the military—I may as well have it painted like everything else."

Back in his own bed, John thought about what Danny had said. *I'm still me. I only have one leg now, but I'm still me.*

John appreciated the guy's attitude. Danny had been injured six weeks ago, and he'd had some time to adjust. John knew that he needed some time to adjust, too. He buzzed the nurse, and when she came up to his bedside, John indicated that he needed a shot for pain. She left to get him one. The consoling injection would provide time to help accept what happened to him. Yes, he needed more time.

After five days in the Philippines, John was put onto a litter and again carried onboard a C-141. Like his flight from Da Nang to Clark Air Base, the Starlifter was filled with stacked rows of litters. John was feeling better and breathing better, but during the flight to Japan the medical technician detected that John had developed a fever. Therefore, instead of returning to the States, he was removed from the aircraft during their stopover in Japan and admitted to an Air Force hospital at Camp Zama.

There were sixty beds on the open bay ward stretched into four, long rows. All the beds were filled with American soldiers who had throat wounds or injuries to their facial features. John's bed was right next to the nurse's station at the front of the ward where the more seriously wounded were located. Although his head was held motionless by bandages and two small pillows propped up against each side of his neck, John was able to rotate his eyes and observe the perpetual activity in the ward from his upwardly angled bed. Doctors, nurses and their assistants were seen everywhere. Patients were constantly being wheeled in and out of surgery with many of them undergoing multiple sessions under the knife. Most were asleep, but the less seriously injured could be seen milling around and visiting with other patients.

John thought the old ward looked like something from the reconstructive years when America first occupied Japan. In reality, some of the buildings in the compound were even older. Camp Zama had been the West Point of the Japanese Imperial Army until it became headquarters of US Army Japan following the bombing of Hiroshima and Nagasaki at the end of World War II.

As John scrutinized the large ENT ward, he perceived that it was divided into two halves. Each side had two rows of beds facing each other, with an aisle running in between. Because John's head was secured in a forward-facing position, he looked straight ahead most of the time. Directly across the aisle, the patient toe-to-toe with John also had his bed elevated at a forty-five-degree angle. This gave John a clear view of that patient—and he was a sight to behold.

John was told the guy had been wounded in a mortar blast. His whole head was burnt crispy black. He had no eyes, ears, hair, nose, or lips. The guy's head looked like a massive, well-done hamburger patty. He had open fragment wounds in his chest with drains inserted in them, but below his shoulders, the man's body was not burned and appeared normal. John had never seen the guy conscious, and there always seemed to be hospital personnel by his bedside.

Once, John awoke and saw that the guy's bed was empty. John figured he had died. But no, later in the day he was brought back. He'd been in surgery. Every time John found the bed empty, he marveled when the guy returned. When John wasn't drugged or asleep, he would often stare over at him. John wondered if the guy knew what he looked like. But what a foolish thought! Of course he didn't know what he looked like—look at his eyes—he has none.

The thought flashed in John's mind that maybe one of their choppers had picked up this patient after he was wounded by the mortar blast. But maybe if that guy knew what he looked like lying there in that hospital bed, well, maybe he would have rather stayed on the jungle floor and died. Maybe Dustoff didn't do this guy a favor after all. For the first time, John questioned whether his own efforts had always been worthwhile. Was it right to save pieces of people that still had life—but no promise of quality of life? Would death have been—if not the preferred conclusion—at least the more humane?

John wondered if the guy across from him had a wife or children. How much time would it take for him to adjust to his condition? He certainly would have huge challenges to surmount. And here John had been feeling sorry for himself. Unable to imagine going through life with that guy's disfigurement, John concluded it would take a better man than he to do so. Closing his eyes, John needed to buzz the nurse for another pain shot.

After a week in Japan, John was feeling stronger. The nurses didn't need to suction his lungs as often, and he no longer had an IV in his arm. It was still painful, but he was able to swallow better, so his feeding tube was removed and he began drinking milk and flavored canned milkshakes—vanilla, chocolate, and strawberry.

At the beginning of his second week in the hospital, John was directed to a side room off the main ward to meet with three doctors. Wearing a hospital robe and slippers, he walked into the room and sat in the empty chair where one doctor had gestured. The doctors were already seated around the small table, which was covered with open files and various reports.

"Specialist Seebeth," the doctor began, "we'd like to update you on your condition and treatment plan."

John listened carefully, unable to nod because bandages still kept his neck immobile.

"John, as you know, during transport from the Philippines, you were found to be running a fever and were admitted to this hospital diagnosed with a low-grade neck infection. You were treated with antibiotics, and your temperature has since stabilized."

Since John couldn't speak, the doctor to his left pushed a pad of paper and a pencil in front of him, instructing John to ask any questions and to please respond to theirs with hand gestures or writing.

After several minutes of penciling responses to questions about swallowing and breathing, John sat quietly as the three doctors discussed his situation.

One looked over at John and explained, "You're going to remain in Japan until we are certain there are no more signs of infection. Then, you will return to the States where more extensive reconstructive surgery will be performed."

John sat across from the doctors, stunned. Until this moment, he really didn't understand the extensiveness of his injury. He felt heat rise in his face.

"NO!" he mouthed.

"John, the type of surgery you need and the care you require is not available for you here in Japan.

"No!" John mouthed again. He picked up the pencil to convey his thoughts, but there was so much he wanted to say, and he didn't know how to spell all the words. Frustrated with trying to record his thoughts on a piece of paper, John tossed the pencil aside.

"That's impossible!" John moved his lips, and air raggedly escaped through his trach, causing him to wince in pain. "You-need-to-fix-my-throat-at-this-hospital-right-here-now!" he gulped while pounding his forefinger on the table.

The doctors looked at each other to see if anyone had understood John. None of them knew what his wheezes of air were trying to say.

"John," the first doctor placated, knowing John was upset. "With reconstructive surgery, we expect you'll be able to live a full life."

"No!" John mouthed emphatically. "I need to get back to my unit! There's a lot of wounded, and my crewmembers are covering my ass until I return. They must be exhausted. I need to pull my load." John was so discouraged at not being able to communicate the totality of his feelings that he began to cry. His eyes pleaded with the doctors to help him get back on the job.

The same doctor stood and put his hand on John's shoulder. He comprehended what John was trying to say, because so many soldiers expressed the same sentiment. "John, your buddies would want what's best for you, and right now that means you need surgery back in the States."

The other two doctors nodded their heads in agreement.

At the end of two weeks, John's temperature was normal, and the lab results revealed no sign of infection. He still grimaced in pain when he swallowed, but he succeeded in taking food orally, adding applesauce, rice pudding, and other soft foods to his diet. The throbbing in his throat had subsided enough to discontinue the shots of Demerol, but he was now given capsules of Darvon for pain. Each night, he was connected to a vaporizer in order to supply warm moist air to his trach. All in all, he had come a long way from when he was unconscious and kept alive by a respirator.

The doctors informed John he was well enough to be flown back to the States. He was issued a Class A uniform—minus the tie—and this time, as an ambulatory patient, he walked onboard the C-141 Starlifter that would carry him home.

Chapter 16

His boot touched ground; John's heart thumped wildly, and emotion choked his throat. He was back in the good ol' US of A. He'd been gone for ten months, and so much had happened. It was late morning of 11 September 1969 when the C-141 landed at Andrews Air Force Base outside of Washington, D.C. John was one of several patients to step off the transport aircraft and back onto American soil.

Near the end of John's two-week stay in Japan, a hospital administrator approached his bed to determine what hospital he would be assigned to back in the States.

"Your records indicate that your hometown is Philadelphia," the man stated. "Do you want to be located there?"

John took a second or two to think about the question. His father had sold their family home and had moved to a different city in Pennsylvania since remarrying. His mother and Eduardo lived in New Jersey. Two months had passed since Karen's last letter, yet he assumed she was still living with her grandmother in West Virginia. John penciled his choice on a piece of paper and handed it to the administrator. He would be sent to the hospital closest to Karen— DeWitt Army Hospital in Fort Belvoir, Virginia.

A First Lieutenant met John on the tarmac at Andrews. The officer instructed John to accompany him to an army sedan, parked off to the side of the huge C-141. John followed him to the vehicle, noting the young officer's pressed and polished appearance. It made John feel self-conscious of his own appearance in a Class A uniform, something he hadn't worn since his wedding a year ago. He couldn't look sharp in his uniform because the top button of his dress shirt had to remain unbuttoned, exposing the metal trach tube and gauze bandage, which was caked with blood and gunk from his wound. Despite the First Lieutenant's crisp exterior, John realized he had something the young officer didn't. The crewmember wings and the two rows of ribbons he wore on his breast—especially the Air Medals and the Purple Heart awarded to him in Japan—were badges of honor and respect. John held his head high as he stepped behind the First Lieutenant toward the waiting car.

Along with a driver, the officer and John were the only passengers in the vehicle. The First Lieutenant didn't have much to say, and, of course, John couldn't speak at all, so there was mostly silence in the sedan during the hour-long drive across D.C. to DeWitt. Gazing out the window at the passing scenery, John was struck by how nothing seemed to have changed. Cars looked the same. People, buildings, signs, signal lights, where the sky met the ground—everything looked just the same. John closed his eyes, overtaken by a tidal wave of emotion crashing over him. How could things be the same? After all he had seen and been through—how could things here still be the same?

The normalcy John saw out the window collided with his recent memories of quite a different reality. Hadn't he just been in a landscape devastated by war? Hadn't he just been in a place where the stench of death was so overwhelming it could make you vomit? Where fear was so palpable it was almost visible? Where the screams of children chilled your bones? And where too much gushing blood and gore could turn a kind heart into stone? Riding along in the vehicle, John felt like his chest could explode. Even though the last ten months had tossed him every which way and landed him upside down, the view framed by the sedan's window made it seem as though time had paused. Nothing had changed much, except for him.

Turning away from the window, John wanted to tell the officer how shocking the contrast was between this reality and the one he knew in Vietnam. We were a country at war. Men were suffering and dying daily, yet it was business as usual outside the car's window. John grimaced as he tried to swallow the turbulent feelings rising in his wounded throat. He used to have a gift for gab. His talkative nature had made social interactions easy and friendly. And for someone who liked to chat, he now had a lot to say. There were so many thoughts churning in his mind, so much he wanted to share with the young Lieutenant, but how could he communicate those thoughts? He hadn't been able to speak a word in four weeks. It took a great deal of time and energy for him to convey even the simplest ideas; how would he ever be able to communicate complicated thoughts and feelings to anyone? To make matters even more difficult, English had always been his worst subject, and now here he was stuck with the written word as his major means of communication.

After arriving at Dewitt Army Hospital, John was assigned a private room where he changed out of his uniform and into a cotton hospital gown, robe, and slippers. He was exhausted from sitting in a jump seat for over twenty hours, so he stretched out on his bed and watched the early afternoon sun angle through the window of his room. Despite his fatigue, John knew he was too revved up to sleep. While being admitted, he had been told that all servicemen returning from Vietnam were entitled to one free telephone call to anywhere in the country. John rose from the bed and paced around the room. He was anxious for the Red Cross volunteer to arrive and assist him in making his call.

Almost a year had passed since John had spoken with Karen. Of course, she would be his one phone call. He'd been told that his next of kin had been sent telegrams about his situation, so Karen surely knew he had been wounded. He also vaguely recalled writing to her from the Philippines during his first week at Clark. A Red Cross volunteer had helped him write a brief note to both Karen and his mother to assure them that he was okay and not to worry. Finally, the moment he'd long been waiting for was almost here. He would be hearing Karen's voice on the phone, and soon he'd be looking into her eyes. By looking into her eyes, he'd really know where things stood between them. Their marriage was in trouble; he knew that. But today, after having been consumed by thoughts of Karen for months, he would finally hear her voice.

John's heart rate increased when the Red Cross worker stepped into his room. The small, gray-haired woman wore a neatly starched uniform and a wide smile as she asked if John was ready to make a phone call.

"Oh!" she softly exclaimed in understanding when she realized John couldn't speak. The smile quickly returned when she told him,

"Well, I am more than happy to help you contact your loved one."

Her exuberance was contagious. The grandmotherly woman provided a heartfelt service to the returning serviceman whose loved ones awaited word of his condition and whereabouts. She had probably helped countless others make similar calls.

Grinning, John handed the Red Cross worker a piece of paper. Below Karen's name and phone number he had written the message he wanted her to say on his behalf, "I'm fine and come as soon as possible. Johnny."

The woman dialed the number while John sat on the edge of the bed, his hands nervously kneading his thighs. It was difficult to maintain composure when the same old questions surfaced in his mind. Questions he had spent so much time wondering about when he was in Vietnam. Had Karen been faithful? What happened to all the money he'd sent? Did she still love him? And he had new questions in his head, too. What was she going to think of his throat and inability to talk? Would she think he looked like a monster?

When the woman began speaking to someone over the phone, John's spine stiffened. He heard her ask for Karen Seebeth. Placing a hand over the telephone's mouthpiece, the volunteer turned to John and stated in a quiet voice, "The person asked me to please hold while they go get Karen." She smiled and arched her eyebrows with excitement.

John suddenly became conscious of a hollow feeling in his stomach.

The Red Cross volunteer's attention returned to the telephone and she began speaking to the person on the other end. It was Karen. John intently watched the woman's face as she explained to Karen

281

that her husband was back in the States at DeWitt Army Hospital in Fort Belvoir.

"Johnny said to tell you he's fine, and I'm sitting right across from him, and he does look just fine," the elderly woman reported. "But due to the nature of his injury, I'm going to speak for him."

John grabbed the pencil and notepad. He quickly jotted down another message and handed it to her.

"Your husband asks that you please come to the hospital right away," she spoke into the receiver and then glanced at John, winking her eye.

The hollow pit in John's stomach grew larger when he watched exuberance fade from the Red Cross volunteer's face.

She again put her free hand over the mouthpiece and declared in a weak voice, "Karen said she won't be coming to see you. She says she has no money."

For the longest moment, John sat and studied the woman's face, searching for truth. From her moist eyes and sad expression, it was obvious the volunteer was almost as upset over Karen's response as he was.

John's mind raced. He suddenly stood up and grabbed the telephone from the startled woman's hand. His own hand trembled as he held the receiver up to his ear. He listened, but there was nothing to hear. He listened longer, but not even the sound of Karen's breathing came across the line. Staring into space, John didn't know what to do. He couldn't even ask the simplest question. Feeling tears well up in his eyes, John lowered the phone to its cradle.

The Red Cross worker mumbled a few words before exiting his room, leaving him alone—dejected and humiliated. John stood upon shaky legs, continuing to stare at nothing. After all he had been through, Karen didn't have the decency to come and see him. Well, he guessed he had answers to his questions. His face was ghostly pale, but his thoughts were red hot. He believed—for a split second—that if his two hands had been around Karen's neck, he would have snapped it.

But really, how could he blame Karen? He couldn't forget how cruel he had been the night before their wedding when he said he didn't love her. And he'd fucked up royally by cheating on her in Vietnam. No, it wasn't all Karen's fault. He'd been an asshole. No wonder she didn't love him. And now, with his disfigurement, he believed no one else ever could.

For the rest of the day, John didn't leave his bed. He refused food because his stomach was in too much turmoil to eat. Vacantly gazing at the wall, he gave up on trying to communicate with anyone, except to ask the nurses for more Darvon. The medication helped maintain his shell of numbness as his soul withdrew into a very dark night.

John might have remained in that place indefinitely, but the next day his mother and Eduardo showed up at the hospital.

"Oh, Johnny! Oh, Johnny," his mother cried as she shuffled into his room. "You have no idea what I've been through. The last couple of weeks have been awful! We've been trying to find out where you were and how you are." Her ample arms encircled John, and she sobbed on his shoulder as she hugged him.

Eduardo nodded. "Your mother's been a nervous wreck. She got your letter from the Philippines before she got the telegram from the Army, so she didn't know what the hell was happening."

"I didn't know how you were wounded or how bad it was." His mother reached for a tissue from his bed stand to wipe her eyes. "Oh, Johnny, it's been awful! The telegram had you almost dead. I'm glad your letter came first or I would have thought for sure you were almost dead."

John blotted tears from his own eyes while his mother pushed the blond lock of hair from his forehead and continued her blubbering.

"As soon as I got your letter, I called your father. He had a lot of questions, but I didn't know anything…oh my god! Eduardo! Look how pale Johnny is! And you're so thin. You're nothing but skin and bones."

"Hey, but at least none of the important equipment got injured, right Johnny?" Eduardo joked.

John would never have expected to be so glad to see his mother. Her words consoled him as she related how they had all responded to the news of his being wounded. She told him that his stoic brother had cried and had to leave work. His sister stayed out of school for a week. Since his mother didn't drive, Eduardo drove her to McGuire Air Force Base each day to see if John was among the patients being brought to Walson Army Hospital.

"I had to stop taking her," Eduardo divulged. "She got too depressed after seeing so many young boys in such bad shape. We didn't know what to expect when we saw you. But here you are looking pretty darn good."

His mother and Eduardo spent the whole day with him, and John was actually sad to have them leave.

The next day, John was surprised to see his father enter his hospital room with tears streaming down his face. He'd never before seen his father cry.

"Son," his father choked as he held him tightly. "How're you doing? I'm so glad to see you up and walking. I'm thrilled to see you looking so good. Really, I'm so thrilled to see you."

His dad and his wife, Anna May, spent the afternoon with him before they had to catch a bus back to Pennsylvania. When departing, his father again showed an unusual display of emotion as he hugged him goodbye.

"I know things will turn out okay," his father gently affirmed. "You're young and you're a fighter. And we don't want to forget your manager—God. He'll bring you through this."

A day later, John was even more surprised to have his high school friend, Eddie, walk into his room. Eddie and his wife, Diane, made the over-four-hour drive from Philly on bald tires in their 1960 Chevy.

"How did you find out about me?" John penciled on a notepad after the friends' joyful reunion.

"Your mother and her husband stopped by our apartment on their way back to New Jersey."

"At three in the morning," Diane added.

"Your mother apologized for waking us up, but she thought I would want to know—and I sure did," Eddie confirmed.

Eddie had been John's best buddy when they were both Vocational Commercial Art students at Bensalem High School. Diane had been a student there as well. They all became friends and had often double-dated. Like John, Eddie had received a scholarship at Hussein Art College, where he was currently a student.

"We brought you a gift," Eddie announced as he gestured for his wife to hand him the small bag tucked under her arm.

"What was your trademark in high school?" Diane questioned.

John shrugged his shoulders, indicating that he wasn't sure.

"Come on. What was one thing you were really known for?" Eddie teased while inserting his hand into the bag. He pulled out his hand, holding a small toy in his palm. Eddie pushed a button on the device, and the sound of hearty, mechanical laughter filled the room.

"Your mother told us that your injuries left you without your laugh," Eddie informed John through his own laughter. "So, we decided this laughing box would be the prefect present for you. It's your crazy laugh!"

"You had the kind of laugh that made other people want to laugh," Diane chuckled. "Until you get it back again, you can use this funny one."

By the time Eddie and Diane said goodbye at the end of the day, John's face was sore from smiling. It had been a long time since he had experienced such levity. Looking back over his life, John realized that some of the difficult times he knew as a teenager were made bearable because he was able to laugh about things. In Vietnam, Zeke's outrageous humor had helped him cope with all the insanity. Humor had saved him, and laughter had gotten him through. Now, the free-spirited, upbeat sound that used to flow out of John's mouth was missing. It made his injury even more difficult to accept.

Later in the week, another unexpected visitor stepped into his room. John hadn't seen Billy since they served a year together in Baumholder with the 565th Ambulance Company. After being redeployed to Fort Polk, Billy left the Army, having fulfilled his 2-year conscription. Billy and John had been close friends in Germany. In fact, Billy had been with John the night he met Karen at the Budapest, and he'd accompanied John to her home on several occasions to have dinner with her family. It was helpful for John to talk to someone who actually knew Karen.

"Remember how brokenhearted I was when Kathy dumped me?" Billy asked. "Remember how I couldn't stand to hear that Everly Brothers' song, "Cathy's Clown"? I reckon you might not think so now, but it does get easier over time."

Billy made the 3-hour drive from his home in Lynchburg to visit John again a week later. John was learning to adapt to his wound by using facial expressions and gestures to communicate. He also began to control the air through his trach, which allowed him to mouth words in a breathy whisper. Billy became adept at understanding John's unclear speech. One sunny afternoon, Billy led John out of his room and over to an outside patio. There, the two comrades sat in the fresh air and reminisced about their shared experiences. Together, they had gone through basic training at Fort Bragg, they'd attended the medic school at Fort Sam Houston, and they had both been assigned to a year of duty in Baumholder. Of course, many more hours were spent talking about Karen, and those long conversations were therapeutic for John.

Nevertheless, as days passed without a visit or phone call from Karen, John became completely disheartened. Though his physical condition was steadily improving, ever since the Red Cross worker's phone call, John's emotional health dropped to a new low. In addition to thinking about his marriage falling apart, he also thought about his friends back in Vietnam. How were the guys in his unit doing? Had the fighting died down? Plus, he had so many thoughts about the uncertainty of his wound. What could the doctors do? Would he ever be able to talk again?

John wasn't aware that his mother had contacted the Army, lobbying to get her son transferred up north to a closer hospital. It was impractical for his family to drive from Pennsylvania and New Jersey to visit him in Virginia. John's doctor's agreed that his reconstructive surgery should be done in a military hospital closer to his supportive family. Since Karen hadn't made any effort to contact him, John had to admit there was nothing for him in Virginia. The doctors submitted the necessary transfer papers, and on 26 September 1969, two weeks after being admitted to DeWitt, John left Virginia and was flown up to McGuire. From there he rode in an Army ambulance to US Walson Army Hospital at Fort Dix, New Jersey.

During his flight to McGuire, John thought about how his family and friends had rallied for him. The emotion expressed by his father had really touched him. And his mother had shown remarkable concern for him by contacting Eddie and Billy. Eddie and Diane's visit had given him the gift of laughter and made John think about how his circumstances could have been different if he had become an art student like Eddie. The many hours spent with Billy reminded him of the importance of having a close friend. John was thankful for those visits from his friends and family. They had given him a glimmer of hope. People still cared about him and made him believe that he might even have a future.

Chapter 17

"Johnny, why don't you come and sit at the table with us?"

"No!" John emphatically whispered, furrowing his brow into an angry expression.

"But, Johnny, you couldn't be here for Thanksgiving, and Eduardo cooked a turkey for you today. No one minds looking at your neck...."

"NO!" John whispered louder, stiffening his arm and holding his hand up to tell his mother to stop bugging him and just leave him alone. He was fine by himself in the living room. He knew how unsightly his neck was, and he wasn't going to eat in front of others and make them sick.

His mother plunked a plate of food down on the coffee table and stomped back to the kitchen where the rest of the family was dining. John heard her say, "He's not the same old Johnny anymore. He used to be happy-go-lucky, like he didn't have a care in the world. That's why people liked him. He was always smiling. But not anymore. He's really changed. Damn that war!"

Yeah, John knew he wasn't the same old Johnny. He really was a different person. His nine months in Vietnam were equivalent to a nine-month pregnancy, and he'd come out of that gestation period—

born again—as a new and wounded person. How could his mother expect him to be the same old happy-go-lucky Johnny after all he'd seen and been through? John pushed the plate of food to the side of the coffee table and slumped back down on the couch, which also served as his bed. With his brother and sister living there, too, the modest house didn't have extra space for him. Still, it was good to be part of a family household this weekend rather than being stuck looking at the same four walls of his hospital room.

It was John's first weekend away from Walson Army Hospital, where he had undergone nine procedures on his neck over the past eight weeks. The surgeries, skin grafts, stenting and acrylic mold changes kept him mostly in bed and medicated. John was grateful that Eduardo had made the 50-minute drive north to Walson to pick him up and bring him back to their home in Lanoka Harbor. However, it didn't take long before being under the same roof with his mother caused old irritations to fester.

On the day John arrived at Walson, he had been pleasantly surprised when his mother and Eduardo walked into his room. John had already completed transfer procedures, met with his doctor, and was settling into the small space that would be his new quarters when his visitors arrived in the late afternoon. After a half-hour of small talk, his mother suggested Eduardo go to the cafeteria for coffee while she and John went outside to take a walk around the hospital grounds. That's when she hit him up for money.

"We could lose the house and all the furniture," his mother bemoaned while wiping her tears as they walked. "Eduardo doesn't make as much as he used to when he was in the Navy," she sniffled. "We can't make ends meet, and we've got a lot of debts."

Of course, John couldn't refuse her plea. He began a practice he would continue for decades and sent his mother money each month.

Earlier that day, John was encouraged after meeting the Army doctor who would be performing reconstructive work on his neck. He felt an immediate trust for the fair-haired, soft-spoken man who wasn't much more than ten years his senior. Major Gerald Bell had only recently finished school and would be applying the newest procedures he had learned during his ENT/Otolaryngology specialization. His professional manner and positive attitude convinced John that he would be receiving the best possible care.

While Dr. Bell was describing the first series of operations, John couldn't fully pay attention, because his mind was concentrating on something else.

"Sir, I have to go see my wife before we begin," John wrote on a pad of paper the doctor had provided for him.

"I'm not at all in favor of you traveling to West Virginia on a commercial flight by yourself," Dr. Bell countered. "You may be ambulatory, but you're essentially very weak." Pointing to the calendar, he emphasized, "You're scheduled for surgery on Wednesday, October 1st, and that cannot be postponed. Too much time has passed. You should have already started your surgeries."

Through hand gestures, breathy words, and written words on the notepad, John expressed the need to see his wife. "It's been over ten months, and I don't know where we stand." How could John communicate his need to look into Karen's eyes? Only then would he really know for sure the fate of his marriage.

The kind doctor was adept at comprehending John's speech and understood the importance of his emotional health. He reluctantly granted John a weekend pass. Dr. Bell wished him luck and sent John off with a warning.

"You need to be back in this hospital by Monday when you're scheduled for your pre-op exams."

Much of the trip to West Virginia became a blurry memory to John, probably because right after returning he began the surgeries and accompanying painkilling medications. However, he remembered waiting for his flight at Philadelphia's International Airport and noticing he was a frequent object of people's attention. He wasn't sure if they were looking at him because—dressed in his Class A uniform—he represented the military at a time when public sentiment about the Vietnam War was shifting. Americans had been stunned when the media exposed the atrocities committed at My Lai. Just a few weeks ago, criminal charges had been filed against Lieutenant Calley for his part in the massacre. Such questionable conduct of soldiers inflamed antiwar protestors. John had heard about protesters harassing soldiers and calling them baby killers, but no one in the airport made any comments to him. They just silently stared, making John believe that—more than his uniform—their eyes were directed at his red, grotesque neck. It made him feel extremely self-conscious of his appearance and added to his apprehension about how Karen would react when she saw him.

John also remembered arriving at the Regional Airport in West Virginia and taking a twenty-minute taxi ride to Karen's residential neighborhood. The driver sprinted to the front door of the two-story brick home with a note from John. He returned to the vehicle and reported that Karen Seebeth did live there and she was on her way

292

out. John thanked him, paid him, and stepped out of the cab to look into his wife's eyes.

When Karen came down the front steps of the entry and walked toward him, John was overwhelmed by her beauty. Truly, he'd never seen her look more beautiful. The sight of her immediately dissipated his anger. Instead of wanting to know why she didn't write more, or why she didn't meet him in Hawaii, or what she did with all the money, and why she didn't come to the hospital to see him—he just wanted to put his arms around her and hold her tightly. He wanted all past misunderstandings forgotten, and he wanted to pick up the pieces of their six-week marriage and assemble them into something better. But when Karen met his gaze, the spark in her eyes was missing. He was used to seeing that special twinkle in her eye whenever she looked at him, but it wasn't there anymore. In reality, John could have headed back to Philadelphia right that moment. Karen's eyes made it clear—she wasn't happy to see him.

Rather than inviting him into her home, Karen suggested taking a walk around the neighborhood. They must have walked for five hours, yet he could hardly recall what they talked about, except for reminiscing about old times. He had to gesture and whisper, and sometimes she couldn't understand him, so he had to pull out his pencil and pocket notepad. She never mentioned his wound. He couldn't remember if she asked about Vietnam. Even if she had, how could he express such deep feelings with his inability to speak?

They walked without stopping to sit or eat. The skies were darkening, and John was tired, but he didn't want to bring things to an end. He didn't want to admit what he knew to be true. He hoped that if Karen had more time to think things through—but in his heart, he knew it was over. He waited on the sidewalk while she went in the house to call a cab. When the taxi arrived, it was time to say goodbye. They didn't hug; they politely shook hands.

As John was about to climb into the cab, Karen quickly questioned, "What about the US Savings Bonds?"

Oh. So that's what this was about. The hours of friendly walking and talking were really about getting him to sign over the bonds to her. John's heart ached as he made the trip back to Walson. In his mind, he couldn't help but wonder if Karen was any different than his mother. Both wanted something from him.

It was almost a relief to check into the hospital. The first day, Dr. Bell found an infection in John's neck, so doses of antibiotics were immediately administered. When the series of surgeries began, the doctor's orders allowed John to receive shots of Demerol and Morphine at his own discretion. Since being wounded, three months of injections had left John's arms bruised from wrists to shoulders. In order to prevent abscesses in his overly pricked arms and butt, the nurses began giving him injections in his hip. Even though his muscles were sore from needle sticks, he continued requesting the numbing narcotics every four hours—and eventually every three. More than for pain, John craved the shots to blur his thoughts and memories and to help cope with his situation—as well as tolerating confinement in the small hospital room.

Some of his nurses, particularly Nurse Rodriguez, became wise to his true intentions. From the 95th Evacuation Hospital in Da Nang all the way to US Walson Army Hospital in Fort Dix, John had warm feelings for the nurses who cared for him. In his mind, they were true angels, and Nurse Rodriguez was no exception. She was a motherly type, and he knew she had his best interests at heart. When he asked for another shot of painkiller, Nurse Rodriguez would give him a disapproving glance that told him she knew what he was up to. Even if she resisted, John would get his painkiller because Dr. Bell's orders permitted. Fortunately, John never became addicted to the narcotics.

"Your healing is a slow process," Dr. Bell made clear to John, during a follow-up appointment in the doctor's cramped office at the hospital. "The last acrylic mold replacement on November 29th was your fifth since last month." The doctor placed three plastic tubes on his desk, each about two inches long. Pointing to the slight difference in their diameters, Dr. Bell illustrated, "We started with #32 French Silastic chest tubing and are working up to a #35 French acrylic mold. The molds are preventing the laryngotracheal fissure from growing together, and the gentle increase in mold size is slowly forcing the opening in your throat to widen."

As John listened to Dr. Bell, his eyes studied the molds. The smallest seemed to be about the width of his pinkie, and the largest no bigger than his index finger. John had grown to respect his doctor, and he had confidence in Major Bell's commitment to restore his neck. Although frustrated by not being able to speak a word in over three months, John trusted he would eventually regain his voice and that the gaping hole in his neck would be closed.

"This last mold change is it for a while," Dr. Bell stated. "I don't foresee another procedure until February. We have to give it time. You'll be followed as an outpatient, but meanwhile, how'd you like to get out of the hospital for the weekend?"

After his first weekend pass, John packed an overnight bag and returned to his mother's house the next weekend, too. He would spend several more weekends there before starting to get back on his own two feet. Surprisingly, the initial interaction with his mother had been favorable. It was almost like she was making up for her absence in his life during his teenage years. Since he couldn't talk, she spoke over the phone on his behalf, helping him reconnect with some of his old friends in Philly. John borrowed Eduardo's car and took his mother along with him to update his civilian wardrobe. He relied on his mother to consult with salespeople and offer feedback on the newest styles. John was a little embarrassed to take his mother shopping, but he'd had the wind knocked out of him, and his self-esteem was sorely lacking.

"What are you looking at?" his mother would shout to a passerby who gazed in the direction of John's neck. "Don't you know there's a war going on? Haven't you heard of Vietnam?"

At first, John actually appreciated his mother's verbal attacks on strangers. It felt good to have someone stand up for him. Yet soon he became humiliated walking beside an obese woman with her loud mouth and aggressive outbursts. In addition, as John's weekend passes extended to weeklong leaves, he took on the responsibility of driving his mother to her many medical appointments. John began to wonder if his inability to talk was going to sentence him to a future based on a mutually dependent relationship with his mother. During the waiting periods between scheduled surgeries, John was either confined to the four walls of his hospital room or confined to his mother's living room. And the more time he spent with his mother, the more he realized that if he had to remain in confinement with her, well, he'd sooner go back to Vietnam.

Nevertheless, John gained confidence as he continued to venture out into the public, first with his mother and then on his own. He still refused to go to restaurants, but he found people were accepting of him and quite willing to make the effort to comprehend his watery and wheezy words. Like most young people, he desired socializing with others of his age group. John borrowed Eduardo's car a few times and drove over 60 miles one-way to Philadelphia to see some of his old buddies. It was great to be in their company—but other than getting stinking drunk together—a lot of miles of road had passed between them.

Being in a state of limbo while waiting for his next medical treatment, John was in and out of his mother's house for weeks at a time. Transportation soon became a major hassle. John disliked inconveniencing Eduardo by frequently asking to borrow his car. Otherwise, he had to depend upon friends to drive long distances to collect him and bring him back. One day in January, when a check arrived in the mail that unexpectedly included back pay, John went right out and bought himself a new set of wheels. He wanted an affordable vehicle, good on mileage.

As soon as John purchased his brand new 1970 beige VW beetle, he steered it to a place that had caught his eye on his weekend trips back and forth to the hospital with Eduardo and his mother. The Satellite Lounge was a huge one-story building with a billboard that advertised live bands from the surrounding area. Philadelphia congestion had spread across the Delaware River into southwestern New Jersey, where an almost continuous belt of cities stretched ninety miles to New York City.

Situated near that belt, the Satellite Lounge featured musicians from Trenton, Camden, Newark, Jersey City, as well as Philly and New York City. The first Friday he had possession of his new car, John made the drive from his mother's home in Lanoka Harbor back toward Fort Dix to the Satellite Lounge. The distance was only about thirty miles, but driving through the winding countryside roads and the Pine Barrens of New Jersey took close to an hour.

The Satellite Lounge was supposed to be off-limits for members of the US Armed Forces. However, located in Cookstown, adjacent to the sprawling complex that included Lakehurst Naval Station, McGuire Air Force Base, and Fort Dix Army Base, the Satellite was an irresistible watering hole. Dressed in their civvies, military personnel joined crowds from the tri-state area and packed the cavernous establishment on Friday and Saturday nights.

John found refuge at the Satellite. Being around music, dancing, young people, and booze recreated familiar, warm feelings. The bouncers got to know him by name as he regularly arrived at about seven or eight o'clock each Friday and Saturday night and stayed until closing. Entering the windowless club, colored lights reflected from a rotating glass ball on the ceiling and transported John to another world. The Satellite Lounge was the place where it was happening. Popular bands performed onstage, and throbbing music beckoned scores of people onto the dance floor. Watching others, John longed to be out there and losing himself to the rhythm. Music had always moved him, and dancing had been a great source of pride. Yet, John felt uncomfortable asking a girl to dance at the Satellite. What would he do, hand her a note?

Occasionally, a female would approach but often ended up asking, "Do you have cancer?"

His neck began to feel like a fence around him. It stood in the way of meeting women, and he had to peer over the top of the fence to make contact with people. Rather than scale the fence, John would sit on a barstool with his back to the dance floor and drink.

In between sets, taped music would filter out of the speakers. When a song like Eddie Holman's "Hey There Lonely Girl" played, John would order another Screwdriver or Bloody Mary. Hearing songs that so strongly captured his feelings glued him to the bar and kept him drowning his frustrations until last call. After six hours of drinking at the Satellite Lounge he would find his car—one of the few remaining in the parking lot—and drive the deserted roads back to his mother's home.

Later in January, John received a call from Tom Hartman, who was home on leave, having finished his one-year tour of duty in Vietnam. He invited John to come visit before he had to report to Fort Devens and fulfill his last year of commitment to the Army. Without hesitation, John agreed to make the 6-hour drive to visit Tom at his mother's house in the Finger Lakes region of New York State. It was an emotional reunion as John and Tom celebrated surviving Vietnam. Tom introduced John to family and friends in his bucolic town, and his mother served them a home-cooked meal in her white-painted, wood-shingled home.

The next night, John drove almost an hour to Rochester, where Tom navigated the VW to a couple of popular hangouts. At Duffy's Tavern, they found a quiet corner in a wooden booth, and—thanks to Tom's ability to understand John—they caught up on old times.

"You got a letter from Pilot Dave Collins?" Tom asked in response to John's breathy speech and hand signals.

John nodded and waved his hand to indicate the past. "October," he mouthed.

After John gestured to make another point, Tom replied, "Yeah, what Collins wrote you is right. The fighting let up a day or two after you were shot. It took about five days, but the ground troops finally reached that C&C chopper that was shot down, and right after that, the push ended and things let up."

Tom paused to sip the foam from his mug of draft beer before continuing, "And it wasn't too long before the 196th vacated Baldy and moved their rear staging area back to Hawk Hill."

John's hand swooped like a fast-moving plane.

"Yeah, that's where the gunships flew out of. Not far from Tam Ky."

Setting his mug on the table that was liberally carved with names and initials, Tom asked, "Did Collins mention how Zeke jumped Stanton?"

"What?"

Tom lit a cigarette before telling the story. "Zeke was so upset about you getting shot—hell—we all were. But Zeke got it in his head that Stanton took too long to lift off and was somehow responsible for you getting hit. So as Stanton was walking across the company area one evening, Zeke jumped on him and started punching him out."

"Zeke?"

"Yeah, he kind of went off the deep end. Roy Reynolds said Zeke found a piece of bone or cartilage of yours inside the chopper afterwards, and he wore it around his neck next to his peace medallion. And he started drinking a lot."

John shook his head and pointed to his mug of beer to indicate that Zeke didn't drink.

"Well, he changed," Tom revealed. "He drank, and got quiet, and withdrawn—not the funny guy we used to know."

John chugged the rest of his beer. He didn't know how to respond.

"Did you know about LaForge almost getting fragged?" Tom questioned.

John's eyes and mouth opened wide with surprise.

"We already knew a lot of guys were disgusted with First Sergeant LaForge because of all his dirty dealings, but when he refused to allow some members of the unit go see you at the 95th, he really pissed guys off. So one morning--ba-boom! A grenade went off in his hooch. It was only a smoke grenade, but the message was clear. Next time it could be the real thing."

Shrugging his shoulders and lifting his palms, John mouthed, "Who?"

"Honestly, it could have been any number of guys," Tom speculated as he butt his cigarette in the ashtray on the table. "But that very day, LaForge was transferred out of there, and we never saw him again."

"Wow!" John exclaimed while catching the bartender's eye and gesturing for another round of beer.

"You would've liked Sergeant Baker—the First Sergeant who replaced LaForge," Tom declared. "He flew his share of missions, and the guys really respected him." Finishing the last swallow in his glass as the bartender came over to their table and set a full one in front of him, Tom divulged, "Baker called LaForge a pig. What a difference it could have made if we'd had him as our First Sergeant instead of LaForge."

John thought about Tom's statement for a moment. Maybe if he'd had a different First Sergeant, things would have been different for him. Maybe he wouldn't have gotten involved with Xuan, which might have prevented problems with Karen, and then maybe he'd still have a marriage. Oh well. It was all water over the dam now.

After finishing their beer, Tom directed John to another club with live music. The crowded room and decibel level at The Glass Onion made talking more difficult.

"You don't smoke anymore, do you?" Tom spoke loudly as he pulled out his pack of cigarettes and lit one.

"No," John conveyed.

"I remember you used to smoke two packs of unfiltered Lucky Strikes a day."

With laughter in his eyes, John held up his index finger and motioned for Tom to watch. He reached hold of Tom's lit cigarette and placed it up to the metal trach tube in his throat. After inhaling deeply, he slowly exhaled a long stream of smoke from his stoma."

"That's great!" Tom laughed. "Next you know, you'll be playing the saxophone."

They left The Glass Onion after only one beer, surprised to find it snowing. During the short time they had spent in the club, almost an inch of the white stuff had accumulated on the ground. With Tom's coaching, John managed to slowly maneuver the unplowed, winding roads along the 50-mile trip back to Tom's home.

"Food," John whispered as he used his right hand to pantomime eating when they arrived at Tom's hometown.

"Gee, it's almost 2 a.m.," Tom noted. "Nothing's open here at this hour, but there's a truck-stop in the next town where we could get a good omelet."

Perhaps because they were accustomed to flying perilous Dust-off missions, John and Tom thought nothing of driving another five miles on treacherous roads with big, heavy flakes continuing to fall. Four inches of snow already covered the ground and had slickened the pavement. As the road began a long descent into the Finger Lakes' valley where the next town was located, the VW bug slid on the snow and ice. John tried to negotiate a tight turn at the bottom of the hill, but the car skidded across the road over to the other lane and crashed into a metal guardrail. The guardrail prevented John and Tom from plummeting over a steep drop.

"Okay?" John gasped when the vehicle came to a stop.

"I'm okay, but I think your new car took a bad hit."

They stepped out and inspected the damages. The bumper and front end were badly crumpled and a headlight had been knocked out. Because it was still snowing hard, they climbed back into the car to discuss what to do. No more than five minutes passed before a police car pulled up behind them with its lights flashing. A New York State trooper came over to John's window and requested his license and registration.

"How did you come to crash your car?" the uniformed man inquired.

Noting John's inability to talk, the officer walked back to his patrol car. Tom bounded out of the VW and went over to the two troopers who were seated in their own vehicle. In a few minutes, Tom returned and handed John his license and registration.

"What...?" John wheezed in disbelief, certain he would be cited for the accident, especially as an out-of-state driver. In fact, he had been worrying about failing a sobriety test.

"I told them the truth," Tom explained. "That we were celebrating surviving the war, and that we were medics together, and you couldn't talk to the officer because you'd been wounded."

The following morning, John decided to cut his visit short and drive back to New Jersey before the roads became increasingly blanketed with snow. Right after breakfast, Tom and John exchanged heartfelt goodbyes, and John began the long drive back to his mother's home.

While the car made the journey without any problems, John was experiencing a post-crash depression. It was great to see Tom, and John was happy that he became officially engaged to his girlfriend, Gail. Yet, seeing the joy in others' lives only reminded him of the confusion and unhappiness in his own. Furthermore, the VW needed to go into a body shop for repairs, which meant John would once again be without transportation. Since he disliked having to rely on others, John refrained from taking his car to the shop and persisted in driving the damaged vehicle around town and to the Satellite Lounge. In March, after the police pulled him over for driving without a headlight, he finally relented and took the Volkswagen in to be repaired.

Stuck in his mother's living room again, it was nothing for John to polish off a six-pack of beer in one evening. He'd lost interest in going out with the guys or possibly meeting girls. John drank by himself, and he drank to get plastered. He used alcohol to forget about his troubles—and he had plenty of those. He drank to forget about his scarred throat and Karen's rejection. He drank to ease his aching loneliness. And he drank to rid himself of anger and soothe worries about his questionable future. Completely drunk, he could fall asleep and escape the nightmares that dragged him back to Vietnam.

Naturally, his mother had a lot to say about his drinking habits. It hadn't been much more than a week, but John was relieved when his car came out of the shop and gave him back his freedom.

Chapter 18

John opened his eyes and saw nothing but blue. Where was he? The steering wheel was in front of him, so he realized he was sitting in his VW. But how could there be nothing but blue sky in the windshield?

"Hey, buddy, are you all right?"

Dazed, John turned toward his left shoulder where he felt someone shaking his arm. It was a police officer. The uniformed man stood next to the open door of John's car.

"Are you injured?" the officer inquired.

John didn't respond. He was still trying to clear his head and make sense of the situation. Why was the front end of his VW beetle pointing toward the early morning sky? Looking down, John saw what must have been the contents of his stomach, now spewed onto his lap. Vomit covered the front of his slacks, as well as his fine new three-quarter-length suede coat.

Detecting that John was finally alert, the officer asked again, "Are you okay?"

John reached up and touched his aching forehead. When he lowered his hand, he saw blood on his fingers and palm.

"You weren't wearing your seatbelt," the police officer remarked. "Your face must have hit the windshield on impact. Do you have any recollection of how you might have managed to drive your vehicle into the middle of a farmer's field?"

Slowly shaking his head no, John wrenched his wallet from his back pocket and passed his driver's license and military I.D. to the officer's outstretched hand. As the man examined the papers, John tried to comprehend what happened. He knew he had just gotten his car back from the body shop and later that same evening had driven to the Satellite Lounge. But he couldn't remember finishing his last drink, probably around 2:30 a.m. when the place shut its doors. He couldn't recall saying goodbye to the bouncers or finding his car in the parking lot and driving away into the darkness. And he definitely couldn't remember veering off the road and onto the frozen soil of a farmer's field.

Soon, a couple of emergency aid workers appeared and removed John from his car, placing him onto a collapsible stretcher. As he was being carried toward the ambulance, John raised his throbbing head to look back at his car. The VW seemed to be impaled upon a tree stump. Goddamn! It seemed to be the only tree stump in the field, and he'd managed to hit it.

"We have one of your boys," the officer radioed Walson from his patrol car. "Do you want him brought there or to a civilian hospital?"

John was treated in the emergency room at Walson. The attending physician reported that John's nose wasn't broken, but it would take several days before the swelling and discoloration would fade.

"We've contacted your doctor, Major Bell," the physician further explained. "Because of your concussion, you're going to be readmitted to the hospital for observation."

Once admitted, John was taken up to the fifth floor and back to his same old room. It's like it was reserved for him. Throughout his six months in and out of Walson, he always stayed in the same room. He just spent a week in this room last month, having surgery on February 4th to revise his laryngotracheal fissure. As John entered the familiar room this morning—even more than other days—he was not happy to be there. He knew the fifth floor staff fairly well. They'd given him medical care and moral support. Today, he was disgraced to be a red-eyed, bruised, filthy, vomit-smelling patient of theirs.

Later in the morning, John was sitting on the edge of the bed in his hospital robe and slippers when Nurse Rodriguez entered his room. She stood at the foot of his bed and gave him a hard stare, slowly moving her head from side to side. John thought he would melt under her intense glare. After a long minute, she walked out of the room without saying a word. John felt a deep pang of shame for disappointing someone who cared about him.

He was standing beside the window, brooding, when another nurse entered his room and set a lunch tray on the bed stand. John went over and picked up the tray of food. He hesitated for a moment and then impulsively slammed it against the wall. A loud crash filled the room and echoed down the corridor. The nurse gaped at John with an open-mouthed, shocked expression on her face. Orderlies and nurses rushed into his room to see what the commotion was about. They spotted the food-splattered wall and then cast a sideways glance at John.

"Go!" John pointed and motioned for the staff to leave. "I want to be left alone!" he sputtered, frantically waving his arms to convey the anger that his strained, whispery voice could not.

The medical staff retreated toward the doorway, justifiably concerned about their own safety.

"I want to be left alone!" John continued raving, even though the room was now empty and his breathy words were inaudible. "None of you understand—I don't understand," he half sobbed. "Just leave me alone!" Seven months ago—back in Vietnam—he had been a god, helping to save lives. Now, he'd hit rock bottom and was spinning out of control.

Within minutes, Dr. Bell walked into the room. John was standing beside his bed, gazing at the mess he'd made on the wall and floor.

"Specialist Seebeth!"

John was jolted by the doctor's formality and tone of voice. Dr. Bell had never before addressed him by military rank or last name. Over the past half a year, John had never seen Jerry Bell get even mildly upset, but today, his stern expression left no doubt that the easy-going doctor was royally pissed off.

"Specialist Seebeth," Dr. Bell repeated as he stood at the foot of John's bed. "I'm working hard to try and restore your voice, but at the same time you seem hell-bent on trying to kill yourself. You better take a good look at yourself and figure out which it's going to be."

Doctor Bell paused momentarily to glimpse the food sliding down the wall and then turned and walked out of the room.

John crawled into his bed, wishing he could disappear under

the covers. Out of all the people in his life, he valued Dr. Bell the most. He knew Major Bell was committed to helping him heal, plus he also cared about John as a person. When John had confided his family problems, the doctor provided encouragement and support. He was a good man—a voice of sanity in John's mixed-up life— and John deeply respected him. But now, John had angered him. And he'd also let down someone else who wanted him to succeed— Nurse Rodriguez. Burrowing deeper under the covers, there was a lot to think about before sleeping off the rest of his drunk.

The next morning, John was told to report to Dr. Bell's office. Leaving his room extra early to be certain he was on time for his appointment, John shuffled along the hospital corridor. He thought about all the miles of hospital corridors he must have walked. From John's limited view, the hallways and rooms of the various hospitals blended together without distinction.

Following the Korean War, the Army Medical Department began an unprecedented decade of construction to provide care and comfort for the sick and wounded. DeWitt Army Hospital in Fort Belvoir, Virginia—where John was first admitted—was the second of nine planned hospitals to be completed during that building program. DeWitt was dedicated in 1957, and Walson opened its doors in 1960. Under Army policy, all new hospitals were to be named in commemoration of personnel who made noteworthy contributions to the Medical Department. Thus, the hospitals were named in honor of Brigadier General Wallace DeWitt and in memory of Brigadier General Charles Moore Walson. Although the facilities were examples of innovative hospital designs of that time, to John, the rooms and corridors were all alike because they were filled with the same array of wounded soldiers.

As he walked down the hallway, something caught John's eye and made him stop. Peeking into the open door of a patient's room, John saw a man rotated upside down in a traction apparatus. The sight reminded John of the extensive care some returning soldiers required. It also made him realize that even though he wasn't restricted by such specialized equipment he, too, needed extensive care. It humbled him to see the patient's situation. At least John could walk down the corridor.

Punctual for his appointment, John started out by apologizing to Dr. Bell.

"I understand your frustration," Dr. Bell responded. "I know it's been difficult to not have a voice for seven months, but this is a slow procedure."

They talked for quite a while, and John was relieved to know Dr. Bell was still with him.

"John, what do you want to do with your life?"

"Be a Pennsylvania State Trooper," John communicated by mouthing words and writing notes.

"Well, why don't you take some police science classes at a community college? You'll have a start on a law enforcement degree by the time your throat is healed."

"College?" John scoffed, shaking his head. "Just made it out of high school. First in family to graduate from high school, let alone college."

"Well, college can be different," Dr. Bell urged. "You're a smart guy. I bet you'd get a lot out of going to college."

It would take a while for that idea to sprout, but Dr. Bell planted a seed in John's mind.

"My mother's husband works at Toms River Industries. They're hiring. I could get a job there," John wrote.

"I don't think that working in a machine shop with metal filings in the air is the right job for you," Dr. Bell countered after getting the gist of John's message. "There'd be chemical vapors in the air—no, that wouldn't be an appropriate environment for you."

Despite Dr. Bell's objections, John did take a job at Toms River Industries. It got him out of his mother's house and in the company of others. At first, John had been worried about how his visible stigma would be received by his fellow workers. The men may have been a rogue's gallery of social deviants and misfits, but they had no problem accepting John. They called him "Cricket", because in order to get their attention, John would make a clicking sound with his tongue against the roof of his mouth. Despite the racist and sexist attitudes in the work place, John enjoyed the joking and laughter. It filled a void in his life. He missed the camaraderie he had known during his military experiences.

John never returned to the Satellite Lounge. Instead, he climbed out of that destructive pattern by filling his life with greater purpose. Through his brother, he made the acquaintance of a woman who was setting up a Crisis Hotline. Toll free numbers providing emergency support had been available in Britain since the 1950s but were just becoming established in the US. The middle-aged woman arranging the local hotline was a nurse. She found a realtor willing to donate space in the basement of his office building in the village of Toms River, about nine miles north of Lanoka Harbor. Soon, a group of committed young volunteers staffed the phone lines of the new Crisis Hotline 24-hours a day. Whether consoling and advising a rape victim or talking someone down from a bad drug trip, the volunteers took their responsibilities to heart. Of course, John couldn't speak over the phone, but he helped in the office and offered support to his new friends. When one of those friends told him about the availability of a small apartment in Toms River, John jumped at the opportunity to rent it for $85 a month. He'd just had a huge fight with his mother and—for his own sanity—he needed to get out from under her roof.

The argument was about a headband.

"What do you think the neighbors think when they see you dressed like that?" his mother repeatedly questioned. "They think this house is some kind of a hippie-den the way you wear those bell-bottoms and tie-dyed shirts and that headband."

"I'm not a hippie. I'm just wearing the latest styles."

Clothing had always been important to John, and by 1970, the hippie look had been integrated into mainstream society. Mustaches, beards, and longer hair became commonplace, and colorful multi-ethnic clothing dominated the fashion world.

"Are you trying to make some political statement or something?" his mother harped. "Because a headband doesn't look good on your big, round head. It looks dumb on you. And you could use a haircut."

"I'm not making a political statement!" John asserted with whispery words, which his mother was adept in understanding and readily disputed. "Everyone wears headbands. Look, I just spent nine months in combat, and if I feel like wearing a goddamn headband, I'm going to wear one."

"Not in my house, you aren't! It looks ridiculous, and I won't have it!"

John wanted to remind his mother that he didn't value her opinions. It scars a boy to wake up and find his mother entertaining a man while her husband was off at work. John would never forget how she beat him with a hairbrush that night because he insisted on knowing who the strange man was. And it scars a boy to come home from school and find his mother had attempted suicide in his very own bed. How could he ever forget his fear that day when the police came to the house and his mother was taken away in an ambulance? John had too many childhood scars to respect his mother's opinion about how he should be living his life.

The attic apartment in Toms River became vacant at the exact time John needed it, and his new friends from the Crisis Hotline had helped him make the connection. Though the apartment was small and a bit rundown, John moved in at the end of April, glad to have his own place on the pleasant tree-lined street. He was doubly happy to be away from his mother's constant criticism.

Working at Toms River Industries gave John confidence that he was still socially acceptable. He also took pride in mastering the noisy machinery—the drill press, lathe, and millers. However, similar to his experience working in the bread factory, John soon became bored with drilling precision holes in pieces of metal. He couldn't forget that he was a trained medic who had provided critical care to the wounded. When some old friends from Bensalem High School phoned and asked if he would be interested in splitting the cost of renting a cottage in Wildwood, New Jersey for the summer, John eagerly accepted the offer. The opportunity allowed him to finally heed Dr. Bell's weekly outpatient advice and quit his job at Toms River Industries. John didn't know anything about Wildwood when he first made the hour-and-a-half drive south on the Garden State Parkway in June. But something told him he was ready for 1970's Summer of Love.

Located along the southern end of New Jersey's coast, John's friends informed him that Wildwood was the place to be. Thousands of young people from Philadelphia, Trenton, and New York City converged in the seasonal resort town. The first thing John observed at Wildwood was the metamorphosis the girls had undergone. When he left for Vietnam, they resembled Doris Day. Now, wearing hot pants and no bras, young women looked more like Cher. And in the carefree surroundings of Wildwood, John looked a lot like Sonny.

One afternoon in August, John stepped back to peer into the small mirror hanging on the wall of his bedroom. The guys would soon be meeting up with some girls they knew from high school who were renting a nearby cottage, and John wondered if the wide-brimmed brown leather floppy hat on his head was too much. He stood there in a pair of faded jeans that were thoroughly frayed along the bell-bottoms. Shirtless, he wore a suede vest with fringed strips of leather hanging down to his knees. He'd gained a little weight, so his wiry body appeared stronger. His sun-tanned face had a healthy glow, and his blond hair twisted into curls just below his ears. John smiled at the image reflected back at him. A year ago, he couldn't stand to look in a mirror. Today, he knew he must be doing better, because he was more concerned about the appearance of his hat rather than the hole in his neck.

For John, it was an incredibly moving experience to be around so many young people who were radiating good vibes of peace and love. It was the opposite of what he had known on the other side of the planet in a place called Vietnam. A couple of guys at their cottage had just returned from Nam, having served as Marines. In high school, John hadn't been part of their popular crowd, but at Wildwood, the ex-Marines understood the role of Dustoff and viewed John with respectful eyes. He was buoyed by their admiration.

All summer long, at all hours of the day or night, John could walk between the rows of cottages and hear 8-track players blaring sounds of Led Zeppelin, The Beatles, and Grand Funk Railroad. Music—always important to John—constantly filled the salty air at Wildwood. Their cottage was only a block from the 5-mile sandy beach where people perpetually gathered. Despite the crowds of young people embracing a rebellious spirit, John never saw any fights break out. There were no arguments about politics or world events. The "now generation" focused on having fun, making the atmosphere at Wildwood feel like one harmonious community. John and his roommates, along with their female companions, strolled along the long boardwalk and ate funnel cakes, saltwater taffy, pork roll sandwiches, and French fries with a toothpick. John laughed more than he had laughed in a year, especially after being introduced to the friendly culture of marijuana.

The summer at Wildwood was a great turnaround for John. He learned that his physical stigma didn't prevent cute girls from flirting with him and finding him attractive. When the summer ended, John had a steady girlfriend and more self-confidence. He still didn't have a voice, but he would be readmitted to Walson next month—on September 9th—for another procedure to bring him closer to that goal.

Despite outer changes, inwardly, John always carried the memories of his brothers-in-arms. He thought about the guys he had served with and wondered where they were and how they were doing. And at least twice a day, when he removed and cleaned the metal trach tube in his neck, the memories of the many wounded he had treated became alive to his five senses. A lot had happened since being shot a year ago. He had a way to go before his throat was healed, but the Summer of Love played an important part in shining a brighter light on John's future.

Chapter 19

John fired up the engine of his 1970 orange Firebird and steered toward a new experience in his life. He'd traded his twice-crashed VW Beetle for the Firebird at the end of last summer—the Summer of Love. When summer was over, John continued driving to Wildwood throughout the winter, because that's where his steady girlfriend lived. The Firebird gave him a better ride and an outstanding sound system during the three-hour roundtrip. Today, on this sunny September morning of 1971, John inserted Santana's *Abraxas* album into the 8-track player, forwarded to the song "Black Magic Woman", and cranked up the volume. He was a little apprehensive as he headed for the student parking lot at Ocean County College.

It was hard to believe that two years had passed since being wounded in Vietnam. He'd gone through quite a metamorphosis since then. For one thing, he'd gotten his voice back—well, sort of. The raspy sound hardly resembled his former voice, but his speech was now audible with better phonation. John remembered when Dr. Bell had given him the early Christmas present nine months ago. The final revision of his laryngeotracheal trough seemed no different than the other fourteen procedures John had already undergone. Lying on the operating table, John was medicated but conscious as Dr. Bell and the medical team performed the surgery.

"Okay, John. Can you try and say something?" Dr. Bell requested.

After sixteen months without a voice, John wasn't sure what his first word should be. He had been waiting for the moment for so long, and now he wondered what to say.

"Bell," John weakly stated. He figured the good doctor deserved to be his first word.

"Again."

"Dr. Bell," John repeated with more courage and determination. Startled by the alien sound coming from his mouth, he said once more, "Dr. Bell."

Beneath his surgical mask, Dr. Bell smiled.

The next day, following the surgery, John went to Dr. Bell's office to discuss the cutting-edge procedure that had given him a voice.

"John, we've come a long way, but there is still more to do before you can breathe and speak normally," Dr. Bell confided. "I plan on eventually completely closing your neck wound, but in the meantime, you'll have to use a Montgomery T-tube to help you speak. One of my professors developed the device about five years ago to support the trachea following laryngotracheoplasty. The T-tube will maintain your tracheal airway and serve as a stent."

It took some coordination for John to master speaking with a Montgomery T-tube. As its name suggested, the silicone rubber tube was shaped like the letter T. The top crossbar inserted vertically into the open and scarred portion of John's tracheostomy stoma, and the stem of the tube projected a couple of inches beyond his wounded neck, held in place by a 5-inch strip of 1-inch wide paper surgical tape. By covering the end of the tube with his finger and forcing air up and out his mouth, John could speak. Because he also had to breathe through the tube, John learned how to release the opening, take a breath, and then quickly reseal the hole with his finger in order to have fluent speech. In addition, he had to practice removing, cleaning, lubricating, and reinserting the tube. Copious amounts of Vaseline were needed to prevent the tube from adhering to his newly built trachea, which had been constructed earlier from a 4x2 inch patch of skin from his thigh.

During his first week of speaking, John couldn't believe that the strange, scratchy-sounding voice belonged to him. It didn't have a familiar ring to it at all. He was relieved when Dr. Bell assured him that more procedures would eliminate the need for the tube.

"Once we get things working, a plastic surgeon will repair your neck so no one will know you had an extensive throat injury."

After being in a medical holding company for a year and four months beyond his 3-year enlistment, in May of 1971 John was placed on the Army's Temporary Disability Retired List as Specialist 5, pay rank E-5. That's when Dr. Bell brought up the idea of college again, informing John that his 100% disability rating would entitle him to educational benefits under the GI bill. This time, John investigated the idea. Discovering there was a community college based right in Toms River, he signed up to take the entrance exam, passed it, and would enroll as a full-time student at Ocean County College in the coming fall. And now fall had arrived, and he was behind the wheel of his Firebird on his way to register for classes.

John had been living in his attic apartment for over a year. Originally, New Jersey had felt like unfamiliar territory, but John had grown comfortable with his surroundings in Toms River. In the spring, he took up jogging and got to know the community more intimately as a pedestrian. It was convenient to go down the hall steps and out the door of his apartment, round the corner to Main Street, and run along the sidewalk of the small village. He passed a variety of shops and offices that flourished in the summer but nearly shut down during winter months. Toms River was located near the highway leading to the Barnegat Peninsula and resort town of Seaside Heights, so the population, traffic, and commerce fluctuated seasonally.

When John first began running, his body was out of shape, and he could scarcely run a mile. His lungs ached as he struggled to take in air through his Montgomery T-tube. One day, out of breath, John stopped in the driveway beside the Toms River Bank. Bent over with hands on hips, he gasped for air, discouraged by his weakness. Huffing and puffing, tears filled his eyes while he stared at the windowless red brick wall of the bank. Just as he was beginning to feel good and sorry for himself, the haunting memories of ever so many wounded soldiers filled his mind. They reminded him not to focus on what he didn't have. How many of those young men didn't even get to come home? Immediately, John was washed over by a feeling of gratitude. He had his eyes. He had his arms and his legs. At that very moment, standing in the driveway of the Toms River Bank, John vowed that he was going to make the most of his life. He was going to do his best to live a worthy life on behalf of those who didn't get the chance.

John continued to provide service through his work at the Crisis Hotline, where he regularly volunteered each week. Now that he had an audible voice, he could help answer the phone lines. And John proved to be a natural counselor.

"Do you hear my unusual-sounding voice?" John would ask someone considering suicide. "Let me explain why my voice is so harsh." From there, the conversations centered on reasons to live—even with something like a physical stigma and strange voice.

As John made more friends through the Crisis Hotline and elsewhere, he became more anchored in his new and different life. Once in awhile, he would drive the ten miles down to Lanoka Harbor to visit his family, but inevitably, he and his mother would get into a shouting match about something. Even less frequently—generally after making the trip to Philadelphia to see old friends—John would stop by and see his dad. Since marrying Anna May his father seemed softer and easier to be around. There were still some old childhood scars between them, but John respected his father's honesty. In fact, his dad had taken the initiative to file papers and dissolve John and Karen's marriage. Although John and his dad didn't argue, his father and Anna May's home never would have endured the raucous beer-drinking lifestyle commonplace at his mother and Eduardo's. And at this point in time, John remained part of the drinking and partying crowd, though never to the extent that he crashed another car.

While waiting for the traffic signal on this bright September morning, John ejected the Santana tape after listening to "Black Magic Woman" two times. He inserted Three Dog Night's *Naturally* into the 8-track player and stepped on the gas of his Firebird when the light changed. Soon he would be registering for classes at OCC—Ocean County College. He was excited about attending college, yet thoughts of Miss Crutcher and high school English made him uneasy about handling the work. Reaching over and forwarding the tape, he stopped when "Joy To The World" began. He would have enthusiastically added his voice to the chorus, however singing along with favorite songs was something he could no longer do. Still, John silently mouthed the words, "Jeremiah was a bullfrog." The song generated a smile, because he heard it often during his trip to Europe this summer when he had a joyful time traveling to new parts of the world.

A friend of a friend from the Crisis Hotline had invited John to join him in hitchhiking around Europe for a couple months. At first John refused, but when he and his steady girlfriend from Wildwood called it quits in June, a trip to Europe seemed to be just what the doctor would order. For one thing, John was still adapting to his alien voice. Really, he hated the sound of it, and lately, Dr. Bell wasn't offering much hope for improvement. John hadn't had a surgery in over six months. The last one had given him a voice—along with a Montgomery T-tube. As John discovered, living with the T-tube proved to be a major adjustment. Invariably, the petroleum jelly would disintegrate, and the tube, though beveled, would adhere to his thin scar tissue. Dislodging the tube drew blood, causing further irritation and soreness to his already sensitive neck. Appearance-wise, the silicone tube was hardly subtle. The longest limb of the T stuck out from his red-scarred wound like Pinocchio's nose. So a trip to Europe offered him the anonymity of being a foreigner in foreign lands. No one would have a preconceived notion of how he should look or sound. As much as exploring the world, John would be free to explore himself and establish a new identity as a person with an odd tube and a peculiar voice.

John and his traveling companion, Chuck, were making the trip on limited budgets. The currency exchange rate favored American travelers, allowing an onslaught of young people to travel throughout Europe with relatively little money. Discounted airfare packages often included U-Rail passes that provided unlimited access to trains that crisscrossed the region. Since John had made his decision to go to Europe at the last minute, he couldn't get a seat on the same flight as Chuck. He had to meet him in Amsterdam a day later. Meanwhile, Chuck had made the acquaintance of two California college girls whose parents were paying for their trip, including their rented bright-yellow VW Beetle.

"Ellie and Marilyn have invited us to travel with them," Chuck announced in the men's quarters of the Amsterdam hostel where he and John were spending the night.

"Really?" John responded, silently wondering if Chuck might have an ulterior motive. Having met the girls yesterday, John thought they were nice, but he'd been looking forward to meeting Europeans. He didn't travel abroad just to hang out with American girls.

"Yeah, they have a whole trip planned, and they're going to Munich first," Chuck elaborated. "Personally, I think it's a great idea! We're on a tight budget, so riding with them would help us out."

John wasn't as enthusiastic, but he liked the idea of seeing Germany again, and he'd never been to Munich. In the morning, John squeezed his large-frame backpack and then his body into the backseat of the VW bug, and the foursome began their journey. Within a day, Chuck was sleeping with Ellie.

Even from the small window of the VW, John was thrilled to view the beautiful German countryside while cruising south along the Autobahn. The scenery brought back pleasant memories of Karen and her family, as well as the realization that a lot had sure happened in the three years since being stationed at Baumholder. After staying at a youth hostel in Munich, the travelers drove ten miles northwest to Dachau. Ellie and Marilyn were Jewish and wanted to visit what was deemed the first Nazi concentration camp.

John probably wouldn't have chosen that destination, but afterward, he was thankful he had gone. He would never forget the sight of scratch marks on the concrete walls inside a gas chamber. Standing in the same space where panicked people had desperately tried to claw their way out with bare fingers, John's body reacted viscerally. His mind's eye could see the horror-stricken faces of the civilians trapped here. He had felt and seen the same fear—etched countless times over—on faces of Vietnamese civilians.

From Munich, the foursome meandered to Heidelberg, staying at campsites and stopping to visit some fascinating castles along the way. They planned to spend two nights in a student dormitory at the University of Heidelberg. Following the first night, John pulled Chuck aside to talk about their plans. John enjoyed visiting Heidelberg Castle the day before and had benefited from all their sightseeing excursions. However, after a week of being cramped in the backseat of a VW bug, he was ready to try something else. He'd had a good time, and now that he was feeling more comfortable interacting with people, he wanted to set his own itinerary. Chuck and John concluded it would be best to go their separate ways. In the morning, Chuck would continue traveling with Ellie and Marilyn, and John would strike out on his own.

On his last afternoon in Heidelberg, John strolled around the campus, awed by the oldest university in Germany. He walked a little taller thinking that he, too, would be a student of higher education when he attended college in September. Of course, Ocean County College was only 6 years old, whereas the University of Heidelberg dated back to 1386. Boasting a long tradition of introducing new ideas to humanity, the University's association with the likes of Martin Luther made lasting impacts on the intellectual climate of the day. John imagined the rousing battles of ideas that must have taken place in this location over the centuries. As he walked the grounds, which were almost empty since the majority of students were on summer break, he stopped after spotting something that felt like a punch to his gut. He reread the words spray-painted on a wall: "Yankee Imperialist Go Home!" and "Long Live Uncle Ho!" Later that evening, the impact of the graffiti resurfaced when John found himself embroiled in his own rousing battle of ideas at the University of Heidelberg.

"Would you care to join us please at our table?" a bespectacled young man asked in heavily accented English. He pointed to a round wooden table where five other young men were seated.

John had gone to the rathskeller, situated in the bottom floor of the dormitory, for some tasty German brew. He had just finished his first beer when the fellow approached. Being eager to meet Europeans, John carried his mug over to where the group sat around a solidly built table. After introductions, John learned the men were university students taking summer classes. Most were

German, but one was Swedish and another Danish. The bespectacled student refilled John's mug from one of the pitchers on the table.

"We are engaged in conversation about *The Pentagon Papers*," a German student called Kurt announced in precise English. "As an American, may we hear your thoughts?"

"I...." John shook his head. "I heard it on the news before I left, but really, I don't know nothing about them."

"*The New York Times* published the reports in June," Kurt further informed.

"But the Nixon administration attempted to repress their publication," another student interrupted.

Facing that student, Kurt related, "Yes, but the US Supreme Court upheld the right of *The New York Times* to make them public." To John, Kurt explained, "The papers reveal the deceptions and cover-ups used by your government to keep its citizens ignorant and misinformed about Vietnam."

"Well, I don't know about that, but I've been in Vietnam, so I think I know something about the subject," John defended, grasping his mug tightly. The students asked questions and listened respectfully as John described the job he had performed and how he had been wounded.

When John finished talking, he was surprised when a student named Norbert bluntly criticized the entire US involvement in Vietnam. "No offence to you, but greatly because you witnessed much blood and horror and you, yourself, obtained such a wound, do you not question the justification of your country's business in Southeast Asia?"

"Of course the war is right and justified," John claimed. "There's a lot of brave American men over there fighting Communism."

"In reality, what is Communism?" Norbert continued. "It is merely an economic and social system. What kind of enemy is that?"

"Well, we're fighting Communism by defending democracy," John insisted. "We're trying to give the people a chance to live free in a democracy."

"The motives of the soldiers are different than the motives of your political leaders," the Danish student commented. "Your government appears more interested to promote capitalism than to defend democracy. For years, you backed the South Vietnamese rule of Diem—essentially a Catholic monarchy, and a cruel one at that. Currently, President Thieu is no more than your puppet."

John gulped his beer. He was frustrated at not being able to reply, but he knew nothing about the South Vietnamese government, and he felt intimidated by how much these students did.

"Yes," a red-haired fellow named Roth chimed in, "The US capitalists vastly profits from this war, for instance, rubber for the automobile industries. *The Pentagon Papers* report of US quests for tin, rubber, and oil. And I read about your former president's wife—the Ladybird—her family business of Sea-Land received the contract for shipping CONEX containers to Vietnam."

"Well, the rest of the world should be glad that America stands up to protect innocent people that can't protect themselves," John charged.

"What about all the innocent Vietnamese citizens who have been killed and maimed by US bombs?" Norbert pressed.

"If we don't fight the Reds in Vietnam, they'd come to our back-yards and rape our mothers and sisters," John argued, fiercely ges-turing with his left arm while his right hand busily controlled the rapid flow of air to his Montgomery T-tube. "It's better to fight the war on their land instead of bringing it back home."

"Many students in your own country are in disagreement, and they protest against the war," Kurt mentioned. "Surely, you must find it appalling to have your National Guard kill four unarmed stu-dents at the Kent Ohio University in May."

"Those longhairs are problems," John objected. He had no toler-ance for antiwar demonstrators. It infuriated him that guys were risk-ing their lives for a cause not fully supported by the whole nation. John expressed the opinion of six out of seven Americans when he stated, "Those students were more to blame than the National guardsmen. Good men are dying in Vietnam because of those pro-tests. The problem with the war is how it's being conducted, and the hippie-dippie longhairs and spineless politicians are fucking it up."

"Certainly as a democracy," Kurt countered, "the students have the right to question the policies of their government."

"Well, I thought the rest of the world stood with us fighting the bad guys," John challenged. "I was surprised to see anti-American messages on your campus—like "Long Live Uncle Ho!". You have no idea how much suffering that motherfucker caused. I was there and I saw it firsthand." John's irritation was building. His face was flushed with anger as he accused, "I think you Germans, you know, you had Hitler, so I think you should fucking know about why we need to fight the bad guys and stand up for what's right."

"Ho Chi Minh was hardly Hitler," Norbert contradicted. "He

organized the Vietnamese people to gain liberty from the French, exactly like the US did with the British. Uncle Ho is more like the George Washington of his country."

"The North Vietnamese are not enemies to the world," Kurt elucidated. "Do you see the man seated over there?" He pointed to a black-haired man engaged in conversation at another table. "He is a student here, and he is North Vietnamese."

John recognized the familiar hair and body stature. The last time he'd seen a North Vietnamese man the guy's stomach was ripped open and John was helping to deliver him to interrogators. At this moment, John couldn't believe that he was sitting and drinking beer in the same room as his enemy. In fact, it was unthinkable that the enemy was allowed to go to school here. John stood up.

"You know," he muttered, "you need to figure out who the fuck the real threat is. I've fucking been there, and I've seen it with my own eyes."

John excused himself and went up to his dorm room. He remained hot under the collar as he repacked his belongings in preparation for his solo departure in the morning. The conversation in the pub disturbed him. John strongly disagreed with the students' position, but he felt stupid because he was unable to express his opinions with anything other than jingoisms. Closing his backpack, John looked out the window of his room at the University of Heidelberg and made another vow. He promised that when he went to OCC in the fall, he would use college to learn more about the war, so he would be able to argue his position better.

Thoughts of that conversation would replay in John's head during the remainder of his time in Europe—and long after that. His thumb took him through Germany, and he took trains through Austria and Switzerland, often hitchhiking there as well. In the auto-free, mountain village of Zermatt, he hooked up with a half-dozen college students from all over—including a couple of Americans. The young men and women were traveling separately, but all had landed at the base of the Matterhorn, where the group hung out and socialized together for an incredible week. There were no political arguments or romances amongst the group. They were there to hike and appreciate the extraordinary surroundings of the deep valley enclosed between steep mountains—nine of the ten highest peaks in Europe. With no automobiles, the silence allowed them to enjoy the fresh Alpine air and glimpse the huge, gracefully curving pyramid of the Matterhorn. One morning, in a restaurant along one of the cobbled paths of the town, John's friends introduced him to granola and yogurt. From Zermatt, he took a train to Paris, where he stayed in an exceptional hostel before eventually flying back to the States. He was ready to return home and eager to start college.

John switched off the music of Three Dog Night after turning his Firebird onto the campus drive of Ocean County College. He easily found a spot in the student parking lot. Opening the door, he stepped out of his car. His feet followed the flow of people toward the Student Activity Center, where registration for classes was taking place. John might not be taking these steps if he hadn't made the trip to Europe. His many experiences and interactions strengthened him and helped him accept his raspy voice. And after thinking about it, he figured that's the way his voice should be. The significance wasn't how it sounded, but what it stood for—a thousand souls whispering in unison, encouraging John to look for answers. He started 1971 with a new voice, and this September day, John entered the doors of Ocean County College determined to understand more about himself and the world around him.

Chapter 20

John hadn't been a student at Ocean County College a week before he bumped into a problem.

"How can I help you?" the Dean of Students inquired, motioning for John to take a seat in his office.

"It's ridiculous for me to take this *Community First Aid and Safety* class," John emphatically sputtered as he worked his T-tube with one hand and passed his course schedule across the desk to Dean Flynn with the other. "Why should I waste my time going to that class? I mean, it's insulting to me."

"All right, let's see now," Dean Flynn clarified while examining John's schedule. "We're talking about *HEPE 160, Community First Aid and Safety*. That is a required 3-credit class in the Criminal Justice program, and I see that you're majoring in Law Enforcement/ Police Science."

"I was a trained medic in Vietnam. I don't need to take a basic first aid class."

The Dean opened the course catalog and read aloud, "*A course designed to prepare the student in basic first aid care to the sick or injured. Classroom drills and practice will prepare the student to react properly in accident situations, plan his/her actions, and exercise good judgment in adapting his/her classroom training to the accident scene.* Hmm." Glancing up at John, Dean Flynn concluded, "This class would serve students just out of high school, but with your experience—you could probably teach it."

"If I have to sit through a class like that," John challenged, "there's no point in me going to college. And I've talked to some other vets, and they don't think it's right to have to take a basic physical education class when they just got back from humping the boonies in Vietnam."

"Well, what you say is valid," Dean Flynn concurred. "This year, we have more veterans than ever before on campus, and others may have similar complaints. John, here's my suggestion to you. Let's talk to Mr. L—he's in charge of the Activity Center—and make arrangements to reserve a room. You can post notices around campus announcing the designated time and place for veterans to meet, and we'll take it from there."

The following week, John was surprised when about sixty vets overflowed the reserved meeting space to standing room only. For John, it was a milestone to speak in front of such a large crowd with his new voice. He'd already met some of the guys, because it was fairly easy for him to pick out vets in the cafeteria. They weren't necessarily much older than other students, but they looked it. A thousand-yard stare on a somber face that had seen it all made some vets unmistakable. Being military, the veterans readily organized into a group and established a chain of command. John was elected President of the newly formed Veteran's Club at Ocean County College.

The Veteran's Club became an important presence on campus, and John enthusiastically accepted his leadership role. The Club's first order of business was to petition the college to credit military training in place of comparable basic courses. It was a respect thing for the vets, and many of them—including John—probably would have quit school if they had to sit through elementary classes without having their experiences acknowledged. Fortunately, the local focus of community colleges facilitated swift responses to diverse student needs. While other campuses might take academic years to enact policy changes, flexible community colleges could respond within days and weeks. Ocean County College soon used DD-214 forms—the veterans' official discharge papers listing their specialization and training—as a basis to transfer appropriate credits in exchange for certain courses. John's medical work was recognized, and he was exempted from taking *Community First Aid and Safety*.

Within the first few months of being formed, the Veteran's Club initiated a blood drive for a local boy with hemophilia. They organized a bike-a-thon to assist nearby flood victims, as well as establishing an annual campus ceremony to honor fallen veterans. Also, they sponsored a community-wide Toys for Tots collection and a POW campaign. Ongoing beneficial functions earned the club a respected reputation, and by association, veterans walked on campus with self-worth and dignity. The men demonstrated by example that they were helping and not destroying; they were rebuilding instead of burning; and they were planting seeds of good will.

As well as being an instrument of change and service, the Vet's Club provided valuable support for its members, because veterans were often unable to relate to other students. In addition to a record number of veterans on campus, college enrollment in general had soared in recent years. Ocean County College was one of over 450 junior or community colleges established in the 1960s to offer an alternative to four-year institutions. Responding to society's desire for a better-educated citizenry, public community colleges provided higher education opportunities at little or no cost. Thus, many high school graduates who might not have considered going to college were registering at local community colleges, including young men seeking student deferments to escape the draft. Vets rarely related to those students but found instant camaraderie with others who had served in Vietnam.

"I don't trust a soul," a veteran named Frankie confided to John over beers one night.

The two had left OCC late that afternoon and driven north to a neighboring town where a pleasant restaurant's bar had become a favorite watering hole for some members of the Veteran's Club. On any given Friday or Saturday evening, half the club's membership congregated in Brick Town at the Ship's Wheel Inn. As friendships grew, war stories were shared, and the club became their medicine for healing, helping many men transition back into society more easily. John and Frankie were drinking and talking at one end of the bar while waiting for others to arrive.

"So, why don't you trust anyone?" John wanted to know.

"We'd be sent out to do recon in teams of two to eight guys, and we counted on our partner to keep watch, ya know? One guy would sleep—or try to—while the other guy kept watch."

"Where were you at?"

"The rubber plantation area of the central plains, south of where you were at. Yeah, we'd sit back to back, huddled in our ponchos at night, trying to protect ourselves from the flies and mosquitoes that were always bothering us. We couldn't use insect spray 'cause the VC could smell it. And those fuck-you lizards about drove you mad. You'd hear them go 'fuck you, fuck you' over and over like everything around you hated your guts. I'd see huge pythons hanging from trees—and there were small poisonous snakes and poisonous spiders—there was a lot of crazy shit out there. Believe me, there was a lot of shit in the jungle that could kill us besides Charlie."

Frankie paused to take a swallow of beer before continuing. "One night, the guy I was leaning against was supposed to be on watch, but he fell asleep. A big explosion woke me up. The VC had tripped a claymore we'd setup on the path earlier, and they were almost on top of us. Holy fuck, I didn't know what was happening. I start firing away. My M-16 got so hot the barrel turned red. My partner took a hit to his leg and had to be dusted-off. So, fuck, when you have to trust somebody with your life like that, well, now I don't trust nobody."

"When did you get out of Vietnam?" John asked.

"Almost two months ago. One day you're trying to stay alive, the next day you're on the streets back in the States."

"How's it been for you?"

"Let's just say that my welcome home party didn't go so good. This jerk—a friend of my sister and a draft-dodging, longhaired asshole—started making some comments about the war." Frankie stopped and lit a cigarette. "I lost it, man. I didn't think about it, I just picked up one end of the dining room table and flipped the fucking thing over. I was about to punch the guy's lights out, but my sister screamed, and my mother started crying. I looked at the broken dishes and food on the floor, and, fuck, I got out of there in a hurry. I went to a bar and got hammered."

"Yeah, man. I hear you, bro," John consoled, remembering when he'd thrown his lunch tray against the wall in the hospital.

"I don't want to listen to that antiwar shit," Frankie asserted. "There's no way that I'm going to believe the US is the cause of all the destruction we saw, ya know what I'm saying? No one in their wildest dreams could ever say that we were responsible for all the shit we've seen."

"Fucking-A, man." John lifted his bottle of beer in salute. "We're the fucking good guys."

Although the Veteran's Club declared itself to be nonpolitical, a large majority of members agreed with John and Frankie. They had little tolerance for antiwar demonstrations that claimed the war was wrong. That would mean their brothers had died in vain, and they weren't about to accept that. Most club members wanted a solution that made them feel their blood, sweat, and tears had been worthwhile, and so they staunchly supported President Nixon's efforts to obtain peace with honor. Yet, some veterans were disgruntled by the government and just wanted the troops home and the war to end. Thus, the club refrained from voicing an official opinion. One time, however, John overstepped the club's neutral political policy and angered some Veteran's Club members.

In January 1972, two members of Vietnam Veterans Against the War (VVAW) had been invited to speak on campus. John hadn't followed the activities of VVAW since its establishment in 1967, but last month their organization made headline news when fifteen activists barricaded and occupied the Statue of Liberty for two days in an attempt to bring attention to the antiwar cause. Simultaneous protests took place across the country, including Valley Forge and the historic Betsy Ross house in Philadelphia. To John and most members of the Veteran's Club, those acts were an unforgivable betrayal that brought disgrace to the troops. They were displeased that VVAW would be allowed on campus, so they arranged to present their own protest at the evening's meeting.

Before speaking, the VVAW representatives showed a film by noted war correspondent David Schoenberg. The film outlined the history of the Vietnamese struggle for independence with special attention to how and why the US became involved.

When the film ended, a VVAW spokesman stepped up to the podium of the lecture hall and addressed the audience. "The American people's awareness about the war is on the decline because of the recent troop withdrawals. Few people are aware that the bombings of the North are heavier now than they have ever been."

As planned, Vincent, a member of the Veteran's Club, stood up and interrupted the VVAW speaker. He read a prepared statement that John had a heavy hand in writing.

"We feel your goal in striving for an immediate withdrawal in Vietnam is detrimental to every life that was ever lost there and evidently no consideration has been given to the mass slaughter of US troops which would occur in a nonstrategically oriented withdrawal," Vincent read. "We feel that the recent actions taken by your organization at the Statue of Liberty and elsewhere were tantamount to the very aggressive force you seek to stop in Vietnam. The mere fact that you physically and illegally assumed control of a national shrine can be described as nothing short of militancy and an act of aggression."

The lecture hall was silent as Vincent concluded, "Therefore, we cannot support your organization or their methods, and we resent the fact that a false connotation has been created between your organization and all veterans in America."

When Vincent finished—as rehearsed—the couple dozen members of OCC's Veteran's Club stood up and walked out of the room. Since only three people remained in the audience, the meeting adjourned. John and the participating club members were pleased with the outcome. Other Veteran's Club members were not.

"We're supposed to be nonpolitical, but you made a political statement on behalf of the club," an angry member accused at their weekly meeting. "We never had a general membership vote to approve what you did."

To keep peace in the club, the next week John submitted a letter to the *Viking News*, OCC's campus newspaper. His carefully worded message stated that the Veteran's Club remained a nonpolitical organization and reading the statement at the Vietnam Veterans Against the War meeting was inconsistent with club policy. However, he made it clear that his letter was not to be construed as an apology, merely an explanation of circumstances.

Throughout his time at OCC, John maintained his same beliefs. He was even given time behind the microphone to expound his views at antiwar demonstrations on campus but made certain to clarify that he was not speaking on behalf of the Veteran's Club. John was usually the lone voice in support of the President and US policies, yet he gained respect for his willingness to come forward.

Personally, the war was a subject best not talked about—unless you were another combat vet. If anyone dared bring up the topic and spoke out against the war, John would point a finger at the person and emphatically sputter, "Fuck you, asshole! If what you're saying is true, then everything I've personally experienced—all the pain and suffering, not only my own but the countless number of people directly touched by that conflict—if everything you say is true, then all that pain and suffering was for nothing. And if that's so, then what you're insinuating is that I was part of some grand evil scheme. But I'm not evil, and the men I served with in Vietnam weren't evil, and neither is our country that sent us over there to fight."

The other person would immediately back off, apparently understanding how painful the issue was for John. Not once did someone get in his face to counter his position—nor to even object to being called an asshole.

The only times John was given a hard time about Vietnam had nothing to do with liberal-minded people or antiwar protesters. Surprisingly, the criticism came from World War II vets. Shortly after being released from the hospital, John had joined the American Legion and Veterans of Foreign Wars out of a sense of comradeship. He'd never attended their meetings, but one Friday after classes at OCC, he decided to stop by the local VFW Hall. Much like the American Legion Hall he'd visited once before, John sat down at the bar and ordered a beer. There were five men around his father's age already seated there, and John looked forward to reminiscing and sharing wartime experiences with them.

Slowly drinking his beer, John became involved in a conversation with the other patrons, and the topic soon turned to Vietnam.

"Let's just say it like it is," one guy bluntly accused, "present company excluded, Vietnam veterans are losers."

The other heads nodded in agreement.

"Why do you say such a thing?" John questioned, frowning his eyebrows.

"Well, as far as wars go, World War II was a good and honorable war. We fought the good fight, and we beat those fascists and we beat 'em bad," the man boasted.

"Absolutely," another vet concurred. "But that ain't gonna happen in Vietnam. Anyway, Vietnam isn't a real a war. And there's a different breed of soldier today. They're drug addicts and society's losers. They bring disgrace to our country by losing this police conflict."

"Sir, I must disagree with you," John objected. "I never saw any drug use when I was there. And I served with some very brave men."

"Nah," the same man continued. "They're not getting the job done. They're not killing off those commie gooks. That's why we're not winning. Those losers are losing it."

John maintained his cool, but it wasn't easy. Feeling uncomfortable, he couldn't think of how to tell these guys how wrong they were. How could they speak with authority about something they weren't a part of? While John wasn't afraid to confront fellow college students about the war, it was quite another matter with older veterans. Just as he had done at the American Legion Hall, John left the VFW Hall without finishing his beer, vowing to never return.

Subsequent to those interactions with WWII vets, John was especially proud to be chosen as Grand Marshall of the Loyalty Day Parade in Brick Town that spring. Through his wound, he knew that wherever he went, he took the troops along with him, so he was deeply honored to represent Vietnam veterans in the parade.

With forty to fifty men attending weekly meetings, OCC's Veteran's Club grew into the largest social organization on campus and became renowned for throwing the best parties and keggers. John personally took satisfaction in organizing dances, featuring live bands that drew large crowds and raised money for charities. The Veteran's Club even had its own following of female groupies. Although there were many parties, John would never forget the one that took place at a house along northern Barnegat Bay when he came dangerously close to drowning.

John thoroughly enjoyed living by the coastal region of New Jersey, where restaurants and shops sported nautical themes and a marine view was never far away. From the upper floors of Ocean County College he could see Silver Bay, an inlet of Barnegat Bay. And from the village of Toms River, where the mouth of the river opened into the bay, it was a short drive across the bridge to the recreation sites on the Barnegat Peninsula. The narrow 20-mile-long barrier peninsula ran between the Atlantic Ocean and the 4-mile-wide tidal lagoon named Barnegat Bay.

As much as John appreciated the seaside environment, it wouldn't take much water to enter the hole in his neck for him to drown, so getting into a boat was something he avoided. But on the night of that party, he'd already been drinking when he arrived at the bayside home of a friend of a club member after 9 p.m. And he trusted Randy, a New Jersey State Policeman and an off-duty regular at the Ship's Wheel Inn.

"I'm going out to look for Frankie and Izzy. Want to come?"

Randy invited John. "They're out in Izzy's boat and should've been back by now. I bet he had engine trouble again." Izzy was also a New Jersey State policeman and a good friend of Randy's.

John glanced at the 30-foot-long, triple-tiered cabin cruiser and thought he'd be safe in a craft that size. Joining Randy and two other guys, John climbed aboard. The men sipped beer while Randy navigated through the northern area of the estuary. John found it exhilarating to speed along in the cool, nighttime, saltwater air.

The search party soon spotted the running-lights of Izzy's boat. Silhouettes of Frankie and Izzy could be seen trying to start the stalled engine of the 18-foot vessel. As Randy's cruiser began to pull up beside it, Izzy succeeded in getting his engine going. He quickly raced off and steered his boat in a big circle around Randy's. Then both boats started messing around and doing donuts in the water. Darkness coupled with drinking was a bad combination and surely led to impaired judgment that night.

John was standing on the lowest deck when he saw the shadow and lights of Izzy's boat speeding toward a collision course with Randy's. "He's headed right at us!" John yelled in a voice that couldn't be heard above the rumbling engines. Plus, Randy—the captain of the cruiser—was up on the third tier.

Crash! John grabbed the railing as the boat rocked and jolted. He couldn't believe what he just saw. Izzy's boat struck Randy's cruiser broadside, slamming into the side of the bow. To John, it looked like someone had flown out of the boat. As the two crafts drifted apart, an upset Randy discovered a sizeable gash below the waterline of his 30-foot cabin cruiser.

"Where are the life preservers?" John nervously questioned, recognizing his imminent danger.

"There aren't any," Randy reported.

"Well, we have an immediate crisis! If I land in the water, I'm a dead man. The hole in my neck will see to that."

The men quickly sobered when the gravity of the situation was realized.

"Let's go!" Randy responded. "I'll speed it up and keep the front end out of the water. We'll drop you off, John, then I'll take the boat across and run it up a ramp."

John appreciated Randy's decision to make the 10-minute ride back to the party rather than risk the half-hour trip across the rough waters of Barnegat Bay. However, when Randy had to slow the craft down to maneuver as close to the bulkhead as possible, the hole in the bow undoubtedly took in water. As soon as John was safely tossed ashore, Randy's boat sped away. John immediately alerted the other partygoers about the accident. A group of them sprinted a quarter mile down the road to the beach where lights of the marine police and an ambulance were visible. John spotted Izzy walking from the shore.

"Are you okay?" John asked when he saw Izzy's bloodied face.

"Yeah," Izzy replied, "I hit the windshield."

"Where's Frankie?" John questioned worriedly. He thought he had seen something fly out of Izzy's boat upon impact, and he hoped it hadn't been his friend from the Veteran's Club.

"He's in the boat." Izzy gestured toward the shoreline and kept walking in the opposite direction.

John ran up to the beached boat where Frankie was still seated.

The front of the 18-footer was severely smashed, and Frankie had a bleeding cut across his forehead. Yet instead of finding his friend hurting, John found Frankie hysterically laughing.

"Can you believe this?" Frankie hooted. "I survived Vietnam but almost bought it in a boat crash on Barnegat Bay."

Everyone assumed Randy was all right but later learned that his boat had taken on too much water and sunk before reaching the ramp. Although John's life had been saved, that was not the case for Randy and Izzy's friendship. The two parted ways in a messy lawsuit. Needless to say, members of the Veterans Club never again partied at that location on Barnegat Bay.

During his second year at Ocean County College, John was elected president of the student government and took on an even greater leadership role. He had already been elected senator his first year, having been urged by Dean Flynn to run for office and represent veterans in the student government. As president, his popularity on campus increased, and despite differences of opinion, John made friends and dated women on both sides of the political persuasion. Girls were no problem for the student body president. He could hardly remember the time when he worried about people accepting him. Befitting his new position and social life, John upped his car payments and traded his Firebird for a new Elkhart-green T-top Corvette with saddle-leather seats.

In the spring of 1973, John and several other students attended a three-day leadership conference at the Fernwood Inn in Bushkill, Pennsylvania. A series of grants through the Kellogg Junior College Leadership Programs helped train many community college leaders during that time. John had already attended previous leadership events, but this would be his last. His reign at OCC would soon be coming to an end. Feeling nostalgic as he walked across the lobby of the conference center, John's attention was captured by a television screen where he saw a familiar sight. He watched as a Huey landed on the deck of an aircraft carrier. Then the camera panned back to show a line of already parked helicopters. John heard the news commentator proclaim the withdrawal of American forces from Vietnam was near completion. Seeing the Hueys was like seeing old friends. The sounds of the engines and interiors of the cargo bays were well imprinted in his mind. How many missions had he flown and how many lives did he and his fellow crewmembers save in those machines? Moreover, John had crashed in a Huey, and, of course, he'd been shot in one. His life at college often kept him distracted from Vietnam, but at this moment, John was instantly drawn back there. His heart raced, and tears unexpectedly filled his eyes. He felt disgust and anger. *All that effort—all that blood—and it all comes down to this?*

"Hey John-John!" a female workshop participant diverted his attention when she called him by his campus nickname. "*The Styles and Methods of Effective Leadership* lecture starts in five minutes. I'll walk there with you."

John turned and left the images on the TV screen behind. In a few months, he would be leaving Ocean County College behind, too—forever changed. He'd met professors he respected and who had greatly inspired him. Classes such as *Sociology of the Family, Social Problems and Policies, Deviance and Control,* and *Juvenile Delinquency* had given him insight into his own family situation. Other classes, such as *Introduction to American Politics, Social*

Problems and Policies, and *Sociological Analysis of Society* made him look differently at the culture. He felt confident enough as a student to continue his education and applied to two schools known for their excellent criminal justice programs. John was pleased to be accepted at both American University in Washington, D.C. and Indiana University in Bloomington, Indiana.

On June 10, 1973, John was one of 486 students to graduate from Ocean County College. The same kid who was unsure if he would graduate from high school was about to deliver the commencement address to OCC's graduating class. From the stage at one end of the soccer field where the first outdoor graduation ceremony was being held, John gazed over the block of blue caps and gowns of his fellow graduates. Beyond them sat their friends and families. John recognized Eduardo and his mother in the crowd of over 2,000. His mother was vigorously trying to stir the air, using her program as a fan on this very warm day.

"It gives me great pleasure to introduce a member of this year's graduating class," OCC President Dr. Andrew Moreland began his introduction of John. "John Seebeth's success story is worth repeating. As a wounded veteran and holder of several medals, including a Purple Heart and a Distinguished Flying Cross, John became involved in activities on campus and has been an inspiration to all who have had the privilege of working with him."

John proudly listened as President Moreland cited his achievements—his work with the Veteran's Club, his placement on the men's varsity tennis team....

Dr. Moreland continued, "...earlier this year John was named to *Who's Who Among Students in American Junior Colleges.* And

350

he was recently awarded the James George Inman Award for demonstrating outstanding qualities of scholarship, loyalty, citizenry, as well as contributing to extracurricular activities. I am very glad to present to you—the President of the Associated Students of Ocean County College, and one of the outstanding students in college history—John Seebeth."

"Thank you!" John bowed his head to acknowledge the thundering applause and whistles and cheers. "Thank you very much!" he said into the microphone. When the audience quieted, John read the speech he had prepared.

"Looking back and reflecting on my two years at Ocean County College, I feel that this experience has been a meaningful one marked by personal growth and academic development.

"Being new in the Ocean County area, I started at OCC not knowing anyone. Also, I look a bit different because of a tube in my throat, resulting from a wound I received in Vietnam. Having spent four years in the Army, I wondered how I could relate to other students, many of whom were recent high school graduates.

"But during my two years at OCC, I found my doubts being replaced by optimism and a growing sense of accomplishment. The education I received and the acceptance by students, faculty, and administration helped me to find myself and bring my full potential to the surface. Above all, I came to understand that an individual's goals are limited only by the degree of effort that he or she puts forth to attain them.

"For me, Ocean County College represented another chance to receive an education that I was not able to get before. I am glad I chose to take advantage of that opportunity."

Chapter 21

Everything John possessed was crammed into his Corvette and on the way to Indiana. He and his two cats departed Toms River at 3 a.m. so he could pick up the key to his apartment in Bloomington before the real estate office shut its doors for the day. Since John knew he didn't want to live in Washington, D.C., it had been an easy decision to attend Indiana University.

"Marblecake, move!" John ordered as he tried to scoot the cat away from his feet. John had meticulously set up food, water, and a litter box on the floor of the passenger's seat for his cats' comfort during the over-12-hour drive. However, Marblecake decided that she preferred to lounge near John's feet while the Corvette cruised west along the interstate. "Go on, Marblecake! Lie down next to Spot. Because if it ever came to your head getting between my foot and the brake pedal—you better get over next to Spot."

Relocating to America's heartland was a leap of faith for John. He was giving up the best home he had known—his convenient little apartment in Toms River. And he was leaving behind an assortment of friends who valued his company. Now, he headed off to unknown horizons. Literally, horizons were unknown in view of the fact that he hadn't made a trip to Bloomington beforehand. Other than photos in the college catalog, he didn't know what to expect. All arrangements had been made via phone or mail, including finding an apartment near campus. With Marblecake settling upon the Corvette's console, things were in order for him to make it to the rental agency on time.

Although John was a little sad to leave the familiar behind, he welcomed the opportunity to reinvent himself in new surroundings. He'd become a mighty big fish at Ocean County College, and even though the whirlwind of activity was exciting, it wasn't completely fulfilling. John looked forward to leading a quieter life at IU where—with 30,000 students—he was definitely in a bigger pond. Entering as a junior, he was eager to focus on his studies rather than expending so much energy on extracurricular activities.

John graduated from OCC with a fresh quest for truth. He'd learned new ways of looking at the world that helped him put some things in perspective. For instance, he'd been introduced to the term *dysfunctional family* and immediately knew it applied to his childhood experiences. Viewing his situation as a case study allowed John to stay positive when he said goodbye to his mother, which proved to be no easy task considering the dismal forecast of failures she warned would befall upon him if he moved out of state.

John also graduated from OCC with greater confidence in his academic abilities. In high school, he never read a book from cover to cover. Something about Miss Crutcher and English made reading feel more like punishment than pleasure. However, when John was stationed in Germany and grew tired of playing pinochle, he picked up a few paperback novels and was surprised to discover how much he enjoyed getting lost in a spy adventure. He continued to read other books in the Nick Carter-Killmaster series and then widened his reading to police action and crime stories. After graduating from OCC, John's summer reading included Truman Capote's *In Cold Blood, The Valachi Papers* by Peter Maas, and a few of Joseph Wambaugh's heroic police novels. *The Blue Knight* and *The Onion Field* kindled his resolve to further his studies in criminal justice.

And John could use some inspiration, because last month he hit a stumbling block. It had been over two years since any procedures had been performed on his neck, and a determination needed to be made about what else could possibly be done. On 13 August 1973, the Army sent John to Chelsea Naval Hospital in Boston to be evaluated by leading medical specialists for laryngotracheal reconstruction. Dr. William Montgomery, designer of his T-tube, was one of the expert consultants. Upon admission to Chelsea, John underwent a series of tests, including surgical exploration. Unfortunately, results of the examination did not reveal positive news. The medical team found no evidence of any vocal chord tissue or neurological functioning within John's larynx, only the presence of mature, skin-covered granulation tissue within the fistula. In layman's terms, the extent of involuntary nerve damage was so severe that John was left with insufficient mechanism to be able to breathe through his nostrils. That made closing the hole in his neck impossible. The Medical Examiner concluded that John would be required to wear the T-tube indefinitely, and he would not benefit from any other surgery unless a new valve device was designed at some point in the future.

As he drove toward Indiana, John was still coming to terms

with the fact that his neck could not be repaired. For so long, he had lived with the belief that the T-tube was temporary and the hole in his neck would someday be closed. Now he had to face life with a permanent stigma and the uncertainty of its ramifications. While the recent medical evaluation was a disappointing blow, John wouldn't allow it to defeat him. He was committed to pursuing his education and determined to take things one day at a time.

The Corvette safely transported John and the cats to Bloomington hours before the real estate office closed. Although his apartment came furnished, the formal-looking chairs and couch made him feel like he was in a doctor's waiting room instead of a home. Marblecake must not have been pleased with the new surroundings, because she sequestered herself in a closet for the first month and rarely came out of hiding. Like Marblecake, John kept a low profile at first, too.

Outside his stark apartment, he found Indiana University strikingly beautiful. Indiana literally meant *land of the Indians*, and John thought about the state's history as he observed the gentle landscape. Majestic trees decorated the rolling hills in this southern part of Indiana, and this year, the fall foliage's brilliant display of red and golden hues was breathtaking.

Walking the university grounds and exploring the layout of his new school, John thought the campus seemed to extend for miles and miles. Compared to the modern buildings at OCC, the stately, towering ones at IU reminded him of Heidelberg. In reality, Indiana University was founded nearly 500 years after the University of Heidelberg. In 1823, it was the first college west of the Allegheny

Mountains. The Allegheny range is the central region of the nearly 2,000-mile long Appalachian Mountain chain of eastern North America. Considered to be the oldest mountain system on the planet, the Appalachians stretch from Newfoundland to Alabama. During the early years of the country's development, the mountains presented a barrier to further expansion; therefore it was a landmark to establish a university to their west. Locally quarried limestone from the karst area was used for the original construction on campus. In fact, Indiana limestone was widely used in other famous constructions, such as the Empire State Building, the Pentagon, Washington National Cathedral, and a number of state capital buildings.

To John, the graceful, historic structures of the Old Crescent in the central part of campus were remarkable, reminding him that he followed a long tradition of scholars who burned bright for truth. The library had the ambiance of a lofty cathedral, and John soon located a quiet nook on the ground floor that became his favorite place to study and do research. While he chose IU because of its excellent forensics program, it was a pleasant surprise to be enveloped by such a picturesque backdrop.

His criminal justice classes were thoroughly absorbing and far more demanding than his work at OCC. Knowing the American people were paying for his education, John took his schoolwork seriously and was committed to doing his best. Consequently, he devoted much more time to studying, which kept John mostly to himself during his first semester at IU. And that suited him just fine. Wherever he went, people always wanted to know about his neck, and John had never minded telling his story. But right now, he needed a break from it. Physically, it took a lot of energy for him to speak;

yet he knew it wasn't just that. Emotionally, he hadn't had enough time to accept the permanence of his wound. Having to repeat his story would certainly evoke those unresolved feelings. So other than occasionally socializing with neighbors, John was content to be out of the limelight and concentrating on his studies. Marblecake and Spot were content to have his company.

By second semester, John moved out of the waiting room and into an apartment in Bloomington better suited to his and Marblecake's liking. Stores, restaurants, and the university were all within easy walking distance from the newly built Jo-Mar apartment complex. John ventured to new arenas and became a regular at the Field house, where he frequented the racquetball courts, concluding he wasn't tennis team level at this university. Since Red Beach, where the guys had built their own court, John enjoyed a good workout of handball or racquetball. He also began to jog on the indoor track, where he eventually noticed another routine runner. Respectful eye contact and nods of acknowledgement led to introductions.

"Yo, bro. Were you in Nam?" John inquired when he initially approached the tall man and gestured toward his calves. The medic had no hesitation in asking such personal questions. He'd noticed scars on the guy's legs and wondered how this young man could have acquired what looked like shrapnel wounds. Plus, there was a certain depth behind his dark eyes, which made John speculate he might be a veteran.

The curly black-haired head nodded affirmatively. "9th Infantry, '69–'70."

John pointed to his neck. "Me too. I flew with Da Nang Dustoff, '68–'69."

The two men laughed as they improvised a dap. John ended the complicated handshake by cuffing the guy on the shoulder.

"Hey man, do you want to grab a hamburger?" the smiling face invited. He told John to call him Rocco, as most everyone else knew him by his nickname. "I'm finished here and was just heading over to Hinkles."

"Hinkles?"

"Yeah, over on South Adams. They have the best burgers."

John's new friend spoke the truth about the burgers. Mounded with onions and pickles, they were hefty but so tasty John managed to wolf down two. Drinking milkshakes and eating cheeseburgers and fries, the men became better acquainted. Like John, Rocco attended IU with help from the GI Bill. He relocated to Bloomington four years ago, after deciding to take the long-term track to graduation. Part-time jobs and a simple lifestyle allowed Rocco to pursue his studies in journalism.

Over time, Rocco introduced John to a great deal more than Hinkles' hamburgers. He started by acquainting him with the best of the few drinking establishments in Bloomington. They often met for a beer at the Red Dog Saloon, where the sounds of bluegrass filled the air. Rocco corrected John, informing him that although the music might not resemble the soul sounds of Philly, it was not to be referred to as shit-kicking hillbilly. The Bluebird on Walnut Street became another stop on their weekend entertainment circuit. There, John met local residents Rocco had befriended over the years. John especially enjoyed going to a much larger club that featured live rock-and-roll bands similar to the Satellite Lounge back in New Jersey. At the Timeout, Rocco shared John's exuberance for dancing.

They both worked it out on the dance floor, boogieing with cute coeds in the crowded room. No matter where John and Rocco went, an abundance of laughter accompanied them.

Rocco also introduced John to Tony, owner of Tony's Pizza, a popular gathering place in town. Pizza became a staple food item for John as he and Rocco normally stopped by Tony's several times a week. It turned out that Tony's apartment, behind the pizzeria, was the place where bongs and friends congregated. John was pleased to be accepted into this new social group.

"Let's eat our burgers in the cemetery," Rocco suggested one sunny spring afternoon.

John followed Rocco across the road into Rose Hill Cemetery. Hinkles was located near the southwest edge of the cemetery, and the small house Rocco rented was on a quiet street along the northeast margin. John and Rocco enjoyed taking a diagonal shortcut through the 15-acre burial ground.

"Wow!" John exclaimed while walking beside the grave markers of former US Senators and other statesmen. "Look at this one," he noted after spotting a worn stone. "This guy was a Civil War Union Brevet Brigadier General."

Rocco led the way into the center of the graveyard to a cluster of fir trees, uncommon to the region. Although there were a variety of stately trees throughout the cemetery, John appreciated the fragrance, sight, and sound of breezes rustling through that distinct stand of evergreens. They ate their food in silence, marveling at the gentle giants of the vegetable kingdom.

"It doesn't bother you to be in a cemetery?" Rocco questioned after lighting a joint and passing it to John. "Darla won't set foot in here. It spooks her."

John spread his arms wide before taking the marijuana cigarette from Rocco. "After all the death I've seen—these are like my friends." He covered the hole in his T-tube and inhaled.

The two sat comfortably without talking. Their stomachs full of Hinkles, they pleasantly enjoyed the moment. Rocco was a man of few words, making stillness easy between them. John recognized how different his seven months at Indiana University had been from his time at Ocean County College. Back in Toms River, he always seemed to be busy rushing from one place to another. Here, he no longer possessed the constant desire for activity. He was satisfied to just lounge back and watch the wind gracefully sway the fir branches. Also, at OCC nearly all of John's friends had been veterans. In Indiana, Rocco was the only other vet in their social group.

"Nope, death doesn't bother me," John mused, breaking the quiet. "Considering all I saw in Vietnam, I'm no stranger to death. And I, myself, had two near death experiences." After a long pause he added, "For awhile, I began to wonder if death was following me, or I was attracting it or something."

"How so?" Rocco questioned while leaning back and stretching his long legs.

"At the end of my first year at OCC, I was on the dance floor, and the oddest thing happened—a guy dropped dead right beside me."

"A student died?"

"No, not a student. He was the father of a student. His son was graduating, and the man was dancing with his wife right next to me and my date, when all of a sudden, he fell to the floor."

Another lengthy pause elapsed before John proceeded. "I didn't even think about it. It was like I was back in Vietnam. Next I know, I'm down on my knees on the floor. I heard the people around me gasp when I ripped the guy's shirt open to administer heart compressions."

John recalled the intensity of that incident. He had been eagerly anticipating the Viking Ball—the big end-of-the-year campus event. Making arrangements for a fun night, he'd dressed sharply in a rented tuxedo with satin trim on the lapels. Yet, right at the beginning when he picked up his date, the evening got off to a bad start, though not through any fault of hers. She was a fellow student at OCC and a very sweet gal. Nonetheless, when John drove up to her parents' home—located in a decidedly poor side of town—his flashy Corvette felt embarrassingly opulent. He was invited into the modest house where he met her parents and her brothers and sisters. The pleasant people were all very kind to him. As he chatted with them while waiting for his date, his own outfit suddenly seemed superficially showy. It made him contemplate his plans for the evening with these nice people's daughter. Still, it was the man collapsing at his feet on the dance floor that truly destroyed the night.

"Really, I was pissed at the corpse," John confessed. "I don't know how long I worked on the guy. It was like I was in Nam. I bent over the patient and concentrated on getting the job done. Once I started working on him, I forgot about the crowd of people circled around. Then a nursing student came over and she started giving him mouth-to-mouth. That's something I can't do." John waved his hand in front of his T-tube to indicate the reason. "We kept a rhythm going, you know, five beats, two breaths, five beats, two breaths," he mimicked the motion with his left hand as he spoke. "But after awhile, I sensed death. I can't explain it, but I've been around it so much—I got the feeling—this guy's gone and he's not coming back."

Rocco relit the remainder of the joint and handed it over to John. Taking a long draw, John passed it back and carried on with his story.

"As soon as I sensed death, I got up off the floor and walked away. It's like I became aware I wasn't in Vietnam. Dean Flynn sort of panicked. He shouted to me and wanted to know what I was doing—stopping before the ambulance arrived. So he knelt down, and he started to administer heart compressions."

"What did the guy die of?" Rocco wanted to know.

"He had a massive coronary. Afterward, I learned his heart blew out so bad nothing could have saved him. I could have performed pulmonary resuscitation all night, and it wasn't going to bring him back. I found that out because I was a pallbearer at his funeral."

John reached for the stub of joint Rocco passed back in his direction. He took a puff and continued, "Can you believe I was a pall bearer? I'd never met the man, and I hardly knew his son, yet I ended up being a pallbearer at his funeral because he dropped dead at my feet. I mean, on that whole big dance floor—and all the hundreds of feets out there—why did he keel over next to MY feets? How many times does a thing like that happen? That's when I wondered if I was attracting death."

"That's pretty wild," Rocco sighed. Silence hung in the air before he concurred, "And I know what you mean about automatically going back to Vietnam. Not long after getting back, I took my car to the shop to get new tires. I was standing at the counter, and I heard a big crash. I didn't see it happen, but someone had knocked over a display of hubcaps. As soon as I heard the crash, I dove on the floor, flat on my belly, like I was taking cover."

Rocco rapidly extended both arms to demonstrate how quickly he had dropped to the floor of the tire shop. "People looked at me, like what the fuck is he doing? I was embarrassed as hell, but months earlier that same response could have saved my friggin' life. At least in your case, you weren't diving on the floor for no reason. You took command of the situation, and your actions were heroic. I imagine the wife and son appreciated your efforts—even if they were futile."

"Yeah, well it sure put a crimp on the evening. I wasn't in the mood for anymore dancing—or anything else," John lamented.

"Hey, did anybody else drop dead around you? 'Cause maybe it's time for me to be someplace else besides a cemetery with you," Rocco jested. Folding his arms and gazing at the treetops, he pondered, "Seriously, isn't it amazing how our instincts reflect our training? It was kind of scary the way my body reacted and I ended up on the floor of the tire shop. Guess that's part of the military method. The best soldier is the man who follows orders and doesn't ask questions. And at eighteen, you're pretty impressionable. That's how old I was when I went in the service."

John remained in Bloomington over the summer, and under the shade of the trees of Rose Hill Cemetery, he and Rocco had many more meaningful discussions. In addition to socializing with his new circle of friends, John took a couple of summer school classes. A psychology class and a class entitled *The Black Man in America* provided plenty of fodder for their cemetery conversations.

In August, John went to New Jersey during the 2-week break before fall semester. Marblecake and Spot happily stayed in Bloomington under the care of friends. Back in Lanoka Harbor, his mother was proud her son would be a senior in college; however she had no difficulty identifying numerous deficiencies in other areas of his life. In Toms River, John enjoyed visiting with old friends from the Veteran's Club. He also made the drive to Philadelphia to see some of his childhood chums. Nearly all of those guys were veterans now, too. Many had attended Father Judge High School and volunteered for Vietnam. The Roman Catholic school had more graduates lose their lives in service to their country during the Vietnam War than any other non-public school in the nation. And Thomas Edison High School, in north Philadelphia, lost more students than any other high school in the United States. Altogether, Philadelphia lost 630 of its men to the war. Twenty-seven of them were from Father Judge and sixty-six from Edison. John and his old friends exchanged war stories, and they laughed and joked while reminiscing about the familiar topics of girls and times past. But when John brought up a subject he and Rocco might deliberate, one friend put him in his place.

"Don't get uppity on us, John. You're getting too highfalutin' for your own good."

Sort of on a whim, John traded his Corvette for a car he had never before seen. Driving by the same dealer that had sold him both his Corvette and Firebird, John couldn't miss the unusual white sports car prominently displayed in the front of the lot. Stopping to admire the black vinyl top with a sunroof and the soft leather interior, John decided to up his car payments once again. He drove back to Indiana in his brand new British Leland TVR. Although his friends and family in Jersey had been duly impressed by his new means of transportation, back in Indiana, Rocco and friends weren't particularly moved. They didn't share the pop culture's worship of wheels.

Upon reflection in the cemetery with Rocco, John concluded he probably bought the TVR to assuage a crushing blow. This summer, he'd been forced to accept the fact that his longstanding dream of becoming a Pennsylvania State trooper was unattainable. Ever since his busboy days, he'd wanted to emulate the troopers that stopped by Howard Johnson. Admittedly, their power-status uniforms held appeal, but John was just as impressed by how nice the guys were and how they appeared to handle their authority responsibly.

"I'm thinking of filing a lawsuit," an agitated John related to Rocco. "How can those assholes say I'm not qualified? Their letter said they couldn't use me on the streets. But I would never want a desk job. I didn't want to be a medic who polished ambulances, and I don't want to be a trooper who sits behind a fucking desk."

"John, you sound like you're still fighting the war," Rocco accused. "Did they explain why? Don't flip out, but I could see why your neck might cause problems."

Later, a conversation with a police officer revealed how John's condition could put another in jeopardy.

"In all honesty," the officer said to John, "I wouldn't want to partner with you. If you got into a struggle involving both your arms—and that kind of thing happens all the time—you wouldn't be able to use your hand to talk. You wouldn't be able to issue a command to stop, and if your partner faced an imminent threat, you wouldn't be able to yell a warning. John, have you ever met—or even heard of—a police officer with a trach? No, sir. Not being able to verbally communicate could put your partner's life at risk."

No one had explained it quite that way before. As soon as he understood his condition could potentially harm another, John accepted that his dream had to die. Now, he wondered what other types of jobs would be suitable for him in the field of law enforcement.

Delving into his course work, John took a class from a professor who had been a convicted felon. Dr. Walters did his time, got out, went to school, and now offered valuable insight—from both sides of the bars—into the operations of the criminal justice system. The students in his upper-level class had already traced the history of prisons in human society back to antiquity. Dr. Walters emphasized that for as long as wars have occurred some vanquished persons end up being held captive instead of being killed.

The Revolutionary War led to the establishment of prisons in America. Boston's forefathers first recognized the practical necessity of allocating a portion of public soil for a cemetery and another portion for a site to house prisoners of war. Thus, jails were among the first public structures built in the New World. Eventually, nearly every American city and county was legally required to establish a jail at public expense. Early prisons were not much different from dungeons of medieval Europe where people were confined while awaiting sentencing. Thieves, murderers, debtors, adulterers, and blasphemers—be they man, woman, or child—sane or insane—were all confined together in one large space. Overcrowded conditions made prisons dirty and dangerous, breeding disease and resulting in even greater iniquity.

John was proud to learn that prison reform initiated in his hometown of Philadelphia where the humanistic influence of the Society of Friends was strongest. Perhaps the Quakers developed an interest in the treatment of criminals after they, themselves, had been jailed by Massachusetts Puritans for speaking against the public burning of witches. Common criminals generally met justice via hangings or mutilation, although forced labor, social ostracism, and public disgrace were other widespread forms of colonial punishment. The Quakers introduced the idea of incarceration as punishment itself, claiming that restricting a person's liberty would be retribution enough. Thus, prisons built according to the Philadelphia system became known as *penitentiaries*, denoting the prisoners to be religious penitents serving time for their sins. The prisons were constructed in a hub-and-spoke design in order to isolate prisoners 24 hours a day—basically shutting them in a cell with a Bible. The Quakers hoped that solitude would prevent degrading association with other criminals, as well as promoting earnest Christian self-reflection. Penitentiaries gained acclaim for their goals of perfecting society through imprisonment and became models for hundreds of prisons worldwide. However, despite high moral aims, more prisoners in solitary confinement ended up insane instead of reformed.

Alternative systems were introduced in the US, and in 1816, a prison in Auburn, New York initiated a new design. The Auburn type of prison was constructed in the form of a cell-block of several tiers of stone or brick cages. Individual sleeping cells were sometimes as small as 2½ by 6 ½ feet. Prisoners left their cells during the day and went to congregate shops, where they worked in silence. The Auburn plan proved to be most economical to erect and administer, and most subsequent American prisons were merely refinements of its original cellblock/cage construction.

"Why do prisoners rebel?" the average-looking man asked his class. Dr. Walters was introducing the topic of the bloodiest prison riots in American history—the Attica Prison riots of 1971.

"Because of the wardens' cruel treatment," a young woman suggested.

"Yes, definitely," Dr. Walters nodded as he wrote *treatment by guards* on the chalkboard at the front of the classroom.

"Because social and cultural movements outside prisons encourage rebellion," a white male student responded. "For instance, the Black Panthers and black militancy."

"That's a valid answer," Dr. Walters recognized while gesturing with the piece of chalk. "Prisons are not isolated from the culture. In fact, the culture dictates how we design prisons, treat prisoners, and who we incarcerate."

Another male student spoke up, "It said in one of the articles that a member of the Black Panther Party who was imprisoned in San Quentin died at the hands of white prison guards a few days before the riot in Attica. It said his death might have sparked the riots."

"Prisoners could riot if they're treated badly," a woman contributed. "I mean, like inadequate living and sleeping conditions."

The professor asked the student, "What did your reading assignment reveal about the conditions they were living under in Attica?"

"Well, their mail was read, and their reading material was

restricted," the same female student replied. Her eyes widened as she added, "And they were only allowed one shower a week and one roll of toilet paper per month!"

"Wouldn't overcrowding also play into riots?" a young man asked. "One of the articles reported that Attica was a facility designed to hold 1,200 inmates but was actually housing 2,225."

Dr. Walters vigorously nodded his head as he added *overcrowding* to the list on the chalkboard. "We know even rats get agitated when they're too crowded."

"What about race relations?" John inquired. "I read that 1,281 prisoners in the riot were black, while all the guards were white. And some guards had nicknamed their batons 'Nigger Sticks' and had been using them liberally long before the riots."

"Absolutely," Dr. Walters responded. "As we will see, race and class are disproportionately represented in our prisons. The incarcerated population is vastly skewed toward low income and dark skin." To the entire class, Professor Walters pointed to the list on the front board and summarized, "Prisoners rebel for various reasons. Whatever the reasons, the act of rebellion brings public attention to the conditions."

Later in the semester, Dr. Walters offered five of his keenest students the opportunity to tour two of Indiana's correctional facilities. John was pleased to have been chosen for the field trips. The group climbed into Dr. Walters' sedan early one morning to make the 4-hour drive toward the state's northern border to Indiana State Prison in Michigan City. Situated on the southern edge of Lake Michigan, aptly named Michigan City was about fifty miles east of Chicago and positioned between the industrial cities of South Bend and Gary, one of the world's centers for producing iron, steel, and petroleum products. During the drive, Dr. Walters informed the three men and two women about the group discussion he had arranged with five inmates.

"I'm not going to tell you about the men beforehand, because I don't want you to form preconceived notions," Dr. Walters explained. "But all of them have been given life sentences for committing multiple homicides. And all of them have been in prison for years—I believe the shortest time served is eight or nine years."

Approaching the facility along the outskirts of Michigan City, the students first noticed a massive wall that enclosed the entire prison complex. Indiana limestone and red brick created a city behind walls, preventing the public from seeing in and the inmates from seeing out.

"Behind this protective fortress is where society houses its repellent," Dr. Walters remarked as the students observed the wall. "Most American prisons are surrounded by walls that are higher and thicker than the walls that protected ancient cities or medieval castles."

He also explained that Indiana State Prison was originally built by convict labor around 1860 to house Civil War prisoners. Other industries contracted Indiana prisoners at the rate of about thirty cents per day until convict labor became illegal in 1904.

The old buildings felt heavy and repressive when the students and Dr. Walters entered the first set of gates. They silently passed through the various security checkpoints and procedures required to gain entry. Bags were hand-inspected, and each person was patted down. Only one gate was opened at a time, so all eyes were on the group as they proceeded through the highly complex maze of bars, locks, and protocol. Later, the two female students described how their knees literally knocked when they stepped inside the prison. The collection of people and circumstances, as well as the bricks and stones and cold, clanging metal gave the place a chilling feeling. Nothing about it felt like a warm fuzzy.

John would never forget the experience of sitting in a room with five murderers. Dr. Walters directed the group to sit student-inmate, student-inmate, around the circle of chairs. Guards prominently stood in the corners of the conference room and were visible outside the doors. Reiterating the guidelines for the group discussion, the professor told the students they could not ask any questions about specific crimes, since all cases were under appeal, and the men had been advised to not talk about them. Otherwise, students and inmates could ask each other about anything else. Following first-name-only introductions, Dr. Walters invited someone to ask the first question.

A man with black sideburns extending to his jowls raised his heavily tattooed arm and pointed at John, "What happened to your neck?"

On the long drive back to Bloomington, the students engaged in a lively conversation. Dr. Walters related the charges against each man and wanted to know who they thought committed what crime. It was impossible for the students to conclusively identify the man who killed three policemen or the one who shot two people during a robbery or even which one was known as the infamous Mad Dog Killer who had committed a string of six murders and left a seventh victim blind and crippled. Appearance-wise, harsh lives played havoc on the men's faces. Pockmarks, scars, and grim expressions verified their attendance in the school of hard knocks. Their outer shells were so similar the students couldn't discern any distinguishing differences in the group of downtrodden, hardcore criminals—except for one man. The students had no trouble identifying the man convicted of molesting and strangling his neighbor's two children.

"Without question," a female student asserted, "it has to be the skinny guy. You know, the one whose shoulders were bent over and who sat with his legs crossed and his arms folded across his chest the whole time."

"Yeah, that nutty guy with thinning hair and sunken cheeks," another student offered. "I noticed how he was off by himself when they entered the room. The other inmates seemed to keep their distance from him."

One student ridiculed a prisoner's claim of being an innocent bystander. "Don't most prisoners insist on being innocent even if they aren't?"

"Actually," John countered, "I know what it's like to be an innocent victim of the criminal justice system."

The students and Dr. Walters listened attentively while John related how he had been beaten up by cops and then thrown behind bars when he was stationed in Louisiana back in 1968. He explained how he and Mike, a fellow medic from the 565th, had gone into Leesville to have a few beers—something they had done in Germany countless times. While John used to frequent the guest houses in Baumholder almost every night, during his three months at Fort Polk he hadn't gone into Leesville more than a half-dozen times. Instead of foosball, the bars in Leesville had pool tables, so Mike and John inserted a few quarters in the jukebox, ordered a couple beers, and played a friendly game of 8-ball at the first saloon they entered. They repeated the same routine at two more places and then decided to hit one more bar before calling it quits for the night.

"We weren't looking for any trouble," John justified. "I'd just been assigned to my new job with the 236th Helicopter Ambulance Detachment, so I sure didn't want to mess that up. We didn't go to town to get drunk or raise hell. Anyhow, it was a weeknight, and we planned to wrap things up by midnight."

Leesville, like other military towns, had a love/hate relationship with soldiers. While their purchases contributed to the local economy, their presence led the town morally astray. Since Fort Polk specialized in advanced infantry training, most of the young—and often undereducated—soldiers had been trained to kill in Tigerland. The vast majority would soon find themselves in the deadly rice paddies of Vietnam. So who could blame them for the everything-goes attitudes they carried into Leesville—the place that served their basic animal needs with liquor and whores? On any given weekend, Leesville turned into a place of debauchery where fights and other lewd conduct required civilian and military police intervention.

Local residents considered the soldiers to be disrespectful intruders. Of course, they frequently saw the soldiers at their worst: drunk, obnoxious, oversexed, rude, and sometimes violent. Apparently, some of the town's people harbored such hostile feelings toward the soldiers they sought occasion to act them out.

As John recounted the story to Dr. Walters and his fellow students, he accentuated how normal everything seemed when he and Mike entered the bar that evening. It was a slow night, and similar to the three preceding establishments, about a dozen or so people were seated around tables and country-western music twanged from the jukebox. Although one pool table was in use, a second one beckoned. Mike went over to rack the billiard balls while John headed to the counter to order a couple of beers. John noticed the woman bartender stood across from two men seated upon stools at the other end of the lengthy bar. Full glasses sat on the countertop in front of them. There were no other customers at the bar and no sight of a waitress.

"Did you yell over to the bartender or something?" one of his classmates inquired.

"I didn't say a word. I just waited for her to end her conversation with those two guys."

John would never understand what happened next or why. When the barkeep finally turned in his direction and started moving toward him, she unexpectedly stopped and climbed on top of the bar. The heels of her cowgirl boots made clicking sounds as she strutted his way. Watching her walk upon the countertop, John thought her behavior was a little odd. When she stopped and pivoted in front of him, John focused his gaze upward. Beneath blond hair framed by ceiling rafters, angry eyes glared down at him. Not knowing what to make of the woman's performance, John stepped back from the bar but kept his attention fixed on those fierce eyes.

John observed the young woman crouch down like a huge cat and abruptly lunge at him as though he were her prey. John couldn't believe what was happening. She came down on him with her full weight, knocking him backwards to the floor. Frantically, he tried to wrestle himself from underneath while struggling to keep her hands away from his face, because she was viciously clawing at his eyes.

Pandemonium broke out in the room. Chairs, tables, broken glasses, and spinning bodies flew about in a blur of chaos. It seemed that everybody who had been minding his own business a few moments ago was now intent on kicking John's ass. Punches were coming at him from all directions. Knocked back down to the floor, and overwhelmingly outnumbered, John curled into a fetal position to protect himself from the onslaught.

"Didn't your friend run out and call the police?" a female student interrupted.

"Mike had a mob after him, too. The last thing I saw before losing consciousness was two men pulling on Mike's legs, dragging him out from under the pool table."

John related that when he regained consciousness, he and Mike were lying on a dank, piss-smelling sidewalk. Trying to make sense of his whereabouts, John recognized the pulsating red glare from several police cars. He also identified the neon lights of the bar, surmising that both he and Mike had been beaten unconscious and then dragged out the front door and tossed onto the sidewalk.

As soon as Mike came to, he became distraught. Tears streamed down his blood-caked cheeks.

"Are you seriously hurt?" John asked, perceiving his buddy's bruised and bloody face. Mike's lip was badly split and one of his eyes was nearly swollen shut. "Do you need to be taken to a hospital?"

"I'm okay," Mike stammered. "But you...John, I failed to protect you."

Unable to see his own face, John didn't know it was even more battered than his friend's.

"The police didn't take you to a hospital?" the same woman questioned.

"No!" John emphasized. "They never even approached us to see if we were okay. My head was throbbing and I had a deep cut that was still bleeding and probably could have used a couple of stitches. So I waved a cop over, and I asked to be taken to a hospital. The cop didn't say a word. He turned and walked away. Then they shoved us in the back of a patrol car—Mike in one and me in another—and drove us to the police station. At the station, I showed another officer my head wound and again asked to be taken to a hospital."

John dredged up the unpleasant memory of sitting on a wooden bench in the reception room of the police station. Across the room sat ten of the rowdies involved in the brawl—including the bartender. Compared to Mike and John, that gang appeared physically unscathed. Only one or two of them exhibited traces of blood, probably from John or Mike's strikes of self-defense. That crazed female bartender seemed to take pleasure in yelling verbal taunts from the opposite side of the room. She proudly shouted that she was the one to knock John unconscious. Evidently, as he was lying on the floor trying to protect himself from the free-for-all of punches and kicks pummeling him, the woman had knelt down and clocked him on top of his head with a billiard ball. No mercy in that crowd.

Around 2 a.m., an officer approached and notified Mike and John they were going to be booked and put into jail. They were shocked! They had never even been asked their side of the story. Yet Mike and John were even more shocked when the same officer declared that all the townies were free to go. Mike responded by stomping over to the counter and demanding to make a phone call. It probably didn't help matters for the Chicagoan to threaten to call his Illinois Senator and report the mistreatment of US servicemen by the Louisiana police—if only he could remember one of his senators' names.

Following Mike's bluster, two cops grabbed John, one holding each arm. Another two restrained Mike in the same manner. The cops marched them outside to a fenced walkway, all the while pounding their heads and upper bodies.

"I had a bleeding head wound, but I had a cop on each side throwing punches at me with their free fists," John imparted to the students and Dr. Walters. "We were shoved up against a chain-link fence and ordered to put our arms over our heads and spread our legs. They frisked us and confiscated our wallets and cigarettes."

John remembered being led to the adjacent gloomy-looking brick building, which was the county jail. An officer unlocked and opened a thick metal door. From the doorway, the two cops holding Mike shoved him so hard, he went flying into the dark room. Next, John received the same forceful thrust from his handlers. Like Mike, he landed face first on a concrete floor.

"Had you ever been in jail before?" the other female student questioned.

"I'd never been in any kind of trouble with the law before."

"Well, what happened?" the student seated beside John in Dr. Walters' car asked.

"It was dark in there, so I didn't try to stand up. I crawled over to a 55-gallon trash bin and curled up beside it. Mike and I weren't put in a cell. We'd been thrown in a hallway that had about six cells off it. When I woke up, Mike was gone. I didn't know what happened to him. And I didn't know if anybody in my new unit even knew I was missing. I didn't know anything except my head was splitting in pain."

John recalled the worry he felt. The events of the evening had been so bizarre, he wondered if he could find himself stuck in the jail without anyone knowing. And if he did get out, would the 236th still want him after this incident?

"The cells weren't locked. Men milled around," John reported to his classmates. "The hallway led to other hallways of cells, but I didn't wander around, so I don't know how big the facility was. I never saw any guards inside or any people of authority to even ask a question. Someone eventually came and took me across the street to the courthouse. I was really relieved to see the Commanding Officer from my new company standing there. The judge told me that if I didn't plead guilty to the charges of disorderly conduct and pay the $55 fine, I'd have to remain in jail until the next court date, which would be in two or three weeks, give or take a week. Well, my commander, Major Jackson, paid the fine, and not long after I was on my way to Vietnam."

"John," Dr. Walters addressed. "Did you interact with any of the other prisoners?"

"Yeah, I talked to a guy named Jimmy. He was probably in his late thirties. I went into the latrine area to wash up because dried blood was in my hair and all over me. I was asking around for aspirin, and another prisoner pointed to a corner cell. That was Jimmy's quarters. At first he wanted me to pay $15 for advice and protection, but when I told him the police had emptied my pockets, he gave me the aspirin and advice anyway. He also lent me a shirt to wear to court. He said my bloody one would make a bad impression on the judge."

John paused and pictured the mustard-colored v-neck velour shirt Jimmy had pulled out of the chest of drawers in his cell. "Jimmy was an interesting character. And he sure knew a lot. He talked about how there's supposed to be a one-year time limit of being in the county jail, but he'd already been there for over two years. And he told me about a black prisoner who had allegedly hung himself a year before in an upstairs area of the jail. And Dr. Walters, I remember noticing that at least half of the prisoners were black, while all of the people in authority were white."

"What was Jimmy jailed for?" a student inquired.

"He never said, and I didn't ask. But he did tell me I was lucky because I would've been stuck in jail until the circuit court judge came back to town—and that's the same thing the judge said. And Jimmy advised me to plead guilty just to get out of there. I told him I absolutely wouldn't since I didn't do anything wrong. But, in the end, I did end up pleading guilty because Major Jackson ordered me to."

"Can you describe the conditions of the jail?" Dr. Walters requested. "And some things you learned from the experience?"

"Well, the jail was disgusting. It stank terrible, and there was trash all around. It was obvious no one had swept the place in a while. And some of the windows were broken. They were covered with bars, but there was jagged glass in the frames, so flies and mosquitoes could get in. Jimmy said the place was overrun with rats, mice, and lice. He said it gets real cold in the winter, and with those broken windows, I can see how. I didn't get a meal, but Jimmy said the food wasn't fit for a dog.

"Also, I noticed there was a cell with a solid metal door that had a waist-high slot in it. Jimmy said it held a woman prisoner serving a 6-month sentence for prostitution. There was a wooden chair right by her door, and Jimmy said her pimp husband was also in jail, and he'd sit there and play cards with his wife through the slot in the door. It made me wonder if all women prisoners were confined behind metal doors like her. She had to stay her in cell and wasn't able to roam around like the other prisoners."

"She was probably isolated for her protection, don't you think?" a female student suggested.

Dr. Walters nodded and stated, "Indiana was the first state in the nation to build a separate correctional facility exclusively for females."

"Jimmy talked about how unfairly he and other prisoners had been treated," John further mentioned. "He said some of them had been there six months or longer but they'd only had an initial hearing and had no idea when their court date was going to be. He also asked if I could inform somebody on the outside about his predicament— how he was legally supposed to be moved out of the county jail and into a state facility to finish serving his time. A state prison would give him access to work training and other services. And maybe if I hadn't experienced the police brutality, I might not have believed anything he said about the wheels of justice."

"It's sort of hard to believe," the student who made the comment about convicts proclaiming their innocence balked. "Are you sure you didn't provoke the people in the bar? And you're sure you didn't agitate the police?"

"Hey, why would I make this up? Trust me, they crossed a line. And even if I offended the bartender—which I didn't—what crime would Mike and I have committed that would have deserved having a gang of people beat us to a pulp? I was beat up twice—first by the townies and then by the police. I was never given medical care—and I should have been taken to an emergency room." Touching the crown of his head, he stressed, "I still have a scar from that billiard ball. I could have been lying there in a coma or dead as far as they knew, because nobody in authority ever came in to check on me. And nobody—other than Jimmy—explained what was happening. I wasn't allowed to make a phone call, and I certainly wasn't read my Miranda rights. Really, that experience left me thinking the criminal justice system was screwed up. No doubt about it—there was no justice dispensed in Leesville that day."

Dr. Walters smiled as he suggested, "John, as a result you'll probably always see a person as innocent until proven guilty."

While the conversation inside the sedan turned to a different topic, John sat quietly with his own thoughts. He recalled reporting to Major Jackson's office at 0900 the next morning. As John described the circumstances of his arrest, Major Jackson sat behind his desk and silently nodded. The Old Man must have been satisfied with his explanation, because John never heard another word about it. For his part, John honored his promise to stay out of Leesville during his remaining duration at Fort Polk.

Although John mailed the velour shirt back to Jimmy, he thought it best not to stick out his neck for a man he didn't know. Instead, grateful to be back with his new unit, John fully concentrated on his training with the 236th. For three months he flew onboard Hueys and learned his role as a member of a 4-man Dustoff crew. He also worked under supervision in the emergency room at Fort Polk's hospital. There, he gave injections, started IVs, cleaned and irrigated wounds with saline, and sutured ripped skin back together. The ER was busiest on Friday and Saturday nights when the soldiers had been partying in Leesville. There could be bullet wounds and stabbings, but generally the men arrived in ambulances with head wounds, gashes, and bruises—the results of fistfights and beatings. When treating those men, John wondered about the circumstances of their injuries, reminded of his own experience of being an innocent victim of the criminal justice system.

Later in the semester, the same group of students drove an hour and a half from Bloomington to Pendleton, northeast of Indianapolis. At the Indiana State Reformatory, Dr. Walters pointed out the architectural design of the radial-plan prison. A student noticed how the buildings seemed to allow light and a view of green grass even from the enclosed areas. While touring the facility, John again observed that almost all the guards were white, even though about half the prison population appeared to be non-white.

At Pendleton, Dr. Walters had arranged for the students to converse with a minimum-security prisoner who had already served ten years of his life sentence. Although he'd been convicted of two homicides, this guy was nothing like the hardened thugs the group had met at Michigan City. Most of those convicts had long rap sheets and had done time as juveniles, whereas this man never had a prior brush with the law. He worked in the office of the correctional facility's psychiatrist, which is where the meeting took place. The man appeared quite normal and could have been taken for an employee except for his blue denim prison garb. After Dr. Walters and the psychiatrist made introductions, the man was asked to share his story. He cried when he told the group how in a moment of rage—he snapped—and shot his wife and her brother with a rifle.

"He was my best friend. They were the only people that really loved me," the distraught man stated. Choking back sobs, he dropped his gaze to his feet and whispered in a barely audible voice, "I killed the only people that I ever loved. Now I have no love. I killed the love inside me."

Chapter 22

"I don't want to be in law enforcement anymore," John vehemently pronounced. "In a couple of months, I'll have my degree in Criminal Justice, but now I don't even want to be in the field."

Rocco stepped over the low concrete wall that separated the periphery of Rose Hill Cemetery from the street where he lived. He'd noticed John's moodiness at his roommate's party and suggested going outside for a breath of fresh air. On this night in early May, warm gentle breezes carried the sweet fragrances of spring, and a star-spangled sky shimmered above as the two men strolled to their favorite talking place.

"Was it the movie?" Rocco asked, the sounds of music and laughter fading in the distance behind them.

John couldn't speak for a moment. He was busy holding his quivering lip rigid. Earlier, he and Rocco had seen a showing of *Serpico* at the local theater.

"Didn't you see the movie when it was first released?" Rocco inquired.

"No, but I read the book, and we covered the *Knapp Commission Report on Police Brutality* in class."

"So the subject matter wasn't a surprise."

"Not at all. I was familiar with Detective Frank Serpico and his role in establishing the commission. But watching it on the big screen—you know, seeing him get shot when he was only trying to be an honest police detective."

"I hear you, man" Rocco consoled as he slouched beside John on the grassy knoll.

There were no grave markers in the perimeter of the cemetery where the men sat. The mounded boundary offered a slightly elevated view of the neighborhood. From their darkened perch, and through the arms of a red maple, candles could be seen flickering through the windows of Rocco's house on the street below. The funky beat of Average White Band pulsated upward.

John took a swig from his bottle of Michelob. "To think that men who swore an oath to protect society act like thugs on the street. It brought back memories of that night I was unjustly jailed in Leesville. I used to believe that incident was an isolated event in a soldier's town, but now—well, I don't want to be in law enforcement anymore."

"John, remember last year when we went to see *Soldier Blue*? You had a strong reaction to that movie, too."

John dug his fingers in the grass as he tilted his head upward to gaze at the celestial grandeur. What Rocco said was true. Watching the Colorado State militia—under the leadership of a drunken commanding officer—heartlessly massacre a defenseless village of Cheyenne and Arapaho struck him hard.

"As I recall," Rocco began, "after that movie, we sat here and had a lengthy discussion about the 1864 Sand Creek Massacre and the 1968 My Lai Massacre."

"It's hard to accept that Americans can behave so dishonorably." John heaved a sigh before adding, "I always believed Americans were the good guys."

"Yo man, why wouldn't you?" Rocco surmised. "We grew up watching *The Lone Ranger* and *Gunsmoke* on TV. We read *Batman* and *Superman* comic books. And all those Westerns and war movies taught us about good guys and bad guys. Naturally, we wanted to be like our superheroes and fight the bad guys."

"I guess that's why I wanted to be a Pennsylvania State trooper. I wanted to be a good guy," John considered out loud. After a pause of thought he remarked, "I've met a lot of people in the field of law enforcement—most of them through my classes—and they seem to be sincere people that are really trying to help. So I know there are a lot of upstanding guys who stand on the right side of the law. But when you hear about the bribes, and the kickbacks and extortion that went through the ranks of the New York Police Department—and if you resist it, like Serpico did—well, they called him a rat and set him up." John sipped his beer and muttered to himself, "I don't want any part of it."

"I don't know about the Knapp Commission, but I didn't trust the findings of the Warren Commission," Rocco denounced. "Government investigations aren't above suspicion in my book. And from what I've learned in some of my journalism classes—about the media and propaganda—we're given a whitewashed version of reality. You know, one way of shaping public opinion is to have some important person or commission tell us something. If a big-shot tells us it's true, then the general populace believes it."

Rocco sat up and straightened his back while he emphasized, "There's a big difference between the America we read about in high school history textbooks and America's actual conduct on the world stage. Vietnam's a prime example."

As usual, John's defenses shifted into high gear at the mention of Vietnam. "When you talk about Vietnam, bro, remember I flew Dustoff with some honorable and brave men."

"Bro, I don't argue that. Dustoff is an example of our best. It's about compassion, man." Rocco clenched his right hand into a fist and thumped his chest several times. "Compassion for others is one of our highest qualities as human beings. And maybe some men committed atrocities at My Lai, but didn't some act heroically? Like that chopper pilot who put his Huey between the American troops and the fleeing My Lai civilians—you know who I'm talking about."

"Yeah, Hugh Thompson, Jr. That's his name."

After a long swallow of Budweiser, Rocco admitted, "You know, John, I humped the boonies, and I saw some men behave in very un-compassionate ways. I mean, they did things I'm sure they were taught not to do. But in war—no-holds-barred." Rocco took another gulp of beer before expressing, "Maybe because you were flying Dustoff and on the compassionate, medical side of things, you didn't see the shit some guys did. I was part of the killing machine, and I can tell you, ugly shit happened. And some guys really got off on it. There were times I was more afraid of my fellow Americans than the Vietnamese."

"I heard things, but I never saw any of that shit," John stated. "But inside the cargo bay, I saw the results of it. I saw what hatred and cruelty can do to a body."

388

"I've never told anyone this before, because I'd probably be accused of being a friggin' gook-lover," Rocco confided, stopping to take a guzzle of beer. "One time, my platoon was passing through a village. And while the platoon leader was talking to the chief, I stood off to the side, watching some of the peasants. Right then, it hit me. What a pleasant life the villagers had—if we would just leave them alone. I mean, the village was beautiful. The vegetation was neatly landscaped around the hooches. And the people were doing their thing—old mamasans cooking with young girls. A couple of boys were washing a water buffalo and they were laughing—just like kids anywhere. It looked like fun the way they were sliding off its back. I remember smiling and thinking how even the water buffalo seemed to be enjoying the whole thing. It was a happy, family setting—kind of like a Vietnamese Norman Rockwell scene. Right then, I realized that those peasants weren't hell-bent on overthrowing communism. They probably didn't care who was running the government—or if Vietnam even had a national government. They just wanted to live a peaceful, simple life on the land of their ancestors."

Rocco chugged from his bottle before continuing. "When my platoon was headed for another village, I couldn't believe it. One guy shot a water buffalo just for the hell of it. Fuck! I mean, why?" Rocco's voice quavered as he resumed. "Really, I was outraged. Right then, I knew what a major fuck-up the war was. How were we supposed to win hearts and minds with behavior like that?"

John nodded with understanding before confirming, "Sometimes when we flew over rice paddies, I saw water buffaloes that had been shot. Some were dead and on their sides, but some were upright, still alive and walking. But you could see their innards—or these knobs of fat—bulging out of holes in their hides where they'd been peppered with bullets."

"I'll tell you," Rocco asserted. "It was like a punch in the gut to watch the news last week and see those frantic people swarming the helicopters on top of the US Embassy in Saigon. How many guys died—and we got wounded—for fucking what? I didn't see anything honorable about our government's involvement in Vietnam. It had more to do with making profits and exploiting resources than spreading freedom and democracy. And me—like a lot of other dumb-fucks—got caught up in it all."

In his presence, John did not tolerate people speaking out against the Vietnam War. Painful memories of so many fallen brothers made him feel obligated to stand up for those who had served their country. But Rocco was different. He'd paid his dues. The battle scars on his flesh evidenced that he'd served his time. He was entitled to his opinions. And his views were respected. Listening to Rocco, John was reminded of his conversation at the University of Heidelberg nearly four years ago where those students had made similar points. Rocco could have held his own at that table. Today, John saw President Ford on the news, declaring an end to the Vietnam Era. So it was over—and he had to agree with Rocco—what good came of it?

"I volunteered for Vietnam," John attested. "I took to heart what President Kennedy said. You know, *Ask not what your country can do for you....*"

Rocco contributed his voice and they chimed in unison, "*Ask what you can do for your country.*"

John raked his fingers through his chin-length hair. Not only was his hair longer than ever, he also sported a thick moustache and scraggly beard. And if he felt like it, he sometimes wore a headband. The men sat in silence for a long while. Headlights and the familiar putt-putt of a small gasoline engine captured their attention. They watched as a VW Beetle drove past and then parked on a side street. Five partygoers piled out of the car and headed down the sidewalk to Rocco's house. High-pitched squeals rose from the front porch as his roommate, Darla, greeted the new arrivals and ushered them inside. In the shadows of blossoming trees, John and Rocco remained unseen in their hillside sanctuary.

Rocco broke the silence, "From what I've seen, there's corruption in a lot more places than just the police force. Hell, where isn't there corruption?" Rocco leaned forward and stretched his spine. "Man, it blows your mind to think about it. There's corruption in business, in government, even in goddamn churches. It seems like wherever there's a human, there's the potential for corruption."

"What good are laws if people don't obey them? Social order depends on law and order," John insisted. "We're a country founded on laws."

"Yeah, law is holy here. Americans grow up obeying laws," Rocco agreed. "Starting in kindergarten, we're taught to stand in line and take orders," he cracked. "But really, John, are things so black and white? We have this rigid judgment of how everything would be perfect once the good guys lock up all the bad guys—or wipe them off the face of the earth. But who are the bastards we want to annihilate?"

"In class, we've studied theories that tried to identify the murdering mind," John explained. "There was a popular one, about ten years ago, that claimed mass murderers had an unusual chromosome pattern. You know, females are XX and males are XY, but these guys were labeled 'supermales' because they had a pattern of XYY. They were thought to be overly aggressive and more prone to deviant behavior. But years later, they found out that Richard Speck didn't fit the profile—remember him?"

"Yeah, he was the one that murdered those eight nurses. That was the summer before my sophomore year in high school—1966."

"Well, turns out he didn't have that supermale chromosome pattern." John moved his hand away from his T-tube and snapped his fingers and pointed. "Kaput! That ended that. The chromosome theory eventually fell into disrepute almost as fast as it became popular." John tipped the bottle of Michelob and slugged down the last few drops.

"There's not a physical clue to the criminal mind?" Rocco wondered.

"So far, no theories are absolute. Dr. Walters adheres more to the psychological origins of crime rather than trying to locate a brain defect or find some physical cause. And I know from those field trips to Indiana State Prison and Pendleton, murderers can be very different."

"Oh yeah, I remember last year when you were in an encounter group with five murderers. And you mentioned how Dr. Walters himself is a successful product of rehabilitation."

John paused to pay attention to the music from the party. Someone had put on Earth, Wind & Fire's new album, *That's the Way of the World*. He and Rocco listened to the lyrics of the title song.

A child is born with a heart of gold
The way of the world makes his heart grow cold

When the song ended, John quietly offered, "I used to believe that if someone broke the law, nothing else mattered. They committed the crime and they had to do the time. And I wanted to be a law enforcer who put them away—like the Lone Ranger galloping up to the sheriff's office on Silver with the bad guys in tow. But now, my mind asks why? Why would somebody do such a thing? What would lead somebody to commit such a heinous act?"

"It's complicated," Rocco affirmed.

John nodded his head in agreement. "Earth, Wind & Fire just said it—a child is born with a heart of gold. And so I wonder what happened in a murderer's life that hardened that heart of gold? What were the life circumstances that made him become a calloused killer?"

"Now you're talking about social problems—like poverty, dysfunctional families, oppressed people, and all that kind of shit."

"That's right. I've learned a lot from my psychology and sociology classes about social issues that foster deviant behavior," John reflected. "If we deal with those problems, maybe we could prevent some people from becoming criminals in the first place."

"That makes a lot of sense to me," Rocco acknowledged as he grasped his empty bottle and got up on his feet.

"I'm about to fill out applications for graduate school, but I've changed my mind about my major," John said while stretching and standing. "I'm not going to apply to a criminal justice program. I'm going to look into something else. I want to understand the roots of

393

criminal behavior and help nip it in the bud."

"That sounds like a good move," Rocco concurred. He held up his empty bottle of Budweiser and added, "Speaking of Bud and good moves, why don't we head down to the party and get a couple more cool ones."

"I'm with ya, bro. Time to party!"

Chapter 23

"Okay! Cut it out, you two!" John waved his arms to shoo Marblecake and Spot away from the assortment of papers he had strewn across the living room floor. As soon as skittish Marblecake vanished under the couch, John softened his bristly voice and tapped a ballpoint pen on the rug beside his thigh to coax her out of hiding. He didn't want her to go into seclusion in his new apartment like she had done when he first moved to Bloomington. At present, he especially valued her company because Marblecake and Spot were the only familiar faces he had in his new city of residence.

When John left Toms River two years ago, everything he owned fit inside his Corvette. In Bloomington he'd acquired so much stuff—furniture, books, a lava lamp, larger stereo speakers—his possessions would never squeeze into his TVR. Last week, he rented a U-Haul truck and filled it with his belongings. Rocco drove the U-Haul while John followed in his TVR, and they made the 4-hour journey northeast to Columbus, Ohio. Approaching the metropolitan area, John was astounded by the sheer size of the city. It was definitely covered by a great deal more concrete than Bloomington.

If John had researched Columbus beforehand, he would have

learned that the centrally located city was the State's capital. Historically, Columbus experienced a population boom when the National Road opened the Ohio River Valley for settlement and commerce. Following the Revolutionary War, President George Washington promoted the construction of a road linking cities of the United States from east to west. It was President Thomas Jefferson who actually signed legislation to authorize the National Road—the country's first federally funded highway. Of course, before white settlers arrived, American natives had carved a network of footpaths across the continent, and many modern roads owe their existence to those earlier trails. The National Road started at the city of Cumberland, nestled against the Appalachian Mountains in the far western portion of Maryland. Adjacent to Cumberland, a rocky river valley made a natural gateway to the west, and through it, the National Road crossed the mountains. The road extended to Ohio by the early 1830s and led to Columbus' expanded development. As John and Rocco drove east toward Columbus on West Broad Street, or US Route 40, they were driving on part of the National Road's original route.

The next day, Rocco drove the empty U-Haul back to Bloomington. It was sad for John to say goodbye to his good friend and the pleasant life he had known in Indiana. Yet, once he had been accepted into The Ohio State University's graduate school, John knew there were new horizons he felt called to explore.

Last month, two milestones occurred in his life. On 1 August 1975, John was permanently retired from the Armed Forces of the United States of America. Receiving the certificate marked the end of an official medical waiting period, but John already understood nothing more could be done to his neck. He'd moved on. He accepted his fate and was now focused on his education. When the terms of his retirement and disability benefits were brought up, John was ready to walk away from his military service without any compensation.

"Johnny, don't be a fool!" his mother scolded. "You served your country. The American people sent you over to that God-forsaken place. If you hadn't been there, you wouldn't have got shot. They owe you!"

"I was only doing my job," John protested.

"Well, you'd better think about what it could be like when you get old. Your grandpop was medically retired from the Army, and don't you remember all his problems? What if your neck got worse—then what? If you refuse the benefits now, you won't be able to get them later. And for Christ's sake, the American people should take care of their veterans."

Years later, John would look back and greatly appreciate his mother's insistence that he accept the disability stipend.

Another milestone in his life occurred at the end of the month. On August 31, 1975, he received his Bachelor of Science degree in Criminal Justice. Unlike Ocean County College, where John was center stage addressing his fellow graduates, at Indiana University he didn't participate in a graduation ceremony. Funny how things had changed. Nevertheless, John was proud to graduate from college with a 3.1 GPA. His many hours in the library paid off.

Marblecake finally came over to investigate the tapping pen and then cuddled up beside John's leg. He smoothed her sleek tortoise-shell fur, and a loud purr told him she was content once again.

"So, what am I going to do?" an exasperated John queried his cats as he held up the college catalog.

He hadn't thoroughly investigated the Department of Sociology at OSU when he decided to apply to the program of Race Relations. John chose the course of study because over the last decade the country had exploded with racial tensions. Recently, mandatory busing to achieve school integration had led to violence in Boston and other Northeastern cities. Since John didn't harbor racial prejudice, he believed his unique perspectives would make him a natural mediator. He could be of service to a nation on fire with ethnic conflicts.

John's life experiences hadn't cultivated a racial bias. Certainly, the color of skin didn't matter when flying Dustoff. In the cargo bay, such differences didn't make a difference. This John knew, because he had seen so many men's insides. While outer skin shades varied, inwardly they were all the same red-blooded Americans. Also, he grew up loving music that transcended ethnicity. To John, music and rhythm were everything; skin color of the artist was insignificant. His soul throbbed to the doo-wop love songs where every voice shared an equal role in creating those characteristic muscular harmonies. Some of the singing groups, such as the Crests, the Del-Vikings, and the Jaguars were racially integrated back in the 1950s, well ahead of the times. In addition, over the years, John had developed close friendships with black kids from his grandparents' neighborhood.

During various ages of his life, John's family had lived with his father's parents in their brownstone row house in northern Philadelphia, which his grandmom had inherited from her parents. Even after moving to their tract house in Nottingham, they went back each weekend to be nourished by grandmom's home cooking. Since he was a small tyke, John recalled the loud thumping sounds the cars and trucks made as their tires bumped along the road's uneven, granite-stone surface. Tracks from trolley cars—no longer in use— ran down the middle of the road and added to the resounding clatter rising from the busy one-way street. North Fifth Street contained a combination of businesses and residences. There were mom-and-pop-type grocery stores, drug stores, commercial garages, and taverns all interspersed between the 3-story row houses. Several doors down from his grandparents stood a vacant foundry where horses had once been shoed and wagon wheels repaired. On the opposite side of the street was a large weathered brick building that had served as a banquet and meeting hall. As more immigrants that could afford it made the exodus to the suburbs, old Germantown transitioned to a racially mixed neighborhood. By the time John graduated from high school, his grandparents were the only remaining white people.

Directly across from his grandparents' house was the home of John's friend, Brucie. Since first grade, he and Brucie had walked side by side to John Welsh Elementary School on Fourth Street. After school, they played together from the time John was old enough to cross the street by himself. They also hung out with other neighborhood kids close to their same age. Reggie lived a few doors down from Brucie, and Butch and his brother, Bob, lived beside Reggie. Over the years, the boys spent hours tossing and trading baseball cards—a coveted Willie Mays for a prized Mickey Mantle. The youngsters didn't care if shortstop Chico Fernandez was the first black man to play with the Philadelphia Phillies. They just knew that he and pitcher Robin Roberts were star players and their baseball cards were highly valued when won in a card toss.

Brucie had a number of sisters, and his house seemed to be filled with ongoing activity. John was graciously welcomed into the always open front door. He was treated kindly and offered food. After a while, he wondered why his stout, rosy-cheeked grandmother didn't reciprocate the generosity. His black friends were never invited into her home. John became more aware of his family's discriminatory attitudes when his father drove through the inner city and uttered derogatory insults at the black people on the sidewalk. Of course, his father's racial name-calling could only be heard inside the car, but John would sit there, forced to listen to those unkind remarks. The behavior confused him. The tone of his father's voice implied there was something wrong with black people. But John got along fine with his friends. Sure, they were a different color than he was, but he liked them, and there had never been any trouble between them. From a young age, John couldn't understand how people could be so mean to another just because of the color of a person's skin.

Considering his diverse background, applying to graduate school to study Race Relations seemed like a good fit. However, John hadn't visited Ohio ahead of time and hadn't spoken to anyone in the department. After making the move to Columbus and meeting with his academic advisor, he was flabbergasted to learn that the Race Relations program in the Department of Sociology was heavily weighted toward research and statistics.

Uh-oh. That didn't interest John at all. He didn't want to be studying theories and compiling data. That would be like having a desk job in the police department, and he wanted to be hands-on. Now, here he was, all alone in a new city, thumbing through the college catalog and trying to decide what to do with his future.

"Hey, this looks intriguing," John informed Marblecake and Spot as he highlighted a section in the catalog. "It's a new division. It's called Black Studies."

Rising from the living room floor and heading to the kitchen, John thought his living arrangements were pretty cool. His old Army buddy Roy Reynolds had found the apartment for him. Two years ago, when Roy discovered that John had survived and was attending school in Bloomington, Roy made the drive from his home outside of Columbus to visit his friend. The last time they had seen each other John was being wheeled onto a C-141, and Roy had waved farewell by flipping him the bird.

Roy was ten years older than John and gainfully employed. He insisted on taking his college-student friend out for dinner at a fine restaurant in Bloomington. Roy didn't drink—and still didn't curse—therefore John limited himself to one beer and strictly monitored his vocabulary as they talked about the unforgettable times they had lived through.

"John, besides Hartman, have you seen any of the other guys—like Zeke?" Roy inquired after the waitress refilled his coffee cup.

Swallowing a last bite of apple pie, John replied, "Yeah, one time I did see Zeke. Hartman gave him my number when I was at Walson Army Hospital, and Zeke called and said he had some of my things—like the stereo I bought at the PX at Freedom Hill. So I borrowed my step-dad's car and drove up to Trenton, but it was really odd to see him. He was like somebody else—nothing like the Zeke I used to know."

John stopped to take a swallow of coffee. "It was dark by the time

I got to his place, and it looked like a rough part of town, so I didn't want to linger in Trenton. But it was awkward to see Zeke. His eyes were so distant. I knew my neck looked bad—it was still red and raw—and maybe that's why it was hard for him to look at me. And I couldn't really talk. I didn't have the T-tube yet, so I was hard to understand."

John stared at the black liquid in his cup before murmuring, "Really, it was sad. Zeke used to be such a funny guy, and he used to keep me sane by making me laugh. But seeing him in Trenton was like meeting a stranger." John took another sip of coffee and mentioned, "Hartman said that Zeke blamed Bill Stanton for me getting shot."

"Really?" Roy's voice conveyed surprise. "I heard he blamed himself—for being asleep and not flying as the 5th man who might have protected you."

There was a pause in conversation before Roy stated, "I don't know if you know this, John, but Warrant Officer Stanton was recommended for the Congressional Medal of Honor for flying that mission when you got shot."

"I didn't know that. But when I was in Walson, I was presented with the Distinguished Flying Cross, and I assumed the rest of the crew got one, too."

"I'm pretty sure they did," Roy affirmed while stirring cream into his coffee.

"What about Stanton?" John wondered.

"Well, it was a big deal that he was even seriously considered for the Congressional Medal. I think it had a lot to do with him holding it together and being able to fly that shot-up chopper back to Baldy.

It was really shot to pieces, you know." Roy paused to set his spoon upon the saucer. "Then, when it was deliberated by the higher-ups, the Congressional Medal of Honor got bumped down to a Silver Star. So then, Stanton did receive the Silver Star."

For a brief moment, John's mind traveled back to 1969 and that intense time at LZ Baldy when his life changed forever. The certificate accompanying the DFC stated it was presented for heroism during aerial flight over those days in August. Yet, John knew that many previous missions had been equally as perilous, and no doubt so were many that followed.

After dinner, John and Roy parted ways. It was different to reunite with men who had only known each other through the service. In the Army, they wore the same uniforms, knew the same people, and shared the same daily experiences. In the combat theater, those experiences included frequent rocket and mortar attacks. Brothers readily bonded in an environment saturated with violence and fear. In civilian life, they no longer shared those common denominators. Each passing year carried them a farther distance from their war days. Age and lifestyle differences became more pronounced, and mostly the men had more in common with the past than they did with the present.

All the same, friendships forged during war were unbreakable bonds, thus John didn't hesitate to contact his old Army buddy when he made the decision to attend OSU and needed to find a place to live. Roy seemed overjoyed to have secured an apartment for John in a complex named The Club. Amenities included tennis courts, a swimming pool, a workout/weight room—and as John would soon learn—some very interesting neighbors.

Although the apartment itself was agreeable, John had misgivings about relocating to Columbus. Not only was he disappointed to discover he'd enrolled in the wrong department, he was having a hard time adjusting to a big-city setting. Instead of a pleasant jog along a tree-lined street, which was his normal route to campus in Indiana, John had to drive a 6-lane freeway to get to his new campus. Factories, tall buildings, and busy traffic were part of the atmosphere that neighbored The Ohio State University. And if he thought IU had been large, the sprawling grounds of OSU and an additional 10,000 students were almost staggering.

In 1870, The Ohio State University was founded as a land-grant university. For at least two decades prior, a number of government officials advocated granting land to states for the purpose of building colleges. There was a strong belief that in order for a democracy to function, there needed to be a well-educated populace. Aiming for a citizenry with world-class standards, a Vermont Representative, Justin Smith Morrill, introduced a bill to build colleges where members of the working class could receive practical educations. Congress passed the bill, but President James Buchanan vetoed it. Morrill resubmitted the legislation with the amendment that the proposed institutions would teach military tactics as well as engineering and agriculture. The reconfigured Morrill Act was then signed into law by President Abraham Lincoln in 1862. Sixty-nine colleges were funded by the land grants, including Cornell University, the Massachusetts Institute of Technology, the University of Wisconsin at Madison, and The Ohio State University, originally named the Ohio Agricultural and Mechanical College.

Later in the week, as John made his way across campus, he

noted a variety of architecture and a number of very modern-looking structures. He gave himself plenty of time to locate the building that housed the offices of the newly established Division of Black Studies. John was directed to the dean's office where he took a seat and his interview commenced.

"I see you've taken a number of classes on race relations at Indiana University." The dean made reference to John's application, which was in an open folder upon his desk. "And you wrote a paper on *Racial Attitudes in Martinsville, Indiana.* Why did you choose that topic for your final paper?" The distinguished-looking black man calmly folded his hands and waited for John's response.

"Martinsville is about fifteen miles from Bloomington, and through some classes, I heard blacks were advised to keep away from Martinsville because of Klan activity there. When I read about the unsolved murder of that young black woman in 1968—Carol Jenkins—I thought I'd investigate and see if Martinsville deserved its racist reputation."

"What did you conclude?"

"Well, Indiana's State Constitution sure made it clear that blacks weren't welcome there in 1850. It actually declared that Negroes or Mulattoes shouldn't even enter the state. And any business dealings with them would be illegal."

The dean removed his glasses and leaned back in his chair as John spoke.

"I went to the town and browsed through years of past issues of the *Martinsville Daily Reporter* for clues, and I interviewed the Editor-in-Chief," John explained. "The editor had the same opinion as the police—that the murder was sexually motivated, and that Miss

Jenkins rejected somebody's advances. But it's been seven years since her murder, and they still don't have a suspect," John reported. "And I asked the editor if any black people currently lived in Martinsville. He told me that only a couple of racially mixed families lived on the outskirts of town. He said that blacks would rather go to Indianapolis instead of an area they believed to be hostile."

The dean put on his glasses again and looked down at John's application. "I see you've already read a number of books on the reading list: *Nigger* by Dick Gregory, *Soul On Ice* by Eldridge Cleaver, Richard Wright's *Black Boy* and *Native Son.* And you've read *Jim Crow's Defense* by Newby and *The Souls of Black Folk* by Du Bois." Glancing up, the dean asked, "Did the literature provide understanding into the black experience in America?"

"Yes, sir, very much so. And other books like *Dark Ghetto* by Kenneth Clark and *Rivers of Blood, Years of Darkness* by Robert Conot really gave me insight into what prejudice can lead to."

The dean discussed the details and goals of the new Black Studies Division at OSU and then inquired, "John, you would be the only white person to join this program. What experiences have you had with black people that would connect you to this course of study?"

"A black girl once saved my life," John blurted.

The dean leaned back against his chair again and folded his hands to listen to John's explanation.

"Well, my grandparents lived in a racially mixed neighborhood in Philadelphia, so I had some good friends that were black," John began.

Thinking back on his childhood and teenage years, John realized he had always enjoyed spending time in the old neighborhood.

Naturally, he was warmed by the doting affection his grandmom showered upon her eldest grandson. John didn't interact much with his grandpop, but he understood that Pappy had bravely served his country during World War I. Pappy had been one of over a million Americans who fought the Germans on French soil. He'd participated in several campaigns, including the final and largest American operation of the war—the Meuse-Argonne military offensive of 1918. John had been told that Pappy and fellow soldiers had just finished burying a high number of casualties between the Meuse River and the snow-covered Argonne Forest when they were again struck by a barrage of artillery, resulting in more losses and more body parts to gather and bury. Whether it was the mustard gas he'd been exposed to or the shock of the horrors he'd seen, when World War II broke out, Pappy's mental condition drastically deteriorated. He was no longer able to work at Stetson's hat company, which had been his employer for thirty-seven years. John heard stories of John Neil Seebeth I being a bright and funny man before he went off to war, but that's not the grandpop John ever knew. John only remembered having a very superficial exchange of words with the shell of a man that was his grandfather.

Their row house was a couple of miles north of Philadelphia's historic district, located near the west banks of the Delaware River. There, a web of wharves had developed into the port city's dominant commercial district. In 1682, when Pennsylvania's namesake—the English Quaker William Penn—extended an invitation to the poor and persecuted to join his *holy experiment*, the subsequent settlement contained a diversity of races and religions seen nowhere else in colonial America. Houses of worship of every denomination soon sprouted up in the city of *brotherly love*—the meaning of the ancient Greek word, *Philadelphia*. Both the *Declaration of Independence* and the *Constitution* were adopted in Independence Hall on Chestnut Street. The concepts of *we the people* and *all men are created equal* rang from the Liberty Bell on 6th and Market. John had grown up in a city founded upon the tolerance of differences. He was proud of Philadelphia's heritage, and whenever visiting his grandparents, he looked forward to exploring the busy streets.

John took a breath before describing to the dean how a black girl had saved his life back in 1963. He would never forget that day. He had just finished eating the baked ham and boiled potatoes his grandmother had prepared and served for their lunch, along with ice cream and pretzel sticks she knew John fancied for dessert.

After thanking his grandmom for the meal and praising her cooking, John excused himself from the table where his father, brother, and grandpop remained seated.

"I'm going out," John had announced to his father. Ever since his mother left a year ago, John wasn't beholden to anyone. He was only fifteen, but he would come and go as he pleased.

John headed out the front door toward his favorite destination—Front Street. Industrial buildings and warehouses lined the 3-block route to the busy street. The whole area was rather run down, but compared to the homogenized surroundings of their suburban neighborhood, the hubbub of Front Street offered a captivating and exhilarating experience. Along the sidewalk, colorful displays of fruits and vegetables and a variety of wares were exhibited. Pungent smells from tobacco shops and tantalizing aromas from a multitude of ethnic restaurants mingled with exhaust from cars and delivery trucks, filling John's senses as he strolled down the main arterial. At each intersection, street-corner vendors sold soft, warm pretzels topped with mustard for a nickel. High above, the El transported commuters on the overhead trestles and tracks. About every fifteen minutes, loud metallic screams ripped through the air as the trains came to a screeching stop. Many Saturdays, John would go to the family-oriented theater on Front Street where he would pay a quarter to watch a matinee and enter such adventurous realms as *20,000 Leagues Under the Sea* or *Journey to the Center of the Earth*.

On that particular warm afternoon, John wore a white t-shirt and khaki pants as he set out for Front Street. Turning left at the first intersection onto West Dauphin Street, he stopped to retie the laces of his desert boots before crossing over the railroad tracks. On the same side of the street, a half a block away, John saw about twenty teenagers congregated on the concrete staircase of a large, brick warehouse. Continuing in his same direction toward Front Street, John soon approached the group of teens. As he neared, he noticed that all the girls who had been standing around the stairs quickly moved over to the other side of the street, giving him a peculiar side-long stare as they traversed in front of him. John felt like something wasn't right, but he continued on his route.

He glanced to the left at the group of boys gathered around the concrete steps. They, too, were giving him a hard stare. John's heart raced and his stomach muscles tightened. He sensed trouble coming his way. Just as he was about to pass by, one boy jumped off the bottom step and landed on his feet directly in front of John. The boy appeared to be Puerto Rican, and he stuck his face right up to John's.

"Where you from?" he asked menacingly.

John wasn't a fighter. To him, fighting wasn't rational behavior. He had seen plenty of guys with facial scars and missing teeth as the result of some stupid fight. They ended up permanently carrying the legacy of that fight long after the memory of the reason for fighting faded. Furthermore, girls often commented to John on what a nice smile he had, and he knew his smile depended on the full set of teeth he displayed. To risk losing a tooth in a fistfight over a trivial disagreement made no sense to John. Nonetheless, boys from Philly carried a certain prideful attitude. John wasn't a coward, and if forced into a situation, he would stand his ground.

Refusing to dignify the Puerto Rican boy's affront, John brushed past him and persevered down the sidewalk toward Front Street. He had only taken a few steps when the rest of the teens jumped off the stairs and rushed up behind him. The group corralled him against the brick wall of the warehouse and started punching him. John curled over, trying to protect his face and midsection from the pummeling. When the punches ceased—after what seemed like a very long minute—John stood erect and found himself backed against a wall, facing about ten teenagers. All the boys were white except for the Puerto Rican who stood directly in front of John gripping a knife in his hand.

"I'm goin' to ask you again," the boy challenged in a threatening voice, slowly picking at John's t-shirt with the point of his knife. "Where you from?"

John stared at the half-grin and cocky expression on the boy's face. He was scared shitless, but this punk was really pissing him off. As the point of the knife continued to lightly prick at his chest,

410

John became fixated on wiping the smirk off this guy's face. Backed against the wall and feeling claustrophobic, he made up his mind to make a move, even if it meant getting stabbed. John decided to use the element of surprise and lunge at the Puerto Rican. He would count to three in his head, and then grab the wrist that held the knife with his left hand and clutch and squeeze the boy's neck with his right. Then he'd charge through the circle of guys and break free to crowded Front Street. He began silently counting. One. His rage doubled as the boy persisted in waving the knife in front of John's throat. Zeroing in on the guy's Adam's apple, John determined that's where his right hand was going to go. Two. John watched the cold eyes glaring at him and took a deep breath. Body tensed, John was about to spring into action at the count of "Three!" when all of a sudden, a girl's voice pierced the trance.

"I know him," a young black girl yelled. She seemed to have appeared out of nowhere before shouting and then turning and running down Dauphin Street in the opposite direction.

Everyone rotated toward the youngster who had just prevented John from getting stabbed. He had been ready to go up against the blade, but one of Brucie's sisters had inadvertently saved him.

The teenage girls came back across the street and handed John tissues for the bleeding cuts on his face. Some of them recognized him from when he had attended John Welsh Elementary School. The Puerto Rican went back over to the concrete staircase while the other boys explained how one of their friends had been stabbed at the Front Street movie house a few weeks ago, and they were looking for members of the gang from Fishtown they believed did it. Agreeing that the assault had been a misunderstanding, a couple of boys shook hands with John before he headed back to his grandparents' house.

Halfway up the front staircase of their row house, John stopped when he heard someone call his name.

"Johnny! My sister told me what happened," Brucie hollered as he dodged between cars and ran across the street to where John was standing. "Man, they did a number on your face—it's cut and bruised all over. Go clean up and come back down right quick. And don't let your grandmother see your face," he advised.

"I'm home!" John declared as he ran upstairs to wash. "I'm going out!" he notified two minutes later, slamming the front door behind him.

Across the street, Brucie, Reggie, Butch, and Bob were standing on the sidewalk waiting for him. As soon as the traffic cleared, John joined them.

"How are you feeling?" Reggie asked.

"My ribs and face are sore, but I'm okay."

Through his black-framed glasses that gave him a studious appearance, Reggie scrutinized the marks on John's face. A couple of years older and a few inches taller than the rest of them, Reggie's strong, quiet manner had earned a certain authority among the group of friends.

"A PR did it to him," Butch informed.

"Come on, let's go," Reggie instructed the other four.

Not knowing their destination, John, Brucie, Butch, and Bob trailed behind Reggie as he walked up to Dauphin and made a left. Soon, they were back at the warehouse where John had been attacked. The teenage boys and girls all seemed surprised to see John again.

Without pausing, Reggie strode past the other teenagers and right up to where the Puerto Rican boy was standing beside the steps. Reggie's nose couldn't have been more than an inch away from the surprised teen's face.

In a barely audible voice, Reggie uttered, "I can understand if one of your friends gets stabbed, you want to get the ones that did it." Reggie slowly braced his right foot back a step as he continued, "And I can understand how a mistake can happen."

Right after speaking the word, *happen*, with lightning speed, Reggie sucker-punched the Puerto Rican, who dropped to the sidewalk like a rock. All of the onlookers—black and white alike—gasped at the loud thunderclap of Reggie's fist striking the side of the boy's head.

"But what really irks me," Reggie pressed, "is you pulling a blade on him." He pointed a finger at John to show who he meant. Unexpectedly—without warning—Reggie swung his right foot back and kicked the Puerto Rican in the head.

John's gaze jumped over to Brucie. His friend's wide-eyed, slack-jawed expression mirrored John's own shocked reaction. A half a block away, a high-pitched shriek sounded from an overhead train. When Reggie turned and headed back down Dauphin Street, Butch, Bob, Brucie, and John silently followed. Although easily outnumbered by the white teenagers, no one moved and nothing more was said. John never had any more trouble in the old neighborhood after that.

Perhaps the telling of his story had made an impression on the dean, because John ended up being accepted into the new Black Studies Division. He pursued the topic with his usual academic fervor, completing all assignments and studying hard for the tests. John became friends with some of the two-dozen students in the graduate program. A couple guys were his regular study partners, and sometimes they played basketball or jogged together.

Inside the classroom, John began to feel a bit like an outsider. Class discussions often referred to the *blue-eyed devil*, the symbolic, undisputed oppressor of black people. Since John was the only fair-haired, blue-eyed student in the room, he physically invoked the sins of the father. His ideas were always respectfully received, yet John came to realize that he was approaching the program from a mental understanding. For the black students, the classes also provided an emotional healing. And because John closely resembled that blue-eyed devil, he felt his presence interfered with the group's therapeutic process. After completing the first quarter, John withdrew from the Black Studies Division.

Chapter 24

John resided at The Club for a year, but when his lease was about to expire, he didn't hesitate in searching for a new place to live. Initially, he'd been thrilled with all the conveniences and amenities and the swinging environment of his apartment complex. And swinging it literally was. A group of Ohio State football players lived there, and they exhibited a propensity for Quaaludes and orgies. John never popped a Quaalude—and he was never invited to the orgies—however, he and all of the other nearby tenants couldn't avoid hearing the wild parties. Lounging beside the pool, John had met some other colorful characters, like the two roommates who proudly bragged of their sexual exploits. The men kept detailed records, because they had a $1,000 wager riding on who would score highest in their sport-fucking tournament. John also became acquainted with a few milder residents who he would accompany to a popular fern bar on weekends. Dressed in fine duds, the goal of the evening at TGI Friday's was about meeting women. Yet after a while, the whole scene began to lose its appeal. So when John vacated his premises at The Club, he left a certain lifestyle behind as well.

Since first attending Ocean County College, John had faithfully adhered to the cultural prescription for happiness: he drove a fancy car, he wore stylish clothes, and he usually had a hot babe on his arm. At a time in his life when he believed no woman would find him attractive because of his physical stigma, his popularity and outer successes helped uplift his sagging self-esteem. Sleeping with a lot of women had actually been a healing of sorts. But as John came to realize, following society's prescription for happiness wasn't fulfilling. For one thing, he couldn't be proud of his behavior. He became skilled at sweet-talking the girls and telling them how special they were. The deception required in order to be a man of conquest was something John didn't feel good about. Too often, when the fire of the night's intense hormones cooled in the morning light, it was disappointing to find the attractive female—usually someone he met at a bar—had nothing intellectually stimulating to say. John would make excuses and wriggle out the message of "don't call me, I'll call you."

John was a product of a culture that sold everything from cars, cigarettes, and toothpaste with sex appeal. Bombarded by ads that represented females as sexual objects, he possessed a limited view of women. Furthermore, his interactions with them were greatly influenced by confusing lessons he'd learned from his mother—namely, that a woman couldn't be trusted. John's upbringing hadn't role-modeled anything close to a healthy, intimate relationship. Still, his heart truly longed for a loving connection. His motivation for going to bars and clubs had been driven by the search for that special someone. However, the more John observed his surroundings at The Club, the more he grew tired of the shallowness of it all. He wasn't interested in just obtaining another bed partner; he wanted to find a woman who also moved his heart. Deciding he probably wasn't going to meet her in a fern bar, John quit going out on weekends and retreated to his books and studies. His mind eagerly absorbed new ideas, and his understanding of the world deepened. John began to see women more holistically and soon found himself in an environment more reflective of his new awareness.

"Are you the one who called about the apartment?" the smiling woman inquired.

John introduced himself to Frannie, the current tenant in the upstairs apartment of the beautiful old house.

"This is a great space," Frannie affirmed while giving John a tour.

"Why are you moving out?" John wondered.

"I'm moving in with my boyfriend. He's renovating an old Victorian closer to campus and dividing it into two apartments like this house."

"Are you a student?" John asked.

"Not any more," Frannie replied. "I graduated last year. Now I'm a teacher. I teach third grade. How about you—are you a student?"

"It's a long story, but I was accepted to graduate school in the Department of Sociology last year, but I didn't realize how statistics-oriented the program was, so I transferred to the new Black Studies Division, but that wasn't right for me, and I ended up withdrawing mid-semester. So over the past ten months, I've been volunteering at different agencies."

John didn't hesitate to rent the apartment, which was located in an old area with the familiar moniker of Germantown. Marblecake and Spot were delighted to explore the interesting nooks and crannies of their new home, and they especially appreciated the various views from the upstairs windows.

For John, becoming friends with Frannie and her boyfriend, Shaun, was an added bonus. He was often invited to their place across town for vegetarian meals and lively political discussions. Frannie introduced John to the natural food co-op where she regularly shopped, and there he met a different kind of woman. Like the food in the store, the women were wholesome and natural. Decidedly unpretentious, they exhibited little inclination to paint themselves into the culture's beauty myth. Instead, the women focused more on social concerns, such as boycotting Nestlé's products because of the company's promotion of breast-milk substitute in third-world countries. For the first time in his life, John was able to relate to women without the limiting, sexual-object perspective that had so heavily dominated his past.

John's new neighbors in Germantown were quite unlike his old neighbors at The Club. Jeremy lived below John and was a recent graduate who now worked as an executive with TWA (Trans-World Airlines). Alex lived in the house behind them and was a medical student from Cuba. Occasionally, Frannie would stop by and smoke a doobie with her old neighbors and John. A spirited discussion would usually follow, as Frannie had strong opinions on a wide range of topics. John enjoyed the friendly debates, which often resulted in Alex attacking capitalism while Jeremy supported it.

One evening, John rose from the couch to answer a knock at his door.

"Are you ready to go?" Jeremy asked. To the puzzled expression on John's face he elaborated, "Remember? The woman across the street invited us to her birthday party. It's tonight."

"That's right," John recalled. "Hey, Jeremy, you go ahead. I'm in the middle of a book, so I think I'll just stay home and read." John marked his place and then set the book on the coffee table. He headed toward the kitchen to refill his empty cup of tea.

"Is this what you're reading?" Jeremy sauntered over and picked up the book from the stack on the table. "*Born On the Fourth of July* by Ron Kovic. What's it about?"

"It's about a Marine who comes home from Vietnam paralyzed, and he exposes the disgraceful conditions of the VA hospitals and...."

"Come on," Jeremy insisted as he tossed the book onto the coffee table. "You can read later. Right now, we should be neighborly and go to the party."

Reluctantly, John followed Jeremy across the street to their neighbor's apartment. The woman worked as a secretary in the State Capitol building, so a variety of people attended her party. Jeremy—equipped with a drink and his good looks—made the rounds to meet some of the female guests. John stood off to the side, nursing his beer and thinking about Ron Kovic when a loud commotion entered the room. A man dressed in a pinstriped suit and loosened tie walked in with a woman half his age hanging on his arm. The shrill laughter of the obtrusive couple made it obvious they had been drinking.

"He's a state senator," John heard the woman behind him whisper to her friend. "And he's married—but that's not his wife."

Someone must have told the politician that John was an injured

Vietnam veteran, because he later came over and asked in a raucous voice, "Hey, buddy. How's it been for you since you've been back?"

"I'm not your buddy," John tersely replied, wondering who invited this jerk into his world.

The politician was persistent. Despite John's brush-off, he approached twice more to ask how the war had been for him. By then, John was ready to sound off. In his own rough voice, he let the guy know about the suffering he'd witnessed—and for what? American capitalists had sent them there to fight a needless war. John walked away and took a seat on the couch.

Shortly, the politician came over and sat down on the other end of the couch. His female companion wedged beside him.

"So, who is paying for your education?" the state senator pointedly questioned John. "Is the government paying for it?"

"Yes, it is," John responded.

Leaning over the lady, the senator extended his arm and shook his index finger at John, cautioning, "Well, if the government's paying for your education, how'd you like to make half that amount?"

"Are you threatening me?" John sprang from the couch and riveted his gaze to the man's eyes. "I don't want to waste my breath talking to you," he asserted while inhaling and speaking through his T-tube. "If this is how *you* serve your country," John glanced at the young woman who was almost sitting upon the senator's lap, "then you have no business talking to someone who really did serve."

To John, this arrogant, overindulging, hypocritical loudmouth represented most of what he found wrong with America. Unable to remain in the same room with the man, John bolted out the front door. He slowed his pace when Jeremy called his name.

"I heard that asshole threaten to take away your GI benefits," Jeremy hissed as he caught up with his friend. "Could he really do such a thing? It's not right!"

"You know," John sputtered. "I had a gut feeling he was going to say something like that before he said it, but when he actually said it, I couldn't believe what I was hearing!"

"Well, if he ever did anything like that—John, I promise you right now—I'd pay the difference out of my own pocket."

"Thanks, man. I really appreciate you saying that." John playfully punched Jeremy in the arm, knowing he would never accept his offer.

"Come on back inside," Jeremy requested. "I met a couple of nice ladies and…."

"You have fun, Jeremy. I'm gonna go back and read."

John and Jeremy clasped hands before heading in opposite directions.

In autumn of 1976, Frannie and Shaun invited John to be the first tenant in the downstairs apartment of their newly remodeled home. Marblecake and Spot were pleased to have Frannie and Shaun for upstairs neighbors. The new location would allow John to walk to campus when he returned to school next year. John had postponed beginning his graduate studies for another year, as he knew he needed time to assimilate the many changes in his life.

A big change in his life centered on food. Part of his membership with the food co-op entailed volunteering four hours each month in the store, stocking shelves or wrapping cheese or whatever needed doing. Besides learning about whole foods, John was introduced to the politics of food. After reading *Diet for a Small Planet* by Frances Moore Lappé, he became a vegetarian and enrolled in a macrobiotic cooking class. After reading *Back to Eden* by Jethro Kloss, John decided to try fasting to detoxify his body. To be safe, he went to a doctor for a pre-fast physical exam.

"I do not recommend fasting," the oversized doctor had advised from his chair.

"Well, some of the books I've read suggest it's a good way to cleanse the system, so I'm going to give it a try."

"If you do fast, you'd better be certain to drink plenty of liquids—like Coca-Cola or Pepsi," the doctor earnestly warned as he leaned back and took a draw from his pipe.

John chose to ignore the doctor and embarked on a 5-day water fast. When his urine turned brown, he felt like years of built-up toxins were being eliminated from his body. On the sixth day, he drank juices before gradually resuming his normal eating. For months afterward, John continued to fast one day a week.

One morning, John dug his spoon into a bowl of granola and yogurt—his routine breakfast—and considered how much he'd learned since first being introduced to yogurt at the base of the Matterhorn five years ago. Even if not presently a fulltime student, his mental cultivation never ceased. Reading outside the classroom from the growing library of books in his living room supplied a diversity of knowledge that broadened his mind. John also took several classes through OSU's continuing education program, including woodworking and dance. In addition, he persevered with his volunteer work in order to narrow his interests and determine what course of study to pursue for his Master's degree.

With a B.S. in criminal justice, John was a welcomed volunteer at every social service agency where he applied. He started off volunteering at a juvenile detention facility. However, he became alarmed when some of the youth confided that they were being mistreated and even sexually abused by staff members. Whether or not the kids' allegations were true, John's concern for the young people caused friction with his supervisor. After several months, he left that position and began volunteering in the dayroom at a mental hospital. It only took a couple of months before John knew that the field of mental health wasn't for him. From there, he began his present volunteer assignment at Children's Hospital.

One afternoon, John set the remaining carrots on the kitchen counter and turned off his Champion Juicer when he heard the phone ring.

"Johnny, I've got something to tell you."

"What is it, Mom?"

"Remember when you were telling me about your volunteer work at the Children's Hospital? Well, I—just a second."

John listened to his mother shout to someone else in the house. "I'm in here on the phone!" he heard her yell.

"Mom, do you want me to call you back?" He always returned her calls so she didn't have to pay the long-distance charges.

"Johnny, call me back in five minutes, will you?"

John went into the kitchen and finished juicing the last bunch of carrots. His mother's tone of voice made him think that "the something she had to tell him" was not good news. If he still smoked cigarettes, he probably would have lit one up right now, but smoking was a habit he quit on the day he was shot. He opened the refrigerator and set the container of fresh juice on a shelf. No beer in the fridge. Changes in his diet had greatly reduced his beer consumption. Instead, John went over to a cupboard and took out the ceramic bong he had purchased from a door-to-door bong salesman in Bloomington. The longhaired young man had claimed to be working his way through college, so John felt obliged to help him out by buying two. Taking a nerve-calming inhalation, John sat down and dialed his mother.

"Okay, Johnny. I can talk now," his mother sighed.

Sniffles accompanied her voice and he knew she was crying.

"What is it, Mom?"

"Remember when you were telling me about how so many of the children that came to the hospital were sexually abused?"

John's volunteer work at Children's Hospital included compiling statistics for federal funding. The reason for each child's admittance to the emergency room was recorded and entered onto IBM punch cards. The results of the data processing were distressing. A high number of admissions involved the mistreatment of children, including physical and sexual abuse. When John questioned his supervisor, he was taken aback by her response.

"This is just the tip of the iceberg, John. These are only the cases that got reported," his supervisor had proclaimed.

John was deeply disturbed to learn that child neglect and abuse was so prevalent in America's heartland. Perhaps because he associated the core of the nation with strong family values and good Christian people, it made the information all the more upsetting. And perhaps because his mother never missed the opportunity to find fault with his life, he felt compelled to draw attention to inconsistencies in her own. At any rate, John made a point of mentioning to his mother that the supposedly pious Christians—who she always loudly professed to be—were mistreating and molesting their kids.

"I still volunteer at Children's Hospital," John reminded his mother.

"Well, Johnny, I guess it's time I tell you this—I was sexually abused as a child."

John listened to his mother's sniveling across the phone line.

"It was my own father," she managed to say.

"When did it happen?"

"It started when my mother died. I was only seven and I missed Mommy so much. Of course, you know I was sent to live with Aunt Agnes and Uncle Gus. My father would be gone for months with the merchant marines. When he came to see me, he slept in the same bed with me. It went on for almost three years before Aunt Agnes figured out what was happening. Then, he disappeared and I didn't see him again for over ten years—after you were born. He'd remarried and had a couple of kids. But my own father had sex with me! It's like I'm one of those statistics at the hospital where you volunteer."

John was stunned at his mother's revelation. It shed light on the erratic behavior she'd demonstrated throughout his childhood. Following the phone call, he promised to make a trip east at the end of summer before beginning fulltime graduate studies. His mother reminded him that he hadn't been back to visit in over three years.

Rather than chancing driving his TVR, John decided to fly to Philadelphia. He'd enjoyed his unique sports car, but lately—with overheating problems—it was becoming more hassle than pleasure. Not only was it difficult to find a mechanic to work on the British machine, procuring replacement parts could take many weeks and cost many dollars. Furthermore, John often parked the TVR on the street across from Shaun's house where an Appalachian family with about six kids had recently moved into an un-renovated row house. Seeing his car parked in front of the impoverished family's residence left him with an uneasy feeling—similar to the time he picked up his date for the Viking Ball in his Corvette. The TVR now represented a former side of himself that no longer had meaning in his life. John doubted the vehicle would make the over 8-hour drive to Philadelphia without trouble, so he booked a flight.

Although John hadn't made the trip east for years, he occasionally phoned his old friends to keep in touch. When he called his buddies from Bensalem High School, Jay and Stevie made party plans and offered to pick John up at Philadelphia's International Airport. The guys were glad to reunite and boasted they had even chipped in and bought a gift for John. Entering Stevie's converted utility van, John soon learned what that gift was. In the back, on a custom-built platform bed, sat an ordinary woman who looked like she might have been washing dishes or doing housework before stopping and climbing into the van. In actuality, she was a prostitute the guys had hired for $150.

"Our welcome home gift to you, Johnny!" Jay announced.

With Jay and Stevie in the front seats, John sat in back with the woman, who appeared to be in her late twenties. As the van pulled out of the airport's parking lot, John introduced himself and discovered the woman was a single mother with two children. Prostitution was how she supported her family.

"How do you want it?" she questioned John.

"Look—you know—I appreciate my friends' thinking of me, and nothing against you personally, but—it's not going to happen," John declared. He proceeded to explain where he was coming from—how he had friends in Columbus who were women's libbers and after knowing them, he could no longer see women as simply sexual objects. John chatted about the female friends he had met at the co-op, and the conversation soon led to healthy foods, with John asking about what she fed her kids. When the woman described her son's behavior problems, John recommended eliminating sugar from his diet. They continued talking until Stevie drove up to the woman's house.

"Are you sure you don't want anything? After all, they paid for it," she reminded.

"Thanks, but no thanks," John held. He shook the disbelieving woman's hand, and she departed.

Awkwardness filled the van as Stevie and Jay wanted to know what the hell was wrong with John. Did he go homo or something? It was difficult for John to communicate his thinking. Eight years had passed since he and Hartman hired women in Saigon, which was the last time John had been with a prostitute. In fact, the only times in his life he'd seen one had occurred when he was in the Army—first in the Red Light district of Amsterdam and then in Vietnam when surrounded by war and unsure if he'd live to see another day. Since then, he hadn't had to pay for sex, and lately, he'd become altogether more discriminating about physical intimacy.

The next morning, Stevie threw a pair of lacy underwear at John's face. He said there was no sense wasting their money, so he returned to the woman's house later that night and collected on his investment. John laughed, but inwardly he thought his welcome-home gift had been a stark reminder of how much he'd changed over the last few years.

The rest of his stay prompted him to draw the same conclusion. It was fun visiting with old friends from the Vet's Club at OCC while they reminisced about their days of glory, yet like John's friends from high school, there was a yawning gulf in their worldviews. As expected, time with his mother was intense. Despite having an understanding of her childhood circumstances, it didn't take long before John's buttons were pushed and old wounds revisited. And even though he considered himself a changed person, John couldn't believe how quickly he slipped back to the same ingrained family patterns of interaction. When John boarded the plane to Columbus, he knew he wouldn't be going back east for a long, long time.

In September 1977, John resumed fulltime graduate school at The Ohio State University, majoring in Child Abuse and Neglect in the Department of Social Work. His volunteer experiences had convinced him of the need for early childhood intervention to facilitate breaking the cycle of abuse that often led to criminal behavior. And taking his own family's situation into consideration provided personal understanding into the ramifications of being raised by a product of sexual abuse. John became thoroughly engrossed in his course work and was inspired by a sharp professor he had for eight of his sixteen credit hours.

Professor Meenahan was different than other professors. Outwardly, he was younger and dressed and acted more casually. Thought-wise, he was less entrenched in stodgy methodology and more committed to open-minded discourse. John felt as though he had found a fellow researcher of truth. His one-on-one meetings with Professor Meenahan delivered weekly jolts of new awareness.

"Yes, that is right," Professor Meenahan responded to a student's question during the final moments of class one November day. "Foreign policy directly impacts social policy. Wars cost money. If a large percentage of tax revenue goes toward the military and defense industries, then dollars are siphoned away from domestic concerns—such as health care and education."

Most of the students quickly exited the room when class ended, but John and Kate lingered to gather their belongings and dialogue with the professor. John was glad to have acquired a friend in his social work classes. Kate was a minister's daughter and a dedicated student who shared John's compassionate humanitarian outlook, along with an admiration of Professor Meenahan. Kate and her husband, Timothy—a minister's son—frequently joined John and Frannie and Shaun for potluck dinners and world-saving conversations.

"Did you see the news about the Shah of Iran getting tear-gassed?" Kate asked John and Professor Meenahan with a smirk.

"You're referring to the incident at the White House the other day—the 15th," Professor Meenahan clarified. "I read that the D.C. police used tear gas to quell protests and that it drifted over to the south lawn."

"Yeah," Kate confirmed. "President and Mrs. Carter and the Shah and his Empress were standing at attention as both national anthems were being played, and the tear gas drifted over and burned their eyes."

"It was the biggest clash near the White House since Vietnam," John added. "The thousands of protestors were trying to bring attention to the human rights violations in Iran. I think over 100 were injured, including policemen."

"I don't understand why Carter invited the Shah to our country!" Kate charged. "I mean, Iran's secret police—the SAVAK—are one of the worst human rights offenders in the world! They've tortured and executed thousands of the Shah's political opponents."

"Our history with Iran is curious," Professor Meenahan suggested. "Back in 1953, Iran's elected Prime Minister Mossadegh made moves to nationalize Iran's oil for the benefit of the Iranian people. Of course, that would have cut into the profits of Western oil companies, so Mossadegh had to be stopped. The CIA stepped in and overthrew his more democratic government and installed the Shah's brutal dictatorship. And since then, the US continues to provide generous support to Iran, particularly by supplying arms." To Kate, Professor Meenahan made clear, "And it was the CIA that helped train the SAVAK."

"It's really a rude awakening," John grumbled. "It's hard enough to believe our government lied to us about Vietnam and then the illegal bombing of Cambodia, but to find out that we support cruel dictators like the Shah when we're supposed to be promoting democracy—it's ludicrous!"

Professor Meenahan snapped his briefcase shut and replied, "John, I'm afraid our Presidents have a long history of lying about foreign policy. Most Americans believe we're promoting democracy and sending humanitarian aid to countries, but in reality, our foreign policy is based on promoting American business interests and often takes the form of armed intervention."

"I knew that business controlled foreign policy from a pretty early age," Kate informed John and the professor. "Our church's missionary work sponsored two families from Guatemala in 1954 when I was 8 years old, and I kept hearing the families talk about *el pulpo*. I got the message that they had to leave their homes because of el pulpo. And when I found out that el pulpo meant *the octopus*, I pictured a monstrous octopus with tentacles long enough to reach land and snatch the children."

John and Professor Meenahan smiled as Kate moved her arms in an exaggerated manner to illustrate.

"That left a deep impression on me," she snickered. "For years, I thought the families had to escape from a giant sea monster. Of course, later, I found out that el pulpo referred to an American business—the United Fruit Company. The people called it *the octopus* because it had its hands in everything—it controlled the railroads, the police, the mail delivery system, all banana exports, and most of Guatemala's land—but it didn't pay any taxes. So, it's just like you said about Iran, Professor Meenahan. When the people elected a more democratic government that made moves to control the United Fruit Company, a CIA-led coup overthrew it and put a brutal military regime in place that eliminated any dissenters. That's why our church sponsored those families."

"That's quite a story, Kate," Professor Meenahan remarked. "I'm afraid there's a long list of countries in Latin America—and all over the globe—where US foreign policy supports some of the most oppressive governments in the world. It's shocking, but our history makes it obvious—profits have trumped human rights."

Professor Meenahan paused to check his watch and then announced, "I've got to run, but see you in my office next week.

And John, I found another book I think you'll like."

For the rest of the year, John avidly immersed himself in his graduate studies. Some of his research proved to be staggering, such as the American corporations' abuse of people for profits. As he ascertained, colonial-style exploitation didn't just occur on foreign lands. John wrote a paper documenting the unfair treatment of fellow Americans entitled, *The Causes and Effects of Appalachian Poverty.*

He chose the topic to help understand the circumstances of the family across the street. Through Frannie's urging, John became a Big Brother to one of the older boys of the relocated Appalachian family. Coordinating with the family's caseworker, he took the extremely shy fellow on various outings, such as the zoo and science center. As they ate together at different restaurants, John found himself doing most of the talking. The withdrawn young man scarcely uttered a word. John's relationship with the boy lasted just a few months, because social services moved the family to another location. During his time with the youth, John discovered the family had been forced to leave their mountain lands in eastern Ohio because their wells had been contaminated by slurry—a waste product of coal processing.

John's term paper traced a dismal and exploitative history of the Appalachian people by Northeast industrialists. As he came to understand, King Coal ruled Appalachia. Historically, coal companies had employed hundreds of men from the region to tunnel coal in traditional underground mines. However, recent legislation permitted a highly mechanized, manpower-eliminating form of surface mining known as MTR—Mountaintop Removal and valley-fill.

John recalled the petroleum crisis of 1973 that spawned the legislation. He remembered the long lines at fueling stations and waiting for as long as an hour to fill his gas-guzzling Corvette. He later learned the gas shortage occurred because OAPEC (Organization of Arab Petroleum Exporting Countries) declared an oil embargo against the US for its role in supplying arms and support to Israel during the Yom Kippur War. Consequently, the US made efforts to become more energy independent, and the Surface Mining and Reclamation Act of 1975 was passed. The act allowed widespread use of MTR—the most environmentally destructive but most profitable form of coal mining. The technique involves shaving a ridgeline of its dense forest of hardwood trees. Next, massive amounts of dynamite blast as much as 1,000 feet off the top of a mountain. Enormous shoveling machinery then scrapes away rock to expose the layers of coal. The remaining rubble—tons of excess rock and dirt—is bulldozed into valleys and streams. MTR radically alters the scenic Appalachian landscape because mountain peaks are literally flattened. And like the family across the street, residents are often forced to relocate, generally becoming welfare dependents of the state.

John's research revealed little reason for optimism. With mining companies, large land corporations, banks, railroads, and public officials all profiting, the simple Appalachian people didn't have a prayer. His paper concluded that the existing inequality of power would continue to allow business interests to take dominance over human needs. He summarized that when America finally came to grips with itself and decided that the greatest resource we have—as a nation among nations—is our people, only then will we treat human beings accordingly.

In reflection, John thought about the many Dustoff missions he had flown and the amount of energy exerted to save just one life. Each and every life was deemed important and worthy of rescue. Inside the cargo bay of the helicopter, John had recognized a sameness of being in the eyes of every human he treated—no matter what their race, gender, age or nationality. He came to believe that every single life on this earth had a purpose. John had once been proud to perform a job that represented the compassionate, highest qualities of his country. But now, he was coming face-to-face with quite the opposite sort of conduct. As he learned more about heartless US policies in Appalachia and around the globe, it was hard to accept that the beacon of democracy placed profits above human life. John loved his country, but it was painful to discover America wasn't all he believed it to be. This certainly wasn't the America he went to war for.

Chapter 25

It was a really bad beginning. As he turned the key, pushed open the door, and rolled his bicycle onto the worn shag carpeting of the modest motel room, John wondered if he'd bitten off more than he could chew. A few weeks ago, a bike trip to Alaska seemed like an excellent idea. John had been inspired by an excursion he took early last summer, before flying back to Philadelphia. He didn't know the former infantry captain very well, but when the fellow Vietnam vet extended an invitation to camp at Grand Teton National Park, John welcomed the opportunity. From the passenger window of the guy's truck while driving west to Wyoming, John occasionally saw cyclists along the road with heavily laden panyards strapped to their bike frames. Arriving at the 80-mile-long and 15-mile-wide valley of Jackson Hole, John was awestruck at his first glimpse of the Teton Range, the youngest of North America's Rocky Mountains. The sight of pointy peaks abruptly rising 7,000 feet from the surrounding sage-covered valley was nothing short of breathtaking. When they stopped at the resort town of Jackson, John noted that it appeared to be a magnet for hikers, climbers, and cyclists. He struck up lengthy conversations with various people, including two guys from Germany touring on bicycles. However, when he and the captain hiked around the base of The Grand Teton for four days, words were seldom spoken. Tenting beside pristine glacial lakes and observing extraordinary wildlife provided a restorative refuge. Following that ten-day trip, John was left with a desire to experience more of the rugged North Country and challenged by the physical rigor a bicycle tour would require. At the completion of his first year of graduate school, John was ready for a change of scenery. He bought Kate's blue ten-speed Concord English racer for $110, and from his apartment, he'd set out for Alaska early this morning.

John leaned the sixty pounds of his fully loaded bicycle against the wall and went over to close the curtains. He started to pull the drapery cord but paused when he saw the man who had rented him the room standing beside a flagpole in front of Pinewood Lodge. The man was lowering the American flag that flew high above the circle of red geraniums and painted white rocks. As the flag traveled down the length of the staff, the stripes remained unfurled, parallel to the ground. John faced the flag and stared at the enemy he'd battled all day. How could he not have anticipated the prevailing Northwest wind?

With curtains drawn, John was overwhelmed with discouragement. Tears and tremors shuddered his body. It had been an exhausting, nerve-wracking day, but he'd scarcely biked twenty-five miles outside of Columbus. The cruel and persistent wind seemed to be doing everything it could to push him back to the place he was anxious to depart. When he came upon Pinewood Lodge on Highway 33 West, he knew he had to stop and sort things out. John was on a campground budget, but here he was renting a room on the very first night of his trek.

Hobbling into the bathroom, he peeled off his biking gloves and washed his hands before removing his encrusted T-tube. The lubricating layer of Vaseline had melted away, so the silicone device stuck to his skin. Jostling it loose, John held it under the faucet to rinse off the dried mucous as well as the coating of exhaust fumes and road grime. He then moistened a washcloth and washed his neck. Better able to breathe, he took a fast shower but could barely touch the outside of his left calf or the inside of his right. Tender red skin let him know he'd acquired a serious sunburn. Plus, his whole body ached, especially his wrists from the tense grip he maintained on the handlebars all day, particularly when being chased by two Doberman pinschers. And John had become painfully aware of the difference between a leather bicycle seat that offered some flexibility and his plastic shell seat, which proved to be unyielding.

More than anything, John felt defeated by the bicycle itself. Not long into the trip, it began to wobble and shake and literally fall apart underneath him. A tire blew, and it took an hour to change it alongside a busy road. He rode for maybe five miles before a second tire went flat. In his motel room, after washing and eating, John repeated the same procedure he had already performed twice that day while fixing flats. He disconnected the bungee cords and removed his tent, sleeping bag and insulite pad from the bike frame. He unclamped and removed the bright yellow panyards, which were stocked with food, a camping stove, a container of fuel, cooking utensils, a tire-repair kit and spare tire, bicycle tools, a first-aid kit, a poncho liner, rain parka, towels, extra biking apparel, a pair of jeans, two shirts, a sweater, a pair of Birkenstock sandals, toiletries, and a few other items, including eight paperback books he intended to read while biking for two and a half months. After removing the two plastic water bottles from their holders and unfastening the front handlebar bag, John turned the bicycle upside-down, uncoupled the chain from the derailleur, and removed the rear tire. He adjusted the brakes and fine-tuned each spoke with the spoke wrench, trying to figure out what was causing both wheels to vibrate. In addition, he had to patch the punctured inner tubes from the flats in his heavy-duty touring tires. Laboring for hours, John humbly came to realize how much he didn't know about bicycle mechanics. Late that night, frustration overpowered him when he couldn't get the bike reassembled.

Utterly demoralized when he finally went to bed, John grappled with his predicament in the morning. Yesterday had been a hard day. But he knew there was no going back to Columbus. He needed time away from his life in that busy city. In the light of the new day, the bicycle was back together and sleep had restored John's spirits. Originally, he had been motivated to experience Alaska as a result of hearing the enthusiasm of others who had been there. His curiosity about its wilderness was further aroused after reading John McPhee's *Coming Into The Country*. Today, John was again filled with conviction to continue his over-4,000-mile journey to Anchorage. Anyway, now he was only about 3,975 miles from his destination.

Coated with sunscreen, John wheeled his loaded bicycle out of the motel room and clicked the straps of the Bell helmet under his chin. He cut his shoulder-length hair soon after moving to Columbus, yet it had been years since he wore it as short as the military buzz the barber gave him in preparation for his trip. Thinking about the military, John remembered the times in Vietnam when his body trembled in fear prior to a mission. He would experience a victory by jumping into the cargo bay of the helicopter despite his body telling him otherwise. This morning, John felt another inner victory as he climbed on the bicycle and continued peddling northwest.

> 9 June 1978
> Hello Mother Dear,
> Arrived in Madison yesterday. Things are going well. Have been biking it for a week now. I'm going to take a three-day rest break and then move on. Will keep in touch.
> Love,
Johnny

John slid the postcard—featuring a photo of the University of Wisconsin campus sprawled along the shore of Lake Mendota—into the mail slot and then strolled over to Memorial Union and the actual scene represented on the card. Entering the arched passage to the student union's rathskeller, the wooden tables and décor made John feel like he had just stepped into a German Gasthaus. Since it was a sunny afternoon, he carried his mug of beer to the outside terrace, where many people were gathered. Sitting upon the concrete steps that curved beside the lake, John watched a dozen single-person sailboats circling offshore, apparently part of a class. A half-dozen noisy ducks swam right up to his feet, quacking interest in his pretzels.

Last night, he checked into an affordable nearby motel, glad to rest in such a pleasant city. John thought the capital of Wisconsin was a fantastic place. Located on an isthmus between three lakes, it was convenient to get around the attractive, bicycle-friendly city.

Strolling along State Street, he welcomed interaction with people as he went to a Laundromat and food co-op. He restocked his supply of granola and gorp and also bought Fig Newtons in bulk. John ate heartily in Madison's natural food restaurants, not knowing when his travels would come across such fine cuisine again.

Relaxing this afternoon, John took more refreshing swallows of beer. It was gratifying to have successfully bicycled 500 miles. Fortunately, none of his days on the road was quite as difficult as the first one. He hadn't faced the same brutal headwind the second day. In fact, the wind was to his back, so he cruised along and made excellent mileage. Yet, other days, the wind returned and once again slowed progress. It had been grueling to bike through the stinky steel towns that neighbored Chicago. John didn't have much of a sense of smell, since he really didn't use his nostrils, but even he couldn't miss detecting the acrid industrial stench—actually tasting it—as he stopped to fix a flat tire near Gary. Following his night at Pinewood Lodge, he'd tented at campgrounds, but after biking around the southern edge of Lake Michigan through busy Chicago traffic, John had rented a second motel room to wash away road grit. Staying at another motel in Madison, he looked forward to resting for a couple of days.

Finishing his beer and stretching his legs, John noticed that his sunburned skin had turned into a bronzed tan. Flexing his foot, his calf muscle flaunted the strength and stamina he'd gained from an intense week of peddling. While he'd been a regular runner for years, cycling employed different tendons and tissues. Even though he'd trained by biking around Columbus, it definitely hadn't prepared him for the level of physical endurance the trek in fact demanded.

Muscling against the wind had been a supreme bodily challenge, and it was a mental challenge, too. John had to work with his mind, giving himself pep talks in order to stay positive while peddling against that formidable force. He also had to rustle up his faith in humanity to trust that cars and trucks approaching his back would safely pass by him. Initially, he had to struggle with his wobbly bicycle, but he took pride in getting it tuned and working satisfactorily again. He continued to make adjustments as he went along, like using his thick wool sweater to cushion the plastic shell seat. For the first time in many weeks, as John unwound in the enjoyable setting of UW's campus, he was feeling exceptionally robust and confident.

While it had been an accomplishment to complete his first year of graduate school, John now had even more questions about what he wanted to do—or was capable of doing—with his life. Although he continued to appreciate his classes with Professor Meenahan, things did not go well in his field placement. He and two other students were assigned to an agency that was in the middle of a transition, thus leaving the agency without clients at the time. When John's assignments included moving boxes and furniture, he complained to his supervisor. He wanted to know how his field placement was honing his hands-on skills with clients. Perhaps because John felt such a strong commitment to help others who were suffering, he possessed an urgency to get the job done. Therefore, he had no patience when he observed inefficiencies. For his fieldwork, John was given a grade of "D" and told to change his attitude. To his annoyance, he had to spend time over the next semester filing a complaint and defending his position. The D was eventually changed to a B, but the grade had never been the issue. It was the principle of the matter that counted to John. As a result of the whole experience, he became disillusioned with the effectiveness of some social service programs and began to doubt his role in the field of child neglect and abuse. Truthfully, he didn't know for sure if he'd be able to contain his anger and remain impartial when meeting face to face with a suspected child abuser. Furthermore, social service programs focused on the *casualties* of abuse and neglect. John strongly believed that efforts should be directed toward the *causes*—such as poverty inflicted by the power elites.

Going off by himself on a bicycle trip, he hoped to gain clarity in his mind. In reality, he was still plagued with memories and images from Vietnam. Every so often, he might be having a conversation with someone when—out of the blue—that person's face would transform into something from John's memory bank. Vivid, life-threatening wounds would suddenly be superimposed on the cranium of the person talking. John usually wouldn't mention what he was seeing for fear of sounding crazy, so he dealt with the bloody and gruesome flashbacks in his own heart and mind. He wished he could thrust aside those moments of horror in the cargo bay—but how could he forget the way frantic eyes had locked on his? Whether a Vietnamese civilian, a child, or an American—through the windows of his patient's eyes—John had repeatedly watched the life force depart the body as a result of the grisly and ghastly circumstances of war. People's desperate pleadings made it known—they weren't ready to go. Those traumatic images were impossible to forget, and he never knew when one might pop into the present moment.

In his gut, John carried the heavy toll of having seen young lives violently snuffed out before their light had a chance to shine. The roiling inside him demanded that he give his all to help make the world a better place on their behalf. However, the more he became aware of what was happening in the world, the more frustrated and angry he grew. Surely, patriotic Americans hadn't died for the sake of corporate greed and capitalist corruption. Recent headlines indicated there was much in the world to be disturbed about: a hole in the ozone layer, growing tensions in the Middle East with Iran, the suspicious death of Karen Silkwood, and an arms race that seemed to have the world headed for nuclear destruction. John questioned his future in this bewildering and uncertain world.

He did know one thing for certain. He didn't want to be in Columbus if war broke out in the Middle East and the price of gasoline skyrocketed. Life in a big city—along with a dependency on cars—wasn't for him. In some ways, John remained staunchly committed to obtaining his Master's degree at Ohio State University. In other ways, he felt prodded to move elsewhere and pursue a different course of action. John embarked on the bicycle trip to distance himself from the nuts and bolts of his life. He hoped that spending the summer cycling would help clarify his personal direction.

June 17th
Hello Mother Dear,
Hope this finds you in fine health. Things
with me are good. Arrived in this city a couple
of days ago. Heading for N. Dakota next.
Wisconsin is a beautiful state.

Love,
Johnny

"Uh-oh," John mumbled when he saw the pick-up truck slow

443

down and pull over to the shoulder of the road, parking in front of him. "What does this guy want?" he questioned under his breath.

John was just finishing changing a flat tire in the pouring rain when the truck stopped. After biking 260 miles through northern Wisconsin, John had stayed at a hostel at the YMCA in St. Paul for three days to catch up on laundry and restock supplies. The Mississippi River runs through the city and forms a western municipal boundary with Minneapolis. John had enjoyed exploring the pleasant setting of the Twin Cities and eating at some excellent natural-food restaurants. Before departing, he had mailed his mother a postcard of Peavey Plaza in downtown Minneapolis. He also sent one to Frannie and Shaun, as they were caring for Marblecake and Spot. Back on the road, biking for hours, John saw signs for Lake Itasca—the source of the Mississippi River. He was within a hundred miles of where the great river began its 2,320-mile course from northwestern Minnesota, flowing south through ten states to the Gulf of Mexico. He'd been on the road for about four hours when a tire blew.

"Hey there!" the lanky man called out as he slammed the door of his pick-up truck and walked toward John.

So far on the trip, people had been remarkably kind to John. They approached with respect for his cycling endeavors and curiosity about his journey. Next, they usually wanted to know about the circumstances of his neck. John took a breath and trusted this guy would be no different.

"Not the most pleasant weather to fix a flat," the guy declared as he pulled the hood of his rain parka over his head.

Turns out, the man was a biking enthusiast, and after exchanging introductions and conversing a while, he invited John to crash at his house that rainy night. Rather than accept a ride in the truck, John peddled for a couple more hours and then found the man's home—conveniently located along the same road. John was grateful for a hot shower, dinner, and a bed in the spare room. He also appreciated hearing about his host's biking adventures.

The next morning, the sun was shining when the man offered John some parting advice.

"Like I was telling you last night, I strongly encourage you to take a train from Fargo," the man suggested. "Otherwise, you're going to be fighting the wind the whole way across the flatlands, and the wind is tough—it'll weaken you. You've gotta save something for the mountains, because you don't want to miss seeing those places I was telling you about." Pausing to shake John's hand, he wished him well, "Hey, I'm excited for ya, man. You're in for a mind-blowing experience."

> June 22, 1978
> Hello Mother Dear,
> Things with me are great. Arrived in Fargo
> earlier today. I'm taking a train to Glacier
> National Park in Montana because of the wind
> and time elements. Then I'm heading north by bike.
> > Love,
> > Johnny

John mailed the postcard of an aerial view of Fargo before boarding the Amtrak. His mother had pleaded to keep her updated with postcards.

"Do you have any idea how worried I'll be about you?" she grilled when John announced his summer travel plans. "I mean, anything could happen to you out there and no one would ever know.

445

Johnny! Why are you doing this?"

Jotting off a fast postcard was a lot easier than making a phone call to his mother. Over the phone, he heard nothing but complaints. Even though John had insight into his dysfunctional childhood and his mother's abusive past, it still didn't make it any easier to have her continually rain on his parade. Keeping in touch by postcard was a concession he could abide.

Like the guy had suggested, John would rest on the 18-hour train ride and save his strength for the mountains. Slumping down into the passenger seat, the outside scene rarely changed. Sometimes rolling, mostly flat, the endless prairies induced a feeling of spaciousness, even when framed by the window of the train. Bordered by the Rocky Mountains on the west and the Appalachians to the east, the interior of the country consists of a vast lowland known as the North American Interior Plains. The western portion is called The Great Plains, and John was relieved he hadn't fought the wind across the hundreds of miles of mainly unvaried grasslands. He would shave about 900 miles off his trip by taking the train, and since he had already biked 1,000, John figured he would be almost halfway to Anchorage when he arrived at Glacier National Park.

About to shut his eyes and nap, music from a nearby radio drifted across the aisle. John recognized the familiar piano introduction of a song that pulled at his heartstrings. He glanced over at a young couple whose radio was softly playing. The guy had his arm around the girl, and when Michael Murphey began to sing the first words of his song, "Wildfire," the couple tenderly kissed. John blinked hard and snapped his attention to the darkening landscape outside the window. A wave of emotion washed over him.

John would very much like to be traveling with a female companion, but that hadn't been in his cards. Although he'd had a few steady girlfriends over the years, there had been no relationships of significant duration. Admittedly, when problems arose, he was quick to throw in the towel and call it quits. He was cautious about getting too attached to anyone personally. Getting close involved emotions, and emotions were something he tried to bury. So, over the years, he'd mostly managed to avoid close human entanglements. Anyway—even before Vietnam—he hadn't been taught how to deeply relate to another. After the war, things were assuredly worse. He bumped up against his own emotional walls and confused sex with love and closeness. Women gave him feedback that he wasn't that easy to get along with. They let him know that his verbal outbursts of anger were intolerable—along with his complete lack of patience. The slightest thing could set him off, and sometimes even John didn't know exactly what or why. He couldn't deny that since the war he was angry about a lot of things happening in the world, so of course he'd lost patience for what he considered trivial matters. As much as he longed for a life partner, John concluded that before entering relationship with another, he had a lot to learn about himself. And on the trip—biking alone—mile after mile—hour after hour—day after day—John was beginning to learn a great deal. This much he knew already: he was committed to living a path with heart.

June 24
Hello Mother Dear,
Things with me are great. Met 2 other
guys who are going to go north to Alaska.
So now there are 3 of us. Leave tomorrow to
ride on this road.

Love,
Johnny

John had met the two guys when they all stowed their bicycles in the baggage compartment of the train. Todd and Dan were from Sioux Falls, South Dakota and also spending the summer bicycling. Onboard the train, the men discussed their biking adventures.

"Are you taking the Going-to-the-Sun Road?" Todd asked.

"I heard of it," John replied, recalling his conversation with the cyclist he'd stayed with in Minnesota. Minimally preplanning, John bought a map each time he entered a new state. Since he hadn't yet arrived in Montana, he hadn't yet plotted his route.

"It's supposed to be one of the world's most scenic roads," Todd explained. "It's 50 miles long, and it connects the east and west sides of the park. But it's cut right into the mountains and it's really steep and narrow and winding."

When the train stopped at the West Glacier Railroad Depot, the three cyclists claimed their bicycles and cycled a couple miles to the visitor center. There, John picked up a park map and bought a copy of the *Milepost,* the indispensable travel guide Todd had recommended. Now, John would be able to plan ahead on where to camp and restock supplies. Setting up his tent in the campground at the foot of Lake McDonald, John spent the remainder of the evening enthusiastically mapping his route and studying the *Milepost.*

In the morning, John had broken camp and was packing his panyards when Todd walked over from the neighboring campsite.

"We're not taking the Going-to-the-Sun-Road after all," Todd informed. "Dan doesn't think he's up for it. We're going to take the long way and start along the railroad grade and go round through the Great Bear Wilderness Area."

John had to admit; the sight of the high mountains where the road climbed was rather intimidating. However, once he had read about the road, he knew he wasn't going to miss seeing the engineering marvel that took eleven years to build. Besides, he already mailed a postcard to his mother saying he'd be biking the road pictured on the card. And John knew he was physically ready, having built strength and stamina over the last few weeks. Plus, the Going-to-the-Sun-Road would bring him closer to two destinations he didn't want to miss—Banff and Jasper. John wished Todd well and took off. The road would close to bicyclists later in the morning, so he had no time to lose.

Skirting Lake McDonald, John stopped a few miles ahead and unzipped his front handlebar bag to remove his 35-millimeter camera. He took a picture of a sign that read "Going-To-The-Sun Park Road Completed 1932". The lake's calm water mirrored snow-capped peaks against a cloudless blue sky, along with an assortment of colorful wildflowers adorning the landscape. The scenery was so magnificent John could have stopped every ten minutes to take a postcard-quality snapshot. But he had to peddle hard to make his way up the narrow winding road. At the summit, John paused to take another picture of a park sign. "Logan Pass Continental Divide Elevation 2033 M".

John knew that the Continental Divide represented the border between two watersheds. Crossing west to east over Logan Pass at 6,680 feet, precipitation would now eventually travel to the Atlantic, rather than the Pacific Ocean. Mountains were the water towers of the world, as almost all major rivers of the Earth have their sources in mountains. From the first time he had witnessed the Swiss Alps— and then the Tetons—John was stirred by the power and majesty of mountains. He concluded that the wilderness—like one's spiritual beliefs—couldn't be taught, but needed to be personally experienced. Mountains had to be felt with the heart. Biking past glaciers, waterfalls, and cedar forests, and surrounded by snow-capped pinnacles, John felt part of something vast and mysterious.

After toiling to the high country, John enjoyed the descent to St. Mary Lake. He mostly freewheeled from the summit, laboring to control his downhill speed.

> July 3
> Mom
> What's Happening!
> Things with me are great.
> Seeing some nice sights and
> meeting some real nice people.
> By myself again.
>
> > Love,
> > Johnny

John glanced at the picture of the Three Sister Mountains before inserting the postcard into the mailbox. It had taken him over a week to get to Banff. He had been excited to cross the border into Canada and onto Alberta Highway 2, where the terrain mellowed into rolling hills and rather unexciting cattle country. The day before heading into Calgary to intersect with Trans-Canada Highway 1, John spent the night at a government campground on the bank of the Sheep River. Relatively hilly, Calgary is located at the transition zone between the foothills of the Rockies and the Canadian Prairies. On the road, John had noticed that many bicyclists used safety flags and pennants, and that made a lot of sense to him. Since Calgary's population was close to half a million, he figured the large metropolis would have a store that sold such gear.

John didn't have to enter the actual downtown area of Calgary, as there were plenty of shopping plazas in the suburban outskirts before the junction with Highway 1. Luckily, he spotted a sandwich board with a colorful display of bicycle flags attached to long fiberglass poles, and he made a quick turn into the shopping area. His attention was immediately drawn to the activity at the far end of the huge parking lot. Signs and banners made known that a truck rodeo was taking place. John rolled closer to observe the driving competition. He watched as several fully loaded logging trucks masterfully maneuvered around an obstacle course of orange traffic cones. Prior to his bicycle trip, John had never before seen a logging truck. The first time a loaded truck rumbled past him on the highway the sight of masses of timber jolted him. He couldn't explain his reaction, but there was sadness in the air, particularly when a big rig was filled to capacity by only three huge circumferences—all sections of one felled giant.

The aroma of meat cooking on a grill overpowered the diesel fumes, so John moseyed over to the food vendor area of the rodeo and ordered fried potatoes, a cheeseburger with everything on it, and a vanilla milkshake. He had no qualms about eating meat while on the trip, as he needed all the calories he could get. John went back and ordered a second burger, finishing it before coasting toward the store. There, he bought a bicycle flag and pole, which he attached to his rear axel. A safety shield—a bright orange triangle mounted on the back of the seat—seemed like a good way to increase visibility, so he bought one of those, too. John also bought a couple of inner tubes and decided to purchase a radio that ran on the same C-size batteries as his flashlight. He rested the radio on top of his handlebar bag and fastened it to his handlebars. After stopping at a grocery store to stock his panyards with bread, peanut butter and jelly, and a package of cookies, John was then ready to conquer the eighty miles leading to Banff.

As others had extolled, Banff was an exceptionally beautiful place. It was also a popular tourist center, so John decided not to stay there. He biked through Main Street just long enough to mail a postcard to his mother before continuing toward Eisenhower Junction and Lake Louise.

"It's Baker Street again," John mouthed to the atmosphere. Whenever he turned on his radio, the haunting saxophone solo from Gerry Rafferty's hit song always seemed to be playing. Ever glad to hear it, the music supplied impetus to keep his tired legs peddling, while some of the lyrics repeated in his head:

> *But you know he'll always keep moving*
> *You know, he's never gonna stop moving*
> *Cause he's rolling, he's the rolling stone*

When John saw a sign pointing to Vermilion Pass, he realized he would eventually be crossing the Continental Divide again—this time from east to west.

Out of the clear sky, he heard his mother's critical voice clanging, "Johnny, why are you doing this?"

Then he heard a different voice. It carried no judgment as it asked—why am I here—why am I alive?

John knew the trip was a challenge to himself. Like a mission in Vietnam, he wanted to see if he could accomplish his goal. He'd set a high bar, and so far his physical abilities had been tested and proven. Mentally, he was learning to slow down and appreciate the incredible power and beauty of the landscape. In his daily existence—so close to the natural world—there had been many profound, tranquil moments. The shear number of stars that dazzled a wilderness sky was astounding. Camping beside turquoise Alpine lakes, he never failed to be enchanted by a loon's magical serenade. And whether sun-kissed or cloud-clad, the tremendous presence of mountains moved his soul. John was inspired by an aliveness in the world that made him think about his place on this planet and this planet's place in the universe.

Yet, every day he would get on his bicycle and it was the same thing. He would see a new peak in the distance and bike toward it. Throughout the day, as he followed along the meandering road, he would see different angles of the same mountain. In time, he would pass it and view another perspective over his shoulder. Although it wouldn't be accurate to say that once you've seen one razor-sharp peak you've seen them all, still, John had been in the company of so many lofty, finely etched, snow-covered precipices that mountains were becoming landmarks just to bike past. As he came to realize, it might take an entire day for him to travel the same distance a car could drive in an hour and a half. He was definitely learning about scale and patience.

Conquering steep roads was not as demanding as sharing roads with motorized vehicles. So far on the trip, his route mostly traveled along fairly busy highways. Trucks—especially 18-wheelers—wreaked havoc on his nerves. He had to brace himself whenever he heard the roar of a big rig approaching from behind. He'd tighten his grip on the handlebars so the truck's wake wouldn't shake his bike like a branch in a windstorm. He looked forward to getting farther north where he anticipated a less-traveled wilderness.

When Highway 1 swung west, John continued north on provincial Highway 93 toward Jasper. From Bow Summit at 6,787 feet, the 140-mile road was known as the Icefield Parkway. Considered to be one of the premier mountain roads on the planet, John bicycled along the rugged ridgeline, passing the Columbia icefields on his left and paralleling the Continental Divide.

July 10
Mom,
Hope this card finds you in good health.
Things with me are great.
I'm at Mount Robson Provincial Park.
Weather has been damp, but all is well.
Going to Prince George.

Love,
Johnny

John didn't stop in Jasper, as it was a large recreation center, but its surrounding beauty was quite evident. He caught Highway 16, The Yellowhead, and crossed the boundary from Jasper National Park in Alberta to adjacent Mount Robson Provincial Park in British Columbia. He camped in view of the matriarch of the Canadian Rockies. At 12,972 feet, Mt. Robson was the highest peak. When John pulled into the groomed campsite, he did what he did most every day. He dismounted his bike and leaned it against the picnic table. Unfastening and removing his helmet, he set it on top of the table, grabbed his toiletry bag and a washcloth, along with his plastic water bottles, and immediately sought a source of water. Sometimes, in more primitive campsites, the source could be a nearby stream. Since Mount Robson was a popular area, it offered pit toilets and washrooms with showers. John went into the men's room and removed his T-tube. Holding it under the faucet, he rinsed it—manipulating and squeezing it to remove the encrusted gunk. Earlier in the day, John had already stopped to clean the tube and relubricate it with Vaseline—once beside a creek and again at a rest stop. After washing road dirt from his neck with a washcloth, John reinserted the freshly lubricated T-tube and then wiped the sweat and grime from his face, arms, and legs. He filled his water bottles and headed back to his campsite. Retrieving a bag of gorp and the *Milepost* from a panyard, John sat at the table, munching while marveling at where he'd traveled that day.

He rested for about half an hour, then removed the equipment from his bike and set up his tent. The weather was cloudy, so he hitched up the rain fly. Unrolling his sleeping bag, he aired it by draping it over the top of the tent. He then stretched a bungee cord between two trees and hung yesterday's still-damp towels and garments. Next, he set up his stove to make dinner. If he happened to be camping in the vicinity of a restaurant, John would usually eat there in order to simplify his evening. Not only would he enjoy a substantial hot meal, he'd buy cookies and milk for later. However, in a busy recreational area, John was self-conscious of his T-tube and grimy appearance, so he opted to eat a meager meal at his campsite.

Before zipping his tent shut for the night, John stored all his food in his ditty bag and hung it from a high branch a good thirty feet from his tent.

John thought the Canadian campgrounds were very well designed. They were clean and tended, and they blended with the natural surroundings, allowing privacy between campsites. Some of the provincial parks had areas specifically reserved for cyclists. At almost every campground, he met friendly people who often offered him food and a seat around their campfire. Of course, they asked about his neck, and after telling his story, people always expressed esteem for his work as a medic. A few Canadians—just like the cyclist in Minnesota—had even invited him into their homes. John was impressed by Canada's openness and overall friendliness toward bicyclists. Pleasantly, the roads were kept clean of debris—quite a contrast from the glass and metal scraps he frequently had to dodge on the sides of US roads. And some Canadian roads—especially near tourist areas—had extra-wide paved shoulders.

In the dawn's early light, John unzipped the mosquito netting that also protected him from horseflies and no-see-ums. The insects were intense, attacking whenever he wasn't pedaling. As he opened the tent door, the high-pitched ripping sound of the zipper was followed by a loud snort. Stepping out of the tent and looking left, a chill ran down John's spine as he came face to face with the origin of the snort. He'd seen bears at campgrounds before—mostly scavenging around dumpsters—but this was the first time he was within ten feet of a 300-pound black bear. For a second, John's eyes locked with the magnificent creature's dark ones. Standing motionless, John thought of something a park ranger once said at an interpretive program.

The ranger told of witnessing a black bear rip a fully inflated high-grade Michelin tire off the rim of a BMW. However, at the moment, John felt no fear—only awe. Suddenly, the bear's twitching snout lifted upward, and the animal sniffed as though reading a newspaper of wind. Then, unhurriedly, it ambled across the clearing of John's campsite and disappeared into the woods.

August 1
Mom,
Hope this card finds you in good health.
Things with me are great. Arrived in
Prince Rupert 3 days ago. Catching a
seaplane to Stewart, B.C. From there,
I'm biking up the Cassiar Highway to the
Yukon, then up to Alaska.

Love,
Johnny

By the time John had bicycled a couple hundred miles west across British Columbia on the Yellowhead Highway, any sight of the Canadian Rockies was left far behind. The terrain softened as the road began to follow along three river valleys. Although there were no longer any high summits to surmount, John had to battle strong westerly winds and rain. On through Prince George and surrounding farmlands, there were long distances between sizable towns. Small communities sometimes offered private camping facilities where John would set up his tent on a grassy lawn behind a simple mom-and-pop-owned general store. Such places often included showers and laundry services. He appreciated the conveniences and the friendliness of the folks, along with the cookies and milk—sometimes chocolate—available in the stores.

Meticulously studying the *Milepost,* John planned on taking the Cassiar Highway 37 north to Watson Lake, where he would intersect with the Alaska Highway—or the Alcan as it was known. According to his calculations, he could catch the Cassiar at Kitwanga, which would be a shorter route. Or, he could follow the Yellowhead Highway west until it met the Pacific, fly to Stewart, and meet up with the Cassiar farther north. Since he'd never seen the Coast Mountains, and he didn't want to miss seeing the sun set over the Pacific Ocean, John chose to bike an extra seventy-five miles to Prince Rupert.

Excitement grew when John spotted the coastal mountains. He'd been told that The Pacific Coast Ranges, like most of the world's mountains, run in broad belts, or cordilleras. In the Western Hemisphere, the American cordillera is an essentially continuous sequence of overlapping and parallel mountain ranges, forming a western backbone from Alaska to Argentina. The character of the ranges widely varies, but along the coasts of British Columbia and Alaska, the mountains intermix with the sea in a complex maze of fjords and islands. Located on Kaien Island, Prince Rupert is titled the *Gateway to Alaska.*

As if on cue, the saxophone melody of "Baker Street" blasted from the radio as John glided down McBride Street toward the sparkling azure water of Prince Rupert Harbor and the Pacific Ocean. Gleefully swaying, almost dancing on his toe clips aboard his 2-wheeled companion, John felt proud that he had bicycled a distance of 700 miles across the Yellowhead, making his total biking distance over 2,000 miles. He'd made it to the western coast of North America.

He camped high on a knoll in the center of Prince Rupert at Roosevelt Park, where each evening he had a splendid view of the setting sun. Resting while exploring the small port city, he ate at restaurants, restocked supplies, and stopped by the ferry terminal at Fairview Dock. There, he watched an Alaska State Ferry loaded with cars and passengers depart for its 90-mile route to Ketchikan. After a few days, he left his hilltop campsite and made his way to Seal Cove, where Trans-Provincial Airlines offered charter services to Stewart. Having never flown on a seaplane, John thought the shiny, bright-yellow aircraft almost looked like a toy. Yet, following the hours he clocked in Vietnam, he had no fear of flying when he boarded the small 6-seater. During the short ride to the old mining city of Stewart—covering a distance of approximately 100 miles—John was gifted with a different perspective of the coastal mountains: a glorious aerial view.

The seaplane touched down on the Portland Canal, a long saltwater fjord that formed the boundary between British Columbia and Alaska. At the dock, John unloaded his bicycle, which had been stripped down in order to fit on the aircraft. He reattached the front wheel, as well as his camping equipment, panyards, and flag. After repositioning the handlebars, John mounted the bike and started out toward Watson Lake—a distance of about 400 miles. From Stewart, he had to bicycle a 39-mile spur east before reaching the main Cassiar Highway that would take him north. He'd anticipated a gravel road, but the large rocks hardly resembled gravel. A sharp shard soon blew a tire. This leg of highway had originally been built to accommodate seagoing freight hauls from the asbestos mine in Cassiar, located over 300 miles north. Instead, the fiber ended up being trucked along the Alaska Highway to other ports, so the spur from Stewart was not a heavily used route.

The road may have been challenging to negotiate, but it offered unforgettable sights. Passing within spitting distance of Bear Glacier, John was fascinated by the brilliant greens and blues of the river of ice. The melting glacier formed the beginning of Bear River, and along the road, John could discern evidence of past washouts caused by glacier melt. Cycling past peaks of the Cambria Icefield, spectacular icefalls, and more glaciers on his right, it took most of the day to traverse the rough road's strenuous climb over Bear Pass and finally reach the junction where the spur met the Cassiar Highway's more traveled route. Although still not paved, the gravel was better compacted and easier on the tires.

The next day, John bicycled through a depressingly large burned area. He remembered flying over land in Vietnam where everything had been burned to shit. And there were areas that hadn't been charred by incendiaries but were just as devoid of life after being sprayed by a defoliant. Unable to receive radio reception in this remote area, John's mind began to wonder as he peddled along. Had the fire been caused by Nature or man? And what happened to all the animals that had been living there? In Vietnam, the devastation had definitely been caused by man—and his instruments of war. John knew a vet who had cancer, and the guy swore his cancer—along with his child's birth defects—had been caused by his exposure to Agent Orange. The weapons of war had become so powerful they didn't discriminate between the victor and the vanquished. Biking through the bleak landscape, John got to questioning if there was an equivalent to war in any other species, or was man alone the designer of such organized violence? And what did war really achieve—other than death and ruin? Pumping hard as he approached an incline, John shifted gears, relieved to finally pass through the fire-torched land. The new horizon reminded him that—even though there was a lot of tragedy and suffering in the world—there was also infinite beauty.

August 4, 1978
Dear Mom,
Hope everything is fine with you.
I'll be in the Yukon Territory in a few
days. Lots of beautiful scenery.

Love,
Johnny

When John was nearly halfway to Watson Lake, he stopped at the small town of Iskut. The *Milepost* indicated that Iskut had a post office, and he'd decided to lighten his load. Even downhill, biking on the Cassiar Highway's gravel was far more demanding than cruising on paved surfaces. He didn't need a pound of extra weight. Snickering as he sorted through his panyards, John realized he hadn't opened even one of the paperback books he'd planned to read. At the end of a strenuous day, he was too tired to peruse anything but the *Milepost* before falling asleep. While packing his unneeded items in a cardboard box, John stopped to thumb through notes he'd made in the margins of Schumacher's *Small Is Beautiful* when he started reading it back in Columbus. Positioning more books in the package, he paused again to read the back cover of *The Greening of America* by Charles Reich. Removing the last two books from his panyards, John placed Erich Fromm's *Escape From Freedom* in the box and then hesitated when he came to *Anti-Intellectualism in American Life*. John considered himself to be an intellectual in the making, so he was keen to read Hofstadter's Pulitzer-Prize-winning book. Books had become beacons of knowledge for John. His mind thirsted for understanding, and reading the ideas of visionary thinkers helped quench that thirst. John sighed as he finished packing the stack of books he would eventually read—but not during the course of the trip. Regrettably, he detached the radio from his handlebars and set it inside the box. Radio reception had become nonexistent as he traveled in more isolated areas, so there was no sense lugging a useless item. Taping the package shut, John addressed it to himself and sent it to his apartment via parcel post. He also sent his mother a postcard of a panoramic view of the Skeena and Cassiar Mountains.

Even with a lighter load, biking the steep, dusty road demanded John's full concentration. Nonetheless, he appreciated the views of deep-gorged rivers and the wide valleys and lakes composing the area. Many of the roads and communities sprang from early gold mining operations. Today, quite a few were now ghost towns. Approximately 100 miles from the Yukon border along a remote stretch of highway, John set up his tent at a private campground beside beautiful Cotton Lake. A man with a long white beard and rosy cheeks introduced himself as Mighty Moe, the proprietor. Like the man, the place was rustic but captivating. A potbelly stove fired hot water for showers, and the interior of the old outhouse was papered with outdated calendars. Mighty Moe was a memorable character, and John got a big kick out the guy's nonstop telling of tales.

John silently celebrated when he left British Columbia and crossed into the Yukon Territory. The last twenty miles of the Cassiar Highway were paved, so he made good time before reaching the junction with the Alaska Highway. Similar to intersections of other major routes, there was a collection of gas stations and stores where the Alcan met the Cassiar. John pulled over into the parking lot of a food store. He needed to clean his neck and hunt for something good to eat. Dismounting his bike, John sipped from a water bottle while kicking his legs to get the circulation flowing in his feet—numb from the pressure against his toe clips. Looking around, he saw a scattering of signs along the highway, announcing that Watson Lake—about six miles east—had modern motels with color TV. Judging from the advertisements for fishing tackle and Yukon fishing licenses, he surmised the area was popular with fishermen. John noticed a sign pole with boards attached that listed the mileage to various destinations. Right then, a car sped by, spreading a cloud of dust. John's gaze followed the dusty wake of the vehicle as it traveled west on the Alaska Highway, the same direction he was headed. Damn! The dust kicked up by passing vehicles—predominantly trucks—only meant more frequent stops to clean his T-tube and a dirtier body at the end of the day. Looking back towards the sign pole, John had to smile at a sign pointing southeast on the Alcan to Chicago—2,911 miles away. He observed that he would arrive at Whitehorse in 280 miles. Heaving a sigh when he read that Anchorage was over a 1,000 miles from here, John walked toward the store.

"Sad news about the Pope, eh?" the elderly woman behind the register asked when John paid for his food.

"What's that?" John wondered. Without his radio, he had completely lost touch with what was happening in the world—quite a contrast from his life in Columbus, where he was regularly plugged-in to current events.

"Pope Paul VI—you know, the pontiff of the Roman Catholic Church—he had a heart attack," the woman elaborated.

John glanced at the newspaper on the counter. The headlines did indeed proclaim that the Pope was dead.

Back on his bicycle, John realized that time was beginning to run short for him. It was already the 7th of August, and he'd planned on being back in Columbus by the middle of the month to register for classes. He contemplated his predicament as he peddled. Biking the remaining 1,000 miles to Anchorage appeared to be an impossibility within this summer's time frame. He considered delaying school to finish his trek, but it was also growing late in the season, and he wasn't prepared for camping in colder weather. Maybe he'd been a little ambitious in embarking on a journey that actually turned out to be closer to 4,600 miles. Anyway, he knew this wasn't going to be his last bicycle trip.

He was so absorbed in his thoughts that the speeding 18-wheeler's air horn nearly made him lose balance. John quickly steered right, and his tires sank into the soft shoulder of the dirt and gravel road, almost throwing him over the handlebars. *ping ping ping.* Stones kicked up by the big rig struck John's helmet and bike frame. In an instant, he was back in Vietnam and the helicopter was taking bullets. Pulling off to the side, John had to stop and take a few breaths. The Alcan would not be considered a busy highway, but—unpleasantly for a bicyclist—the majority of passing vehicles were big fast-moving trucks. The highway had originally been built to relieve Alaska from the wartime hazards of shipping. Constructed by the US Army Corps of Engineers according to an agreement between the US and Canadian governments, the 1500-mile Alaska Highway officially opened in 1942 and provided an overland route for war materials and equipment.

On the road again, in the quiet of his own thoughts, the headlines about the Pope flashed in John's mind. Not that he had any personal feelings about the Pope being dead. Truthfully, it meant nothing to him. But the headlines reminded him of a commonly quoted pronouncement of Nietzsche: *God is dead.* Maybe Nietzsche was referring to man's concept of God, or the belief that God was a fearsome old man with a white beard who lived up in heaven, passing judgment on his creations below. For John, that God had died years ago. As a young boy, his mother insisted that he attend Sunday school, even though she rarely attended church herself. Most every Sunday and several weeks each summer, a small white school bus—emblazoned with a depiction of three crosses on a hilltop—would pick him up and transport him to Calvary Memorial Church. John didn't remember much, except for making crafts out of Popsicle sticks. Of course, he loved the music and singing hymns like "For the Beauty of the Earth". His soul was stirred when the congregation rang out all the verses to "My Country 'Tis of Thee". John's voice would earnestly belt,

"Land of the noble, free...
Long may our land be bright
With freedom's holy light...."

Even though the music was inspiring, the Bible stories seemed a far cry from what was happening in his daily life. And what happening at home was frightening: his parents' fighting, his father's beatings, and his mother's erratic behavior filled John with fear and confusion. He had prayed and prayed and prayed to God about his home life. Yet his prayers went unanswered and the craziness continued. John eventually gave up on praying and never attended church again, except to marry Karen. Years later, instead of believing in some distant God, he came to believe in the power of the human spirit. John concluded that how we live and conduct ourselves as human beings *is* our expression of divinity. His beliefs were strengthened after discovering that many of America's Founding Fathers shared a humanistic philosophy, affirming the dignity and worth of all people.

Still, the news about the dead Pope also made him think about a conversation he had with Professor Meenahan several months ago.

"You've read a number of books about the Vietnam War—or the American War, as the Vietnamese call it," Professor Meenahan stated in his office that day. "This one offers a unique point of view." The professor handed a slim paperback to John.

John stayed home that night to read the 100-page book, *Vietnam: Lotus in a Sea of Fire*. It was a Buddhist proposal for peace written by a South Vietnamese monk, scholar, and poet named Thich Nhat Hanh. For the first time, John was presented with the religious implications of the war. He hadn't known that 80–90% of the country practiced Buddhism, while the minority ruling class and wartime government had been Roman Catholic. The book included the monk's remarks from 1966 when he met with the recently deceased Pope Paul VI at the Vatican to request the Pope's help in stopping the religious and political persecution of Buddhists. Ironically, the monk was never granted an audience with President Johnson. John's heart was moved by the clear message of the gentle man and couldn't wait to discuss the book with Professor Meenahan.

"I didn't know," John began, hesitating for words as he took a seat in Meenahan's office the next day. "The killing of monks! I mean, I don't understand how Catholics—or any Christian—how can they act so contrary to their beliefs and support such violence and destruction?"

"You forget about the Crusades," the professor quipped as he opened his thermos and filled two cups.

"How difficult can it be to understand the meaning of *Thou shall not kill*?" John insisted.

"I related to what Thich Nhat Hanh said about the real enemies of man," Professor Meenahan shared after taking a sip of peppermint tea. "He said that evil isn't a person—and our enemies aren't a particular people—our enemies are the intolerance, and the hatred, and fanaticism, and discrimination that live in all of our hearts and minds."

For a long time after that conversation, John was troubled by a particular memory. Sure, back in Vietnam, he'd participated in the name-calling of the enemy. All Vietnamese became gooks, dinks, slope-heads, or something sub-human that made it okay to be killing them. But the recollection of that North Vietnamese Army officer festered in John's memories. Most of the time in Vietnam, John had tried to support life, even when surrounded by death. But he'd handed this patient over to others, knowing that the young NVA officer would be tortured. Such an action completely went against his medic training. He was ashamed of what he did, but realistically,

John knew he wouldn't have done anything any differently. He'd followed his orders like a good soldier. Just the same, the fate of that officer would ever trouble him.

August 15
Dear Mom,
I'm flying back from Whitehorse.
Not enough time to get to Anchorage.
Sure have learned a lot on this trip.

Love,
Johnny

I've got to get out! I've got to get out! John madly thrashed around inside his sleeping bag. Something was coming at him, and—in his dream state—he clawed and fought to get out of his confinement. When he awakened from his nightmare, he was pissed.

"You asshole!" John admonished himself. "What the fuck is wrong with you?" his internal voice berated. Not only had he ripped a big hole in his mosquito netting, he almost broke a finger in the process. Lying back down to gather his wits, John couldn't decipher the dream. Was he onboard a crashing helicopter? Or was it the exhaustion of dealing with 18-wheelers on the Alaska Highway? Following that nightmare, John decided it was time to end his bike trip, especially when he learned that the 722 miles of highway from Whitehorse to Anchorage had long distances between the few services. He'd postpone that journey for another day. According to the *Milepost*, Whitehorse had an International Airport with service to major cities. John packed up his campsite amidst the lodgepole pines in the Teslin Lake government campground, climbed on his bicycle, got back on the highway, and headed toward Whitehorse.

John was elated as he cycled the remaining 100 miles to White-horse. He'd survived the laws of nature and was filled with conviction to return to his studies and work on the laws of man. Back in gradu-ate school, he would learn more about promoting conditions that would help life prosper. Throughout the trip, people had been kind to him, reinforcing his genuine regard for all members of the human family. Some would say that life had dealt John a difficult hand, but he didn't see it that way. Yes, fate had flung him into a war and he'd been permanently wounded, but without that wound, he wouldn't have had the opportunity to go to college. And he'd certainly become a different person because of the knowledge he'd acquired. In John's opinion, a free education for all people would be the best possible use of taxpayer money. If more citizens became aware of the work-ings of the world, a greater society could be attained. After reading about Rousseau's *Social Contract*, John thought that a guaranteed income would go a long way in relieving social problems. Without struggling to survive, people could contribute to society by realizing their own talents and unique expression of life.

Cycling by the Yukon River as it boiled through rocky walls, John recalled the writings of a man who had become a hero to him— Thomas Paine. John balked when Professor Meenahan first sug-gested that he should read the *Age of Reason* and the *Rights of Man*, along with the pamphlet credited for influencing America to become a free and independent nation—*Common Sense*.

"Those pamphlets were like bestsellers of their day. They were the most widely read tracts of the 18th century," Professor Meena-han informed. Chuckling, he added, "Besides, you and Thomas are both Philly boys. And your stubborn genius is a lot like his—I think you'll appreciate his thoughts on religion. He believed freethinking trumped dead religions, and he said that his own mind was his own church."

John read Paine—albeit with some difficulty—and was impressed by the writings that had spread a fire amongst the colonists of early America. John strongly believed in Paine's opinion that a person's religious duties should "consist in doing justice, loving mercy and endeavoring to make our fellow creatures happy." And John agreed that the purpose of government should be to protect each person's *inalienable rights,* because some people most definitely needed protection from the barracudas out there. As Paine proclaimed—"only when the poor are happy, and the jails are empty, with no beggars on the streets, and children and the aged are not in want—only then can a country boast about its constitution and government."

When John spotted the sign that read "Welcome to Whitehorse", he stood up on his toe clips in joy. He didn't have a radio, but in his head, he clearly heard a saxophone playing the melody of "Baker Street". John was proud of his accomplishment. He'd set out from his apartment with little more than determination and had traveled a distance of approximately 3,900 miles—having actually pedaled nearly 3,000. Even though he was just an average guy from Philadelphia, he was doing the best he could each moment. And despite a brutal introduction to war, John knew—with all his heart—that for the rest of his life, he would pursue a path to peace.

*John behind the wheel of his ambulance
in Baumholder, Germany.*

Bored with diapering the "crackerbox."

Standing by a 236th Dustoff helicopter ambulance.

Acting First Sergeant, Senior Medic C Co 23 Med Battalion 196 Lt Inf Bde AMERICAL, SFC Gary Weaver at LZ Baldy aid station.

Crew chief Spec 5 Robert Long inside his chopper.

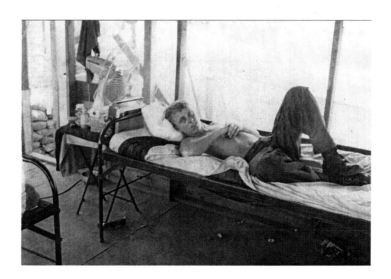

An exhausted John in the perpetually dirty
Dustoff hooch at LZ Baldy.

John seated on floor of cargo bay as
Dustoff ship arrives at LZ West

A pickup at LZ West or Hill 445 (John standing outside
of cargo bay moving litters. 5th man seated in hell hole
beside John and holding M-16. Crew chief Robert Long
seen across the cargo bay.) Photo taken by Joe Kralich in
August 1969--the day before John was shot.

Spec 5 John Seebeth.

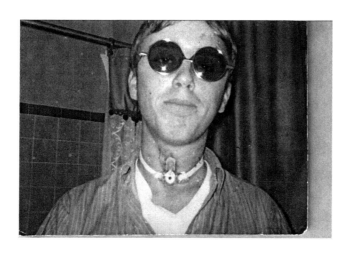

At Walson Army Hospital with a tracheostomy.

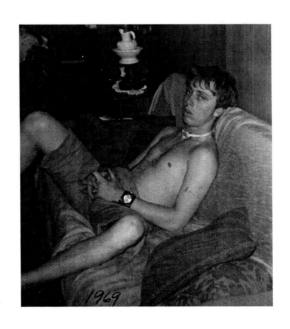

John's first weekend leave from Walson, December 1969.

*John wearing fringed suede
vest in Wildwood, New Jersey.*

John and the Montgomery T-tube. This was his passport photo.

Hitchhiking through Europe 1971.

President of the Student Association at
Ocean County College.

John and bicycle along the
Icefield Parkway, Canada.

About the Author

Linda Seebeth grew up in a suburb of Rochester, NY as Linda Nifenger. After earning a degree in Education with an emphasis in Special Education, Linda balanced a teaching career with mothering her two daughters. Over the years she has taught and tutored students from elementary through college. Like her husband John, Linda has a long history of environmental and social activism.

Above all, Linda strives to live a loving life of mindfulness, and it is with this spirit that she listened to and recounts the journey of a soldier's heart.

Please visit the Seebeth's website:

http://seebeth.com/default.aspx

Made in the USA